Democratic Governance and European Integration

Democratic Governance and European Integration

Linking Societal and State Processes of Democracy

Edited by

Ronald Holzhacker

Assistant Professor, University of Twente, and
Fellow for Political Science and International Relations,
University College Utrecht, the Netherlands

Erik Albæk

Professor of Political Science and Journalism,
University of Southern Denmark

Edward Elgar
Cheltenham, UK • Northampton, MA, USA

Published by
Edward Elgar Publishing Limited
Glensanda House
Montpellier Parade
Cheltenham
Glos GL50 1UA
UK

Edward Elgar Publishing, Inc.
William Pratt House
9 Dewey Court
Northampton
Massachusetts 01060
USA

A catalogue record for this book
is available from the British Library

Library of Congress Cataloging-in-Publication Data

Democratic governance and European integration : linking societal and state processes of democracy / edited by Dr. Ronald Holzhacker and Erik Albæk.
p. cm.
Includes bibliographical references and index.
1. European Union. 2. European Union countries–Politics and government. 3. European Union countries–Economic integration. I. Holzhacker, Ronald, 1961- II. Albæk, Erik.
JN30.H665 2007
341.242'2–dc22

2007001401

ISBN 978 1 84542 448 0

Printed and bound in Great Britain by MPG Books Ltd, Bodmin, Cornwall

Contents

About the Editors vii
About the Contributors viii
Foreword xii

1. Introduction: Democratic Governance and European Integration 1
Ronald Holzhacker and Erik Albæk

PART I OPINION FORMATION AND INTEREST INTERMEDIATION IN MULTI-LEVEL GOVERNANCE

2. Visibility and Framing of European Integration in the Media 25
Claes de Vreese
3. Europeanization of Expert References in the Media? Researchers as Sources in Danish Daily Newspapers 1961-2001 44
Erik Albæk, Peter Munk Christiansen and Lise Togeby
4. National Election Campaigns and European Issues 53
Ronald Holzhacker and Andrea Römmele
5. Resisting Change: European Integration and National Party Systems 69
Tapio Raunio
6. Interest Organizations and European Integration 88
Ove K. Pedersen

PART II EXECUTIVE DECISION-MAKING AND NATIONAL PARLIAMENTARY SCRUTINY

7. Undermining Democratic Governance in the Member States? The Europeanization of National Decision-making 113
Tanja A. Börzel and Carina Sprungk
8. The Europeanization of National Executives: Changing Capacities and Ambivalent Effects on Democracy 137
Ignacio Molina and César Colino
9. Adapting to Europe: Strategic Europeanization of National Parliaments 157
Katrin Auel

10. National Parliamentary Scrutiny: Comparing Rules, Institutions and Behaviour 180
Ronald Holzhacker
11. A Model for the Strictest Scrutiny? The Danish European Affairs Committee in a Party Group Perspective 207
Henrik Jensen
12. The Southern European Pattern of Parliamentary Scrutiny of EU Legislation: Emulating the French Model 229
José M. Magone
13. The Role of ECE Parliaments in EU Integration 249
Attila Ágh

Index 269

About the Editors

Ronald Holzhacker is Assistant Professor for Political Science at the University of Twente and Fellow at University College Utrecht, the Netherlands. He received his Ph.D. from the University of Michigan and his J.D. from the University of Minnesota Law School. He is founding director of the European Research Colloquium of the Netherlands Institute of Government. He has published in such journals as *Party Politics, European Union Politics*, and the *Journal of Legislative Studies*. He is currently a co-editor, with Markus Haverland, of *European Research Reloaded: Cooperation and Integration among Europeanized States* (Kluwer, 2006). In 2005 he was a Visiting Professor at the University of Paris 1, Sorbonne and a 2005-2006 recipient of the Jean Monnet Fellowship to the Robert Schuman Centre, European University Institute, Florence.

Erik Albæk is Professor of Political Science and Journalism at the University of Southern Denmark. He has been a visiting fellow at M.I.T., Harvard University, and the University of Potsdam, Germany, and a visiting professor at Vilnius University, Lithuania. Between 2001 and 2005 he was Chairman of the Danish Social Science Research Council. His most recent publication is a 2004 book on the role of expertise in public policy making.

About the Contributors

Attila Ágh is Professor at the Political Science Department, Corvinus Budapest University, Hungary. His major field of research has been comparative democratization and EU accession in East Central Europe. He has published several books and papers in English on this topic and also produced edited volumes in collaboration with West European colleagues. Currently, he is the director of the 'Together for Europe' Research Centre at the Hungarian Academy of Sciences.

Katrin Auel is University Lecturer in Politics at the University of Oxford and Fellow at Mansfield College, Oxford. Her research interests include legislative studies and democratic theory, especially the democratic legitimacy of systems of multi-level governance. Her publications include: 'Multilevel Governance, Regional Policy and Democratic Legitimacy in Germany', in: Arthur Benz/Yannis Papadopoulos (eds.) *Governance and Democracy – Comparing National, European and Transnational Experiences*, London: Routledge 2005; *Regionalisiertes Europa – Demokratisches Europa? Eine Untersuchung am Beispiel der europäischen Strukturpolitik*, Baden-Baden: Nomos 2003.

Tanja A. Börzel completed her Ph.D. at the European University Institute, Florence, Italy, in 1999. Between 1999 and 2002, she was Senior Researcher at the Max-Planck-Project Group on the Study of Common Goods, Bonn and the Humboldt University of Berlin. In April 2002, she accepted the position as Associate Professor of International Relations at the University of Heidelberg. Since December 2004, she holds the chair of European Integration at the Free University of Berlin. Her teaching and research interests include international institutions, compliance, European politics, comparative federalism, and the implementation of EU policies. She has published several articles on these subjects. Her current research project is on member state compliance with Community Law. She published a book on *States and Regions in the European Union* with Cambridge University Press in 2002. Her second book *Environmental Leaders and Laggards in Europe* was published in March 2003.

Peter Munk Christiansen is Professor of Public Policy and Administration at the Department of Political Science, University of Southern Denmark. He was a member of the board of directors of the Danish Power and Democracy Study (www.magtudredningen.dk). Among his recent books are *Eksperter i medierne*; *Dagspressens brug af forskere 1961-2001*, Århus: Magtudredningen, 2002; (Experts in the Media; Researchers in the Danish Daily Newspapers, 1961-2001), with Erik Albæk and Lise Togeby. *Hvem skriver lovene? Interesseorganisationer og politiske beslutninger.* Århus: Aarhus Universitetsforlag, 2004; (Who Writes the Law?), with Asbjørn Sonne Nørgaard and Niels Chr. Sidenius), and *Power and Democracy in Denmark: Conclusions.* Århus: Magtudredningen, 2003, with Lise Togeby, Jørgen Goul Andersen, Torben Beck Jørgensen and Signild Vallgårda.

César Colino is Lecturer in Politics and Public Administration at the Autonomous University of Madrid. He holds a B.A. in Political Science from Universidad Complutense Madrid and an M.A. in Social Sciences from the Juan March Institute, Madrid. His post-graduate studies were undertaken at the Humboldt University and the Free University of Berlin. He was Visiting Researcher at the Max-Planck Institute for the Study of Society in Cologne (1996-1997) and Institut d'Etudes Politiques, Bordeaux (2004). He was Research Officer at the Institute for Research in Public Administration, Speyer, Germany (1997-2000), where he specialized in comparative public administration and the Europeanization of environmental policies. Other research and publications have dealt with European integration and comparative federalism.

Claes de Vreese is Professor and Chair of Political Communication at the University of Amsterdam and scientific director of the Amsterdam School of Communications Research. He is also Adjunct Professor of Political Science and Journalism at the University of Southern Denmark. He has published on media coverage of European integration, European elections, EU referendums, public opinion about the EU, media effects, and journalism in journals such as the *European Journal of Political Research*, *West European Politics, EU Politics, Communication Research, European Journal of Communication*, and the *International Journal of Public Opinion Research*. His most recent book *Political campaigning in referendums: Framing the referendum issue* (London: Routledge) deals with the role of the media in referendum campaigns on issues of European integration.

Henrik Jensen is Associate Professor in the Department of Political Science, University of Copenhagen. He has published several articles and books on the Danish Parliament, including a book on the Danish European Affairs Committee: *Europaudvalget – et udvalg i Folketinget*, 2003.

Ignacio Molina is Lecturer in Politics and Public Administration at the Autonomous University of Madrid. He has been Fulbright Visiting Fellow at Harvard University, and Junior Visitor at Nuffield College, Oxford University. He has participated in several national or international research projects and has written on the contemporary transformations of the Spanish State (including economic reforms and multi-level governance), on European integration and on nationalism. He has published in various journals such as: *Revue française d'administration publique; Public Administration;* and *Revista de Estudios Políticos* and he is the author of the dictionary *Conceptos Fundamentales de Ciencia Política* (Madrid, 1998). He has also contributed to several chapters in comparative volumes by Palgrave Macmillan and Oxford University Press.

José M. Magone is Senior Lecturer in European Politics at the Department of Politics and International Studies, University of Hull. Among his research interests is Europeanization of southern European political systems. Among his most recent publications are: *The Politics of Southern Europe* (2003); *The Developing Place of Portugal in the European Union* (2004); and *Contemporary Spanish Politics* (2004).

Ove K. Pedersen is Professor of Comparative Political Economy and director of International Center of Business and Politics, Copenhagen Business School. He has been Professor of Comparative Politics at Copenhagen University, Professor of Public Administration at Aalborg University and is honorary professor at Aalborg University. His work includes *National Identity and Varieties of Capitalism: The State of Denmark* (McGill University Press, 2006), *Europeanization and Transnational States: Comparing Nordic Governments* (Routledge, 2004), and *The Rise of Neoliberalism and Institutional Analysis* (Princeton University Press, 2001).

Tapio Raunio is Professor of Political Science at the University of Tampere, Finland. He is the co-author of *Finland in the European Union* (2003) and has published articles on various aspects of European integration in journals such as *European Journal of Political Research; Journal of Common Market Studies; Party Politics;* and *Scandinavian Political Studies*. His current research focuses on the role of national legislatures in the European Union.

Andrea Römmele is Professor for Communication Management at the International University Bruchsal in Germany. She was formally a Research

Fellow at the MZES, University of Mannheim. She is Secretary of the Research Committee on Political Sociology of the International Political Science Association and the International Sociological Association (2002-2006). Her research interests are in the field of comparative political parties and political communication. Her recent publications include *Electronic Democracy* (Routledge, 2004) and *Direkte Kommunikation zwischen Parteien und Wähl-ern* (Wiesbaden, 2002).

Carina Sprungk is a Ph.D. candidate at the Free University Berlin and is currently affiliated to the University of Victoria, Canada, as a visiting professor for European Politics. Her teaching and research interests include compliance, parliamentarism, European politics, and the implementation of EU policies. She has published on the effects of Europeanization on national decision-making, on compliance with law beyond the nation state, on the ratification processes of the EU Constitutional Treaty and on national parliamentary scrutiny of EU politics.

Lise Togeby is Professor in Political Sociology at Aarhus University, Denmark. She was Chairman of the board of directors of the Danish Power and Democracy Study (www.magtudredningen.dk). Among her recent books are: *Eksperter i medierne: Dagspressens brug af forskere 1961-2001*, Århus: Magtudredningen, 2002 (Experts in the Media: Researchers in the Danish Daily Newspapers, 1961-2001), with Erik Albæk and Peter Munk Christiansen; *Power and Democracy in Denmark: Conclusions*. Århus: Magtudredningen, 2003, with Jørgen Goul Andersen, Peter Munk Christiansen, Torben Beck Jørgensen and Signild Vallgårda); and *Man har et standpunkt. Om stabilitet og forandring i befolkningens holdninger*, Aarhus Universitets-forlag, 2004 (You have a standpoint ... About stability and change in public opinion).

Foreword

This book emerged from a series of discussions called the 'Dialogue on Democracy', which recently took place in Denmark and the Netherlands. The discussions were designed to deepen our understanding of the impact the process of Europeanization is having on democracy in the member states of the European Union. By combining both a societal- and a state-centric approach to the research on 'Europeanization', we hope that a broader understanding of the impact multi-level governance is having on the national institutions and domestic politics of the member states can be achieved.

Our first meeting took place at the University of Copenhagen in October 2002, concurrently with the COSAC (*Conférence des organes spécialisés dans les affaires communautaires*) meeting of national members of parliament assembled in the Danish parliament. In addition to the invited scholars, several members of parliament and their staff from various European affairs committees of the member states attended the academic conference.This interaction between scholars and practitioners enriched our debate on governance in the EU and the member states. Our second conference, this time with completed research and final papers, took place at the University of Twente, the Netherlands, in October 2003.

Scholars in the fast developing field of 'Europeanization' research have contributed chapters for this discussion and the subsequent book manuscript. Participants were chosen to include a broad selection from the four corners of the new Europe: from the original core of the European project, the Nordic countries, the Mediterranean South and the new accession countries in East and Central Europe. We would like to thank the Danish Social Science Research Council and the Netherlands Organization for Scientific Research for their generous assistance in funding these international 'Dialogue on Democracy' meetings. Finally, we would like to thank Annette Andersen and Christine Pihlkjær Jensen for their careful review and preparation of the final manuscript.

Ronald Holzhacker and Erik Albæk

1. Introduction: Democratic Governance and European Integration

Ronald Holzhacker and Erik Albæk

Many new institutions are being created beyond the nation state to solve problems that transcend the ability of individual states to address effectively. As the power and scope of the European Union (EU) moves further and further beyond traditional forms of international cooperation between sovereign states, it is fruitful to analyse how these developments have impacted national institutions and processes of democratic representation and legitimacy in the member states.

In this introductory chapter, we introduce some key concepts which will be addressed by the other chapters in this book. The idea of the book emerged from a desire to think broadly about the impact the EU is having on national institutions and domestic political processes which provide representation and legitimacy in the multi-level system of governance. Thus both the Europeanization of national institutions and political processes and the impact this is having on democracy within the emerging political system will be discussed.

Let us begin with a longer historical perspective on the development of democracy within nation states and beyond. Robert Dahl discusses three great democratic transformations in his work: the first, the transition to the democratic city state in ancient Greece; the second, the transition towards republicanism, representation, and the logic of equality within European nation states; and the third, the democratization of institutions beyond the nation state, in transnational institutions.

> The boundaries of a country . . . are now much smaller than the boundaries of the decisions that significantly affect the fundamental interests of the citizen. A country's economic life, physical environment, national security, and survival are highly, and probably increasingly dependent on actors and actions that are outside the countries boundaries and not subject to its government (Dahl 1989, p. 319).

Dahl suggests two strategies as a response to these changes in the scale of political life. One is to encourage the gradual development of truly transnational political associations. The second is strengthening the control democratic institutions *within countries* have over delegates to transnational bodies.

Dahl is sceptical, however, about the wisdom of duplicating the second transformation in the third – that is merely applying institutions and processes from democracy in the nation states to democracy in a transnational state. In the countries where democracy emerged, 'the structures and consciousness of nationhood were already rather fully developed, but transnational political structures and consciousness are likely to remain weak' (p. 320). Nevertheless, Dahl is a bit more optimistic about this occurring within the EU, and he says that incipient institutions of a democratic transnational political community are visible within the EU. But Dahl argues that efforts in the shorter term should be directed at strengthening the democratic institutions within countries, particularly democratic control over the authority delegated to transnational decision makers. This is important to preserve democracy and avoid de facto guardianship within these new organizations (Dahl 1989).

The continuing evolution of the system of multi-level democracy in the EU and the member states, with executive decision-making and parliamentary representation occurring at different levels, makes it necessary to consider its impact on democratic decision-making in the member states. A great deal of the focus by scholars, political elites and the public on the 'democratic deficit' in the EU has concentrated on the institutions of the EU itself. The EU is criticized for its complex and non-transparent decision-making process, weak mechanisms of representation and absence of a European public sphere (Börzel and Sprungk, Chapter 7, Scharpf 1999, Schmitter 2000). But to understand the new political system, one must also understand political processes within the member states themselves, which may have changed as a result of the shifting divisions of decision-making competencies, and the subsequent interaction between decision-making levels. The core puzzle is how multi-level governance has changed democratic processes in the member states and whether these changes are consistent with maintaining democratic principles. We believe that by reflecting on the interactions between societal and state processes inherent to the democratic process we can begin to address this question.

Competitive elections have traditionally been seen as the premier institution linking citizens and the government, with political parties competing for the support of the citizens in periodic elections. But in modern democracies, many organizations have evolved that provide a linkage between society and the government, and that play a pivotal role in democracy, including interest groups and the media. As new levels of decision-making are created above the level of the nation state, the whole range of democratic institutions and societal processes within the nation states will likely evolve and respond to new challenges.

Decision-making within the evolving system of multi-level governance is an inherently political one. It is a process involving competing actors and institutions at different levels, with different preferences and strategies for attaining their goals. Thus it is important not to view the EU as merely a bureaucratic process played out in the supranational institutions in Brussels or just an inter-governmental process played out between ministers of the national governments. Instead, the decision-making process must be seen as beginning with a political process in each country involving competing political parties, the social partners – business and union groups – other types of interest groups, the media, as well as citizens.

While most of the thinking to date has focused on the EU institutions themselves and has found a democratic deficit, we believe that democratic governance must be sought in linking democratic processes between the different levels of decision-making. The ideas of democratic governance have been developed within the context of nation states; we desire in this book to reflect on whether these concepts can also be used to understand national processes occurring within the context of multi-level governance. We will not be considering the EU institutions in great depth, but national institutions and processes that are linked in the system. We identify four core processes of democratic governance in any democratic political system that link societal and state processes of decision-making: opinion formation, interest intermediation, national executive decision-making and national parliamentary scrutiny.

We thus ask in this book, first empirically, how have societal and state democratic processes been impacted by multi-level governance – is there evidence of a process of Europeanization?

Second, we ask from a normative perspective, what impact does this process of Europeanization have on democracy in the evolving system of multi-level governance?

Of course, considering that the impact of Europeanization on democratic governance is a broad question, we will only be able to provide empirical research on selected cases or comparisons of groups of countries at one or several points in time. We also suspect that we will be able to give a better answer to the first question than the second in this book. While the scholars in this book are known for their empirical research, we have tried to push the authors to consider the normative implications for their observed developments of multi-level governance. One reason it is difficult to make normative evaluations towards the evolving political system is the wide disagreement among scholars, practitioners, and the broader public about the EU and the proper criteria for evaluating its democratic qualities.

INTERGOVERNMENTALISM, SUPRANATIONALISM AND MULTI-LEVEL GOVERNANCE

Decision-making within the EU has traditionally been seen as occurring in one of two ways; intergovernmentally or supranational. Institutions such as the Council of Ministers operate intergovernmentally, with ministers from each member state's government gathering to reach decisions. Institutions such as the European Commission and the European Court of Justice operate supranationally, and have been given powers of decision-making that transcend that of individual national governments. Both these perspectives on decision-making emphasize the interaction between states or state-like actors, that is the member states and the institutions of the EU itself (see Haas 1958, Moravscik 1999).

Newer perspectives on the EU have emphasized additional relationships and connections in the evolving political system of the EU and the member states. For example, institutions like the Council of Regions promote trans-governmental relations – that is cooperation between units of government below the level of the nation state. Furthermore, institutions such as the Council of Ministers often operate in cooperation with organized interests in society, like business organizations and non-governmental organizations (NGOs), that is transnationally (Risse-Kappen 1996, p. 57). Thus, the EU is quite rightly referred to as a multi-level structure of governance (Marks et al. 1996, Jachtenfuchs and Kohler-Koch 1996).

> The EU is a complex entity without a clearly defined core and compared to a state, with a far less hierarchical system of governance. It is a mixture of supranational, transnational, transgovernmental, and intergovernmental structures (Schmitter 1996, p. 4).

The two formal modes of decision-making within the EU, supranationalism and intergovernmentalism, have ramifications for how one conceives and evaluates democracy within the EU. For decisions made under the supranational approach, it is important that the EU develop a democracy of its own if it is going to enjoy support from the citizens of Europe. For example, a European level democracy could have a pan-European electorate and a parliament with important powers over the leadership of the union. Under an intergovernmental approach, national democracies must be adapted to the task of legitimizing the union, with national electorates and national parliaments ratifying treaties and forming governments that make decisions in the European Council and Council of Ministers (Beetham and Lord 1998, p. 59).

This book concentrates on a consideration of the mechanisms of national representation and legitimacy within the intergovernmental mode of decision-making, operating within the new and evolving context of multi-level governance. Beetham and Lord discuss the best means for achieving the authorization, representation and accountability for the democratization of the EU through the member states when working within the intergovernmental framework. In terms of legal authorization, they posit ratifications of treaties by the democratic institutions of each member state and the election of national governments whose members will then serve on the European Council and the Council of Ministers. In terms of representation, they argue that this should occur through the national governments acting in the Council and through the national allocations of Commissioners and Members of the European Parliament (MEPs). Finally, in terms of accountability, they state that this should occur by the members of the European Council and the Council of Ministers being accountable to national parliaments and electorates (Beetham and Lord 1998, p. 60). If this is not done, they warn of the danger that 'The intergovernmental model may even lead to the de-democratization of the state rather than the democratization of the Union' (Beetham and Lord 1998, p. 74).

But Beetham and Lord argue that even if the best means for achieving democratization within the intergovernmental chain of representation is followed, democratic shortcomings would remain. For example, while they focus on the role of the Council of Ministers for the authorization of power within the EU, they acknowledge that the Commission has a very strong agenda-setting role, even in areas where the Council of Ministers has final power. In terms of representation, although they argue the best way is for national electorates to take into account the actions of their national government in the Council of Ministers when voting in national elections, they acknowledge the difficulty in voters having only one vote to be used to evaluate actors operating in two different arenas. Finally, while they state that national parliaments should hold their government accountable for votes in the Council of Ministers, they acknowledge the lack of transparency of Council deliberations.

As valuable as the contribution of Beetham and Lord is, it is apparent that their perspective is very state-centric, stressing obligations of states in treaties and the actions of national governments and parliaments. Little emphasis is placed on societal institutions and the interaction between state and societal institutions in the national democratic decision-making process over the EU.

Recent research on the EU has tried to move: '. . . beyond the simple supranationalism embedded in neo-functionalism and the state-centric view of intergovernmentalism, to conceive of the EU as a system of multi-level governance which consists of multi-tiered, geographically overlapping structures of governmental and *non-governmental elites*' (Eriksen and Fossum 2000, p. 14).

Here we wish to take into account not only institutions stressed in a state-centric approach, but also the political processes that occur between these state institutions and societal actors. Why is this important and why has it become increasingly necessary to consider not only formal institutions but also societal processes? We believe that the EU has entered a new phase in its development since the late 1980s and early 1990s, a point which coincided with the attainment of two long-term goals of the Western European political community: the fundamental completion of the single economic market and the ending of the division in Europe after the fall of communism in Eastern Europe.[1] Political debate was bound to increase as the EU changed to incorporate the new realities of Europe and began to address more diverse political and policy objectives.

> The decade from 1985 to 1995 was a watershed in the political development of the EU, for it introduced more intense public scrutiny of European decision making, more extensive interest group mobilization, and less insulated elite decision making. The period beginning with the Single European Act and culminating with the decision to establish economic and monetary union created the conditions for politicized-participatory decision making in the EU by increasing the stakes of political conflict, broadening the scope of authoritative decision making, opening new avenues of group influence, and creating incentives for a quantum increase in political mobilization (Hooghe and Marks 2001, p. 126).

Multi-level governance sees three main features characterizing the emerging political system incorporating the EU and the member states:

1. Decision-making competencies are shared by actors at different levels, national and the supranational institutions of the EU.
2. Collective decision-making among states involves a significant loss of control for individual national governments.
3. Political arenas are interconnected, not nested, thus transnational arenas emerge (Hooghe and Marks 2001, p. 3).

We thus ask, what impact does this shift of competencies, loss of control by individual national governments and interconnectedness of political arenas have on democratic processes in the member states? Let us first review the rapidly expanding existing literature on Europeanization.

EUROPEANIZATION

What has existing empirical research discovered about how the EU has impacted the member states and the underlying causal mechanisms for the process of Europeanization? (See Cowles et al. 2001, Featherstone and Radaelli 2003, Goetz and Hix 2001).[2] A relatively clear understanding of the direct and most visible effects of the EU has emerged from this research. The EU impacts the member states directly by imposing a European policy on the member states to which the member states have to adapt. Another direct effect concerns the establishment of an administrative infrastructure in the member states, in the national capitals as well as in offices in Brussels, to deal with European affairs. Relatively underexplored, however, are effects that are by definition indirect, for instance on democratic input processes such as cleavages, parties and patterns of democratic legitimization (Hix and Goetz 2000, p. 15).

Indirect effects of European integration, if they occur, are transmitted by quite different mechanisms than those resulting from direct effects. The establishment of a new set of institutions at the European level with legislative, executive and judicial powers, provides actors with a new layer of access to political decision-making. The EU creates new exit, veto and informational opportunities for domestic actors and therefore changes the national opportunity structure for exerting political influence (Börzel and Risse 2003, Hix and Goetz 2000, Knill and Lehmkuhl 2002). Another indirect mechanism is the cognitive impact of European integration and issues of framing. European integration may alter the beliefs and expectations of domestic actors and may lead to cognitive convergence about the appropriate modes of governance (Börzel and Risse 2003, Kohler-Koch 2002, Knill and Lehmkuhl 2002, Radaelli 2000).

DEMOCRATIC GOVERNANCE

How can a democratic system be evaluated? Let us begin very broadly. Dahl states that in a political unit as large as a country, the following political institutions are necessary to satisfy the democratic criteria of full inclusion, voting equality, enlightened understanding, effective participation and control of the agenda (Dahl 1998, p. 92):

1. elected representatives
2. free, fair and frequent elections
3. freedom of expression
4. alternative information

5. associational autonomy
6. inclusive citizenship

It is clear that in a democracy, elections play a key role. Many emphasize the double role of elections in engendering representation: a government may act because it is responsive or because it is accountable (Przeworski et al. 1999, p. 10). These mechanisms work at least partially due to the fact that voters may vote prospectively for the government they want, or may vote retrospectively and punish incumbents for past actions.

Because elections can be a blunt instrument of control – for example voters after all have but one decision to make with regard to the entire package of government policies – additional mechanisms of public accountability have evolved in modern democracies. A control mechanism qualifies as public accountability if the following conditions are met: the actor is required to give account, there is public accessibility of the account given, the actor explains and justifies the conduct in a specific forum and there exists the possibility of judgement, including the imposition of formal or informal sanctions (Bovens 2004, p. 4). Bovens furthermore discusses traditional vertical hierarchical forms of accountability, like those mechanisms between parliament and ministers (and more broadly with ministries as institutions), but also horizontal forms involving interest groups and the media. Both types will be addressed here.

In this book, we are focusing on the linked societal and state processes of representation and accountability in the member states for its decision-making towards the EU. We set out the following criteria for evaluating the democracy in this political system:

1. *The chance for the people to be informed, to understand and to have their voice heard.* Here we focus on opinion formation and interest intermediation at the national level concerning the EU by such institutions as political parties, interest groups and the media.
2. *The chance to have effective and responsible steering of EU policies.* Here we focus on national decision-making towards the EU within executive structures.
3. *The chance to hold public officials accountable for their actions.* Here we focus on national parliamentary scrutiny of executive decision-making in the member states.

MODEL OF SOCIETAL AND STATE PROCESSES OF DEMOCRACY IN MULTI-LEVEL GOVERNANCE

We need now to present a model that illustrates the various institutions and the political processes involved in the multi-level system of governance of the EU. A democratic political system attempts to have government policy reflect the interest, values and preferences of the citizens. The model illustrates the institutions involved in the four key political processes identified earlier: opinion formation, interest intermediation, national executive decision making and national parliamentary scrutiny over the entire democratic process. In this way, societal actors are involved in the process with the state in forming, shaping and scrutinizing decision-making national and EU issues.

The model presented in Figure 1.1 shows the linked societal and state processes in the multi-level political system incorporating the EU and the member states. The state-centric processes are illustrated in the top half of the figure and the societal-centric at the bottom half.

Beginning at the base of the figure with the electorate, the diagram illustrates an abstracted and simplified view of the two chains of representation, the intergovernmental and the supranational within the formal institutional system of democracy within the EU and the member states. A chain of representation should link voter preferences through a series of deliberative (parliamentary) and decision-making (government) institutions to the policy outputs of the system to assure democratic representation.

Between the formal institutions of the member states and the EU involved in national, intergovernmental and supranational decision-making, are placed the organizations and institutions of civil society, including political parties, interest groups and the media, which provide democratic inputs and legitimacy to the various strands of decision-making. The numbers next to the various institutions indicate the chapter in this book that presents empirical research on the processes linking these institutions of multi-level governance.

If one first follows the path of representation indicated on the right through the EU institutions, one sees the input of the views and preferences of citizens (at least those who chose to vote) being expressed during the elections for the European Parliament. Then, to the extent that the European Parliament has various rights and powers, from consultation to co-decision within the institutional structure of the EU, the voice of the citizens is heard through the individual members of the European Parliament and the party family groups they form. However, because the European Parliament does not directly decide and elect a European government like a national parliament does, but instead is given only limited (but gradually and systematically expanding) rights and powers vis-à-vis the European Commission, the chain

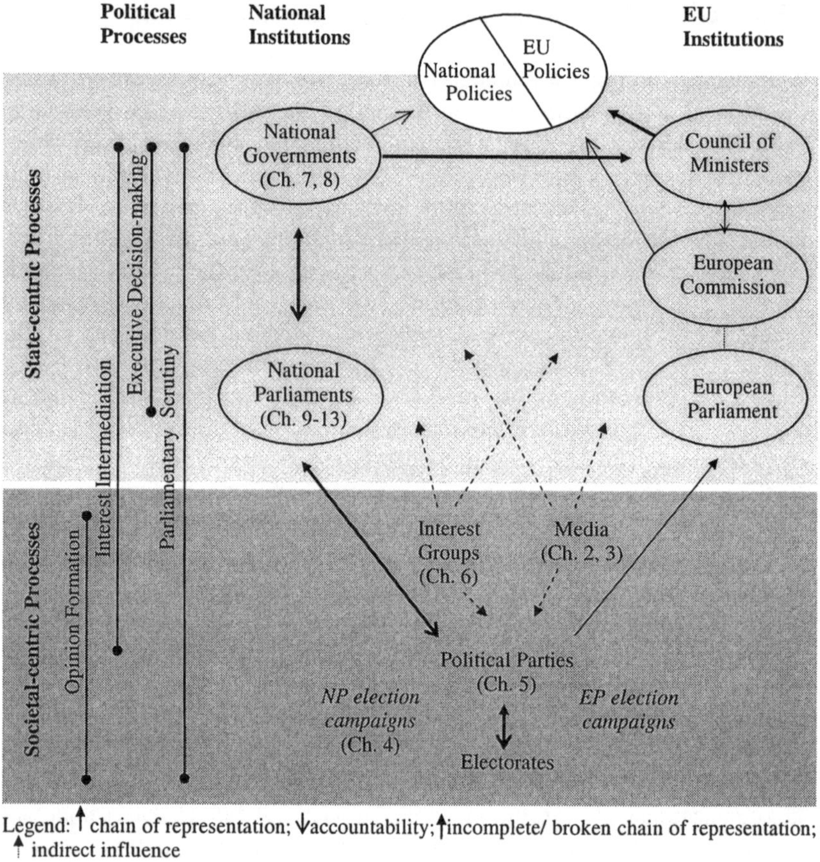

Figure 1.1 Societal- and state- centric processes of democratic governance in the EU: Intergovernmental and supranational chains of representation and accountability

of representation is incomplete (or indeed, broken). This means that the chain of representation through the EU institutions, linking voter preferences and choice expressed during elections to decision-making and policy outputs, is incomplete because of the limited powers of the European Parliament over the two executive institutions of the EU, the European Commission and the Council of Ministers. This institutional structure is one of the primary causes of the 'democratic deficit' in the EU. This book will not further address this chain of representation through the EU institutions themselves. Theorizing that concentrates on the EU institutions and democracy is found elsewhere, including recently in a theory of complex democracy (Scharpf 1998, Schmidt 2000) and compounded representation in multi-level governance (Benz 2003).

We instead follow another chain of representation that could potentially link the Council of Ministers in a democratic chain of representation; one that passes through the core of the traditional democratic institutions of the member states. If one now follows the left-hand side of Figure 1.1, a chain of representation that exists in each of the member states is illustrated. Here the citizens' preferences are expressed in national elections, in a process in which political parties are competing for the national parliament. This national parliament then elects a national government, a prime minister and a cabinet, which is responsible for both national policy making and casting its vote in the Council of Minister meetings of the EU. These national parliaments not only directly elect a government at the beginning of the term and have law-making powers, but also have the power to scrutinize the government's positions to be taken in the Council of Ministers.

Of course, some matters are decided exclusively within the EU institutions, principally the European Commission, and do not typically appear on the agenda of the Council of Ministers. Democratic representation through the national parliaments does not occur for these matters.

ORGANIZATION OF THE BOOK

The first section of this book concerns the societal-centred democratic processes, first opinion formation in the EU and the member states, including the role of the media and expert references in the media, followed by interest intermediation between various levels in multi-level governance by political parties and interest groups. The second section concerns the state-centred processes of democracy, beginning with the impact the EU has on executive decision-making in the member states. Here the changing executive structures in the member states will be discussed, as well as changes to national policy-making processes. This section also has a rich comparative focus on national parliamentary scrutiny over EU decision-making in the member states. The discussion includes parliamentary practice in some of the original members of the European Community, including Germany, France, the Netherlands and Italy. We also discuss parliamentary scrutiny in the UK, one Nordic country – Denmark – the southern Mediterranean countries – Portugal, Spain and Greece – and the largest of the new member states in East Central Europe – Hungary, the Czech Republic and Poland.

The research contained in this book uses a wide variety of research methods and includes both in-depth single country case studies and comparative studies. The methods used include institutional analysis, interviews with elites, content analysis of TV news and newspaper coverage, experiments to gauge audience effects of media exposure, surveys to administrative agencies, expert surveys and the analysis of party programmes.

SOCIETAL DEMOCRATIC PROCESSES – OPINION FORMATION AND INTEREST INTERMEDIATION

In the first section of the book, De Vreese investigates the visibility and framing of the EU in the media by conducting a content analysis of TV news programmes. He does this for all 15 (at the time) member states by investigating the visibility of the 1999 European Parliament elections during the nightly news as well as the extent that national politicians were visible during the European Parliamentary election campaign. He then uses an innovative experimental design to judge the impact media exposure and 'framing' has on public opinion towards the EU.

Next Albæk, Christiansen and Togeby use content analysis of newspapers to investigate expert references in the media, so-called 'opinion elites' cited by the media to inform and guide mass opinion, to ascertain whether national or European references are made. To do this they conducted an analysis of Danish newspapers over four decades to see whether the public debate in Denmark has remained predominately national or has become more Europeanized over time. They ask whether Europeanization has created a transnational corps of experts on which the media draw, or if instead national experts are drawn upon.

Holzhacker and Römmele in their chapter on national election campaigns and European issues investigate the positioning of political parties towards the EU during national election campaigns. They present empirical data from two long-standing EU members, Germany and the Netherlands, and two applicants (at the time), Poland and the Czech Republic, countries which recently held national elections. They consider just how much information is provided by the media during national election campaigns that would allow citizens to distinguish the parties' positions on Europe.

Next we consider the processes of Europeanization and democratization on political parties and interest groups. Raunio uses expert surveys, public opinion surveys, and content analysis of party programmes in all 15 (at the time) member states to look at party system change. Raunio explores the impact of the EU on three key aspects of national party systems – the number of parties, government formation and the internal cohesion of parties. He seeks an explanation for the limited impact of European integration on national party systems.

Finally, Pedersen in his chapter on interest organizations and European integration uses a large survey of administration agencies to consider the relationship between state administration and private interests in four Nordic countries – Sweden, Denmark, Norway and Finland. He theorizes about three possible strategies for managing public and private interests in relation to the EU, a 'within strategy' in which the government itself determines policy, a 'go-through' strategy in which private interests are encouraged to go through the government in a system of national coordination, and a 'by-pass strategy' in which private interests choose to avoid the national authorities.

STATE DEMOCRATIC PROCESSES – EXECUTIVE DECISION-MAKING AND NATIONAL PARLIAMENTARY SCRUTINY

In this section we move from a primarily societal-centred approach to instead considering decision-making by the state. Börzel and Sprungk ask in their chapter whether the Europeanization of national decision-making has undermined democratic governance in the member states. They assert that the debate on how to democratize the EU tends to overlook that the EU institutions and processes themselves have a significant impact on democratic governance in the member states. They question whether the Europeanization of national decision-making undermines one of the core mechanisms for ensuring democratic representation and legitimacy in the nation state – the horizontal and vertical division of power. More specifically, they ask whether Europeanization has strengthened the centre in federal systems and the executive over legislative and judicial power.

Molina and Colino present a chapter on the changing executive structures in national decision-making and discuss domestic processes of executive decision-making that have been altered as a consequence of EU membership. They ask whether there has been convergence in institutional responses as a result of the external pressure of the EU, or whether national variation persists in executive decision-making and the impact this has on democratic legitimacy of national decision-making towards the EU in the member states.

Next we discuss a parliament's role in linking societal-centred democratic processes to decision-making by the state. Auel presents a strategic dilemma faced by national parliaments when scrutinizing their government prior to international negotiations and bargaining. She argues that parliaments are aware that an overly close coupling of parliamentary scrutiny in the member states might collide with the need to bargain and compromise during intergovernmental decision-making, to avoid structural dilemmas in the overall system. To avoid these dilemmas and overcome the difficulty in reaching a common position across countries, parliaments develop strategies to assure parliamentary scrutiny without losing international influence. This is necessary so that national interests are reflected upon within the light of their transnational consequences.

Next Holzhacker in his chapter uses institutional analysis and interviews to develop criteria for comparing the power of national parliaments to scrutinize decision-making over EU matters in the member states. He sets out these criteria in three categories: rules, institutions and party behaviour. He then uses these criteria to evaluate parliamentary scrutiny in four countries; one with majoritarian government, Great Britain, two with coalition governments, Germany and the Netherlands, and one with minority government, Denmark.

We then begin to focus in more detail on scrutiny in particular countries and areas in Europe. Here Jensen reports on a model for the strictest form of parliamentary scrutiny, the case of Denmark. While many parliaments have studied the Danish system, it emerges from the rather unique setting of a tradition of minority governments and a Eurosceptic electorate. He focuses on the incentives of the parliamentary party groups to become actively engaged in the scrutiny of EU decision-making by the national executive.

In the next chapter, Magone discusses the southern pattern of parliamentary scrutiny, based on institutional analysis of the parliaments in Portugal, Spain, Italy and Greece. He cites a tradition of executive dominance in legislative-executive relations within the state and the high degree of support for the EU in the society for the rather marginal role the parliaments in these four countries play in scrutinizing their government's EU decision-making. He asserts that there are sound reasons why these parliaments have developed soft modes of scrutiny such as scheduling of public debates and hearings, the mobilization of civil society and their engagement in inter-parliamentary cooperation.

Finally, Agh reports on the cases of parliamentary adaptation to the EU in the new member states in East Central Europe, focusing on Hungary, the Czech Republic and Poland. His chapter is concerned with the organizational capacity of these parliaments to consider their countries' decision-making in EU matters, their aggregation capacity to create a position of national interest from conflicting interests and their ability to mobilize the population concerning EU accession. Agh argues that political parties have been strong actors in the process of leading the democratic transition, because the organizational density of civil society has been rather low in these countries. Thus political parties acting in parliament have connected citizens to 'high' politics through their representative, communicative, socializing and communicative functions.

CONCLUSION

We now turn to our conclusion and present this here to guide the reader through the empirical and theoretical conclusions from the individual chapters.

What do we conclude from this research on democratic governance and European integration? We first return to our empirical question introduced at the beginning of this chapter.

How have societal and state democratic processes been impacted by multi-level governance – is there evidence of a process of Europeanization?

We must acknowledge that any conclusions discussed here must be considered tentative, even speculative. The conclusions that may be drawn from the empirical data are to be found in the chapters which follow. Those conclusions are of course strictly limited not only geographically – to a single country, region, the 15 member states prior to enlargement or to selected countries East and West – but also by time frame, and by other inherent limitations of the research design and methodology chosen by each author. But here, we will try to make speculative hunches based on the research discussed in this book. Some readers will certainly view this attempt as foolhardy for scholars to take. But others may view the following discussion as, at best, an educated guess from our research, perhaps helpful to practitioners who have to function and navigate in the world of multi-level governance even before all of the evidence is in from 25 member states at multiple points in time. Others, for example social science researchers, may use the following hunches as possible hypotheses for further research.

Given the broad scope of this book and its attempt to analyse the Europeanization of democratic processes in the member states and begin to evaluate the impact this has on democracy, we submit the following as our 'hunches' from the research presented in this volume.

First, the opinion formation process within European societies appears to have remained overwhelmingly dominated by national processes. In the media, national issues predominate over EU issues, and journalists draw on national experts to help in explaining and interpreting news events to the broader public. National election campaigns barely mention European issues, even though the national government, which is elected, must take important positions towards the EU.

Second, in terms of interest intermediation processes, the existing national political parties in most of the member states have been able to defend their traditional role linking society and the state. Few political parties have formed exclusively because of the EU. More change is seen at the level of interest group representation. Although many groups continue to aggregate their interests with others to assert a national position, some groups are beginning to bypass their national government and express their concerns directly to the EU level.

Third, Europe is impacting the balance of powers within the various institutions of the member states. The role of the executive has been strengthened vis-à-vis the legislative and judicial branches. Additionally, inside the executive branch itself, the process of Europeanization has had a differential impact on power distributions and processes within the executive, but little evidence is seen as to a convergence of these impacts. Once again, the process of Europeanization is filtered through the institutions and processes of the member states, leading to divergent impacts.

Finally, more change as a result of 'Europeanization' is seen within the area of national parliamentary scrutiny. Parliaments across Europe have responded to the loss of power which Europeanization brought, and have attempted to claw back some of the lost influence. The response has not been the same in each member state, but has ranged from requiring strict scrutiny over the government's negotiation positions to the implementation of softer mechanisms of influence. Parliaments have been careful to avoid tying the hands of their executive too closely, in order to allow international bargaining and cooperation at the EU level.

These conclusions suggest that state-centric democratic processes have been more impacted by the process of Europeanization than societal-centric ones. This is not to suggest that this is because they have been more susceptible to the process of Europeanization, but instead that often these institutions have been able to strategically respond to the new environment to preserve their power or role. We see this in the response of national exe cutives to continued EU integration. We also see it in the attempt of some national parliaments to wrestle back power lost to their executive.

But much less Europeanization is seen within the societal-centred democratic processes. Voters continue to cast their vote, in national elections and in elections for the European Parliament, overwhelmingly based on national issues and concerns. The media seem to reflect this interest of the electorate, and concentrate their reporting on national issues. The main institutions of interest intermediation also have been able to respond strategically to their environment. In most European countries, the traditional political parties have been able to keep competition at a minimum on European issues. In addition, at least the largest and best organized interest groups have been able to turn the advent of multi-level governance to their advantage.

What should we conclude then about the Europeanization of the linked processes of opinion formation, interest intermediation, executive decision-making and national parliamentary scrutiny? Organized institutions with a high capacity for adaptation have been able to respond effectively to Europeanization, but the broader public seems to have been left behind. Groups and organizations with lower adaptive capacity have not fared so well.

In summary, we see 1) little change in the process of opinion formation as a result of Europeanization, 2) existing political parties maintaining their role in interest intermediation, but with interest groups beginning to choose the best venue to assert their influence, 3) a strengthening and adaptation of the executive to demands of European integration, and 4) national parliaments beginning to regain some of their influence over the executive, but with differential responses entailing different institutional mechanisms of control, scrutiny and oversight. Thus more change is seen within the state-centric processes than in the societal-centred processes, and the responses of the state actors to the pressures of Europeanization have been shaped by existing national institutions and circumstances.

We now turn to the second main question of this book.

From a normative perspective, what impact does Europeanization have on democracy in the evolving system of multi-level governance?

We return here to our three criteria we presented from a normative perspective.

Criteria 1: The Chance for the People to Be Informed, to Understand and to Have Their Voice Heard.

We first present information in this book on opinion formation through the media. The research presented here shows that the media provides some, but minimal information to the people about Europe and national decision-making over the EU. While the visibility of the EU in TV news was 3 to 5 per cent during routine periods, during EU summits it took up around 10 per cent of total TV news time (EU Council Meetings held in 2000, compared to routine periods in 2000 measured in five countries, see De Vreese, Chapter 2). De Vreese is also interested in the degree to which national politicians and members of the national parliaments were engaged in discussions on EU affairs. Here de Vreese finds that the degree to which national politicians were part of the discussions and visible in the news programmes depended on whether elite opinion in the country was polarized or consensual. Countries with polarized elite opinion towards the EU had much more coverage of national politicians during the EP election campaign than those with consensual elite opinion.

He also finds that the way the media 'frames' issues involving the EU has a considerable bearing on how citizens understand and react to the information.

De Vreese finds that exposure to news framed in terms of strategy of the political actors produces a higher level of political cynicism compared to exposure to issue-based news (De Vreese, Chapter 2). De Vreese from a normative perspective asserts that the presence of European affairs in the news is a prerequisite for a viable public debate and contributes to the legitimization of political action and policy making. He concludes: 'given the changes in . . . power from the nation state to internationalized levels of governance, it appears that the EU is too peripheral on national news agendas' (De Vreese, Chapter 2).

Albæk, Christiansen and Togeby find that the Danish print media often use national experts to help the people understand the EU (evidence, four time points between 1960 and 2000). That may be helpful for the electorate to understand and take an interest in events in Brussels from a 'national' perspective, but makes it hard to understand how other Europeans may understand these same events.

Holzhacker and Römmele find that during national election campaigns people are provided with very little information about the stances of political parties towards Europe. This means that national elections do not provide a good vehicle for citizens to have 'their voices heard' concerning the positions their national government will take in the European Council, Council of Ministers or in Treaty negotiations (cases Germany, Netherlands, Poland, Czech Republic), national issues predominate, and very, very few articles deal both with the campaign and the EU. Voters are not provided enough information through the print media to allow them to distinguish the parties based on their stances towards the EU.

Elections are an important time for the voice of the citizens to be heard in their casting of a ballot for a particular political party. Raunio researched (all 15 member states at the time) the impact of the EU on three key aspects of national party systems – number of parties, government formation, internal cohesion of parties. The observed stability in party systems is due to the vested interests of the established parties in defending the status quo and their ability to control the electoral and legislative arenas.

The chance for the people's voice to be heard occurs not only in political parties but also through interest groups. Pedersen researched the influence of European integration on the relationship between state administration and private interests in four Nordic countries (cases Sweden, Denmark, Norway and Finland). The focus is on the national policy processes involved in managing EU issues.

He concludes that in the Nordic countries, private interests have been integrated with political administrative agencies and political institutions as a precursor for national governments to take part in EU policy processes. In all four countries, private interests have participated with a significant voice and this has assisted in the aggregation of the public and private interests.

From a normative point of view, Pedersen finds four democratic challenges linked to the interplay of private and public interests. Here we focus on just one of those mentioned – the coordination process between administration agencies, political institutions and private interests empowers the administration to take political decisions. This is because often the 'administration determines who is to be included in the coordination process, which interests (private and public) are to be taken into account, and when, how, and whether political institutions are to be consulted...' (Pedersen, Chapter 6). This means that there is at times a role for the citizens to be a part of the decision-making process, but the administrative agencies decide when this shall occur.

All in all, in answer to our first normative question, we conclude that the people are given some, but a rather minimal chance to be informed, to understand and have their voice heard in the multi-level political system.

Criteria 2: The Chance to Have Effective and Responsible Steering of EU Policies.

Börzel and Sprungk find that EU institutions and processes have a significant impact on the democratic governance in the member states. It has affected the horizontal division of power between branches of government, strengthening the executive over the legislative. The EU has also impacted the vertical division of power in decentralized member states, empowering the central state vis-à-vis the subnational levels of government. This has changed the federal nature of German federalism. Molina and Colino also find that executive structures have been strengthened vis-à-vis the national parliaments.

Thus, in response to our second normative criterion for judging the democracy, we conclude that steering over EU decision-making has become concentrated in the national executive, to the detriment of federal or regional bodies in the member states and to national parliaments.

Criteria 3: The Chance to Hold Public Officials Accountable for Their Actions.

Last, we turn to our final criterion for evaluating democracy in the emerging political system. The chance to hold public officials accountable for their actions. Here we focus on the ability of parliaments, traditionally the institution closest to the people, to hold governments accountable for decision-making towards the EU. Of course, accountability includes links back to the people, and the lack of media attention and other constraints on the ability of the people to be informed and understand EU decisions previously discussed are applicable here as well.

Auel finds that when national parliaments have considered institutional changes to better scrutinize the government over EU decision-making, they have had to confront a structural dilemma (cases the UK, Germany, France), which constrains them from only acting in the national interest. She finds that the more effectively they influence and scrutinize their government, they bind the ministers negotiating at the EU level to national interests. But this ties their hands in multi-level negotiations, and they face the possibility that the outcome of the negotiations will be inferior to compromises that might have been obtained if their government had more room to manoeuvre.

Holzhacker proposes a model with a set of eight criteria – legal, institutional and party behaviour criteria – to comparatively assess the power of scrutinizing their government's decision-making over EU matters. He concludes that parliaments with minority governments have the most power, followed by coalition government and then by majority governments. So accountability through parliament varies based on government formation and traditions of executive-legislative relations.

Jensen when discussing the Danish Parliament stresses the importance of parliamentary party groups for understanding scrutiny – scrutiny is carried out not so much by the committee as such, but by the party groups in opposition. The opposition parties have an incentive to hold the government responsible for its actions.

Magone finds that all four southern parliaments (Spain, Portugal, Italy, Greece) have difficulty holding their governments accountable. However, he argues that the parliaments constitute an important forum for their civil societies, to discuss the latest developments of the European integration process. But they struggle to keep pace with European developments and do not achieve the level of sophistication and continuity achieved even by the French parliament, and certainly not that of the member states to the North.

Finally, Ágh argues that parliaments in East Central Europe play an important role in linking state and society together. He stresses the external communication capacity – how parliaments can mobilize the population to support Europeanization and also to achieve aggregation to create a national interest from the conflicting interests associated with EU accession. Agh argues that whereas societal groups representing the interests of the new middle classes have emerged, a mature consolidation of democracy will require a more intensive social participation also on behalf of the relative 'losers' in the transition process. Here national parliaments will have to play a leading role for the inclusion of these groups into the political and policy-making processes of these new member states.

In answer to our third normative question on whether public officials can be held accountable for their actions, we conclude that this is improving as parliaments have increased their ability to conduct scrutiny, but that it varies widely across the member states. Additionally, this scrutiny is subject to certain structural limitations and dilemmas because of the need for governments to retain some flexibility in bargaining and reach compromises within the EU institutions.

We hope that the empirical research and model presented in this book will further our knowledge concerning the Europeanization of societal- and state-centric processes of democracy within multi-level governance and contribute to the continuing 'dialogue on democracy' in European studies.

NOTES

1. For a fuller discussion of this argument based on Fritz Scharpf's (1999) concepts of input and output legitimacy in the EU, see the introductory chapter to Holzhacker and Haverland (2006).
2. There are many different usages of the term Europeanization (for overviews, see Eising 2003, Olsen 2002, Radaelli 2000). Europeanization is here broadly defined as the effect of European integration on the member states. European integration is characterized by two interrelated processes: 'the delegation of policy competencies to the supranational level to achieve particular policy outcomes; and the establishment of a new set of political institutions; with executive, legislative and judicial powers' (Hix and Goetz 2000, p. 3).

REFERENCES

Beetham, David and Christopher Lord (1998), *Legitimacy and the European Union*, London: Longman.

Benz, Arthur (2003), 'Compounded Representation in EU Multilevel Governance', in Beate Kohler-Koch (ed.), *Linking EU and National Governance*, Oxford: Oxford University Press, pp. 82-110

Börzel, Tanja A. and Thomas Risse (2003), 'Conceptualising the domestic impact of Europe', in Kevin Featherstone and Claudio Radaelli (eds), *The Politics of Europeanisation*, Oxford: Oxford University Press, pp. 55-78.

Bovens, Mark (2004), 'Public accountability', in Ewan Ferlie, Larry Lynne and Christopher Pollitt (eds), *The Oxford Handbook of Public Management*, Oxford: Oxford University Press, pp. 182-208.

Cowles, Maria Green, James A. Caporaso and Thomas Risse (eds) (2001), *Transforming Europe: Europeanization and Domestic Change*, Ithaca and London: Cornell University Press.

Dahl, Robert (1989), *Democracy and its Critics*, New Haven and London: Yale University Press.

Dahl, Robert (1998), *On Democracy*, New Haven and London: Yale University Press.

Eising, Rainer (2003), 'Europäisierung und Integration: Konzepte in der EU-Forschung' in Markus Jachtenfuchs and Beate Kohler-Koch (eds), *Europäische Integration*, Opladen: Leske + Budrich UTB, pp. 387-416.

Eriksen, Erik and John Erik Fossum (2000), *Democracy in the European Union: Integration through Deliberation*, London and New York: Routledge.

Featherstone, Kevin and Claudio Radaelli (eds) (2003), *The Politics of Europeanization*, Oxford and New York: Oxford University Press.

Goetz, Klaus and Simon Hix (eds) (2001), *Europeanized Politics? European Integration and National Political Systems*, London: Frank Cass.

Haas, E.B. (1958), *The Uniting of Europe. Political, Social and Economic Forces, 1950-1957*, Stanford: Stanford University Press.

Hix, Simon and Klaus H. Goetz (2000), 'Introduction: European integration and national political systems', *West European Politics*, Special Issue, **23** (4), 1-26.

Holzhacker, Ronald and Markus Haverland (2006), *European Research Reloaded: Cooperation and Integration among Europeanized States*, Amsterdam: Kluwer/Springer.

Hooghe, Liesbet and Gary Marks (2001), *Multilevel Governance and European Integration*, Oxford: Rowman and Littlefield.

Jachtenfuchs, Markus and Beate Kohler-Koch (1996), *Europäische Integration*, Leske + Budrich.

Knill, Christoph and Dirk Lehmkuhl (2002), 'The national impact of European regulatory policy, three Europeanization mechanisms,' *European Journal of Political Research*, **41**, 255-80.

Kohler-Koch, Beate (2002), 'European networks and ideas: changing national policies?', *European Integration online Papers* **6** (6), http://eiop.or.at/eiop/texte/2002-006a.htm.

Marks, Gary and Fritz Scharpf, Philippe Schmitter, Wolfgang Streeck (1996), *Governance in the European Union*, London and Thousand Oaks, California: Sage.

Moravcsik, Andrew (1999), *The Choice for Europe: Social Purpose and State Power From Rome to Maastricht*, Ithaca: Cornell University Press.

Olsen, Johan P. (2002), 'The many faces of Europeanization', *Journal of Common Market Studies*, **40** (5), 921-50.

Przeworski, Adam, Susan Stokes and Bernard Manin (1999), *Democracy, Accountability, and Representation*, Cambridge, U.K. and New York: Cambridge University Press.

Radaelli, Claudio (2000), 'Whither Europeanization? Concept stretching and substantive change', *European integration online Papers*, **4** (8), http://eiop.or.at/eiop/texte/2000.

Risse-Kappen, Thomas (1996), 'Exploring the nature of the beast: International Relations theory and Comparative Policy Analysis meet the European Union,' *Journal of Common Market Studies*, **34** (1), 53-80.

Scharpf, Fritz W. (1998), *Governing Europe, Efficient and Democratic*, Oxford: Oxford University Press.

Scharpf, Fritz W. (1999), *Governing Europe. Effective and Legitimate?*, Oxford: Oxford University Press.

Schmidt, Manfred G. (2000), *Demokratietheorien*, Opladen: Leske + Budrich (3rd ed.).

Schmitter, Philippe (1996), 'Is it really possible to democratize the Euro-polity?', *Arena Working Papers 96/10*, Oslo: Arena.

Schmitter, Philippe C. (2000), *How To Democratize the European Union... And Why Bother?*, Lanham, MD: Rowman and Littlefield.

PART I

Opinion Formation and Interest Intermediation in Multi-level Governance

2. Visibility and Framing of European Integration in the Media

Claes de Vreese

INTRODUCTION

The European Union (EU) relies on a dual system of intergovernmental agreements and on supranational institutions (see Introduction, Chapter 1). For both components of the system, the media are important actors. The media have the potential to contribute to the legitimacy of the decision-making of supranational institutions by covering activities of genuinely European institutions such as the European Commission and the European Parliament. Conversely, the media can also contribute to the transparency and legitimacy of intergovernmental decision-making by devoting attention to national discussions of European politics such as the issues that are addressed by the Council of Ministers and the European Council.

Very few citizens have direct experiences with the EU or the process of European integration. In the system of multi-level governance, most of what citizens know about the European level comes from the media. The media function as the most important intermediary between the political arena and citizens, and they are key sources for citizens for information about European affairs. More than two-thirds of EU citizens identify television as the most frequently used and preferred method for receiving news about the EU (Eurobarometer 56 2002).

Despite the recognition of the centrality of media, extant research has hardly addressed this potential influence for public opinion formation. The debate about the democratic deficit of the EU and studies investigating the antecedents of public support for the EU largely neglect the news media although they may play a crucial role in mediating EU politics to the citizens. Some studies allude to this impact, for example Hewstone (1986), who discusses the role of the press, or Anderson and Weymouth (1999), who analyse the British press coverage of the EU. But only recent research has formally modelled the impact of media and communication variables (e.g., Peter and de Vreese 2004, de Vreese 2002, de Vreese and Boomgaarden 2006, de Vreese and Semetko 2002, 2004).

Being visible in the media is a fundamental feature of public debate, which contributes to legitimizing political actions. Legitimacy as a cornerstone of democratic governance is, also for the EU, conditional upon electoral and public support. While the legitimacy of governance is ensured by elections and referendums (authorizing power holders), legitimacy also includes responsiveness and transparency in the exercise of power and the accountability of power holders (Meyer 1999). Both during and outside election campaigns, the media are central to this process, and we therefore need research investigating (a) to what extent the EU is covered in the news cross-nationally, and (b) the effects and implications exposure and attention to such coverage have in the context of potentially volatile public opinion about the EU. First, this chapter reports on a large-scale content analysis of national news media coverage assessing the visibility of EU affairs in the news. The study looks at how visible key EU events are and how often domestic politicians address EU issues in the news. Second, it provides an individual-level example of how news contributes to public opinion formation by framing issues of European integration.

EUROPE IN THE NEWS: THE EVIDENCE FROM PREVIOUS RESEARCH

Relatively little is known about political communication and news organizations in a comparative perspective and even less about how news differs cross-nationally in terms of the reporting of European political affairs (Semetko et al. 2000). A prerequisite for any subsequent discussion about effects of news is to establish a baseline of the visibility of EU affairs in the news. News is an important input for public opinion; however, this effect is contingent upon visibility of, for example, EU affairs in the news. EU affairs may crystallize on a number of occasions. One is during political events such as the campaigns for the European Parliament elections. The most comprehensive study of these campaigns dates back to the 1979 European elections (Siune 1983). A cross-national analysis of the television coverage showed that 'Europe' did not surface on the media agenda until the last weeks before the elections. In relation to subsequent European elections it was noted that while the first elections received some media coverage because of the novelty of the event, already from the second elections the elections were of modest interest to the media (Leroy and Siune 1994, pp. 52-3).

As an example of the supranational character of the EU, the elections for the European Parliament are important moments to assess media coverage.

To investigate the visibility of EU affairs in the news, a content analysis of the two most widely watched television news programmes in the 15 EU countries (except Luxembourg) was conducted during the 1999 European Parliamentary election campaign.[1] The analysis of the visibility of the 1999 European elections on national television news (see Figure 2.1) showed that the elections took up somewhere between 1-2 per cent (e.g., Belgium, Germany, the Netherlands), 12-13 per cent (e.g., Austria, Denmark, France, Sweden) and up to 27 per cent (Portugal). During the campaign, the EU also appeared in other news, primarily news about the role of the EU in the Kosovo conflict (see Figure 2.1). These results suggest that there is significant cross-national variation in the amount of time devoted to the European elections. As we have argued elsewhere, this variation can in part be explained by a higher level of coverage in countries in which elite opinion is divided over the issue of European integration (de Vreese et al. 2007).

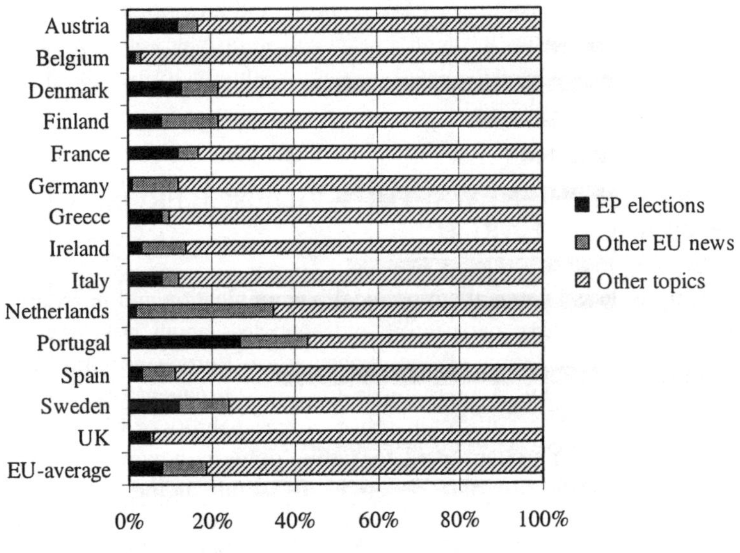

Note: Data entries are percentages of time spent of the topic.

Figure 2.1 Visibility of European elections and other EU news on national television news in the EU countries (June 1-10, 1999)

The visibility of European Parliament elections is an indication of the salience of one of the key institutions representing the EU as a supranational entity. The EU, however, has also affected national political systems and political communications, referred to as Europeanization. We therefore also assessed the extent to which national politicians and members of national parliaments engaged in discussions of EU affairs. For each story about the elections we explicitly coded whether the 'story mentioned or showed members of national parliament discussing EU affairs'. We take this as a measure of the degree to which the EU is made part of the domestic political agenda. Focusing still on television, we found that in on average 27 per cent of the stories about the European elections, a member of the national parliament was commenting on EU affairs.

Figure 2.2 shows that there was considerable variation in the pattern. In Britain, members of the national parliament were part of the election stories in 60 per cent of the cases, while this happened in a bit less than half of the stories in Sweden, Portugal and Italy, and in about one-third of the cases in Ireland, France and Belgium. In Germany and the Netherlands, there was no single case of national politicians addressing EU affairs during the campaign.

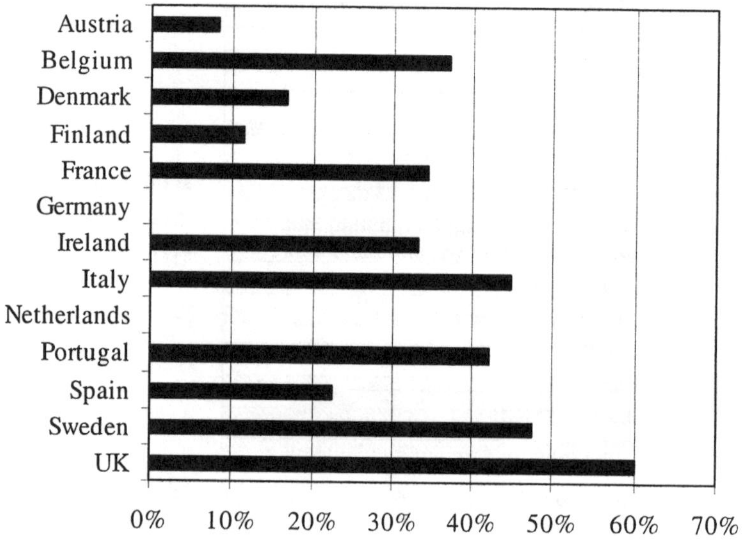

Note: Data entries are percentages of stories.

Figure 2.2 Share of election television news with national politicians discussing EU affairs

What explains this cross-national variation? Again, we may assume that if domestic political elites disagree on issues of European integration, they are more likely to engage in the campaign and thus be part of the news coverage.

Using a country expert assessment (Ray 1999) each country was classified as having either a consensual or polarized nature of political elite opinion about the EU.[2] If we compare the degree to which national politicians were part of the EU coverage in countries with polarized versus consensual elite opinion, we find that in countries with divided elite opinion, national politicians were part of the news stories in, on average, 34 per cent of the cases. In countries with consensual elite opinion the number was 18 per cent.

Moving from the results of the analysis of an EU-level, supranational institution in the news, we next turn to a key feature of the intergovernmental system of decision-making. Intergovernmental agreements are reached by nationally elected delegations at, for example, Council meetings. Therefore we conducted an analysis of news media around key EU Council summits in 2000 and during a routine period in 2000 in five EU countries to establish an encompassing measure of the visibility of EU news.[3] The analysis of the visibility of EU news during the summit periods and in the non-event periods (see Figure 2.3) showed that EU news took up around 10 per cent during the summits (with the exception of Danish news, which devoted more than 20 per cent of the news to EU topics). During the routine periods, EU news took up 3-5 per cent of the news (again with Denmark as an exception).

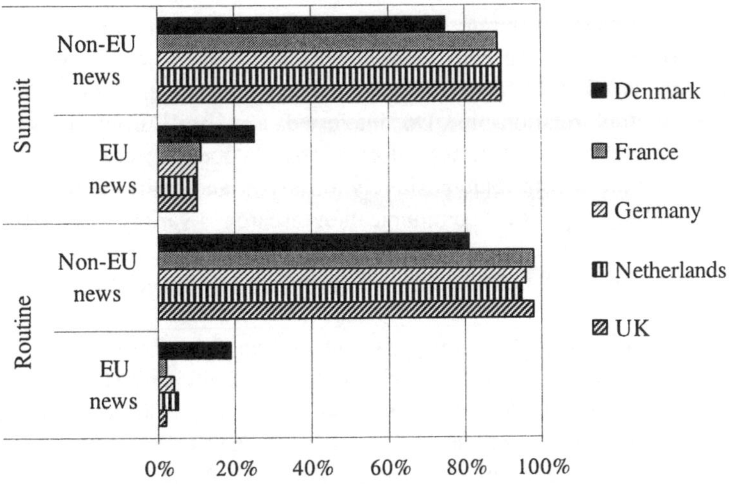

Note: Data entries are percentages of the time spent in television news on EU and non-EU topics.

Figure 2.3 Visibility of EU news during routine and summit period in the UK, Denmark, France, Germany and the Netherlands in 2000

These data suggest that EU news is rather absent from national television news (except in Denmark), but it enters the agenda around the meetings of the European Council. EU news then takes up about 10 per cent of the news time (with more in Denmark). This modest visibility – in which EU topics are rarely covered and EU officials appear only sporadically – can be labelled a 'European Union without Face or Voice' (de Vreese et al. 2007). Determining whether the visibility of the EU in national news is adequate depends largely on rather normative questions about the necessity for the media to report EU news. If legitimacy and democratic governance is preconditioned by media visibility, it is reasonable to conclude that there was too little coverage of, for example, the European elections. Given the changes in terms of legislative, executive and judicial power from the nation state to internationalized levels of governance, it also appears that the EU is too peripheral on national news agendas. A sufficient level of coverage potentially contributes towards public debate and can be a fertile ground for assessing the legitimacy of politics in Europe.

EUROPE IN PUBLIC OPINION

Do the media matter for public opinion formation? Data suggest that citizens who consult several different media sources are generally more positive towards, for example, the euro than citizens who rely on only one source (Eurobarometer 50 1999). Such observations, however, say nothing about the causality of this relationship. Do interested and pro-European citizens turn more to the news media for information? Or does the use of multiple information sources contribute positively to interest and enthusiasm for integration? Looking at political communication research, a variety of effects has been the focus of previous studies. The effects include issue salience (agenda setting), evaluation of political leaders (priming) and issue understanding (framing).

In the specific context of European integration, an emerging strand of research has addressed these types of effects. One study specifically investigated the dynamics of agenda setting during a national referendum on a European issue. Agenda-setting theory posits that the media have the ability to influence which issues citizens consider important. Drawing on the example of the 2000 national referendum on the euro in Denmark, it was found that as the news coverage of the euro referendum increased over the course of the campaign, the issue also increased in salience on the public agenda (de Vreese and Semetko 2004). On the individual level, exposure to news about the referendum increased the likelihood of considering the euro the most important issue, which supports the agenda-setting hypothesis on the individual level.

On two occasions evidence of priming effects were found in relation to key EU events. Priming in the realm of political communication refers to the phenomenon where prior information is used in subsequent evaluations of political leaders. During the 1997 EU Council summit in Amsterdam a two-wave panel study found that attitudes towards the EU became increasingly important for the overall evaluation of the Dutch prime minister and minister of foreign affairs (Semetko et al. 2003). Similarly, during the 2000 Danish euro referendum campaign, the overall rating of the Danish prime minister declined, and this was primarily caused by the fact that citizens rated his performance on handling the euro issue very poorly, which resulted in negative overall evaluations (de Vreese 2004a).

The potential effects of news framing have also been put to the test in the case of European integration. One study suggested that the way news about the euro is framed can have large implications for readers' short-term responses to the euro and can lead audiences to think about political issues along the lines suggested in the news frame (Valkenburg et al. 1999). In subsequent studies de Vreese (2002) found that a news frame, though this is a relatively minor part of a news report, may in fact be as influential for audiences as the core facts and figures of news when conceiving political issues. These studies provide empirical substance to the claim that news about the EU is an important antecedent to consider when understanding public perceptions of and support for the EU.

ACTIVATING MACHIAVELLIAN STEREOTYPES

Various scholars have emphasized the poor image of EU politics in public opinion (e.g., Meyer 1999, Tumber 1995). At the same time, recent studies in political communication have addressed how the media contribute to an increase in political cynicism on the one hand and a decrease in political efficacy, confidence in political institutions and public sentiments to participate in elections on the other (Blumler and Gurevitch 1995, Entman 1989, Fallows 1996, Nye et al. 1997).[4] In particular strategic news, that is news including coverage of politicians' motivations and personalities, focus on disagreement between parties, politicians or voters, and the presence and emphasis on polls in the news (Jamieson 1992) has been blamed for evoking political cynicism and negative perceptions of political campaigns (e.g., Cappella and Jamieson 1997, Patterson 1993, Rhee 1997, Valentino et al. 2001a, 2001b).

The second part of this chapter addresses the question whether strategic news reporting about European integration contributes to political cynicism and negative sentiments towards the EU. Outside the US, little is known about the strategic reporting of politics, though the focus on horse race and game aspects of politics is known from several studies of national election campaigns in, for example, the UK, Germany and the Netherlands (e.g., Brants and van Kempen 2002, Brettschneider 1997, Norris et al. 1999, van Praag and Brants 2000). It remains an open question whether strategic news affects political cynicism in the context of European integration.

An experiment was conducted to explore the effects of strategic television news on political cynicism, issue evaluations and policy support in the specific context of European integration (for further details about the study, see de Vreese 2004b). Previous research has centred on the effects of the strategy frame in election campaigns or in relation to high salience issues such as health care (Cappella and Jamieson 1997, Valentino et al. 2001a). Based on the findings by Cappella and Jamieson (1997) it is hypothesized that exposure to strategic news induces political cynicism compared to issue-focused news, that is, news dealing with substantive dimensions and concrete policies related to a topic. Additionally, based on the findings by Rhee (1997) it was expected that exposure to strategic television news activates negative issue evaluations and depresses positive issue evaluations. Finally, the effects of strategic news on support for European enlargement were also investigated. Previous research indicates that frames in the news may affect public support for various issues (e.g., McLeod and Detenber 1999, Nelson and Oxley 1999). Based on these studies a third hypothesis was cautiously formulated suggesting that exposure to strategic news depresses support for a policy.

Citizens rely on a combination of newly acquired information and existing predispositions when forming attitudes (e.g., Gamson 1992, Neuman et al. 1992). Previous research has pointed to the role of political knowledge and political efficacy when investigating political cynicism. Valentino et al. (2001a) found exposure to strategic news to be associated with lower levels of turnout intention for participants with lower levels of education. Rhee (1997) found political knowledge significantly bolstered readers' use of an experimentally induced frame in their interpretation of an election campaign. Finally, political efficacy, that is citizens' feeling of making a difference in the political process, is negatively related to cynicism, suggesting that efficacious citizens are less likely to be cynical about politics (Pinkleton and Austin 2001). This study therefore includes political knowledge and efficacy in the investigation of political cynicism.

DESIGN AND PROCEDURE

Despite criticisms of impeded external validity, experimentation is superior in an attempt to investigate effects of a key independent variable (Brown and Melamed 1990, Kinder and Palfrey 1993). This study focuses on television because television is repeatedly identified as the most important source of political information (Eurobarometer 56 2002, Chaffee and Kanihan 1997). To address potential shortcomings in previous experimental studies of television news, an entire version of a national evening news broadcast was produced in cooperation with the *NOS Journaal* in the Netherlands. Inserted into this bulletin was a news story on the enlargement of the EU. Two versions of the story were produced for this post-test only, between-subjects experimental design.[5] One version was framed in terms of strategy; the other focused on substantive aspects of the issue.

Participants were recruited to ensure variation in terms of gender, age and level of education as these demographic indicators have proven important for understanding support for European integration (Eurobarometer 49 1998, Gabel 1998). Participants were invited to come to the headquarters of the NOS Audience Research department to participate in a television study. A total of 83 participants completed all steps in the study.[6] Upon arrival, participants were randomly assigned to the two conditions.[7] First, participants filled out a background questionnaire containing demographics, measures of media use, an assessment of political knowledge and feeling of political efficacy. Second, participants watched the experimental bulletin. They were informed that they would watch a proof taping of today's 8 o'clock News, taped in the late afternoon of that day. A post-test was taken immediately after watching the news. Upon completion of the post-test, participants were reimbursed for their travel costs, and they received a gift voucher valued at approximately 16 euro.

A bulletin with the characteristics of the regular 8 o'clock news, including a nationwide known anchorman, was produced. This bulletin, with the experimentally manipulated story as the second story, was made according to common journalistic practices and technical standards at the *NOS Journaal*. The focal point of the experimentally manipulated news story was a (simulated) publication of a report by the European Commission encouraging a fast entry of Poland into the EU. The story was introduced by the anchor. It then contained a brief summary of the report's conclusions. Following this the Secretary of State for Foreign Affairs provided a quote that was scripted in advance. The news story then provided brief background information about the history of the EU. A second quote was then delivered by the Secretary of State before a closing statement about public support for the enlargement in other EU countries.

With the exception of three sentences the two stories were identical in each of the experimental conditions. First, the experimental manipulation consisted of one sentence in the opening section of the story. The journalist's text here referred to a 'charm campaign' and a 'strategic plan' (strategy version) rather than 'concrete policies' (issue version). Second, the Secretary of State referred to a 'battle' (strategy) as opposed to a 'signal' (issue) in his quote. Finally, the closing sentence referred to mobilizing public support (strategy) versus focusing on policies (issue).

THE EFFECT OF STRATEGIC NEWS ON POLITICAL CYNICISM

The first hypothesis suggested that exposure to news framed in terms of strategy produces a higher level of political cynicism compared to exposure to issue-based news. A four-item index formed a scale of political cynicism.[8] Based on previous research political knowledge and political efficacy were included as control variables.[9]

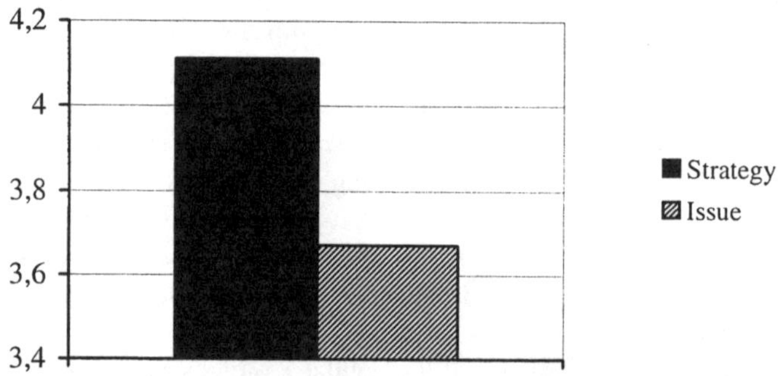

Note: Entries are mean scores of cynicism on a 5-point scale.

Figure 2.4 Political cynicism by experimental condition

Figure 2.4 displays the means of political cynicism in the two conditions. The first hypothesis is supported as participants in the strategy condition (M = 4.11) displayed a significantly higher level of political cynicism compared to participants in the issue condition (M = 3.67) in the immediate post-test (significant difference at $p < .01$).

Introducing political knowledge, political efficacy and the interaction between exposure to strategy news and political knowledge as additional control variables did not affect the impact of exposure to the strategy frame on political cynicism. The effect of exposure to strategy news was still significant in the immediate post-test after adjustment for the controls. Political knowledge was a significant positive predictor of political cynicism, while political efficacy was a significant negative covariate for political cynicism. This suggests that the more politically knowledgeable participants feeling less efficacious expressed higher levels of political cynicism. The effect of the interaction between exposure to strategy news and political knowledge on cynicism was not significant.

THE EFFECT OF STRATEGIC NEWS ON ISSUE EVALUATION

It was secondly predicted that exposure to news framed in terms of strategy activates and renders negative evaluations of the enlargement issue and depresses positive evaluations. To measure the volume of negative versus positive reactions to the issue of enlargement of the EU, an open-ended thought-listing item was used asking participants to list their thoughts about the enlargement issue.[10] The affective tone of each thought was assessed as 'positive' towards enlargement, 'negative' or 'neutral'.[11]

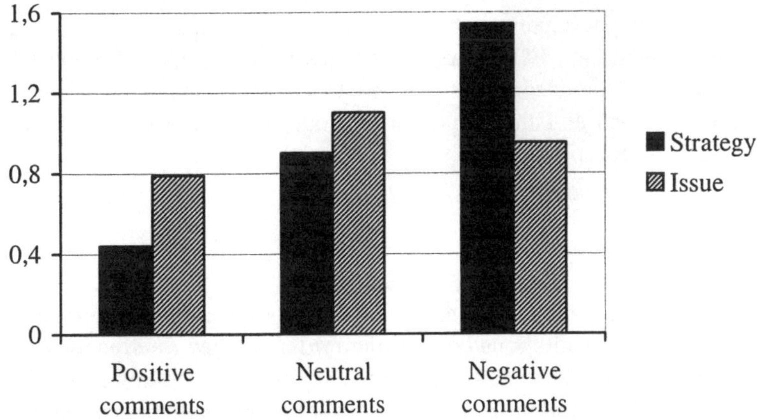

Figure 2.5 Evaluation of EU enlargement by experimental condition

Figure 2.5 shows the valence – positive, neutral and negative – of the thoughts provided by the participants in each of the conditions. As expected, the number of positive thoughts differed between the two conditions with participants in the strategy condition (M = .44) listing fewer positive thoughts than participants in the issue condition (M = .79). Conversely, participants in the strategy condition (M = 1.54) listed more negative thoughts than participants in the issue condition (M =. 95). Both differences are significant ($p < .05$). The volume of neutral thoughts was not affected by the experimental condition so that participants in both conditions listed, on average, a comparable amount of neutral thoughts. In sum, the news frames significantly influenced the likelihood that participants reacted with valenced – both positive and negative – responses.[12]

THE EFFECT OF STRATEGIC NEWS ON POLICY SUPPORT

It was finally expected that exposure to news framed in terms of strategy suppresses support for EU enlargement. To investigate the effect of the two frames on support for advanced European integration in the form of enlargement of the EU, five items were used.[13] The responses to the statements were recoded and averaged to form a scale of 'enlargement support' ranging from 1 to 5 (M = 3.06, SD = .80, α = .83). For the analysis of support for the enlargement of the EU, gender, age, education and political knowledge were included in the analysis (see Gabel 1998). The analysis showed that there was no difference in the level of support for future enlargement of the EU between participants in the two conditions. Political knowledge was a positive predictor for EU enlargement support. The findings suggest that more politically knowledgeable individuals are more supportive of the EU enlargement plans and that exposure to strategic news coverage does not affect policy support.

DISCUSSION

In the dual system of governance in which intergovernmental agreements and supranational institutions coexist, the media is a key intermediary. This chapter investigated the visibility of the EU in the media looking at the EU as a supranational institution in the case of the European Parliament and as a forum for intergovernmental agreements in the case of European Council summits. The study revealed considerable cross-national variation in the extent the EU is covered in the news and the degree to which national politicians are engaging in discussing EU affairs. Coverage was particularly present in countries where elite opinion is divided over the issue of European integration. This suggests that elite cues about disagreement translate into higher visibility on the news media agenda. This presence of European affairs in the news is a prerequisite for a viable public debate which contributes to legitimizing political actions and policy-making.

The chapter also provided an individual-level example of how news media contribute to public opinion formation by framing issues of European integration. The experiment investigated the effects of strategic news coverage of politics on political cynicism. The results corroborate previous research from the US that exposure to strategic news encourages political cynicism (Cappella and Jamieson 1997, Valentino et al. 2001a). Over time, we may for example find that repeated exposure to news framed in terms of strategy produces a cumulative effect. Such a phenomenon would be in line with arguments advanced by Zaller (1992, 2002) suggesting that media effects are likely to be of modest magnitude and most prominent in cases of extensive coverage with consistent directional bias. In fact, the experimental evidence presented here corroborates results showing that high exposure to strategic television news during a referendum campaign on an issue of European integration led to increases in political cynicism and negative campaign evaluations when controlling for both the level of cynicism and negativity at the outset of the campaign and a number of additional predictors of political cynicism (de Vreese and Semetko 2002).

As shown in this chapter, strategic news activated negative evaluations of the EU enlargement and depressed positive issue evaluations. Participants who were exposed to strategy-framed news listed significantly more negative and fewer positive thoughts and comments about EU enlargement compared to participants in the issue condition. Strategic news, however, had no impact on policy support. A similar approval level for future enlargement of the EU was found in the two conditions. That said, it should be noted that the strategic news frame does not offer direct suggestions about whether or not to support a policy. Research investigating the effects of news frames with an inherent valence, that is framing an issue as being 'good/bad' or negative or positive, has found effects of news frames on policy support. Nelson and Oxley (1999) demonstrated this by framing a land development issue as affecting, for example, the environment, which depressed the support for the plans. Similarly, de Vreese and Boomgaarden (2003) found that television news that depicted EU enlargement disadvantageously affected the level of support so that viewers who saw this news were less supportive of the enlargement compared to viewers watching a more positive framing of the issue.

For the process of advanced European integration, the experiment reported here suggests that news coverage may be a very important intermediary for understanding public opinion about and support for European issues. The debate about the democratic deficit of the EU and public perceptions of the EU has largely neglected the news media although they may play a crucial role in this process. While the media is one of several agents in the formation of public opinion, it is certainly a significant source of impact.

As Europe develops further in the process towards shaping multi-level governance, national media are affected in several ways. Europeanization affects news media in several manners: media markets become increasingly competitive and regulations are enforced (see Semetko et al. 2000 for an overview). However, media content is changing too as a result of Europeanization. The EU becomes the source of more news, and European perspectives increasingly become part of news coverage of areas that were traditionally domestic in nature.

The interactions between national and European level actors in the multi-level mode of governance are likely to generate attention in the future. While the role of national parliaments in the integration process has been (see Holzhacker, Chapter 10) and continues to be a point of discussion, national actors, including the parliament, may prove to be media agenda setters in terms of coverage of European affairs. Parliamentary scrutiny of European affairs is a topic in the news, especially in countries where elite opinion is divided over issues of European affairs. Journalists are challenged to act as active agents in this respect by benchmarking competencies between national- and European-level actors.

In terms of public opinion future research needs to focus on the interaction between national and European levels of governance. As 'Europe' becomes more centre stage in politics, research may investigate how national/domestic political leaders are evaluated and judged by their performance on European integration. In other words, what are the domestic political implications of increased visibility of EU events, and does the success or failure of EU pol-icies affect politicians' evaluations in the domestic arena? The European system of multi-level governance not only affects the media, but the system itself is affected by the media's interpretation and evaluation of the system.

NOTES

1. The research was carried out at The Amsterdam School of Communications Research at the University of Amsterdam. All stories in the news programmes were analysed to identify news about the campaign. The unit of analysis was the individual news story.
2. The criterion is a sufficiently visible anti-EU party in the country. An anti-EU party was defined as a party that had, in a survey among country experts (Ray 1999), received on average a score of 2 (*opposed to European integration*) on a 7-point scale. A *sufficiently visible* anti-EU party was defined as parties that gained at least 5 per cent of the votes in the most recent general election (assessed with reference to June 1999). By this classification Austria, Denmark, France, Greece and Sweden has polarized elite opinion. Italy (with Forza Italia) and the UK (with the Conservatives' vigorous anti-EU campaign in 1999) were added as was Belgium given the concurrent national elections which boosted the

visibility of national politicians even in EU news stories. Countries with consensual elite opinion in this analysis are Finland, Germany, Ireland, the Netherlands and Spain.

3. The summits are held four times a year, twice during the spring and twice during the fall, and are hosted by individual EU member states holding the rotating EU presidency. The summits included in this study are Lisbon (March 2000) and Feira (June 2000) during the Portuguese presidency, Biarritz (October 2000) and Nice (December 2000) during the French presidency. For each of the summits, news was collected. For reasons of comparability, seven days are included in each of the summit periods. For further details, see de Vreese (2002) and Peter and de Vreese (2004). News was selected during seven weeks in 2000 to provide the opportunity to investigate news coverage of European affairs in a non-event setting. For details about the sample, see Peter et al. (2003).
4. While the discussion of the role of (news) media in political processes has received considerable scholarly attention both in the US and in Europe, the evidence is not conclusive as to whether exposure to news contributes in a negative or positive direction towards, for example, political cynicism, trust and electoral mobilization. Studies in the US suggest that the media disengage citizens, fuel cynicism and erode social capital (Cappella and Jamieson 1997, Patterson 1993, Putnam 1995, 2000). This perspective is challenged by studies drawing on data from both the US and Europe suggesting that attention to news media is associated with higher levels of trust, knowledge and political mobilization (Norris 2000). Others suggest that effects, either virtuous or vicious, are not omnipresent but contingent upon, for example, type of media use, political sophistication and education (Moy and Pfau 2001, Moy and Scheufele 2000).
5. The design does not include a control group which would have to be treated to a 'frameless' news story. To omit a control group in the design is in line with the procedures used in most experimental framing research (Iyengar 1991, McLeod and Detenber 1999, Nelson et al. 1997, Valentino et al. 2001a). Since this study is designed to test the effects of strategic news, the other group (exposed to issue-driven news) may effectively be considered the functional equivalent of a control group (Brown and Melamed 1990).
6. This sample represents variation (60 per cent males, age 15-67 ($M = 43.8$, $SD = 15.2$), with varying levels of education, but is not representative of the Dutch population, yet preferable to a homogeneous convenience sample given the nature of the issue.
7. The key feature of experimentation is the elimination of intervening variables through random assignment to experimental conditions. In this study the randomization procedure was successful: chi-square tests revealed no significant differences between the different conditions on demographic dimensions: gender ($\chi 2 = .33$, $df = 1$, $p = 57$), age ($\chi 2 = 50.53$, $df = 45$, $p = .26$), education ($\chi 2 = 7.53$, $df = 8$, $p = .48$).
8. The items formed a scale of political cynicism ranging from 1 to 5 ($M = 3.89$, $SD = .79$, $\alpha = .64$).The four items were derived from Cappella and Jamieson (1997) to tap perceptions of politicians' motivations, their character and confidence in the substance of policy debates: (a) Politicians are too superficial when dealing with enlargement, (b) Politicians are too concerned with public opinion about enlargement, (c) The debate about enlargement is more about strategy than content, and (d) Politicians are clear and honest in their arguments about enlargement.
9. Political knowledge was measured by six factual questions, averaged to range from 0 to 1 ($M = .67$, $SD = .28$) ($\alpha = .63$). Political efficacy was measured by three standard items and averaged to form a scale from 1 to 7($M = 3.53$, $SD = 1.43$) ($\alpha = .61$). The questions were: 'Sometimes politics is so complex that people like me do not understand what is going on', 'People like me have no influence what the government does', and' 'I think I am better informed about politics than most others'.
10. The question wording was: 'We are interested to hear how you think about the issue of the enlargement of the European Union. One of the news stories in the *Journaal* was about the enlargement of the EU. Please list your thoughts and feelings about the EU enlargement'. This procedure has successfully been employed in previous experimental research on the effects of frames in the news
11. The thoughts were classified by two coders blind to the experimental condition. The intercoder agreement on the classification of thoughts ranged from r .91 to $r = .95$.

12. Based on previous research, political knowledge and verbosity, that is the degree of issue elaboration measured by the number of words participants listed for the open-ended measure (M = 32.3, SD = 21.7), were included as control variables (Price et al. 1997, Rhee 1997). The control variables did not alter the results. Exposure to strategy news still had a significant negative effect on listing positive thoughts and a positive significant effect on listing negative thoughts after adjustment for the controls. Verbosity was a positive predictor of the number of neutral thoughts. Political knowledge and verbosity were both significant positive covariates for the number of negative thoughts. This suggests that the more politically knowledgeable, and participants elaborating more on the issue, more often provided negative comments.
13. The items (measured on 5-point Likert agree–disagree scales) included positively and negatively framed statements: (a) The enlargement of the EU has more advantages than disadvantages, (b) The enlargement of the EU should happen faster than it is currently happening, (c) I would be willing to sacrifice to help a less strong country in Europe, (d) The EU should be enlarged with former East-bloc countries such as Poland and Lithuania, and (e) The EU should be enlarged with South European countries such as Cyprus and Turkey.

REFERENCES

Anderson, Peter J. and Anthony Weymouth (1999), *Insulting the Public? The British Press and the European Union*, London: Longman.

Blumler, Jay G. and Michael Gurevitch (1995), *The Crisis of Public Communication*, London: Routledge.

Brants, Kees and Hetty van Kempen (2002), 'The ambivalent watchdog: The changing culture of political journalism and its effect', in Raymond Kuhn and Erik Neveu (eds), *Political Journalism. New Challenges, New Practices*, London: Routledge, pp. 168-85.

Brettschneider, Frank (1997), 'The press and the polls in Germany, 1980-1994: Poll coverage as an essential part of an election', *International Journal of Public Opinion Research*, **9**, 248-65.

Brown, Steven R. and Lawrence E. Melamed (1990), *Experimental Design and Analysis*, Newbury Park, CA: Sage.

Cappella, Joseph N. and Kathleen Hall Jamieson (1997), *Spiral of Cynicism*, New York: Oxford University Press.

Chaffee, Steve and Stacey F. Kanihan (1997), 'Learning about politics from the mass media', *Political Communication*, **17**, 421-30.

Entman, Robert B. (1989), *Democracy Without Citizens: Media and the Decay of American Politics*, New York: Oxford University Press.

Eurobarometer (various years/issues), *Eurobarometer: Public Opinion in the European Union*, Brussels, Belgium: Directorate-General X.

Fallows, James (1996), *Breaking the News: How the Media Undermine American Democracy*, New York, NY: Pantheon Books.

Gabel, Matthew (1998), 'Public support for European integration: An empirical test of five theories', *Journal of Politics*, **60**, 333-54.

Gamson, William A. (1992), *Talking Politics*, New York: Cambridge University Press.

Hewstone, Miles (1986), *Understanding Attitudes to the European Community: A Social-Psychological Study in Four Member States*, Cambridge: Cambridge University Press.

Iyengar, Shanto (1991), *Is Anyone Responsible? How Television Frames Political Issues*, Chicago, IL: University of Chicago Press.

Jamieson, Kathleen Hall (1992), *Dirty Politics: Deception, Distraction, and Democracy*, New York: Oxford University Press.

Kinder, Donald R. and Thomas R. Palfrey (eds) (1993), *Experimental Foundations of Political Science*, Ann Arbor: University of Michigan Press.

Leroy, Pascal and Karen Siune (1994), 'The role of television in European elections: The cases of Belgium and Denmark', *European Journal of Communication*, **9**, 47-69.

McLeod, Doug M. and Benjamin H. Detenber (1999), 'Framing effects of television news coverage of social protest', *Journal of Communication,* **49** (3), 3-23.

Meyer, Christopf (1999), 'Political legitimacy and the invisibility of politics: Exploring the European Union's communication deficit', *Journal of Common Market Studies*, **37**, 617-39.

Moy, Patricia and Michael Pfau (2001), *With Malice Toward All? The Media and Public Confidence in Democratic Institutions*, Westport, CT: Praeger.

Moy, Patricia and Dietram A. Scheufele (2000), 'Media effects on political and social trust', *Journalism and Mass Communication Quarterly*, **77**, 744-59.

Nelson, Tom E. and Zoe Oxley (1999), 'Issue framing effects on belief importance and opinion', *Journal of Politics*, **61**, 1040-61.

Nelson, Tom E., Rosalee A. Clawson and Zoe M. Oxley (1997), 'Media framing of a civil liberties conflict and its effect on tolerance', *American Political Science Review*, **91** (3), 567-84.

Neuman, William R., Marion R. Just and Ann N. Crigler (1992), *Common Knowledge. News and the Construction of Political Meaning*, Chicago: The University of Chicago Press.

Norris, Pippa (2000), *A Virtuous Circle: Political Communications in Postindustrial Societies*, Cambridge: Cambridge University Press.

Norris, Pippa, John Curtice, David Sanders, Margaret Scammell and Holli A. Semetko, (1999), *On Message: Communicating the Campaign*, London: Sage.

Nye, Joseph. S. Jr., Philip D. Zelikow and David C. King (eds) (1997), *Why People Don't Trust Government*, Cambridge: Harvard University Press.

Patterson, Thomas E. (1993), *Out of Order*, New York: Alfred A. Knopf.

Peter, Jochen and Claes H. de Vreese (2004), 'In search of Europe – A cross-national comparative study of the European Union in national television news', *Harvard Journal of Press/Politics*, **9** (4), 3-24.

Peter, Jochen, Holli A. Semetko and Claes H. de Vreese (2003), 'Politics on television in Europe: How European is it', *EU Politics*, **4** (3), 305-27.

Pinkleton, Bruce E. and Eroca W. Austin (2001), 'Individual motivations, perceived media importance and political disaffection', *Political Communication*, **18**, 321-34.

van Praag, Philip and Kees Brants (eds) (2000), *Tussen beeld en inhoud: Politiek en media in de verkiezingen van 1998*. [Between Image and Content: Politics and the Media in the 1998 Elections], Amsterdam: Het Spinhuis.

Price, Vincent, Davis Tewksbury and Elisabeth Powers (1997), 'Switching trains of thought: The impact of news frames on readers' cognitive responses', *Communication Research*, **24**, 481-506.

Putnam, Robert D. (1995), 'Bowling alone: America's declining social capital', *Journal of Democracy*, **6** (1), 65-78.

Putnam, Robert D. (2000), *Bowling Alone: The Collapse and Revival of American Community*, New York: Simon & Schuster.

Ray, Leonard (1999), 'Measuring party orientations towards European integration: Results from an expert survey', *European Journal of Political Research*, **36**, 283-306.

Rhee, June W. (1997), 'Strategy and issue frames in election campaign coverage: A social cognitive account of framing effects', *Journal of Communication*, **47** (3), 26-48.

Semetko, Holli A., Claes H. de Vreese and Jochen Peter (2000), 'Europeanised politics – Europeanised media? European integration and political communication', *West European Politics*, **23** (4), 121-42.

Semetko, Holli A., Wouter van der Burg and Patti M. Valkenburg (2003), 'The influence of political events on attitudes towards the European Union', *British Journal of Political Science*, **33**, 621-34.

Siune, Karen (1983), 'The campaign on television: What was said and who said it?' in Jay G. Blumler (ed.), *Communicating to Voters: Television in the First European Parliamentary Elections*, London: Sage, pp. 223-40.

Tumber, Howard (1995), 'Marketing Maastricht: The EU and news management', *Media, Culture & Society*, **17** (3), 511-20.

Valentino, Nicholas A., Matthew N. Beckmann and Thomas A. Buhr (2001a), 'A spiral for of cynicism for some: The contingent effects of campaign news frames on participation and confidence in government', *Political Communication*, **18**, 347-67.

Valentino, Nicholas A., Thomas A. Buhr and Matthew N. Beckmann (2001b), 'When the frame is the game: Revisiting the impact of "strategic" campaign coverage on citizen's information retention', *Journalism and Mass Communication Quarterly*, **78**, 93-112.

Valkenburg, Patti M., Holli A. Semetko and Claes H. de Vreese (1999), 'The effects of news frames on readers' thoughts and recall', *Communication Research*, **26**, 550-68.

de Vreese, Claes H. (2002), *Framing Europe: Television News and European Integration*, Amsterdam: Aksant.

de Vreese, Claes H. (2004a), 'Primed by the euro', *Scandinavian Political Studies*, **27** (1), 45-65.

de Vreese, Claes H. (2004b), 'The effects of strategic news on political cynicism, issue evaluations and policy support: A two-wave experiment', *Mass Communication & Society*, **7** (2), 191-215.

de Vreese, Claes H. and Hajo G. Boomgaarden (2003), 'Valenced news frames and public support for EU: Linking content analysis and experimental data', *Communications: The European Journal of Communication*, **3** (4), 261-81.

de Vreese, Claes H. and Hajo G. Boomgaarden (2006), 'Media effects on public opinion about the enlargement of the European Union', *Journal of Common Market Studies*, **44** (2), 419-36.

de Vreese, Claes H. and Holli A. Semetko (2002), 'Cynical and engaged: strategic campaign coverage, public opinion and mobilization in a referendum', *Communication Research*, **29** (6), 615-41.

de Vreese, Claes H. and Holli A. Semetko (2004), *Political Campaigning in Referendums: Framing the Referendum Issue*, London: Routledge.

de Vreese, Claes H., Edmund Lauf and Jochen Peter (2007, in press), 'The media and European Parliament elections: Second-rate coverage of a second-order event?', in

Wouter van der Brug and Cees van der Eijk (eds), *European Elections and Domestic Politics: Lessons from the Past and Scenarios for the Future*, Southbend: University of Notre Dame Press.

Zaller, John R. (1992), *The Nature and Origins of Mass Opinion*, New York: Cambridge University Press.

Zaller, John R. (2002), 'The statistical power of election studies to detect media exposure effects in political campaigns', *Electoral Studies*, **21** (2), 297-330.

3. Europeanization of Expert References in the Media? Researchers as Sources in Danish Daily Newspapers 1961-2001

Erik Albæk, Peter Munk Christiansen and Lise Togeby

In the autumn of 2001 the Danish media called upon experts in great numbers to comment on various aspects of the September 11 terrorist attack on the US: fire fighting, flight safety, steel construction, Islamic radicalism, Middle East politics, American politics, and so on. Although the number of experts consulted by the print and electronic media may well have been exceptional during that period, the media coverage of September 11 and its aftermath supports the widespread impression among journalists, researchers, and the general public that experts are used much more in the mass media today than in previous decades. It further supports the likewise widespread impression that globalization – economic, political, cultural – has become a prominent feature of modern societies. September 11 in itself became a symbol that political globalization can strike anywhere in the world, even in a country that had not been attacked on its own soil since the War of 1812. The media coverage also demonstrated how fast information about such an attack spreads across the world and how the news media today draw on expert knowledge from around the globe to help explain such unexpected and dramatic events. CNN did it. BBC did it. And the Danish media did it. But how globalized is the media's reference to, and use of, experts? How Europeanized is it?

In an earlier study, we focused generally on the use of experts in the Danish media, without regard to the nationality of those experts (Albæk et al. 2003). In this article we use that study as background for, and as a means of framing, our investigation of globalization, Europeanization, and their impact on the nationality of experts cited in the Danish media.

THE MEDIA'S INCREASED REFERENCE TO EXPERTS

In our earlier study (Albæk et al. 2003) we traced how references in the media to experts have changed over time. Since the term 'experts', both in the social science literature and in the view of the general public, has evolved to include a broader range of actors (Steele 1995), we included in our study only a very specific subset of experts, namely, scientific researchers working at independent research institutions, a subset whose definition has remained constant over the 40-year period of analysis. All articles with references to scientific researchers that appeared in the three largest national Danish newspapers in a month-long period (January 15-February 14) in 1961, 1971, 1981, 1991 and 2001 were included in the study.

The study demonstrated that the number of experts cited in newspaper articles has increased dramatically over the last four decades. There has been an accelerating increase in the number of articles referring to researchers, from 64 in 1961, to 441 in 2001 – a sevenfold increase. If one takes into account that the newspapers have themselves grown in size – thereby providing more space for stories in which journalists might make reference to researchers – the proportional increase is 'only' threefold. Whichever calculation is used, the increase in the number of articles referring to researchers in the three Danish newspapers observed is substantial, and it substantially accelerated during the 1990s.

The study showed that from the 40-year period of study, the number of researchers cited increased in all faculty fields, but that the increases varied considerably from one field to another. Over the entire period, the natural and health sciences increased the least even though in 1961 more experts from these fields were cited than from any of other field. By comparison, whereas social science research appeared seldom in the three newspapers in 1961, the number of social science experts exploded – more than twentyfold – by 2001, at which point they were, by far, the most frequently cited experts. In 1961, social scientists made up 13 per cent of all researchers appearing in news articles, compared to approximately 45 per cent in 1991 and 2001. This rise in the social sciences was matched by a parallel decline in the natural and technical, or engineering, sciences. Humanities researchers made up slightly more than 10 per cent in all years measured.

The study also showed a marked shift over time in what researchers comment on. In 1961 and 1971, researchers' comments on their own and others' research made up two-thirds of all their comments in the three newspapers. Beginning in 1981, researchers shifted from primarily communicating or commenting on research results to commenting on knowledge produced outside the world of science and also on decisions and events not immediately related to new research. In 1991 and 2001, less than half of researchers' comments were about their own and others' research. In 2001, 59 per cent of all researcher comments related to knowledge produced outside of research institutions, to political or administrative decisions, or to other events. In 1961, the corresponding share of comments was 35 per cent.

What researchers comment on varies across faculty fields, which can, in this context, be divided into two main categories. In the first – the hard sciences (the natural, health, agricultural and technical sciences) – researchers overwhelmingly commented on their own and others' research. That is, they primarily communicated information on research, and seldom on knowledge generated outside of research institutions. It would be incorrect to infer, however, that they confined themselves to commenting exclusively on research; to some extent, they – especially the health scientists – commented on political decisions and other events. In the other main group, comprising the social sciences and humanities, the researchers commented much less than hard scientists on their own and others' research.

The academic literature focusing specifically on increased reference to expert sources in the media is very limited. Nevertheless, possible explanations for the increased reference to expert sources in the media may be found in a vast body of literature focusing on the increased role of expertise in modern society in general. The basic theoretic claims of this literature are found in a distilled form in British sociologist Anthony Giddens' book *The Consequences of Modernity*.

Giddens emphasizes two trends that indicate why experts play a greater role in modern society compared to earlier (Giddens 1990, pp. 21-9). First, we increasingly use knowledge, and well as technology produced in highly specialized contexts, for problem solving. The division of labour in modern society is so extensive that we increasingly put our lives in the hands of professional specialists and experts who possess technical knowledge and skills that we do not have. We can no longer imagine a world without specialized knowledge and technology.

Second, modern society is increasingly reflexive (Giddens 1990, pp. 36-45); that is, in modern society we – as individuals and in institutional contexts – reflect increasingly upon ourselves. Whereas in pre-modern societies, tradition made many issues and relations indisputable (even God-given), today nothing is taken for granted. Everything is challenged, including our own actions and choices. By the same token, new information and knowledge can always force us to revise our views, habits and action. And in this context, there is plenty of knowledge available; modern technology allows us to collect, store and process enormous amounts of information, especially within modern sciences.

Increased reflexivity does not necessarily enable us to control the world any better than before. First, knowledge is not automatically converted into action; it must be processed in a social or political system in which interests and power relations determine if and how knowledge is used. Second, human action always has unforeseen consequences. Third, although modern reflexivity has contributed to the dramatic increase in scientific output, it has also – through the associated insistence that the basis for knowledge be consistently questioned and, as necessary, revised – undermined our ability to apply what we know with confidence and without undue caution.

In a modern society as described by Giddens, we would expect increased reference to expert sources in the media, as demonstrated by our study. In daily life, we are dependent on numerous specialized knowledge systems, which we do not immediately understand. If we need to know more about, or reflect upon, the products produced by these systems, it is only natural for the media to contact precisely the experts within those systems. Another factor operating here is that there is typically a range of expert opinion, none of which is conclusive. We therefore expect modern media to present different expert opinions on any particular issue. A final factor is that the media seeks the analysis and opinions of experts largely because new issues have been placed on the political agenda by actors outside the world of science rather than because new scientific ground has been broken and needs to be communicated to the general public. The most relevant experts to consult for comments on such issues are usually social scientists.

GLOBALIZATION AND EUROPEANIZATION OF EXPERTS?

The literature on modernization would predict not only that there would be an increase in expert opinions presented by the media, but that an increasing proportion of experts would be consulted across borders. That is, according to Giddens, globalization is another fundamental dimension of modern societies; modernity has 'stretched' time and space, with the consequence that social relations that formerly took place in local contexts have been reconceptualized, reorganized across time and space (Giddens 1990, pp. 63f). Globalization has made us increasingly interconnected through economic networks, interstate relations, military alliances, and worldwide division of labour. We now have a sense of living in 'one world', promoted not least by modern communication technology, which has created a world in which news and knowledge, in a constant stream, are disseminated across national borders – including, in particular, mediated expert knowledge (pp. 77-8).

The above developments, observed by Giddens on a global scale, have been noticed by other observers at the regional level, especially in Europe, where the economic, political and cultural cooperation engendered by the EU is believed to be accelerating such developments. Analyses of Europeanization have included the impact – observed, projected and normative – on the structure and functioning of the European media. Normatively, it is argued that the EU as a polity resembles a nationstate but suffers from a democratic deficit because it lacks a 'European public sphere' (Habermas 1994, Schlesinger 1997, Kunelius and Sparks 2001). In modern polities, public discussions are conducted in and through the mass media. It remains uncertain, however, whether the European mass media will develop into a common, EU-wide public sphere and to help define, in turn, a post-national European political culture and identity. On the one hand, various initiatives have been taken by the EU to institute a 'European audiovisual space' and a 'European information area' (Commission 1994). Digitalization, in particular, seems to be leading the EU towards a common, technology-driven communicative space. On the other hand, several studies document that, to a remarkable extent, the media are still bound to national contexts and that these contexts continue to frame media coverage of European politics (Kevin 2001, Lund 2002, de Vreese 2003). In this context, however, there is also a countervailing consideration: reference to experts may be expected to transcend national boundaries more than other aspects of media coverage because experts, to an increasing extent, cooperate internationally and also because new communication technologies make experts more accessible to journalists across national boundaries.

Our current study coded the nationality of the researchers referred to in the Danish news media, in ten-year intervals, from 1961 to 2001. This design allows us to survey two interrelated hypotheses concerning references in the mass media to experts – (1) general globalization: a greater proportion of references are being made to foreign experts in general, and (2) Europeanization: that increased European cooperation leads to a greater proportion of trans-European expert references in the media.

Figure 3.1 shows a steady increase over time in the number of references being made to foreign experts in the Danish news media, thereby directly confirming the hypothesis that, at least in terms of absolute numbers, more references are being made to foreign experts in the Danish media today than earlier. Nevertheless, our data, as presented in Table 3.1 – which shows the share of researchers classified by nationality – confirm neither the globalization nor the Europeanization hypothesis. First, no general globalization in expert references can be detected: the proportion of news articles with reference to Danish versus non-Danish researchers has remained fairly constant over the period observed – 78 per cent in 1971, 86 per cent in 1981, 79 per cent in 1991, and 81 per cent in 2001. Only the figures for 1961 deviate from this picture, with only 60 per cent of the researchers being Danish and a

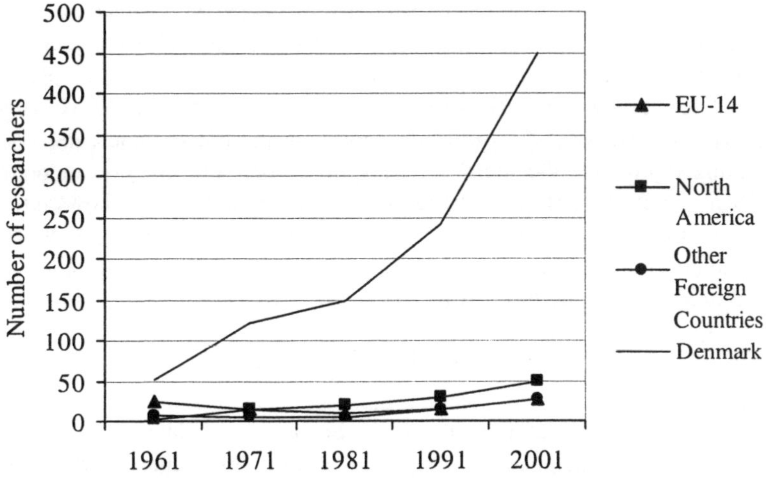

Figure 3.1 Researchers by nationality

corresponding 29 per cent of the researchers being European. This statistical deviation is primarily due to the alleged invention of a truth serum in the UK and the Soviet Union's launching of Sputnik, which was intensively covered by the media. Because 1961 appears anomalous, it will not be included in the following analysis. Second, the Europeanization hypothesis is equally unsupported by our data: the share of articles in Danish newspapers with reference to researchers from the 14 other EU countries has in fact decreased over the period studied, from 9 per cent in 1971, to 5 per cent in 1981, 1991 and 2001.

Table 3.1 Researchers classified by nationality

	EU-14 (%)	North America (%)	Other Foreign Researchers (%)	Danes (%)	Total Researchers (%)	Total Researchers (*n*)
1961	29	3	8	60	100	87
1971	9	9	4	78	100	158
1981	5	6	3	86	100	173
1991	5	10	5	79	100	299
2001	5	9	5	81	100	553

As mentioned earlier, the dramatic increase in the references to researchers in the Danish news media is primarily explained by an increase in the references to social science researchers. The same holds true with regard to references to foreign researchers. Table 3.2 shows that in 1971, 67 per cent of the foreign researchers were technical-natural and health scientists, whereas in 2001, only 51 per cent came from these disciplines; the corresponding figures for the social sciences are 21 per cent in 1971, increasing to 38 per cent in 2001. The change has not been as dramatic, however, for foreign as for Danish scientists: in 1971, 61 per cent of Danish researchers cited in articles came from the technical-natural and health sciences, as compared to 38 per cent in 2001 (Albæk et al. 2003, p. 944).

Table 3.2 Foreign researchers classified by faculty

	Natural, Technical and Agricultural Sciences (%)	Health Sciences (%)	Humanities (%)	Social Sciences (%)	Total Foreign Researchers (%)	Total Foreign Researchers (*n*)
1971	27	40	12	21	100	33
1981	26	35	22	17	100	23
1991	20	22	2	56	100	55
2001	33	18	11	38	100	94

Finally, Table 3.3 shows the geographical distribution of the foreign social scientists cited in the Danish media. The data do not indicate Europeanization. If anything, they indicate a general globalization in that the proportion of references made to social scientists not coming from EU countries or North America has grown.

Table 3.3 Nationality of foreign social science researchers

	EU-14 (%)	North America (%)	Other Countries (%)	Total Foreign Researchers (%)	Total Foreign Researchers (*n*)
1971	14	57	29	100	7
1981	25	25	50	100	4
1991	29	42	29	100	31
2001	22	36	42	100	36

FROM FACTS TO OPINION – IN A NATIONAL CONTEXT

Our study demonstrates that there was a dramatic and accelerating increase in the appearance of researchers in the Danish mass media over the last 40 years. The increase pertains to all types of researchers and supports the idea that experts are playing an ever greater role in modern society. Our study also identifies a significant shift, however, in the types of researchers who appear in the media and in what they comment on. Comparatively speaking, researchers communicate research results much less today than they used to; instead, they increasingly comment on political and other issues placed on the public agenda by actors outside the researchers' ivory towers. This shift is reflected, in turn, in a shift in the types of researchers who appear in the media. Previously, hard scientists appeared most often in the Danish daily press; today it is social scientists. They are, in particular, the commentators most frequently used when journalists need experts to comment on issues whose importance and newsworthiness are defined by the interests of the general public or by the nation's larger political agenda – and not by the researchers themselves. A further factor – one of crucial significance – is that the Danish public has grown increasingly dependent on expert knowledge for 'reflexivity' – that is, for assistance in interpreting modern society.[1]

If measured by the number of references made to foreign experts, the increased 'reflexivity' in the Danish media has become neither globalized nor Europeanized. Rather, the public debate in Denmark has remained predominantly national. Increased Europeanization and globalization have not created a transnational corps of experts on which the national media draw. Instead, they use their national experts, and probably for good reasons: (1) national researchers are easier to access for the national media, and (2) many of the issues on which the national media want expert commentary are indeed national in character. It would make little sense for a Danish journalist to call up a French researcher for a comment on the latest state-local government initiative in Denmark. In this context, it is not at all surprising that Danish newspapers predominantly refer to Danish researchers. What is interesting, however – especially in view of the initial questions concerning Europeanization and globalization – is that the share of references to Danish researchers has not decreased at all. And from the normative perspective of creating a European public space, it is problematic, at best, that, even when it comes to experts, who are among the most internationally well-connected persons in society, no such space can be detected as either present or emerging.

NOTE

1. This development is probably related to a change in the very form that news coverage has taken. Standard models for good news coverage – and therefore for news interpretation, in which experts play a central role – were developed internationally and eventually adopted into Danish journalism. Also a greater incentive for researchers to appear in the media may help explain the development (see Albæk et al. 2003).

REFERENCES

Albæk, Erik, Peter Munk Christiansen and Lise Togeby (2003), 'Experts in the mass media: Researchers in the Danish daily newspapers, 1961-2001', *Journalism and Mass Communication Quarterly*, **80** (4), 937-48.

Commission of the European Communities (1994), 'Communication from the Commission to the Council and the European Parliament, Follow-up to the Consultation Process Relating to the Green Paper on "Pluralism and Media Concentration in the Internal Market – An Assessment of the Need for Community Action"', COM(94) 353 final, 5 October.

de Vreese, Claes (2003), *Framing Europe: News Production, Content and Effects in a Cross-National Perspective*, Somerset, NJ: Transaction Publishers.

Giddens, Anthony (1990), *The Consequences of Modernity*, Stanford, CA: Stanford University Press.

Habermas, Jürgen (1994), 'Citizenship and national identity,' in B. van Steenbergen (ed.), *The Condition of Citizenship*, London: Sage.

Kevin, Deirdre (2001), 'Coverage of the European Parliament elections of 1999: National public spheres and European debates', *The Public*, **18** (1), 21-38.

Kunelius, Risto and Colin Sparks (2001), 'Problems with a European public sphere', *The Public*, **18** (1), 5-20.

Lund, Anker Brink (2002), *Den redigerende magt: Nyhedsinstitutionens politiske indflydelse*, Aarhus: Aarhus University Press.

Schlesinger, Philip (1997), 'From cultural defence to political culture: Media, politics and collective identity in the European Union', *Media, Culture & Society*, **19** (3), 369-91.

Steele, Janet (1995), 'Experts and the operational bias of television news: The case of the Persian Gulf War', *Journalism and Mass Communication Quarterly*, **72** (4), 799-812.

4. National Election Campaigns and European Issues

Ronald Holzhacker and Andrea Römmele

Two developments are continuing to greatly impact the European Union (EU) and the member states. Whereas the processes of deepening and widening the EU were once seen as contradictory, both processes are now occurring simultaneously. The New Europe is rapidly expanding, and ten additional members recently joined the EU. Partially because of this expansion, but also because of new pressures caused by economic difficulties and the world security situation, member states are cooperating in new ways and increasingly bound by decisions taken at the union level. This cooperation is not only in the form of binding decisions through directives, but also through newer forms of intergovernmental cooperation, such as benchmarking and the creation of action plans in a diverse range of policy areas. There are a great many meetings in Brussels in which ministers and other representatives of the member states must gather, stake out positions, discuss, and finally vote on issues facing the EU and the member states. But what role do national electorates play in this decision-making process?

There are two paths of democratic representation and legitimacy within the EU and the member states. One links voters in elections for the European Parliament (EP), through deliberations in the EP, to decision making taken within the supranational institutions of the EU. The other links voters in national elections to national parliaments, and these parliaments across Europe may exercise a degree of parliamentary scrutiny over EU position taking by national governments. These existing democratic institutions in the member states could be strengthened to address concerns that are often expressed regarding the democratic deficit in the EU.

Thus one of the ways to improve the democratic representation and legitimacy within the EU is to assure effective national parliamentary scrutiny of decision making in the member states of decisions prior to the discussions and voting in the Council of Ministers. But there is a link back to the electorate which must also be satisfied if the national parliaments are to fulfil this role in the new multi-level system of governance. To satisfy the demands of representation from a responsible party model of government, discussed below, parties should also be communicating with the public and campaigning on European issues during national election campaigns. Thus scholars should not only be looking at how institutions function when assessing the democratic deficit within the EU and the member states, but also at the political processes that proceed the seating of these institutions.

The growing significance of European politics (compared to politics at the national level) is becoming more evident than ever before, putting the relationship between European citizens and political actors at the European level in a new light and raising new problems and challenges to governance in the European multi-level system. In this context, the aggregation of citizens' political preferences and the extent of their information about European politics take on central importance. But how can citizens gain information about European politics? Particularly with regard to EU issues, citizens display serious information deficits and uncertainty (not least due to the 'remoteness' and minimal transparency of the political system), and are often guided by more general convictions and emotions (Niedermayer and Sinnot 1995). Europe as a subject of the news during national election campaigns has only recently begun to increase. Research on German and Dutch elections in the early 1990s shows that Europe was on the periphery of these campaigns, but played a larger role in the media coverage of the 1998 national elections in each country (Semetko et al. 2000, p. 130). Not only the quantity has increased, but its qualities 'European integration and the EU are not only present in news coverage of genuinely European issues, but are also increasingly an integral part of national political and economic coverage' (Semetko et al. 2000, p. 129).

This chapter discusses theoretically the argument that as the traditional chains of representation proposed in the responsible party model of government for nation states are modified to take into account the realities of the more complex system of multi-level governance within the EU, so too must our conception of the election campaign. Specifically, the focus here is on the need for parties to campaign and receive a mandate, not merely on domestic issues, but also on EU issues on which their government will be asked to take a stand during the next legislative period.

After setting out the argument theoretically, we will present an analysis of the extent that political parties in two long-standing, founding member states of the EU, the Netherlands and Germany, and two accession (now new member) countries, Poland and the Czech Republic, successfully communicated their stance on EU issues during their last national election campaigns, which reached voters through the news media. We present a content analysis of the front section of two daily papers in each country in the two weeks prior to the election, the hottest phase of the election campaign when the electorate may have heightened awareness and interest in the information reaching them because of their upcoming vote decision. The coding scheme first counts the number of articles that appear in the front section (first page until page 6 or 7, before the opinion pages) of the papers concerning the following topics: articles predominately about the national election campaign, articles predominately about the EU and articles in which the EU is at least mentioned. We then look further at those articles identified above, and count the number of articles that combined a discussion of the election campaign and the EU, and this is where our theoretical interests lie. If representation and legitimacy over EU issues is to occur through the national path of representation, voters need to be provided with information about both the national election campaign and the EU so that they can distinguish the positions different political parties are taking on EU issues. This information is a necessary condition, but not a sufficient condition in and of itself for representation to occur on these issues.

INSTITUTIONS AND DEMOCRATIC PROCESSES

Decision making in the EU occurs through both intergovernmental and supranational institutions. Yet recent thought on decision making in the EU emphasizes that it is also a multi-tiered system of government; involving not only institutions created at the EU level, but also an intensified interaction of national, regional and local institutions in the member states (König et al. 1996, Leibfried and Pierson 1995, Weiler et al. 1995). Thus, the institutional structure of the EU is not only intergovernmental and supranational, but also multi-tiered, with implications for key elements of the representative systems in the member states.

The legitimacy and democratic quality of decision making in the EU have been a concern since the earliest days of the European project. As decision making has entered more and more areas and touch more directly on the lives of European citizens, cries about the democratic deficit have grown louder. Beetham and Lord (1998) present the legitimacy claims of both the intergovernmental and supranational approaches to the democratization of the EU in terms of three concepts – authorization, representation, and accountability. For the intergovernmental mode, these include authorization of political leadership through domestic election of members of the European Council and Council of Ministers, representation of national governments through these bodies, and accountability of these bodies to national parliaments and electorates.

What is missing in this discussion and most others is a discussion of the processes of which these bodies are linked back to the electorates in order for representation and accountability to take place. One strand in the literature emphasizes networks in Europe and their function in communicating positions from the society to both European level and national level decision making (Kohler-Koch 1994). But elections among competing political parties are the best possibility that the general interest will be heard, not just narrow special interests.

THE RESPONSIBLE PARTY MODEL OF REPRESENTATION

Schmitt and Thomassen (1999) present a party model of responsible government applicable to democratic processes, designed to make government policy related to the wants, needs and demands of the public. According to this model of representation, the will of the majority of the electorate will be reflected in government policy if the following conditions are met:

1. There are different parties with different programmes.
2. Parties must have sufficient internal cohesion to enable them to pursue the implementation of their party programme.
3. Voters choose the party whose programme is closest to their own policy preferences. This implies that:
   a. voters have policy preferences, and
   b. voters are aware of the differences between the policy positions of different parties (Thomassen 1994, pp. 251-2).

Recently Schmitt and Thomassen have presented an alternative and more realistic model (1999). The model loosens the assumption that voters must have preferences and know where parties stand on a whole range of issues, and instead narrows the preference requirement to the set of issues the voter considers most important. This revision was inspired by empirical research on valence issues in voters (Stokes 1963, 1992), issue saliency by parties (Budge and Farlie, 1983) and mass communication (Iyengar and Kinder, 1987). In this conception, item three above in the responsible party model of government requiring voters to have policy preferences is replaced by the idea that 'voters are concerned about problems . . . voters are aware of differences in issue emphases of the parties . . . and voters choose the party that they believe will best be able to deal with the problems central to them' (Schmitt and Thomassen 1999, p. 116).

Schmitt and Thomassen have used this model in the past to discuss representation in nation states and in their latest book to also understand the European Parliament. Here, we are extending this discussion to the situation of multi-level governance, where it is necessary for representation and accountability to occur for decision making in the members states over EU issues. This is of course fully consistent with their approach. They state that 'questions on political representation and legitimacy in the EU refer as much to the relation between the national governments and the EU and to the institutions and *political processes at the national level* as to the European level as such' (1999, p. 8, italics added).

In this article we want to theoretically explore how one part of the political processes central to the responsible party model of government should be conceived: that is the process of national election campaigns and the role they need to play to provide representation and legitimacy to decision making over EU issues in the member states.

EUROPEANIZATION OF PARTY SYSTEMS: CAMPAIGNS AND PARTY COMPETITION

Election campaigns are a crucial period in the democratic process. It is a time when the electorate is informed about the positions taken on issues by the political parties competing for their vote. If campaigns are going to continue to play an important role in the democratic process, political parties must adapt their campaign communication to the new realities of multi-level governance within the EU and the member states. Because the chains of representation linking the preferences of the citizens, through the decision-making institutions of government, to public policy outputs are changing as a result of the complex and evolving political system in the EU, so should the campaign communication during national election campaigns.

Goetz and Hix recently published an edited volume using European integration as an explanatory factor in domestic political continuity or change (2001). They state that although there has been a long-standing interest in how the 'democratic deficit' in the EU could be overcome, there has been little research into the effects of integration on the defining features of domestic political systems (p. 17). Here, we are interested in the extent to which European issues play a role in national election campaigns. Theoretically, campaign communication on EU issues should be an important component for maintaining democratic representation and legitimacy within the evolving system of multi-level governance in the EU and the member states.

Mair (2001) has written about the impact of Europeanization on the party systems of the member states. He writes that when considering the *format* and *mechanics* of these systems, there has been very little direct impact on these key features of party systems (p. 28). *Format* refers to the number of relevant parties in contention in the national political arena; *mechanics* refers to the way parties interact with one another. His analysis of the mechanics focuses on whether a significant cleavage of competition has opened between pro- and anti- European integrationists, and his conclusion is negative. He notes that parties that have taken strong anti-EU stances also have strong and extreme ideological dimensions. 'Under no circumstances could they be interpreted as being primarily dependent on an anti-European appeal' (p. 34). He concludes that whereas a pro- versus anti-European divide can sometimes be discerned in the party systems of the member states, Europe is neither a necessary nor sufficient condition for that divide.

There is debate in the literature about the appropriate 'division of labour' about which issues are best contested in campaigns and elections for the European Parliament and which for national parliamentary contests. The concept of 'best' or most appropriate emerges from a belief that the contest between the political parties and the public debate should reflect the areas of competence of the elected body. Representation and legitimacy are strengthened when the campaign relates to the competency of the elected body. Mair argues that the 'national political arena is most suited to the contestation of European issues – principally European constitutional issues, but also certain European policy issues – whereas the European electoral arena is perhaps most suited to contestation of everyday policy issues' (p. 46). Yet, Mair concludes, this is not what usually happens; instead national elections continue to be dominated by conflicts over policy alternatives, the exercise of which is severely constrained by the EU. And the European elections tend to be dominated by debates over Europe itself, despite the fact that institutional changes are severely constrained by national governments (p. 46).

So here we look first at the most recent election campaigns in the Netherlands and Germany to see the extent that European issues played a role in the campaign and what types of issues were raised. Thus, do European issues play a strong role in party competition in the weeks before the elections? Others have researched whether Europeanization is having an impact on party systems and state that format and mechanics of party systems are central to this consideration (Mair 2001). However, Mair has reduced the concept of mechanics – party interaction – to the extent that a pro- and anti-European cleavage has entered into party competition. But there are other possible differences between political parties which could become more apparent over time, for example support for a more free market, competitive Europe versus a more socially conscious Europe. Or, some parties might advocate a more supranational Europe with a strengthened European Parliament and others a more intergovernmental Europe. Perhaps a new constellation of issues would be seen with time as an extension of the traditional left–right basis of party competition: the first issue above as part of the traditional economic and social perspectives of left and right parties, and the second issue part of the internationalism of the left versus the nationalism of the right.

REVIEW OF THE GERMAN 2002 AND THE DUTCH 2003 NATIONAL ELECTION CAMPAIGNS

This chapter is mainly an attempt to begin conceiving of national election campaigns as an integral part of the conception of multi-level governance in the EU and the member states. We view these campaigns as a critical time in the life of a democracy. This political process between political parties and voters, and which depends critically on the role of the mass media, must be included in our ideas of the responsible party model of representation.

We will first look at two recent national election campaigns in Western Europe, and later a more preliminary, exploratory look at two recent elections in East Central Europe. The empirical basis of the analysis in the Netherlands and Germany is based on a quantitative analysis of a small sample of newspapers in the two countries in the weeks before the election.

The critical question we ask here is whether the media offered the voters a basis for choosing between the political parties in their national elections based on the parties' stances towards EU issues.

THE DUTCH ELECTION 2003

The Dutch election campaign began after the government coalition consisting of the Christian Democrats (CDA), the Liberals (VVD) and the List Pim Fortuyn Party (LPF) collapsed after 89 days in office and new elections were called. The fortunes of the LPF had risen with its leader, but had great difficulty governing after his political assassination during the previous campaign.

The analysis here consists of a preliminary analysis of two well-respected, quality Dutch daily newspapers, the *NRC Handelsblad*, considered somewhat conservative and free-market-oriented, and the more left-oriented *Volkskrant*.

In general, we conclude from Table 4.1 that although there were a considerable number of articles about the national election campaign in the Netherlands, and quite a few about the EU, very few articles combine the two. Only astute readers of the *NRC Handelsblad* who read on particular days had a basis for distinguishing the position of the parties towards EU issues.

Table 4.1 Dutch newspaper coverage of EU-issues (8 – 22 January 2003)

	Volkskrant	NRC Handelsblad
Articles predominantly about the campaign	116	103
Predominately EU	8	18
Mentions EU	2	3
Campaign discussed in a predominantly EU article	0	0
Campaign discussed in an article which mentions EU	0	2[a]
EU Discussed in a predominantly campaign article	0	2[b]

Notes:

[a] Titles for these articles: 'President van Europa voor 5 Jaar: Partijen Nederland verdeeld' (President for Europe for 5 years: Dutch Parties differ) appeared on 15 January, and 'Ik gruw net zo van klonen als Jan Peter' (I don't support cloning as Jan Peter does) appeared on 18 January. This second article delineates differences between the leaders of the Labour Party (Pvda) and CDA on foreign policy, medical ethics and the policy-making process.

[b] Titles for these articles 'Europa is ondankbaar verkiezingsthema' (Europe is a thankless Election Theme) appeared on 11 January and 'Europa Verdeelt politiek: Europa mag dan geen hoofdrol in de verkiezingscampanne spleen, de politieke partijen hebben daar wel degelijk meningen over.' (Europe divides parties: Europe may not play a main role in the election campaign, but the political parties do have clearly differentiated opinions) appeared on 16 January.

The *NRC Handelsblad* contained a considerable number of articles about the campaign in general, including polls, discussion of party strategy and background articles about issues impacting the country. For example, in the 11/12 January weekend edition there was a large campaign news story on the front page: 'Party Leaders as Persons and as Advertisements'. There was also extensive coverage inside the paper on various issues, including health care, 'No one must wait for an operation', civil rights and police powers, 'Police not allowed to ask for identity', as well as articles on religious schools, education and how asylum works in Australia, Canada and Denmark. There were also articles about the EU, including one about the positions of various member states towards the looming war, 'Objections in EU against attack on Iraq' and EU enlargement, 'Enlargement of the EU to Balkans to Quicken'.

There was one article in this weekend edition in the front section of the *NRC Handelsblad* that discussed both the campaign and the EU, an academic article entitled 'Europe avoids Politics. Political competition is essential for a living democracy, but Europe awakens the impression that politics is not a necessity or is better avoided'. Finally, it also had a special two-page spread (not in the front section, so not included in the quantitative data above) called the 'Party Election Programme', discussing the position of the Dutch political parties organized into 12 subjects: public safety, education, work and income, budget, health care, mobility, housing, agriculture and the environment, foreign policy, integration and migration, public administration, and norms and values. Normally, only one or two lines were devoted under the foreign policy category to the parties' stand towards various European issues. This usually referred to institutional arrangements like increasing powers to the European parliament, but also to issues of enlargement, agricultural subsidies and asylum.

Later in the week, on 15 January there was a major front page article 'President of Europe for five years' and then two articles under this headline titled 'French-German plan for Convention' and 'Dutch parties divided' setting out the three largest parties' (VVD, the Labour Party-PvdA and CDA) reactions to this proposal. Inside the paper on p. 5 there was another article concerning EU foreign policy, 'Solana's unusual critique on the US'.

The following day's paper, 16 January, contained extensive articles on the EU, as well as a major article on the Dutch parties' positions towards the EU. Thus on p. 4 'French-German plan divides Europe', p. 5 'EU police begin in Bosnia', p. 7 'Europe divides politics' with a boxed chart listing the positions of the political parties and 'Schools play EU convention game'. 17 January's paper had three major articles predominately about the EU: 'French-German plan for new EU organ: European Congress for Parliamentarians', 'Recommendations for EU administration' and 'New European ombudsman'. The *Handelsblad* had additional articles in the days that followed, including 18/19 January, p. 5 'Police part of riot at the EU summit in Gothenburg among activists', and on 2 January a large headline 'Resistance against plan for EU president'.

In contrast to the coverage in the *NRC Handelsblad*, the *Volkskrant* had much less news discussing the EU and the political parties' positions on the EU. While a typical edition had articles about the campaign in general, there were only occasional articles about the EU. On 15 January there were two small articles on p. 5 'EU to get a double leader' and 'EU leader: Croatia to join in 2007'. A week later, there were two articles on p. 4 'Benelux is against EU "sun king"' and 'EU commission against EU with two presidents'.

Thus which newspaper voters reads regularly has a large impact on the amount of EU news they are presented with and their national parties' positions towards EU issues. Whereas readers of the *NRC Handelsblad* are presented with some information that would allow them to distinguish between the parties based on their EU stances if they happened to read the newspaper on a particular day, this is not true for the readers of the *Volkskrant*.

MEDIA COVERAGE – PARTY POSITIONS TOWARDS EUROPE

We have seen in this analysis that some differences in issue positions on Europe of the parties competing in the national election were presented in at least one Dutch newspaper, but not in the other. Perhaps the parties' positions on European politics did not play a larger role in the campaign because they do not differ very much? This demonstrably is not true. A week before the Dutch election, an article in the *NRC Handelsblad* was subheaded 'Europe may well not play a major role in the election campaign, but the political parties have clearly differentiated opinions toward Europe. Stark differences exist concerning the ideal federation' (16 January 2003, p. 7). A box accompanying the article delineates differences between the political parties in five key areas, including whether the EU as a federative body should play a stronger role in European initiatives, whether there should be a leader of the European Commission, a referendum on the outcome of the European convention, whether the competencies of the European parliament should be increased and any additional proposals concerning the EU and democracy.

From the list of differences presented, one could see that important differences do exist in the stances of the Dutch parties on Europe. One can also discern a certain consistency of a party's position towards Europe and its traditional stances at the national level. The party that rose to prominence as the party of reform and democratic control in the mid-1960s, D66, thus also takes positions at the European level that can be seen as extensions of this. The party is in favour of direct voting for a leader of the European Commission, the introduction of referendums at the EU level and of strengthening the role of the European Parliament. The VVD takes positions towards the EU that are consistent with their liberal, free-market positions at the national level. Their positions on institutional design at the EU level are intended to limit government and strengthen the intergovernmental institutions of the EU, and are not in favour of strengthening the role of the European Parliament or extending direct participation of citizens with the EU, for example through the use of referendums.

The positions of the other main parties towards the institutional design of the EU seem more varied and perhaps less consistent. The PvdA is not in favour of the EU moving towards being a federation, but would like more cooperation between the member states. But at the same time, it is in favour of strengthening the democratic components of representative democracy of the supranational institutions and introducing forms of direct democracy. Thus it is in favour of elections for the head of the European Commission and for the use of referendums, including on the outcome of the European convention. The CDA is in favour of a federal Europe, and of some measures to strengthen the European Parliament, for example giving it the power to remove members of the European Commission. The party is not in favour of introducing the right of referendum.

There are thus a number of important differences in the Dutch party's stances towards EU issues, but a voter receiving information from reading the daily newspapers might not be exposed to these differences. Readers of some newspapers would be exposed to these differences. Of course, especially concerned and motivated citizens might be able to search out such information, for example by a time-consuming comparison of the election programmes of the parties, available from the parties in published form or on their websites, but most citizens do not.

THE GERMAN ELECTION 2002

Now we turn to the German election of 2002 and ask to what extent EU issues played a role in the campaign. The two major competitors, the Social Democrats (SPD) and the Christian Democrats (CDU/CSU) combined a very personalized campaign focused on Schröder and Stoiber respectively, with an emphasis on foreign policy and economic issues (for further details on the campaign strategy see special issue of FJNSB 1, 2003). The events of September 11 and its consequences clearly dominated the early stages of the incumbent campaign run by the SPD and Schröder. In addition, the ongoing economic crises and the high level of unemployment were the predominant issues. Since the SPD as the incumbent party could not demonstrate a successful management of these issues over the last four years, a mixture of reform perspectives and (modest) achievements was presented. In addition, the SPD and its coalition partner Bündnis 90/die Grünen demonstrated the concept of a modern and open society, that is with different and 'open' family concepts.

The focus of the campaign agenda shifted tremendously during the final six weeks of the campaign. With the flood ('Jahrhunderflut') in Dresden and Sachsen dominating the national agenda, Schröder as chancellor had to demonstrate (and did demonstrate) power and capacity for action. In addition with the definite and clear 'No' on German participation in a war in Iraq, these two issues dominated the final weeks of the SPD's campaign.

The CDU/CSU challenging chancellor Schröder focused on unemployment, lack of economic growth and tax policies. In addition, the CDU/CSU led by Edmund Stoiber, the Ministerpräsident of Bavaria, also aimed at presenting the CDU/CSU as an open, modern party for women. The party hoped that the 'cliché' as a party sticking to outdated values could be overcome with the presentation of a young, single East German mother (Katherina

Reiche) as part of Stoiber's team ('Kompetenzteam') and possible future minister. In contrast to the extreme personalization of SPD's campaign on Schröder, the CDU/CSU underlined the team aspect and not the individual players. Regarding German participation in a potential war against Iraq, the CDU/CSU had a more differentiated view that – according to the campaign management team – could not be as easily communicated as Schröder's definite 'No'.

Whereas the SPD heavily focused on its chancellor candidate Schröder, the CDU/CSU showed aspects of a campaign that concentrated not so much on a single person, but on a team of competent individuals. The personalization of the campaign was also visible in the minor parties. The Liberals (FDP) for the first time nominated a candidate, Guido Westerwelle. Also the Greens built their campaign extensively on Vice-chancellor Joschka Fischer.

Before we begin to discuss the media coverage of the campaign, let us first summarize our findings so far: The campaign strategy with its key issues shows no reference to European matters or to national issues especially related to European matters. Does this picture change if we look at the media agenda? In an empirical content analysis concentrating on two major German newspapers (*Frankfurter Allgemeine Zeitung*, *Süddeutsche Zeitung*) we could hardly find any reference to European matters (see Table 4.2).

Table 4.2 German newspaper coverage of EU issues (7-21 September 2002)

	FAZ	SZ
Articles predominantly about the campaign	172	152
Predominately EU	4	8
Mentions EU	6	5
Campaign discussed in a predominantly EU article	0	0
Campaign discussed in an article which mentions EU	1	0
EU discussed in a predominantly campaign article	1	1

Note: We have coded the headlines of each article on pp. 1-3 in the Süddeutsche Zeitung, and pp. 1-3 +8 in the Frankfurter Allgemeine Zeitung.

THE POLISH ELECTION 2003, AND CZECH REPUBLIC ELECTION 2002[1]

After the research in the Netherlands and Germany found very few articles that combined an analysis of the national election campaign and the EU, we decided to turn our attention to two EU accession countries in East Central

Europe, which recently held elections. Perhaps political parties and the media in countries where the EU is more salient would discuss the EU during a national election campaign? For Poland, we analysed the two newspapers *Rzeczpospolita* and *Gazeta Wyborcza* (see Table 4.3). *Rzeczpospolita* is a daily newspaper with a circulation of about 700,000. It is considered centre-right and focuses extensively on economic issues. *Gazeta Wyborcza* is the most popular and most widely read newspaper in Poland, with an extremely high circulation of over three million per day. This makes it the largest newspaper in the whole east and central European region. It focuses extensively on international issues and is considered liberal.

Here, the picture is somewhat different from what we saw in the Netherlands and Germany. Hardly any articles focus on the national election campaign – during the most intensive period of an election, two major newspapers did not report much on the campaign. Whereas the content analysis indicates that there are very few articles that combine a discussion of the election campaign and the EU, there are a number of articles about the EU or at least mentioning the EU. All in all, both Polish newspapers report on the EU, and given the neglect of the national campaign the readers of the *Gazeta Wyborcza* were given only a minimum of information about party positions on EU issues.

Table 4.3 Polish newspaper coverage of EU issues (7-22 September 2003)

	Rzeczpospolita	Gazeta Wyborcza
Articles predominantly about the campaign	1	0
Predominately EU	8	9
Mentions EU	14	7
Campaign discussed in a predominantly EU article	1	0
Campaign discussed in an article which mentions EU	0	2
EU discussed in a predominantly campaign article	0	3

For the Czech Republic, we were only able to do a content analysis of the paper *Mlada Fronta Dnes* (see Table 4.4). The daily newspaper *Lidové Noviny* was not accessible for our purposes. For the Czech Republic, the empirical findings are very much in line with our findings for the Netherlands and Germany: high coverage on the national campaign, but very few articles give readers in-depth information on the EU: whereas 11 articles mention the

EU in the two weeks prior to the campaign, only three articles talk predominantly about the EU. The voters hardly get any information from this paper on the parties' stands on EU issues.

Table 4.4 Czech newspaper coverage of EU issues (3-14 June 2002)

	Mlada Fronta Dnes
Articles predominantly about the campaign	29
Predominately EU	3
Mentions EU	11
Campaign discussed in a predominantly EU article	2
Campaign discussed in an article which mentions EU	0
EU discussed in a predominantly campaign article	0

CONCLUSION

In the search for representation and legitimacy in the evolving system of multi-level governance in the EU and the member states, we must not only consider voter preferences and the construction of the institutions. It is also very important to analyse the *political processes*, the mass-elite linkages between voters and institutions. Here, we have argued for the importance of analysing the political parties' election campaigns during national election campaigns and the communication that reaches the voters through the mass media. A critical question was whether the mass media provided voters with a basis for choosing between the political parties in their national elections based on the parties' stances towards EU issues.

We first followed two national election campaigns, the German national election campaign in September 2002, and the Dutch national election campaign in January 2003, during the closing weeks of the campaign – the time when many voters start paying attention and make up their minds about which party to support. Our observations focused on a content analysis of newspapers in the weeks before the election.

We find that the timing and context of national election campaigns are critical to the issue focus of the media. There was very little coverage in the German newspapers during the weeks before the election, both concerning the EU itself as well as the parties' positions towards Europe. But because of major developments in the EU, including the French-German announcement of their desire to see two different leaders emerge at the EU level, one for the Commission and one for the Council, and the controversy surrounding a common EU foreign policy concerning the war with Iraq, there was considerably more reporting by the Dutch media on EU issues during the Dutch campaign, although we judge it to be rather limited. The proximity in time of the EU events may have inspired the media to link these stories to their other main story of the period, the national election campaign. Thus, at least one newspaper provided voters with some basis for evaluating the political parties based on their stances toward Europe.

We also did a more limited, exploratory study of the national election campaigns in Poland and the Czech Republic, to see if the media in countries where the EU may be a more salient issue combined the subjects of the campaign and the EU. We wondered if perhaps the EU plays a larger role in national election campaigns among the accession countries, where there has been years of discussion about joining the EU. But again, we found only a limited number of newspaper articles about the two subjects, offering voters little information on which to distinguish the parties' stances towards the EU.

We conclude that at the present, in the selected countries in both Western and East Central Europe, newspapers offer voters very little information during the election campaign that is necessary to distinguish the positions of parties towards EU issues. This means that one of the fundamental bases of the responsible party model of government is not currently being fulfilled, which severely weakens the ability of representation and legitimacy of EU issues to occur through the national path of representation. The most committed voters might be able to compare the stances of their nation's parties towards Europe in the party programmes, but those who rely on the mass media in the final weeks of the national election campaign do not receive much information about the EU on which to base their upcoming vote decision.

NOTE

1. We greatly acknowledge the help of Sabina Woelkner and Michaela Holasova with coding the Polish and Czech papers.

REFERENCES

Beetham, David and Christopher Lord (1998), *Legitimacy and the EU*, London: Longman.

Budge, Ian and Dennis J. Farlie (1983), *Explaining and Predicting Elections: Issue Effects and Party Strategies in Twenty-Three Democracies*, London and Boston: Allen & Unwin.

Goetz, Klaus A. and Simon Hix (eds) (2001), *Europeanised Politics? European Integration and National Political Systems*, London: Frank Cass.

Iyengar, Shanto and Donald R. Kinder (1987), *News That Matters: Television and Public Opinion*, Chicago: University of Chicago Press.

Kohler-Koch, Beate (1994), 'Changing patterns of interest intermediation in the European Union', *Government and Opposition*, **29** (2), 167-80.

König, Thomas, Elmar Rieger and Hermann Schmitt (eds) (1996), *Das Europäische Mehrebenen-System: Konzeptionen und Perspeckitven, Mannheimer Jahrbuch für Europäischen Sozialforschung, Vol. 1*, Frankfurt am Main: Campus Verlag.

Leibfried, Stephan and Paul Pierson (eds) (1995), *European Social Policy: Between Fragmentation and Integration*, Washington, DC: Brookings Institution.

Mair, Peter (2001), 'The limited impact of Europe on national party systems', in Klaus A. Goetz and Simon Hix (eds), *Europeanised Politics? European Integration and National Political Systems*, London: Frank Cass, pp.27-51.

Niedermayer, Oskar and Richard Sinnot (1995), *Public Opinion and Internationalized Governance*, Oxford and New York: Oxford University Press.

Schmitt, Hermann and Jacques Thomassen (1999), *Political Representation and Legitimacy in the European Union*, Oxford: Oxford University Press.

Semetko, Holli A., Claes de Vreese and Jochen Peter (2000), 'Europeanised politics – Europeanised media? The impact of European integration on political communication', Special issue of *West European Politics*, **23** (4), 121-40.

Stokes, Donald E. (1963), 'Spatial models of party competition', *American Political Science Review*, **57**, 369-77.

Stokes, Donald E. (1992), 'Valence politics', in Dennis Kavenagh (ed.), *Electoral Politics*, Oxford: Clarendon Press, pp. 141-162.

Thomassen, Jacques (1994), 'Models of political representation: Failing democracy or failing models?', in M. Kent Jennings and Thomas E. Mann (eds), *Elections at Home and Abroad*, Ann Arbor: University of Michigan Press, pp. 237-65.

Weiler, Joseph H.H., Ulrich R. Haltern and Franz C. Mayer (1995), 'European social democracy and its critique', in Jack E.S. Hayward (ed.), *The Crisis of Representation in Europe*, London: Frank Cass, pp. 4-39.

5. Resisting Change: European Integration and National Party Systems

Tapio Raunio

INTRODUCTION

European democracy is effectively party democracy. However, according to recent literature on political parties, they are gradually undergoing transformation: '. . . it would be an overstatement to write the parties' political obituary, but a pattern of partisan decline – or at least a transformation in the role played by parties – is increasingly apparent in almost all advanced industrial democracies' (Dalton and Wattenberg 2000b, p. 3). The party transformation thesis is primarily based on the eroding linkage between parties and citizens. But while parties may not be as firmly rooted in civil society as before, no similar decline has occurred in the legislature and government. Indeed, the member states of the European Union (EU) continue to be governed by cohesive, disciplined parties.

The rapid constitutional transformation of the EU since the mid-1980s, in part brought about by parties themselves, presents a major challenge for national parties. Since the majority of main political parties in EU member states were established before the start of integration, the European issue has introduced a new dimension to their politics, in terms of ideologies as well as organization. Ideologically, parties both shape European integration by pursuing policy objectives at national and EU levels, and adapt to integration by operating in an environment increasingly influenced by the limits set by the constitution and legislation of the EU. Organizationally, parties have a permanent presence at the European level through Euro parties and the European Parliament (EP), while at the same time the political dynamics of the EU policy process may have consequences for the balance of power within parties (Ladrech 2002, Raunio 2002).

Recently an increasing number of studies have focused on the role of parties in the EU system. This research can be divided into three categories. First, elections to the EP have been subjected to detailed scrutiny, with survey data enabling scholars to analyse voting behaviour in the member states (e.g. van der Eijk and Franklin 1996, Blondel et al. 1998). Second, scholars have analysed party behaviour at the European level, both in the EP and in the context of Euro parties. These works focus primarily on the cleavages at the EU level (e.g. Hix 1999, Katz and Wessels 1999, Schmitt and Thomassen 1999, Gabel and Hix 2002, Pennings 2002, Marks and Steenbergen 2004), and on how and to what extent Euro parties influence the EU policy process (Hix and Lord 1997, Bomberg 1998, Ladrech 2000, Delwit et al. 2001, Johansson and Zervakis 2002). Third, comparative analyses and case studies of national parties indicate that domestic party competition, the national economic and geopolitical context, and ideology shape partisan responses to Europe, with the overwhelming majority of national parties supportive of deeper integration (e.g. Gaffney 1996, Taggart 1998, Ray 1999, Marks and Wilson 2000, Johansson and Raunio 2001, Kopecký and Mudde 2002, Hooghe et al. 2002).

Perhaps the most significant finding of these studies is the divisive nature of the European question. Regardless of the data used – voting behaviour in legislatures, the preferences of citizens and MPs, expert surveys or more descriptive approaches – European integration is clearly a destabilizing factor for national parties. Yet, even just a cursory glance at the shape of the party systems in the EU member states shows that hardly anything has changed at the national level. It is almost as if national party systems were immune to any kind of Europeanization effect.

This chapter offers some explanations for the limited impact of European integration on national party systems. It is structured as follows: The next section briefly examines evidence of the transformation of European parties independent of integration. Then the effect of EU on three key aspects of national party systems is explored: number of parties, government formation and the internal cohesion of parties. The concluding section summarizes the main findings and explains why national party systems are unlikely to change in the near future. The main argument is that the observed stability is explained by the vested interests of the established parties in defending the status quo and by their ability to control the electoral and legislative arenas. However, at the same time there is *some* evidence of European integration contributing to partisan dealignment and influencing citizens' voting behaviour in national parliamentary elections.

TRANSFORMATION OF EUROPEAN PARTIES?

Lipset and Rokkan (1967) argued in their seminal work that the development of European party systems was shaped by critical junctures in history. These junctures resulted in social cleavages (class, religion, centre-periphery etc.), which in turn led to the formation of political parties representing distinct social and economic interests. Lipset and Rokkan, writing in the 1960s, argued that these party systems had become 'frozen'.

But, European democracies have changed rather fundamentally since the Second World War. Economic development has gradually transformed European countries from industrial, or even predominantly agrarian, societies to modern, post-industrial economies that are increasingly subject to global and particularly European regulation. New issues, such as environmental policy, human rights, and globalization and European integration have changed the agenda of politics. The emergence of the welfare state contributed to the weakening of the class structure, which in turn gave rise to parties that – with the help of television – reach out to citizens beyond their normal pool of voters in the hope of gaining votes (Kirchheimer 1966). As class politics has gradually declined, the cleavages structuring party competition and citizens' voting behaviour have also become less stable. These broader societal changes are reflected in European party systems (Bartolini and Mair 1990, Franklin et al. 1992, Nieuwbeerta and Ultee 1999, Karvonen and Kuhnle 2001).

European parties may not be in decline, but scholars agree that the link between citizens and political parties has become weaker in recent decades. The erosion in the traditional linkage between citizens and parties has three main components: turnout, party identification and party membership. First, people turn out to vote less than before. Of the EU member states, the downward trend has been relatively consistent in Austria, Finland, France, Germany, Ireland, Italy, Luxembourg, the Netherlands, Portugal and Sweden (Blais and Dobrzynska 1998, Wattenberg 2000). Second, longitudinal survey data show that identification with and attachment to parties has declined (Biorcio and Mannheimer 1995, Schmitt and Holmberg 1995, Dalton 2000). And third, party membership has declined in the majority of West European countries (Katz and Mair 1992, Scarrow 2000, p. 88, Mair and van Biezen 2001) with also fewer citizens participating in party meetings or election campaigns (Dalton et al. 2000, 2002).

Weaker connection to the voters has in turn increased electoral volatility: 'Fewer voters now come to elections with standing partisan predispositions. Even if they have loyalties to a party, these loyalties are weaker; more voters now make their electoral choices based on the campaign issues and candidates' (Dalton et al. 2000, p. 60, 2002). As a result, national party systems have become more fragmented, measured by the percentage of seats won by non-governing parties and by the number of effective parties in parliaments (Strøm 2000). Electoral volatility is arguably facilitated by ideological convergence, that is the clustering of parties around the centre of the left-right dimension. While scholars disagree about the extent of the convergence, all or at least most evidence shows that parties have become ideologically more alike in recent decades.[1] Ideological distances between parties have diminished, and individual parties and party families have gradually moved towards the political centre, or in the case of left and green parties, to the right (Huber and Inglehart 1995, Knutsen 1998, Caul and Gray 2000, Budge et al. 2001). Such ideological convergence results partially from the dominance of neo-liberal or centre-right economic policies throughout Europe, with European and global agreements further narrowing the policy options available to individual countries (see Mair 1997).

At the same time parties have become more dependent on the state for their collective survival – hence the label 'cartel party' (Katz and Mair 1995). Comparative projects led by Katz and Mair (1992, 1994) indicated that in the majority of European countries the incomes and staff of parties had risen through public funding.[2] The cartel of established parties stifles competition and, through its privileged access to state resources, makes it hard for new parties to enter the legislative arena. At the same time ideology and policy objectives matter less for party elites. Kitschelt has strongly questioned the basic premises of the cartel party thesis. According to him parties are, if anything, more responsive to voters' preferences than before, with the competitive and unpredictable political environment putting 'much greater pressures' on politicians 'to remain representative of their electoral constituencies than in the past' (Kitschelt 2000, p. 164). Dissatisfaction with parties, argues Kitschelt, stems mainly from the inevitable policy compromises parties have to make and from the patronage and the institutionalized privileged position (as Katz and Mair emphasize) that parties enjoy in national politics. Regardless of the validity of the cartel party thesis, parties are indeed firmly entrenched in government (Blondel and Cotta 1996), and their position shows no sign of weakening. According to Strøm, 'parties remain well entrenched in the core executives (cabinets) of most advanced capitalist nations. The farther we move away from this key political institution, the more clearly we see signs of partisan decay' (2000, p. 201).

While the existence of a 'golden age' of mass parties is probably often romanticized, there is no denying that the linkage between citizens and political parties has become weaker. Turnout has fallen, less people belong to and identify with one of the parties, and survey-based evidence shows that anti-party sentiment has increased across Europe (Webb 2002). Class is no longer that important in structuring party choice in elections, ideological convergence has narrowed the distances between parties, and party systems have become more fragmented in the majority of EU countries.[3] While European integration *may* have contributed to at least some of these developments, the tendencies described in this section are nevertheless primarily explained by domestic or cross-national factors not directly related to European integration.

THE IMPACT OF EUROPEAN INTEGRATION

This section analyses the impact of European integration on three key dimensions of national party systems: (a) the establishment of new parties, (b) coalition formation and (c) the internal cohesion of parties. The first indicator examines the shape or format of the national party systems, the second looks primarily at the patterns of contestation among political parties, while the last indicator focuses on the disruptive effect or potential of the EU issue for national parties. Of particular importance here is the partisan dealignment described in the previous section, as it enhances the prospects of European integration altering national party systems. However, much depends on the existence of actors willing to seize the opportunities and their ability to exploit them to their advantage.

Establishment of New Parties as a Result of European Integration

The rationale for examining the potential establishment of new parties is simple. The entry of environmental issues, together with other new policy questions, on the political agenda was a sufficiently large change to result in the establishment of green parties across Western Europe, with some of these parties even achieving government status from the 1990s onwards. So, the question is whether the EU dimension has been significant enough to produce a similar effect.

However, the format of party systems appears to have been almost completely unaffected by integration. The first column in Table 5.1 shows the existence of new parties whose establishment is primarily caused by European integration. Included are parties that get at least 5 per cent of votes in national parliamentary elections and that hold currently (in 2004) seats in the national legislatures of their member states. While in several countries such parties or electoral lists have contested seats in national and/or EP elections, in none of the 15 EU countries have these parties made a more permanent entry into national politics. This general survey confirms the findings of Peter Mair. According to Mair (2000, p. 30), of over 120 parties established in EU member states (excluding Greece, Portugal and Spain) to contest national parliamentary elections after the first direct EP elections held in each country, only three were formed 'with the explicit and primary intention of mobilising support for or against the EU'.[4] Mair also found that these parties were marginal players in their respective political systems, winning an average of only 1.5 per cent of the votes in national elections. The parties were the Austrian No-Citizens Initiative, the Finnish Alliance for a Free Finland and the British Referendum Party (Mair 2000, pp. 30-1). Party members, at least on the elite level, have therefore decided not to defect to other parties despite the often considerable differences of opinion over Europe.

Table 5.1 The impact of European integration on national parties and party systems.

Member state	Establishment of new parties[a]	Two-level party systems[b]	Internal cohesion of parties[c]
Austria	No	No	1.68
Belgium	No	No	1.78
Denmark	No	Yes	2.17
Finland	No	No	1.93
France	No	No	2.03
Germany	No	No	1.96
Greece	No	No	1.53
Ireland	No	No	1.71
Italy	No	No	1.60
Luxembourg	No	No	1.86
The Netherlands	No	No	1.66
Portugal	No	No	1.85
Spain	No	No	1.55
Sweden	No	No	2.44
UK	No	No	2.35

Notes:

[a] The establishment of new parties that get at least 5 per cent of votes in national parliamentary elections.

[b] A different party system in EP elections than in national parliamentary elections, with the parties not contesting national parliamentary elections winning at least 10 per cent of the votes.

[c] Level of party unity over integration in 1996 (Ray 1999). Ray asked country experts to estimate the internal cohesion of parties on a scale of 1 (complete unity) to 5 (leadership position opposed by a majority of party activists). The entries in the cells are the average cohesion levels for the parties in that country.

These findings should not come as a surprise. Indeed, there are very strong reasons to expect that we would not witness the entry of new parties as a result of European integration – or any other issue for that matter. The main explanatory factor for the observed stability is that the established national parties have an interest in sustaining the status quo and the prevailing structures of party competition. It would be dangerous and potentially costly for parties to change existing structures of electoral contestation. After all, despite the gradual partisan dealignment, parties still have their 'natural' pools of voters, and they have reputations for particular programmes and policy objectives. Giving the EU dimension a stronger role in the competition for votes would potentially lead to instability that might weaken the role of the main national parties (Marks and Steenbergen 2002, pp. 881-2). As Hooghe et al. argue:

> Parties that are successful in the existing structure of contestation have little incentive to rock the boat, while unsuccessful parties, that is, parties with weak electoral support or those that are locked out of government, have an interest in restructuring competition. The same strategic logic that leads mainstream parties to assimilate the issues raised by European integration into the Left/Right dimension of party competition leads peripheral parties to exploit European integration in an effort to shake up the party system (2002, p. 970).

Indeed, time series data show that the old parties have proven quite successful in withholding challenges from new entrants such as green parties, and the European dimension is perhaps the most impressive example of the ability of parties to incorporate or absorb new ideological dimensions into their policy profiles without losing their share of the votes. Fighting successful election campaigns is also increasingly costly, and – as the cartel party thesis argues – the established parties are privileged in that they are the beneficiaries of public funding as in most European countries the amount allotted to political parties depends on their success in previous parliamentary elections. This brief survey hence confirms that European integration has not altered the basic structure of national party systems by resulting in the formation of new parties.

The second column in Table 5.1 examines the existence of a 'two-level' party system, operationalized as a different party system in EP elections than in national parliamentary elections, with the parties not contesting national parliamentary elections winning on average at least 10 per cent of the votes in European elections. A two-level system exists in only one of the 15 countries, Denmark. The Danish EP election system features two Eurosceptical lists, the June Movement and the People's Movement, that do not contest seats in national parliamentary elections. In 1994 they won 25.5 per cent of the votes, in 1999 23.4 per cent, and in 2004 14.3 per cent of the votes. In France the party system in the EP elections has also differed partially from that found in national parliamentary elections. European elections have resulted in splits within parties, particularly among the Gaullists, with representatives from the same parties running for the Parliament from more than one list. Moreover, the Hunting, Fishing, Nature and Traditions list, which does not compete in national parliamentary elections, won 4.1 per cent of the votes in 1989, 3.9 per cent in 1994 and 6.8 per cent in 1999. In addition, in the 2004 elections Eurosceptical lists performed well in several countries, notably in the UK and in Sweden.

However, the second-order logic of the EP elections implies that new or smaller parties are advantaged at the expense of larger, particularly governing parties. The second-order nature of the elections enables voters to try new parties, and several parties have indeed made their breakthrough into national politics through success in European elections, with these parties then consolidating their positions in subsequent national or regional elections. Prominent examples are the Front National in France in 1984, the Vlaams Blok in Belgium in 1989, the Italian Democratici in 1999, and several green parties. De Winter (2002) has also shown that regionalist parties on average get more votes in European than in national parliamentary elections.

Apart from the opportunity to enter national politics, gaining representation in the EP is potentially very beneficial for small parties such as most green and regionalist parties. First, because these parties are normally out of government in their national political systems, seat(s) in the EP provides them with at least the opportunity to influence public policy. Second, seats in the EP also give greens, regionalist or other small parties much needed visibility that they can use to distribute their message. And third, financial benefits derived from the Parliament are also potentially very important. Obviously larger parties are the main beneficiaries of EP funds, but such subsidies are arguably more important for smaller parties and especially for new parties that have largely been excluded from public financing of parties or have received only minor public funding at the national level. Indeed, comparative studies of green and regionalist parties indicate that even relatively minor financial benefits can be of considerable importance to smaller parties (Bomberg 1998, De Winter and Türsan 1998, De Winter and Gomez-Reino Cachafeiro 2002).

While several small parties have indeed been able to exploit the potential offered by the second-order logic of EP elections, such impact is again mitigated by the strategic action of established national parties. Considering the disruptive potential of EU issues (see below), established parties have an incentive to compete in the elections along the familiar left–right dimension and downplay contestation over European integration (Hix 1999, Marks and Wilson 2000, Hooghe et al. 2002). So national politics is reproduced in EP elections, with the same set of actors and largely also the same set of issues.[5] By controlling the EP elections the established parties ensure their own survival and their dominant role in politics and are by and large successful in blocking the entry of new competitors. This is indeed an old phenomenon in European politics, with also local elections subject to similar control by national parties (Mair 2000). Also, research on Euro elections has shown that parties have a very good reason to take these elections seriously. Electoral success is important, not least in terms of credibility, with performance in Euro elections having an impact on vote share in the following national first-order elections.[6]

Coalition Formation

Turning next to coalition formation, we are interested in whether European integration has altered the politics of 'making and breaking governments'. Considering the increased salience of the EU,[7] we could expect to find European integration changing traditional patterns of coalition politics, particularly in countries where there is disagreement between the main parties about European integration.

But, again we see little evidence of the direct impact of European integration. For example, the recent large-scale study on European coalition governments showed that the European issue was not the *primary* dimension in explaining the (non-)emergence of cabinets in any of the 13 countries. To be sure, integration issues have resulted in cabinet terminations, resignations of prime ministers and junior coalition partners leaving the cabinet, but the EU issue has not changed the traditional patters of coalition formation (Müller and Strøm 2000). By and large, governments continue to be formed as they would be if the EU did not exist at all. One reason for this observed continuity is probably the fairly broad pro-integrationist consensus between the main governing parties in the majority of the member states. Parties classified as 'Eurosceptical', that is parties that are against increased integration or want to reduce the EU's powers or even call for their country's withdrawal from it, receive low shares of the votes in the majority of EU countries. Outright opposition to integration is mainly the reserve of ideologically extremist or populist parties, that is more or less the same group of parties that are excluded from government in their member states (Taggart 1998, Hooghe et al. 2002). These parties would remain outside of national governments even without European integration (Mair 2000, pp. 31-7).

Moreover, in recent years Eurosceptical parties have entered the government in at least three member states. In Austria the Freedom Party has been a junior partner in a coalition with the People's Party (ÖVP) since 2000. In Italy the National Alliance and the Northern League have been in two Forza Italia-led cabinets, in 1994-95 and in the current coalition formed in 2001. In the Netherlands the List Pim Fortuyn was in the government with the Christian Democratic Appeal (CDA) and the People's Party for Freedom and Democracy (VVD) from July 2002 to May 2003. And, in Sweden the minority government of the Social Democrats has ruled with the support of two Eurosceptical parties, the Greens and the Left Party, the former of which is still calling for Sweden to leave the EU. So, at least in these cases the European issue has not been salient enough to prevent cooperation.

Nevertheless, aspirations to enter national government probably contribute to ideological change, particularly in countries with multi-party coalition governments. The inclusion of Eurosceptical parties in the government is illustrative of the problem facing parties that want to hold executive office. Europe imposes severe constraints on parties and governments in terms of the policies they can realistically pursue. There is an inevitable trade-off between representativeness and governmentability: that is, parties must be seen as capable of efficient government, especially in countries that are members of EMU. Thus participation in government and EU decision-making may distance the party leaders from their electoral promises, the rank-and-file party activists and voters, and also from other members of the party elite such as MPs (Ladrech 2002, p. 398). For example, the majority of green, radical left and social democratic parties have tempered their views, at least partly in order to be recognized as responsible parties fit to govern. Parties may of course also adopt anti-EU/EMU postures in order to differentiate themselves from their competitors, but this could weaken their chances of gaining government office (Christensen 1998, Sitter 2001). Examining the evolution of green parties, Bomberg (1998, 2002) noted that Europeanization had resulted in the 'mellowing' or softening of green ideology throughout Europe, with initial rejection and radical criticism changing to pragmatic recognition and even strong commitment to European integration. Discussing the policy change of the British Labour Party, Daniels noted that 'the "Europeanisation" of the party may be seen as a response to its long exclusion from national office and as a key element of a broader electoral strategy designed to convey the image of a party which is modern, credible and fit to govern' (1998, p. 79). So, becoming recognized as a potential party of government may be a significant factor in modifying or de-radicalizing the policies – also on European integration – of ideologically more extremist parties.

Internal Dissent

Despite the relatively broad pro-EU consensus among the mainstream political parties, there is no shortage of research confirming the disruptive impact of integration matters within parties. The penetration of EU issues into domestic party competition has led – particularly in Denmark,[8] France, the UK and Norway[9] – to losses in elections, back-bench rebellions, factionalism, leadership resignations[10] and the breakdown and formation of new parties.

The last column in Table 5.1 shows the level of party unity over integration in 1996. The figures are from an expert survey conducted by Leonard Ray (1999).[11] Ray asked country experts to estimate the internal cohesion of parties on a scale of 1 (complete unity) to 5 (leadership position opposed by a majority of party activists). The entries in the cells are the average cohesion levels for the parties in that country, and hence they are not weighted taking into account the respective sizes of the parties.[12] The highest levels of internal dissent were in Sweden, the UK, Denmark and France. Parties appeared to be most cohesive over integration in Greece, Spain, Italy, Austria and Ireland. Ray observed that, when looking at individual parties, 'record levels of internal dissent are found primarily in nations which have had referenda, and occur in parties across the political spectrum' (1999, p. 293). Indeed, referenda had been held before 1996 in Sweden (1994), the UK (1975), Denmark (1972, 1986, 1992 and 1993) and France (1992). While it would be spurious to argue that there is a significant direct causal mechanism at work, it is nevertheless clear that referendums can thus reveal splits within parties – and loosen voters' ties to their parties in similar fashion as EP elections do.

Expert surveys and public opinion data indicate that the parties are ideologically less cohesive on integration than in traditional left–right issues (Hix 1999, see Thomassen and Schmitt 1999b). Moreover, within parties the elected representatives are considerably more supportive of integration than their voters. On left–right issues parties are fairly representative of their supporters (Klingemann 1995, Widfeldt 1995, Thomassen and Schmitt 1999a). However, the European dimension reveals a wide gap between citizens and MPs. According to a survey carried out in the mid-1990s, there was considerable divergence between MPs and voters: 'Across the board, voters' attitudes appeared to be less pro-European than those of the political elites, whether they were members of the European Parliament or of the national parliaments' (Thomassen and Schmitt 1999a, p. 206; see however Schmitt and Thomassen 2000). Hence party leaders have an electoral incentive to marginalize EU issues and focus on socio-economic matters in order to avoid irritating their voters.

Aware of the potential damage caused by European issues, parties have resorted to a variety of tactical manoeuvres. The best example is the so far largely successful strategy of downplaying EU issues in both national and EP elections and focusing on more familiar and less dangerous left–right matters. The strategy of playing the EU card in election campaigns is risky business, and its success depends on the unity of the parties over European integration. Van der Eijk and Franklin (2004) argue that the EU issue is a 'sleeping giant' in European politics. Comparing the preferences of voters and parties on the left–right dimension and on the EU dimension, they show that the diversity of opinion among the electorate is not reflected at the level of the parties, with the latter far more pro-integrationist than the citizens. There is thus 'potential for contestation' on EU issues, but this contestation depends on the salience of the European question and on the ability of parties to play the EU card to their advantage.

However, we know relatively little about the independent effect of EU on party choice in national elections (Gabel 2000), but at least in the UK the European issue emerged during the 1990s as a significant cleavage driving citizens' voting behaviour. The Conservative Party failed to increase its vote share by adopting a highly Eurocritical position in the 1990s, because voter perceptions of the party's position on the EU influenced its electoral support negatively (Evans 1998). In his subsequent work, Evans (2002) shows that as the ideological differences between the two main British parties on traditional left–right axis have diminished, the European issue has emerged as a significant factor influencing voting behaviour in elections to the House of Commons. Tillman (2004) also argues that around the time (1994-96) when Austria, Finland and Sweden joined the EU, the membership question influenced voting behaviour in the three countries. However, as Tillman admits, this may be due to the fact that the European issue was particularly salient in those countries at the time.

Moreover, governments and the main parties in several EU countries have tried to 'depoliticize' the European issue through cross-party cooperation behind closed doors in parliamentary committees with the aim of manufacturing consensus in national integration policy (Maor 1998). Such consensus building has arguably been more pronounced in smaller member states, based on the logic that national unity and policy consistency increase their negotiating power in EU institutions (see Hanf and Soetendorp 1998). This way of manufacturing national unity has effectively removed the EU issue from domestic party competition, as all or most parties share the responsibility for the outcome.

DISCUSSION

The impact of European integration on the national party systems of the EU member states has been modest. The format of the party systems has remained largely intact, with the establishment of not a single electorally successful party directly related to European integration. Specific anti/pro-EU parties or movements have remained marginal and often only compete in European elections. European issues have also failed to alter traditional patterns of coalition politics, with the left-right dimension still the most important dimension in structuring party competition and coalition formation. Examining individual parties, we note that the introduction of EU issues has increased internal dissent within parties, particularly within parties whose electorates remain divided over the benefits of integration.

According to the argument advanced in this chapter the observed stability is first and foremost explained by the interests of the main national parties in defending the status quo. The national parties owe their existence to issues unrelated to European integration, and hence they seek to contain competition over EU issues. So far this strategy has worked fairly well, and there is no reason to expect any kind of radical change in this respect in the future. National mainstream parties will continue to do their best to control the agendas in both national and EP elections, and most likely they will also be successful. Nor does the EU dimension appear to be salient enough to most of the electorate to change traditional voting patterns.

Finally, the future of national party systems, and the impact EU will have on these systems, to a large extent depends on what course integration will take. Regardless of whether we examine national parties' ideology, organization or behaviour, the present situation of limited change is likely to persist as long as there are no reforms that either substantially strengthen the policy competence of the EU (e.g., by giving the EU the power to raise taxes and to carry out major redistributive policies) and/or lead to the formation of a genuine EU executive. Without any EU president or parliamentary government vested with significant policy-making powers, the identity and dominant position of national parties are not threatened by the Euro parties (Hix and Lord 1997, Ladrech 2000, Mair 2000).

NOTES

1. Scholars have employed a variety of measures (expert judgements, survey data and content analysis of party programmes) to examine the development of party ideologies. Expert judgements have deployed a scale of 1 (left) to 10 (right), with country experts placing parties on that dimension. Comparing the findings of the two major studies carried out in 1982 and 1993 respectively (Castles and Mair 1984, Huber and Inglehart 1995) both Knutsen (1998) and Mair (1995) found evidence of partisan convergence, particularly among the main parties of the left (social democrats) and the right (conservatives/Christian democrats). Content analysis of party manifestos, analysing the development of party positions between 1945 and 1998, showed restricted change. Left–right distances decreased between the 1940s and 1960s, increased between the 1970s and 1980s and decreased again between the 1980s and 1990s. From the 1940s to the 1960s many party families moved leftward, whereas they moved rightward from the 1970s until the 1990s (Budge et al. 2001, Volkens and Klingemann 2002). However, regardless of the method used, the research does show that despite convergence there are still notable differences between the parties.
2. Katz and Mair (1994) differentiated between party in public office, that is government and parliament; party on the ground, including members and loyal party voters; and party in central office. According to them only the party on the ground had really been weakened:

the erosion of links to civil society coincided with growing ties between the state and the parties. Also the party in central office had arguably seen its position weaken in relation to the party in public office. With the exception of Italy (and perhaps the UK), the growth of parliamentary staff had consistently outstripped that of central office (see also Farrell and Webb 2000, Heidar and Koole 2000, Helms 2000).

3. For more detailed information on the transformation of national parties, see the volumes edited by Dalton and Wattenberg (2000a), Luther and Müller-Rommel (2002) and Webb et al. (2002).
4. Mair thus excludes anti/pro-EU parties that compete exclusively in EP elections. However, it is probable that a large share of the remaining new parties that compete in national parliamentary elections were formed as a protest against or as alternatives to the ruling cartel of mainstream parties. Their establishment is therefore indirectly linked to European integration, as the EU, and the EMU in particular, are key elements of the policies of government parties.
5. The lack of discussion on the constitutional aspects of integration (more or less integration) is potentially very damaging. However, the current situation is arguably not without its merits (Mair 2000). By reproducing the ideological cleavages dividing party families at the national level, and by offering the electorates familiar faces and themes, national parties have probably facilitated electoral mobilization in EP elections. One could also argue that focusing on left–right issues is a positive factor when considering EP's powers and the representation of citizens' opinions: the Parliament has no formal say over constitutional questions, the group structure of the EP is based on the left–right dimension, and the congruence of opinions between the representatives and the voters is higher on left–right matters than on integration issues (Thomassen and Schmitt 1999a).
6. When government parties did better in the European election than expected based on the location of that election in the national election cycle, the same parties also did better at the ensuing national election. When they did worse than expected at the European election they did worse at the ensuing national election' (Marsh and Franklin 1996, p. 29; see Marsh 1998).
7. According to Leonard Ray's expert survey (1999), the importance of European integration for the parties increased between 1984 and 1996. In 1996 the EU was an important issue to 52.2 per cent of the parties. On a scale of 1 to 7, the mean was 2.71 in 1984 and 3.18 in 1996.
8. In Denmark the membership issue produced a notable cleavage after the membership referendum held in 1972, with the 'earthquake election' held in 1973 substantially reshaping the national party system. The support of the four traditional parties dropped in that election from 84 per cent to 58 per cent. Three parties – the Christian People's Party, the Progress Party and the Centre Party – entered the parliament for the first time, and the Danish Communist Party and the Single Tax Party made a comeback. Since then the Danish party system has been more fragmented than before the 1973 elections, with at least eight parties in the Folketing. However, European integration was not the main factor producing change in the 1973 elections. Instead, voters changed their party allegiance mainly because of domestic issues (the welfare state).
9. In Norway several parties suffered severe internal splits or tensions in connection with the membership referendum held in 1972. The Labour Party was internally divided and suffered a heavy loss in the national elections held in September 1973. The Liberals split into two parties, but finally managed to reunite in 1989 (Heidar and Svåsand 1997, Saglie 2000).
10. The most famous example is Margaret Thatcher. The European issue, more specifically the increasingly Eurosceptical views adopted by Thatcher, was the leading factor in bringing about her resignation. Attitudes over European integration were also the primary factor in explaining the choice of John Major as Thatcher's successor (Garry 1995, Cowley and Garry 1998).
11. The elite surveys of MPs carried out in 1996 would have provided more satisfactory data, but unfortunately the dataset covers only 10 out of 15 national legislatures (see Katz and Wessels 1999, Schmitt and Thomassen 1999).

12. The exact wording of the survey question was: 'Please use the form attached to evaluate the positions taken by political parties on the issue of European integration. Please evaluate the parties using the following scales. ... C: The *degree of dissent* within the party over the party leadership's position: 1 = Complete unity, 2 = Minor dissent, 3 = Significant dissent, 4 = Party evenly split on the issue, 5 = Leadership position opposed by a majority of party activists' (Ray 1999, p. 295).

REFERENCES

Bartolini, Stefano and Peter Mair (1990), *Identity, Competition, and Electoral Availability: The Stabilization of European Electorates 1885-1985*, Cambridge: Cambridge University Press.

Biorcio, Roberto and Renato Mannheimer (1995), 'Relationships between citizens and political parties', in Hans-Dieter Klingemann and Dieter Fuchs (eds), *Citizens and the State*, Oxford: Oxford University Press, pp. 206-26.

Blais, André and Agnieszka Dobrzynska (1998), 'Turnout in electoral democracies', *European Journal of Political Research*, **33** (2), 239-61.

Blondel, Jean and Mauricio Cotta (eds) (1996), *Party and Government: An Inquiry into the Relationship between Government and Supporting Parties in Liberal Democracies*, London: Macmillan.

Blondel, Jean, Richard Sinnott and Palle Svensson (1998), *People and Parliament in the European Union: Participation, Democracy, and Legitimacy*, Oxford: Clarendon Press.

Bomberg, Elizabeth (1998), *Green Parties and Politics in the European Union*, London: Routledge.

Bomberg, Elizabeth (2002), 'The Europeanisation of Green Parties: Exploring the EU's impact', *West European Politics*, **25** (3), 29-50.

Budge, Ian, Hans-Dieter Klingemann, Andrea Volkens, Judith Bara and Eric Tanenbaum (2001), *Mapping Policy Preferences: Estimates for Parties, Electors, and Governments 1945-1998*, Oxford: Oxford University Press.

Castles, Francis G. and Peter Mair (1984), 'Left-right political scales: Some "expert" judgements', *European Journal of Political Research*, **12** (1), 73-88.

Caul, Miki L. and Mark M. Gray (2000), 'From platform declarations to policy outcomes: Changing party profiles and partisan influence over policy', in Russell J. Dalton and Martin P. Wattenberg (eds), *Parties without Partisans: Political Change in Advanced Industrial Democracies*, Oxford: Oxford University Press, pp. 208-37.

Christensen, Dag Arne (1998), 'Foreign policy objectives: Left Socialist opposition in Denmark, Norway and Sweden', *Scandinavian Political Studies*, **21** (1), 51-70.

Cowley, Philip and John Garry (1998), 'The British Conservative Party and Europe: The choosing of John Major', *British Journal of Political Science*, **28** (3), 473-99.

Dalton, Russell J. (2000), 'The decline of party identifications', in Russell J. Dalton and Martin P. Wattenberg (eds), *Parties without Partisans: Political Change in Advanced Industrial Democracies*, Oxford: Oxford University Press, pp. 19-36.

Dalton, Russell J. and Martin P. Wattenberg (eds) (2000a), *Parties without Partisans: Political Change in Advanced Industrial Democracies*, Oxford: Oxford University Press.

Dalton, Russell J. and Martin P. Wattenberg (2000b), 'Unthinkable democracy: Political change in advanced industrial democracies', in Russell J. Dalton and Martin

P. Wattenberg (eds), *Parties without Partisans: Political Change in Advanced Industrial Democracies*, Oxford: Oxford University Press, pp. 3-16.

Dalton, Russell J., Ian McAllister and Martin P. Wattenberg (2000), 'The consequences of partisan dealignment', in Russell J. Dalton and Martin P. Wattenberg (eds), *Parties without Partisans: Political Change in Advanced Industrial Democracies*, Oxford: Oxford University Press, pp. 37-63.

Dalton, Russell J., Ian McAllister and Martin P. Wattenberg (2002), 'Political parties and their publics', in Kurt Richard Luther and Ferdinand Müller-Rommel (eds), *Political Parties in the New Europe: Political and Analytical Challenges*, Oxford: Oxford University Press, pp. 19-42.

Daniels, Philip (1998), 'From hostility to "constructive engagement": The Europeanisation of the Labour Party', *West European Politics*, **21** (1), 72-96.

Delwit, Pascal, Erol Külachi and Cédric Van De Walle (eds) (2001), *Les federations européennes de parties: Organisation et influence*, Brussels: Editions de l'Universite de Bruxelles.

De Winter, Lieven (2002), 'Ethnoregionalist Parties and European Integration at the 1999 European Elections', in Gérard Grunberg, Pascal Perrinnau and Colette Ysmal (eds), *Europe at the Polls*, London: Palgrave, pp. 130-45.

De Winter, Lieven and Margarita Gomez-Reino Cachafeiro (2002), 'European integration and ethnoregionalist Parties', *Party Politics*, **8** (4), 483-503.

De Winter, Lieven and Huri Türsan (eds) (1998), *Regionalist Parties in Western Europe*, London: Routledge.

Evans, Geoffrey (1998), 'Euroscepticism and conservative electoral support: How an asset became a liability', *British Journal of Political Science*, **28** (4), 573-90.

Evans, Geoffrey (2002), 'European integration, party politics and voting in the 2001 election', *British Elections and Parties Review*, **12**, 95-110.

Farrell, David M. and Paul Webb (2000), 'Political parties as campaign organizations', in Russell J. Dalton and Martin P. Wattenberg (eds), *Parties without Partisans: Political Change in Advanced Industrial Democracies*, Oxford: Oxford University Press, pp. 102-28.

Franklin, Mark, Tom Mackie and Henry Valen (1992), *Electoral Change: Responses to Evolving Social and Attitudinal Structures in Western Countries*, Cambridge: Cambridge University Press.

Gabel, Matthew (2000), 'European integration, voters and national politics', *West European Politics*, **23** (4), 52-72.

Gabel, Matthew J. and Simon Hix (2002), 'Defining the EU political space: An empirical study of the European elections manifestos, 1979-1999', *Comparative Political Studies*, **35** (8), 934-64.

Gaffney, John (ed.) (1996), *Political Parties and the European Union*, London: Routledge.

Garry, John (1995), 'The British Conservative Party: Divisions over European policy', *West European Politics*, **18** (4), 170-89.

Hanf, Kenneth and Ben Soetendorp (eds) (1998), *Adapting to European Integration: Small States and the European Union*, London: Longman.

Heidar, Knut and Lars Svåsand (eds) (1997), *Partier uten grenser?*, Otta: Tano Aschehoug.

Heidar, Knut and Ruud Koole (eds) (2000), *Parliamentary Party Groups in European Democracies: Political Parties behind Closed Doors*, London: Routledge.

Helms, Ludger (2000), 'Parliamentary party groups and their parties: A comparative assessment', *Journal of Legislative Studies*, **6** (2), 104-20.

Hix, Simon (1999), 'Dimensions and alignments in European Union politics: Cognitive constraints and partisan responses', *European Journal of Political Research*, **35** (1), 69-106.

Hix, Simon and Christopher Lord (1997), *Political Parties in the European Union*, Basingstoke: Macmillan.

Hooghe, Liesbet, Gary Marks and Carole J. Wilson (2002), 'Does left/right structure party positions on European integration?', *Comparative Political Studies*, **35** (8), 965-89.

Huber, John and Ronald Inglehart (1995), 'Expert interpretations of party space and party locations in 42 societies', *Party Politics*, **1** (1), 73-111.

Johansson, Karl Magnus and Tapio Raunio (2001), 'Partisan responses to Europe: Comparing Finnish and Swedish political parties', *European Journal of Political Research*, **39** (2), 225-49.

Johansson, Karl Magnus and Peter Zervakis (eds) (2002), *European Political Parties between Cooperation and Integration*, Baden-Baden: Nomos.

Karvonen, Lauri and Stein Kuhnle (eds) (2001), *Party Systems and Voter Alignments Revisited*, London: Routledge.

Katz, Richard S. and Peter Mair (eds) (1992), *Party Organizations: A Data Handbook on Party Organizations in Western Democracies, 1960-90*, London: Sage.

Katz, Richard S. and Peter Mair (eds) (1994), *How Parties Organize: Change and Adaptation in Party Organizations in Western Democracies*, London: Sage.

Katz, Richard S. and Peter Mair (1995), 'Changing models of party organization and party democracy: The emergence of the cartel party', *Party Politics*, **1** (1), 5-28.

Katz, Richard S. and Bernhard Wessels (eds) (1999), *The European Parliament, the National Parliaments, and European Integration*, Oxford: Oxford University Press.

Kirchheimer, Otto (1966), 'The transformation of the Western European party systems', in Joseph LaPalombara and Myron Weiner (eds), *Political Parties and Political Development*, Princeton: Princeton University Press, pp. 177-206.

Kitschelt, Herbert (2000), 'Citizens, politicians, and party cartellization: Political representation and state failure in post-industrial democracies', *European Journal of Political Research*, **37** (2), 149-79.

Klingemann, Hans-Dieter (1995), 'Party positions and voter orientations', in Hans-Dieter Klingemann and Dieter Fuchs (eds), *Citizens and the State*, Oxford: Oxford University Press, pp. 183-205.

Knutsen, Oddbjørn (1998), 'Expert judgements of the Left-Right location of political parties: A comparative longitudinal study', *West European Politics*, **21** (2), 63-94.

Kopecký, Petr and Cas Mudde (2002), 'The two sides of Euroscepticism: Party positions on European integration in East Central Europe', *European Union Politics*, **3** (3), 297-326.

Ladrech, Robert (2000), *Social Democracy and the Challenge of European Union*, Boulder: Lynne Rienner.

Ladrech, Robert (2002), 'Europeanisation and political parties: Towards a framework for analysis', *Party Politics*, **8** (4), 389-403.

Lipset, Seymour Martin and Stein Rokkan (1967), 'Cleavage structures, party systems and voter alignments: An introduction', in Seymour M. Lipset and Stein Rokkan (eds), *Party Systems and Voter Alignments: Cross National Perspectives*, New York: Free Press, pp. 1-64.

Luther, Kurt Richard and Ferdinand Müller-Rommel (eds) (2002), *Political Parties in the New Europe: Political and Analytical Challenges*, Oxford: Oxford University Press.

Mair, Peter (1995), 'Political parties, popular legitimacy, and public privilege', *West European Politics*, **18** (3), 40-57.

Mair, Peter (1997), *Party System Change: Approaches and Interpretations*, Oxford: Oxford University Press.

Mair, Peter (2000), 'The limited impact of Europe on national party systems', *West European Politics*, **23** (4), 27-51.

Mair, Peter and Ingrid van Biezen (2001), 'Party membership in twenty European democracies, 1980-2000', *Party Politics*, **7** (1), 5-22.

Maor, Moshe (1998), 'The relationship between government and opposition in the Bundestag and House of Commons in the run-up to the Maastricht Treaty', *West European Politics*, **21** (3), 187-207.

Marks, Gary and Carole J. Wilson (2000), 'The past in the present: A cleavage theory of party response to European integration', *British Journal of Political Science*, **30** (3), 433-59.

Marks, Gary and Marco Steenbergen (2002), 'Understanding political contestation in the European Union', *Comparative Political Studies*, **35** (8), 879-92.

Marks, Gary and Marco R. Steenbergen (eds) (2004), *European Integration and Political Conflict*, Cambridge: Cambridge University Press.

Marsh, Michael (1998), 'Testing the second-order election model after four European elections', *British Journal of Political Science*, **28** (4), 591-607.

Marsh, Michael and Mark Franklin (1996), 'The foundations: Unanswered questions from the study of European elections, 1979-1994', in Cees van der Eijk and Mark N. Franklin (eds), *Choosing Europe? The European Electorate and National Politics in the Face of Union*, Ann Arbor: The University of Michigan Press, pp. 23-45.

Müller, Wolfgang C. and Kaare Strøm (eds) (2000), *Coalition Governments in Western Europe*, Oxford: Oxford University Press.

Nieuwbeerta, Paul and Wout Ultee (1999), 'Class voting in Western industrialized countries, 1945-1990: Systematizing and testing explanations', *European Journal of Political Research*, **35** (1), 123-60.

Pennings, Paul (2002), 'The dimensionality of the EU policy space: The European elections of 1999', *European Union Politics*, **3** (1), 59-80.

Raunio, Tapio (2002), 'Why European integration increases leadership autonomy within political parties', *Party Politics*, **8** (4), 405-22.

Ray, Leonard (1999), 'Measuring party orientations towards European integration: results from an expert survey', *European Journal of Political Research*, **36** (2), 283-306.

Saglie, Jo (2000), *Standpunkter og strategi: EU-saken i norsk partipolitikk, 1989-1994*, Oslo: Institutt for Statsvitenskap, Universitet i Oslo.

Scarrow, Susan E. (2000), 'Parties without members? Party organization in a changing electoral environment', in Russell J. Dalton and Martin P. Wattenberg (eds), *Parties without Partisans: Political Change in Advanced Industrial Democracies*, Oxford: Oxford University Press, pp. 79-101.

Schmitt, Hermann and Sören Holmberg (1995), 'Political parties in decline?', in Hans-Dieter Klingemann and Dieter Fuchs (eds), *Citizens and the State*, Oxford: Oxford University Press, pp. 95-133.

Schmitt, Hermann and Jacques Thomassen (eds) (1999), *Political Representation and Legitimacy in the European Union*, Oxford: Oxford University Press.

Schmitt, Hermann and Jacques Thomassen (2000), 'Dynamic representation: The case of European integration', *European Union Politics*, **1** (3), 318-39.

Sitter, Nick (2001), 'The politics of opposition and European integration in Scandinavia: Is Euro-scepticism a government-opposition dynamic?', *West European Politics*, **24** (4), 22-39.

Strøm, Kaare (2000), 'Parties at the core of government', in Russell J. Dalton and Martin P. Wattenberg (eds), *Parties without Partisans: Political Change in Advanced Industrial Democracies*, Oxford: Oxford University Press, pp. 180-207.

Taggart, Paul (1998), 'A touchstone of dissent: Euroscepticism in contemporary Western European party systems', *European Journal of Political Research*, **33** (3), 363-88.

Thomassen, Jacques and Hermann Schmitt (1999a), 'Issue congruence', in Hermann Schmitt and Jacques Thomassen (eds), *Political Representation and Legitimacy in the European Union*, Oxford: Oxford University Press, pp. 186-208.

Thomassen, Jacques and Hermann Schmitt (1999b), 'Partisan structures in the European Parliament', in Richard S. Katz and Bernhard Wessels (eds), *The European Parliament, the National Parliaments, and European Integration*, Oxford: Oxford University Press, pp. 129-48.

Tillman, Erik R. (2004), 'The European Union at the ballot box? European integration and voting behavior in the new member states', *Comparative Political Studies*, **37** (5), 590-610.

van der Eijk, Cees and Mark N. Franklin (eds) (1996), *Choosing Europe: The European Electorate and National Politics in the Face of Union*, Ann Arbor: The University of Michigan Press.

van der Eijk, Cees and Mark N. Franklin (2004), 'Potential for contestation on European matters at national elections in Europe', in Gary Marks and Marco R. Steenbergen (eds), *European Integration and Political Conflict*, Cambridge: Cambridge University Press, pp. 32-50.

Volkens, Andrea and Hans-Dieter Klingemann (2002), 'Parties, ideologies and issues: stability and change in fifteen European party systems 1945-1998', in Kurt Richard Luther and Ferdinand Müller-Rommel (eds), *Political Parties in the New Europe: Political and Analytical Challenges*, Oxford: Oxford University Press, pp. 143-67.

Wattenberg, Martin P. (2000), 'The decline of party mobilization', in Russell J. Dalton and Martin P. Wattenberg (eds), *Parties without Partisans: Political Change in Advanced Industrial Democracies*, Oxford: Oxford University Press, pp. 64-76.

Webb, Paul (2002), 'Political parties and democratic control in advanced industrial societies', in Paul Webb, David Farrell and Ian Holliday (eds), *Political Parties in Advanced Industrial Democracies*, Oxford: Oxford University Press, pp. 438-60.

Webb, Paul, David Farrell and Ian Holliday (eds) (2002), *Political Parties in Advanced Industrial Democracies*, Oxford: Oxford University Press.

Widfeldt, Anders (1995), 'Party membership and party representativeness', in Hans-Dieter Klingemann and Dieter Fuchs (eds), *Citizens and the State*, Oxford: Oxford University Press, pp. 134-82.

6. Interest Organizations and European Integration

Ove K. Pedersen

INTRODUCTION

This chapter examines the influence of European integration on the relationship between state administration and private interests in the four Nordic countries – Sweden, Denmark, Norway and Finland. By private interests I mean interest organizations, private corporations and independent experts.[1] The chapter focuses exclusively on the national policy processes that are involved with managing European Union (EU) issues. More specifically, the chapter discusses two aspects of multi-level governance. First, the important role of private interests in the coordination of decision-making at the national level preceding their government's representation of national interests in the European Council of Ministers and other EU organizations. Second, the effect of all this on national democratic systems.

I show that in all four countries private interests have been integrated with political administrative agencies and political institutions as a precursor for national governments to take part in EU-related policy processes. Some of these EU-oriented institutional arrangements create new forms of corporatist relationships between private interests and public agencies. I also show that these new forms of corporatism challenge existing democratic ideals. Furthermore, new democratic ideals have developed in an effort to legitimize the delegation of political authority to the new corporatist relationships between private interests and public agencies.

RESEARCH QUESTIONS

Theories of corporatist decision-making processes often describe the relationship between political institutions and private interests as one in which special interests have either attained the opportunity to manage their own interests at the cost of the common interest (Lowi 1979, Williamson 1989), or conversely have been subordinated to the interests of administrative or political actors. Recent theories about corporatism provide a third possibility, raising questions as to whether the corporatist decision-making process can be considered to be one in which interests meet '. . . in mutual dialogue [to] achieve compromise concerning which policy is best for both parties' (Rothstein and Bergstrøm 1999, p. 12). This chapter assumes that interest organizations and private firms, similar to political institutions and administrative agencies, have pre-given and opposing interests. However, it is an empirical question whether these are independent of or dependent on other interests, whether these opposing interests are coordinated at the national level, and whether these interests are somehow aggregated so as to establish a truly national interest.

In turn, this is first a question of whether private interests are included or excluded – that is, integrated with – administrative and political interests. In other words, are private interests *in* or *out* of EU-related policy processes? Next, it is a question of whether administrative agencies, while attending to EU-related matters, engage in internal coordination. Are EU-related policy processes coordinated between the political administration's different agencies? Does *politico-administrative coordination* take place? Furthermore, it is a question of whether coordination of private and public interests takes place. Does *corporatist coordination* take place to the degree that private interests in an institutionalized way are involved with administrative agencies in negotiating EU-related national policies? Finally, it is a question of whether such coordination leads to the formulation of a national interest. Is a coordination of public and private interests taking place in such a manner that interests are aggregated into a *national interest*?[2]

It follows that there are potentially three means of managing public and private interests in relation to EU issues and organizations. In the first instance, the political institutions may single-handedly make decisions on behalf of the common good. This is called the *within strategy* insofar as private interests are held outside the national coordination of policy-making. In the second instance, private interests cooperate with public authorities in various ways to coordinate public and private interests. This process subsequently enables the national authority to manage interests in relation to EU organizations. This is labelled the *go-through strategy* insofar as multiple parties are granted a voice in national deliberations on EU-related policies and strategies (Averyt 1977, Greenwood 1997, Hayes-Renshaw and Wallace 1997, Pedersen and Pedersen 2000, Pedersen 2001, Wallace and Wallace 1996). In the third instance, private interests circumvent national authorities and go directly to the European institutions to influence them. This is called the *bypass strategy* insofar as private interests choose to avoid the national authorities altogether (Averyt 1977, Pedersen and Pedersen 2001, Pedersen 2001).[3]

As such, this chapter is guided by two sets of research questions. The first set involves the role of private interests in EU matters at the national level: Are private interests engaged in national policy processes related to EU matters? Is corporatist coordination taking place? Is a national interest formulated?

The second set of questions relates to the democratic input of private interests. In theories about how multi-level governance influences national democratic systems the role of corporatist arrangements at the national level is seldom addressed. Instead, these theories have been concerned mainly with the EU as an institutional ensemble and with the demands this places on it, such as its legality and legitimacy (Lodge 1994, Hayward 1995, Laffan 1996, Obradovic 1996, Weiler 1996, Hansen and Williams 1999). Moreover, these theories have dealt with considerations of the standards of legality and legitimacy to which the EU should conform and how the EU often fails to live up to these ideals. In this chapter I take a different approach. First, I only deal with the democratic consequences of EU-related policy-making for *national* democratic systems and not for all of EU as an institutional ensemble. Second, I assess the democratic consequences instead of evaluating the degree to which the EU does or does not live up to a set of ideal or abstract ideas of how a 'good democracy' is supposed to be organized and function. As such, the second set of research questions involves how national policy-making around EU issues affects democracy. Specifically, based on a historical and empirical analysis, how can the democratic consequences of the involvement of private interest in national coordination be assessed? Are national democratic ideals and traditions being challenged?

METHODOLOGY

This chapter is based partly on a comparative investigation conducted in 1998 in which a questionnaire was sent to 1,323 administrative agencies in the central administration of Denmark, Finland, Sweden and Norway.[4] It concerns the central administration of these four relatively small states, which are all integrated in the Nordic community, but where factors like EU affiliation, EU strategies, general administrative systems, and historical and political circumstances vary considerably. The Nordic states thus provide a first-rate laboratory in which to study the development of corporatist arrangements in connection with European integration. Results of the comparative analysis indicate that private interests in all four countries have gained a voice in the politico-administrative processes preceding national representation in European organizations. Furthermore, results show that there is a significant difference among the four countries as to whether this has evolved into a process of *corporatist coordination* involving political parties and state agencies as well as private interests. There are also differences among these four countries as to whether an aggregation of interests occurs establishing possibilities for national governments to represent a *national interest* in EU policy processes. Finally, results indicate that the relationships between the parties are influenced by the way in which the national coordination system has been constructed and by whether a country is a formal EU member and, if so, for how long it has been a member.

To evaluate the democratic consequences of corporatist coordination the assessment will be divided into two parts (Jacobsson et al. 2004, pp. 131-2). The first part is concerned with democracy. It addresses the question of which democratic ideals form the basis for evaluating the consequences for national states of multi-level governance. This stems from the claim that European integration has led to changes in democratic ideals and, consequently, in the ideals upon which the evaluation is based. The second part is concerned with politics. It addresses the question of who actually controls democratic government in these Nordic countries when it comes to EU-related issues. This stems from the claim that European integration has changed the scope of politics. My analysis will be based on the ideals of everyday integration, that is, the European integration undertaken within the framework of the acquis communautaire, which had been established by 1998. It will also be based on an examination of the real distribution of political authority in connection with everyday integration. In this way, I will carry out two analyses: one that deals with democratic ideals, which were formulated in connection with the entry of Nordic countries into the EU (Denmark, Sweden, Finland) or at least their adaptation to it (Norway is not a formal EU member); the other examines to whom political authority has actually been delegated or granted in connection with the performance of EU-related tasks. Results indicate that democratic ideals are challenged, even if ideals have been transformed in the light of experiences with European integration. Results also indicate that corporatist coordination is one aspect of a general trend towards a bureaucratization of the national EU-related politics and politicization of the national EU-related bureaucracy.

COORDINATION – ARE PRIVATE INTERESTS IN OR OUT?

The first question to answer is: Are private interests included in or excluded from EU-related national policy processes? This question will be answered in several steps. The first is to compare the extent of the *contacts*[5] between authorities and private interests in connection with managing EU-related issues as well as whether private interests are *represented* in committees where matters related to the EU are attended to.

In Denmark the most intensive contact between authorities and private interests is with organizations (35 per cent to organizations, 23 per cent to private firms at least once a month); in Sweden and Norway it is equally with organizations as with corporations; in Finland to a greater degree with corporations. Norwegian authorities have the least intensive contacts – to organizations as well as corporations. There are also major differences between the four countries when it comes to the form of contact. 54 per cent of the responding agencies in Finland indicate that the contact is informal while a mere 12 per cent believe that they are of a formal character (i.e. takes place in writing, in formal meetings or in hearings). In contrast, 64 per cent in Denmark regard the contact as formal, while 39 per cent see it as informal.[6] The contact is most formal in Denmark followed by Norway, while it is most informal in Finland followed by Sweden.

However, private interests are not integrated via contact alone. Involvement also occurs through representation in public committees of varied character.[7] There are significant differences in terms of the extent to which the administration utilizes public committees and ad hoc groups in connection with the handling of EU-related matters. Sweden and Finland rely heavily on ad hoc groups for the management of EU matters; Denmark and Norway to a lesser degree. In contrast, private interests are to a higher degree represented in ad hoc groups and public committees in Denmark than in Sweden and Norway. Private interests are only represented in 28 per cent of these committees in Finland, while in Denmark the same goes for 54 per cent.

Based on these primary findings it can be assumed that all four nations have chosen to involve private interests, both through representation in public committees and through contacts. None of the four countries accordingly have chosen to let the national administrations handle EU-related policy processes single-handedly. Neither the *within* nor the *bypass* strategy is predominant. Even so there are differences between the countries, and they are found on at least three levels: First, Denmark involves private interests more often in administrative working groups and committees than the three other countries. Second, Sweden and Norway provide both organizations and firms with representation, while Denmark unambiguously emphasizes organizations. Third, Sweden has the most open administration in the sense that total involvement through contact and representation is highest. In the Swedish case openness builds on a combination of informal rather than formal contact, and involvement via representation rather than via contact.

Other important distinctions become apparent if we include independent experts as a third category of private interests.[8] Regarding the involvement of experts, Norway is at the absolute top, and Denmark at the absolute bottom. In general the numbers indicate that organizations are better represented than firms and experts, but also that the traditional notion that corporatist representation typically will involve associations and not individuals and collective organizations and not single companies is now challenged – both by individual experts and single firms.

NATIONAL COORDINATION

The second step in answering the first research questions will deal with the extent to which contact with and representation of private interests can be said to be a part of efforts to develop corporatist coordination of national-level decision-making about EU matters. This will be done from three angles. First, are the agencies that have contact with private interests and that are engaged in public committees with private interests also in contact with EU organizations? Is the coordination with private interests part of a broader effort to coordinate relations with EU organizations? Second, do the agencies with contact to private interests also have contact with other national administrative agencies? Is the coordination of private interests part of a broader effort to coordinate public and private interests and, therefore, to be defined as corporatist coordination? Third, do private interests bypass national authorities by going directly to the European organizations? Is corporatist coordination a dominant strategy or merely one among several alternative strategies of coordinating interests vis-à-vis the EU?

Table 6.1 shows that in general coordination has increased in the four countries, which further indicates that all Nordic countries have chosen to grant private interests voice instead of allowing the national administration to handle EU issues alone. Even if Denmark is the country where the EU has increased coordination the most, differences among the countries are not dramatic, but nevertheless show a divergence between the 'full' members (Denmark, Sweden and Finland) and the 'half' member (Norway is not a full member, but part of the Single Market by special agreement). Table 6.1 shows that 64 per cent of the Danish agencies indicate that it is correct that coordination between the agency and private interests has increased. Norway is in a class unto itself.

Table 6.1 In the last year has EU work increased the coordination between the agency and interest organizations/corporations in agencies that actually have contact with interest organizations and firms in connection with EU issues? 1998. Per cent

	Norway	Denmark	Sweden	Finland	Nordic countries
Quite correct	2	6	10	8	7
Correct	36	58	36	47	44
Incorrect	26	20	20	17	21
Quite incorrect	15	2	17	9	11
Do not know	22	14	17	20	18

To determine whether the coordination with private interests is part of corporatist coordination, I compare the number of agencies that have contact with EU institutions with the number of agencies that are also in contact with private interests. At the same time I compare the number of agencies that are in contact with other state agencies as well as with private interests in the same context. The purpose in both cases is to determine whether the relationship between the agency and private interests can be considered to be part of efforts designed to coordinate a plurality of public and private interests in connection with the management of EU-related issues. In other words, the idea is to determine whether coordination with private interests is part of a broader effort towards coordination of private and public interests, and whether coordination can be defined as corporatist coordination.

Generally speaking, Table 6.2 suggests that there is a significant relationship between the agencies in contact with private interests and those in contact with EU organizations. Differences between the countries are limited, but in all four countries only a segment of all agencies is in contact with private interests as well as with EU organizations. In all countries this segment stands out compared to the central administration in general and to the part of the administration that is involved in handling EU-related issues (the EU administration). The segment is roughly the same size in the respective countries, though slightly larger in Norway and Denmark than in Sweden and Finland. The same conclusion is evident when it comes to which agencies are in contact with EU organizations while at the same time in contact with private interests and other state agencies. In all countries a segment of the administrative agencies are involving private interests in their contacts with EU organizations and other state agencies and are doing so more intensively than the rest of the state agencies.

Table 6.2 Agencies in contact with EU organizations and national private interests (interest organizations or corporations) in connection with the management of EU issues in the course of the last year

	Norway	Denmark	Sweden	Finland	Nordic countries
General administration					
Total	69	62	67	68	67
Never	31	38	33	32	34
Often	28	35	36	38	34
EU Administration					
Total	93	94	87	87	90
Never	7	6	13	13	10
Often	59	67	53	55	59
Core-segment					
Total	100	99	91	91	95
Never	0	1	9	9	5
Often	79	75	62	56	68

Note: 'Total' encompasses all declarations of participation, regardless of intensity in the course of the last year. 'Often' is defined as 'once a month or more frequently'.

As such, it is possible to draw three conclusions thus far. First, it is evident that coordination takes place in all four countries. Second, only a fraction (a segment) of the administrative agencies takes part in this coordination. Third, even if agencies in contact with EU organizations are also in contact with national private interests, not all agencies in contact with private interests concerning EU matters are in contact with EU organizations.

CORPORATIST COORDINATION – A DOMINANT STRATEGY?

Even if coordination does take place, it has yet to be shown whether corporatist coordination is a dominant strategy, or if it instead merely represents one among several alternative types of coordination. Taking this third step I examine the degree to which private interests choose to *go through* the public authorities or *bypass* them. Generally speaking, only 13 per cent of the administrative agencies believe that private interests 'often' seek to circumvent the administration; 33 per cent believe that they 'occasionally' or 'rarely' do so. On average, 18 per cent report that interests do not do so, while 36 per cent do not know. Even if these numbers are based on assessments from administrative agencies, they confirm that private interests choose corporatist coordination as the dominant strategy.[9] The second question is the degree to which state agencies also choose this strategy as the dominant one. Are private interests included or excluded to the extent that coordination must primarily be viewed to be politico-administrative and only secondarily corporatist? Comparing the four countries indicates that coordination in Sweden and Finland is predominantly politico-administrative with less emphasis on coordination involving private interests. In the Danish case a more balanced integration of administrative agencies and private interests is apparent. The data also show that not all coordination involves just interests; it may also include coordination between state agencies *both with and without* private interests. As such, there are important differences regarding the extent to which private interests are integrated in coordination. These differences become particularly evident when comparing the extent to which agencies believe that coordination with other authorities (within their own area or in other policy fields) has been increased in relation to their coordination with private interests.

Finland is a special case in this context. In Finland there is a significant difference in the assessment of the degree to which coordination has increased within one's own ministry (67 per cent), with administrative agencies in other ministries (69 per cent), and with private interests (41 per cent). At the same time, however, the Finish agencies report that contact with interest organizations is relatively low. Relative to other countries, few Finish agencies believe that organizations and corporations are represented to a 'great degree' or 'somewhat' in groups and committees that have managed EU-related matters. Sweden differs slightly, but with the same conclusion. So there is evidence that in these two countries the formal integration with the EEC has continued a tradition for corporatist cooperation, but that the internal politico-administrative coordination in particular has been increased and, as a result, has become the dominant strategy. In the Danish case a greater balance between politico-administrative coordination and coordination involving private interests is evident. Sixty-one per cent of administrative agencies report that coordination within the ministry has been increased; 50 per cent report that coordination between ministries has increased; and 47 per cent report that coordination with private interests has increased. At the same time Denmark is the country where coordination with private interests is believed to have increased the most, just as contact with private interests is reported to be among the most intensive and the most comprehensive.[10] Data then indicate that in the Danish case EU integration has increased both politico-administrative coordination and corporatist coordination. For this reason it can be argued that only in Denmark has integration led to corporatist coordination being as important as politico-administrative coordination.

There are several possible explanations for this. First, it can be claimed that EU integration runs along traditional paths for corporatist cooperation (i.e. corporatist path dependency). This can explain why private interests in all four countries have been granted voice in EU-related decision-making, and why the difference between politico-administrative and corporatist coordination is limited under any circumstances. Second, it can be claimed that EU integration depends on traditional paths for the organization of the relationship between government and administration (i.e. administrative path dependency). This can explain why contacts with private interests in Sweden and Finland are predominantly informal, but also more intensive, whereas in Denmark and Norway they are predominantly formal and less intensive (Jacobsson et al. 2004, pp. 93-5). Third, it can be claimed that the form of association with the EU has significance. In the three full member states (Denmark, Sweden and Finland), coordination in general – including with private interests – has increased more than in Norway, which is by special agreement allowed to participate in the EU Commission's expert committees and working groups, but not in the Council of Ministers. Nevertheless, the difference between the four countries is modest.

NATIONAL INTEREST

In the fourth and final step answering the first research questions I now examine the character of corporatist coordination. The question is whether coordination leads to an aggregation of interests into a national interest (Almond and Powel 1978, p. 198). In this context I distinguish between two forms of 'national interest'. First is the national interest as determined by a *national standpoint.* Here coordination occurs such that participation in the Council of Ministers allows the government to represent an established majority in the national parliament based on an institutionalized aggregation of administrative, political and private interests prior to the government's participation in the Council of Ministers. Second is the national interest as determined by the *government's standpoint.* Here coordination occurs such that the government can represent itself without a documented majority in the parliament, but based on politico-administrative coordination that the government itself has deemed necessary prior to participation in the Council of Ministers.

First, let us look at the individual agencies' assessments of whether it has become more frequent to develop a national interest in the management of

EU matters. The difference between countries is significant – mainly between Finland on the one side and Norway on the other. In Finland, 65 per cent believe that it has become more common to develop a national interest. In Norway only 27 per cent believe the same. In Sweden and Denmark the distribution is more moderate – around 45 per cent believe that it has become more common. In this context it becomes apparent that formal membership plays a role, just as the organizational arrangement of the coordination system possibly does so. However, the most important factor in this context is that between 45-65 per cent in countries with full membership report that it has become more common to develop a national interest, which serves to indicate that coordination is oriented towards aggregation as a means of defining a standpoint.

Second, let us look at the agencies' assessments of the degree of disagreement in the decision-making process between public authorities and private interests. In the four countries 61 per cent believe that the degree of disagreement is 'small' or 'quite small'. Similarly, there is only a limited difference in terms of whether the disagreement is 'quite large' or 'large'. The numbers indicate that interplay between authorities and interests involve much consensus, which also suggests that coordination is oriented towards aggregation.

Third, let us look at whether administrative agencies have succeeded in winning the acceptance of private interests for their views and formulations as an indicator of the extent of coordination. The extent to which the agencies report that they have succeeded 'quite well' or 'well' to win private acceptance for public interests indicates that the processes are 'dominated' by the administrative agencies and therefore politico-administrative rather than aggregative. In the event that they are more mixed in their assessment (i.e. that there is greater balance between 'very good' and 'good' on the one side, and 'bad' or 'very bad' on the other side) indicates that the processes involve an aggregation of public and private interests. The numbers reveal that agencies have had some success in winning the acceptance of interest organizations to the agencies' views and formulations. Hence, coordination is somewhat more aggregative than politico-administrative. That said, there is still an element of the latter at work insofar as there is no assessment of whether the politico-administrative agencies unilaterally ('very well' or 'well') succeed in realizing their views in relation to private interests.

Fourth, let us look at the degree to which administrative agencies consider opinions put forward by the affected parties, consumer groups and clients in the execution of EU-related issues as an indicator of the extent of coordination. If agencies grant such opinions less weight than the technical and professional opinions forwarded by the government, this indicates that coordination is more politico-administrative than aggregative and vice versa. The data show that agencies grant technical and professional perspectives greater weight than opinions offered by the government and affected parties. Conversely, however, they place greater weight on the opinions of special interests than on those offered by the government. While professional and political perspectives, on the one side, and those of special interests, on the other side, do not necessarily have to be opposed to one another, the data suggest that the views of special interests are granted greater weight than are those of the government. Moreover, the views of the professionals are granted greater weight than those of anyone else.

Based on all of these findings, it is apparent that coordination involves an aggregation of public as well as private interests. The evidence at hand does not allow a more precise conclusion. Nevertheless, it seems clear that coordination does not take place exclusively in politico-administrative terms (*within*), but that both public and private interests are combined (*go-through*). Over all, this suggests the following: Corporatist coordination takes place within the framework of politico-administrative coordination where in all four countries private interests have participated with a significant voice and that this has helped to aggregate politico-administrative and private interests. That said, it is probably only in Denmark that a system of corporatist coordination has been established, and only in Denmark are politico-administrative and private interests in general combined. In Sweden, Finland and Norway it is equally clear that the politico-administrative coordination is relatively more significant than corporatist coordination. Therefore, it can – with some hesitation – be concluded that a national standpoint is formulated in Denmark, while in Sweden and Finland a government's standpoint is put together and that between the three countries there are varieties of defining national interests.

There are several explanations for these differences. The most important is probably that the national coordination system in Denmark is constructed in such a manner that the government is obliged to integrate private interests in the administrative coordination prior to its participation in the Council of Ministers, and that the government is obliged to have a mandate from a majority in the national parliament before negotiating in the Council. Hence, the formal character of the coordination system as well as the politically binding power of the mandate leads to the formulation of a national standpoint through a process of aggregation of public and private interests (Pedersen 2002). In Sweden and Finland it is different. In these two countries the government alone is obligated to hear or inform the parliament, but in the Council the government can represent itself without a documented majority in the parliament. Instead, these governments need only engage in whatever coordination and consultation they deem necessary prior to participation in the Council of Ministers.

DEMOCRATIC CONSEQUENCES

European integration, full membership or not, entails that the relationship between private interests and public authorities is intensive. Integration also leads to the construction of new and more national channels for contact with the public administration. Corporations and organizations have the opportunity to utilize these channels in two ways: By circumventing or *bypassing* the national administration and initiating contact directly with European institutions or by *going through* the national administration to take care of interests in the European decision-making process. The same is true for public authorities. They can choose to bypass private interests and attend to the common interest through politico-administrative processes or by granting voice to private interests through contact and representation. Let us now consider the democratic consequences of these alternative possibilities for national political systems. This evaluation will be based on a historical and empirical comparison of democratic ideals with the scope of political authority. Are EU-related policy processes under the control and management of politicians – that is, elected members of parliament – or by appointed members of the government?

In the Nordic countries since the 1970s everyday integration has given rise to the development of at least five democratic ideals (Jacobsson et al. 2004, pp. 133ff.). All five deal with questions related to the distribution of political authority and, consequently, with the national division of power. In identifying these five ideals and in comparing them with political reality, the following three methodological requirements must be followed: (1) the assessment must be *contextual*. It must be based on the fact that the scope of politics as well as the democratic ideals will always be country-dependent and conditioned by the period under study. (2) The evaluation must be *dynamic*. It should take account of the fact that political power, like democratic ideals, is subject to continual change. (3) Finally, the evaluation should possess an *authoritative basis*. It must be based on interpretations of the democratic ideals as well as of political authority laid down by political agencies such as parliament, government and judiciary (Pedersen, 1998, 1999, Jacobsson et al. 2004). The five ideas in question are as follows:

1. *The ideal of parliamentary government.* This is based on the idea that while the government has the power to represent national interests in the EU, this must occur within the framework of the overarching authority of the parliament assigned to it by the national constitution or by specific legislation.
2. *The ideal of sovereignty.* This is based on the idea that national governments – and not the EU – should determine how the government and the

administration ought to be organized with the aim of representing national interests in the EU.

3. *The ideal of adaptation.* This is the idea that the government, understood as an organization, and the national administrative system – its organization, procedures and processes – should be adapted to European development and that it is the responsibility of the government to decide and to implement this adaptation.
4. *The ideal of neutrality.* This is the idea that there must be internal coordination within policy areas as well as between ministries, and that this coordination must follow professional standards of political neutrality. There are two associated secondary ideals: one deals with objectivity, and the other deals with the efficient furthering of interests. *The ideal of objectivity* implies that the most objectively competent authority should assume responsibility for the coordination. *The ideal of efficiency* implies that the most important private and public interests should be coordinated and that this should result in an efficient representation of national interests in the EU as well as the most efficient implementation of EU legislation on the national level.
5. *The ideal of transparency and participation.* This is the idea that the relevant parties in particular should be given sufficient insight and participation to permit their interests to influence the coordination of the government's or the national standpoint and that the public should be given insight into the political decision-making process. A secondary ideal of consensus is associated with this fifth ideal. *The ideal of consensus* implies that interests should be coordinated via negotiation and compromise rather than by voting and instruction. This ideal also implies that private interests are included in coordination on a voluntary basis. Private interests are free to participate, and when participating they cannot be instructed (i.e. by decision or decree be ordered to) by neither parliament nor government. They are also free to bypass national public organizations at there own will.

On the one hand, these five ideals show how the number of those who are considered legitimate participants in the political and administrative representation of national interests is extended – all relevant political and administrative, regional and local, private and public interests should be able in principle to participate, and the most important interests should be coordinated in principle. On the other hand, they also show that only very general and imprecise norms have been developed with regard to procedures involving democratic government. For example, there are differences between the four countries in the extent to which norms detail which political institutions, administrative agencies and private interests should be regarded as relevant and important. In sum, this produces a situation where the group of legitimate participants is in principle unlimited, but where it remains unclear who is responsible for delimiting the number of relevant parties. The domain of politics can expand without this necessarily implying the concurrent extension of democratic government.

In the following section, I compare political reality with these democratic ideals. I evaluate whether a gap has developed between the democratic ideals and the real world expansion of politics, and, if it has, I assess the consequences for democratic government. In other words, I address how everyday integration challenges (or not) democratic government. I argue that governments are using their sovereignty to decide the organization of the administration and the government itself in adapting to EU integration. Finally, I also argue that there are indications that administrative agencies are following the ideal of objectivity in the distribution of responsibilities, that the distribution of representation is efficient, and that the implementation of EU norms and rules is relatively high compared to other EU member states. Consequently, it would not be reasonable to describe national-level EU policy-making as undemocratic. Even so, the comparison of ideals and reality reveals four democratic challenges linked to the interplay of private and public interests. The two most important challenges are bureaucratization of the national EU-related politics and politicization of the national EU-related bureaucracy.

FOUR CHALLENGES

1. *Bureaucratization.* In all four countries the bureaucratization of EU issues is a general phenomenon, which reveals the extent to which civil servants and not governments or parliaments manage EU questions. In general the administrative agencies (i.e. the civil servants or the bureaucracy) possess considerable freedom to draft and prepare (and in certain instances even to decide) policies and legislation. For example, a considerable surfeit of informal contacts is undertaken autonomously from parliaments and even sometimes detached from the government's (or the minister's) participation and insight. Even in the Danish case, where there are more formal than informal contacts and where the informal contacts generally comprise a 'shadow' (Scharpf 1997) to the formal ones, there are several examples of corporatist coordination not oriented to the mandating procedure. There are also several examples of administrative units handling EU matters independently from parliamentary supervision and from control from the side of governments (Esmark 2002, Højbjerg 2002). According to the ideal of parliamentary government,

any activity that involves the formulation, ratification or implementation of rules with general application must follow specific legislative procedures. Instead, politico-administrative processes take place autonomously from the parliament and from government control. It is against this background that the first challenge to democratic governance arises: The administrative agencies possess considerable freedom and autonomy in handling EU matters, greatest in countries where no mandating procedure exists and where coordination is not concentrated in formal committees. Accordingly, the democratic challenge is greatest in Norway, Sweden and Finland, but is not inconsiderable in Denmark.

2. *Politicization*. There are differences from country to country and from case to case in the factors administrations take into account in preparing a governmental or a national standpoint. In most instances it is left open to the administrative agencies themselves to decide the extent to which the political agencies should be consulted; when it is to take place; and how such contacts should be organized. This also applies to contacts with other administrative authorities and with private interests. Only in the Danish case have limits been set on the independence of the administration in this respect. The point at which the line has been crossed between administrative coordination (in which only public authorities are required to be consulted), political coordination (in which political institutions, e.g. parliaments, parties and party groups, must be consulted) and corporatist coordination (in which private interests must be consulted) is something that the administrative agencies normally decide for themselves (Jacobsson et al. 2004). This is where the second challenge to democratic government stands out: The coordination process empowers the administration to make political decisions. This may occur when the administration determines who will be included in the coordination process, which interests (private and public) will be taken into account, and when, how and whether political institutions are to be consulted as well as offered the possibility to exercise control. Against this background, the challenge is that political processes are taking place in detachment from parliamentary supervision and from government decisions. Furthermore, administrative units possess considerable autonomy to organize working practices and to formulate the standpoint to be represented by governments in EU organizations, but also to decide which interests should be consulted, which interests will be taken into account and when political control will take place.
3. *Exclusion*. We have seen that many private interests have access to the national systems of coordination. However, this openness is not systematic and does not follow predetermined procedures. The openness that occurs thus depends on factors that have little to do with the ideal of

transparency and participation. The administration is made open as part of an attempt to efficiently represent national interests, not in order to enable the transparency and participation of the general public. At the same time, it is to a large degree left up to the administrative agencies themselves to decide how open they should be. Besides the formal rules giving external interests the right to consultation and hearings, it is left up to the administration to decide in which contexts consultation should occur and what status parties to these consultations should enjoy. The EU-related administration, on the other hand, seems to be less transparent than other parts of the national administrations. In Denmark and Norway, the special committees are inaccessible to the general public. The same applies, to some degree, to the European Affairs Committees of the Danish Parliament (*Folketing*) and the Norwegian parliament (*Storting*). Naturally, the many informal contacts are closed to public insight or participation. It is against this background that the third challenge to democratic governance arises: There are no procedures by which the general public can gain insight into or participation in the national systems of coordination. At the same time, however, the EU administration is open, but only in relation to special interests selected by the administration.

4. *Captivity*. Empirical studies have shown that national administrations can become dependent on external, that is private, interests (Esmark 2002). Interests can capture the administration (Lowi 1979). This challenge is made more acute by the fact that private interests are able to bypass the national public authorities and present their interests directly to the European organizations. In all four Nordic countries, it is the assessment of national administrations that companies and interest organizations take advantage of this opportunity, although not on a large scale or in a systematic manner. But the possibility exists, and this raises the final challenge: The opportunity for private interests to bypass the national government and go directly to the EU's organizations in order to further their own interests. This allows organizations to avoid contact with the national authorities and, as a result, limits governmental control over the interests that are allowed to influence initiatives that may later become national law. This 'detention' limits pluralism just as bypassing alters the conditions for consensus. Private organizations can as a 'threat' use their ability to bypass the national administrations (Pedersen 1998).

Over all, then, it is apparent that there are indicators pointing in the direction of democratic challenges, but also that the democratic ideals have developed in a dynamic fashion to adapt to European integration. With only the four Nordic countries in mind, it is too early to talk about a 'democratic deficit' at this level of multi-level governance. Nonetheless, important challenges are evident insofar as politicians are absent to a very great extent from shaping EU-related national policies. This leads to the conclusion that EU politics are becoming bureaucratized and the national EU-related bureaucracy is becoming politicized, while the bureaucracy to some extent has become capable of determining the extent to which it wants to be subject to political control from parliament and/or the government. This is occurring with a considerable degree of closure with respect to the general public as well as in the relationship between the administration and special interests as illustrated by the fact that the latter can 'capture' the administration (Jacobsson et al. 2004).

SUMMARY

The results presented in this chapter are supported by other national studies concerning the development of the relationship between administration and organizations in connection with the management of interests vis-à-vis EU organizations (Sidenius 1998, 1999, Pedersen 2002). They are also supported by descriptions of the development of the relationship between authorities and interest organizations in general (Christiansen 1998; see also Christiansen and Sidenius 2000, Christiansen and Nørgaard 2003a, 2003b, Pedersen 1995), but are contrary to Swedish studies that indicate that a general 'de-corporativization' has taken place since the 1980s (Hermansson 1993, Hermansson et al. 1999, Lewin 1992, Micheletti 1994, Rothstein 1992, Rothstein and Bergström 1999). On the basis of the data presented here it is difficult to confirm general claims about a 'de-corporativization'. EU integration does not seem to have weakened the relationships between authorities and interests. Not in the Swedish case either, where studies have shown a general trend towards de-corporativization. On the contrary, with European integration the number of channels between administration and interests has increased; the means of managing interests have been combined; contacts are more intensive and extensive; and representation has taken new forms (i.e. has become more informal than formal).

I have also presented evidence indicating that administrative agencies engage in relationships to organizations at the same time as organizations adopt a bypass strategy and circumvent national administration by tying contacts to European organizations. And that the authorities are providing interests with voice while at the same time adopting a *within* strategy whereby they are undertaking significant coordination without including these interests. In all four countries the coordination of a plurality of private and public interests is taking place. However, there are significant differences among countries regarding the extent to which different interests participate in coordination of EU-related policy-making. There are also differences among countries in terms of how coordination produces a national standpoint or a governmental standpoint.

Several indicators provide evidence that the organization of the national coordination system influences the formulation of the standpoint. In Denmark and Norway, the majority of contacts between authorities and interests are formal, which is in harmony with the organization of the coordination systems. In Sweden and Finland, the majority of contacts are informal, just as there are more internal working groups and public committees with EU-related matters, as an indication of the organization of the coordination system in the two countries. Finally, several indicators point to not only a coordination of interests, but also an aggregation of interests to form a national interest. This is most clearly the case in Denmark, where the national government is obligated to attain the Folketing's mandate in matters related to the Council of Ministers and is, therefore, obligated to represent the views of a majority in the national parliament.

NOTES

1. By experts I mean people from universities and business colleges who, similar to organizations and corporations, are neither subordinate nor superior to a minister or political leadership.
2. Aggregation of interests is to be understood in the sense that Almond and Powel, among others, utilize the concept: 'Political aggregation, then, consists of the processes that combine demands into policy alternatives and mobilize resources behind these policy alternatives' (Almond and Powel 1978, p. 198). Aggregation, therefore, simply means that interests are combined to form political alternatives that can be forwarded for decision in the parliament, for the government or in another decision-making organ. The reason for raising the question about aggregation is therefore to assume a difference between coordination and aggregation of interests, and that it is only when interests are both coordinated and aggregated that the result can be referred to as a national interest. In that context, coordination is defined as a relationship in which administrative, political and private interests are involved without necessarily being combined; just as aggregation is defined by the relationship in which administrative, political and private interests are involved, but are also combined to form political alternatives.
3. In both instances, exit is the foundation for the chosen strategy. In the second instance (corporatist coordination) a number of parties are drawn into stable and sustained corporatist coordination and are thereby granted a voice (Hirschman 1970, 1981).
4. The response rate was 82 per cent. The agencies were all part of the state, directly subordinate to the national government, operated in the entire nation and had permanent administrative staff. Municipalities and local agencies were not included in the investigation. Further details of this investigation can be found in Jacobsson et al. (2001, pp. 36ff.), and in Jacobsson et al. (2004, pp. 21ff.).
5. 'Contact' is here defined as formal or informal, oral or written communication between public and private (national and European) agencies dealing with EU-related matters within the framework of the established acquis communautaire. The number of communications per timeframe assessed by the administrative agencies measures the intensivity of

these contacts. The extensivity of contacts on the other hand is measured by the number of agencies involved in contacts, that is are administrative agencies in contact with private interests as well as with other agencies and EU organizations or only for example in contact with other administrative agencies.

6. The combined response is more than 100, as the respondents provided multiple answers to the individual question.
7. By 'involved' we mean the private interests' representation in public committees, established formal-sized or ad hoc. Interest organizations in Denmark are formally involved in the coordination system through their participation in 13 of the 32 special committees. Norway has followed the Danish example and has also established special committees; however, these do not include representatives from private interests. Instead, they are involved in so-called reference groups, which are established ad hoc by the special committees. Sweden has not introduced a formalized system with special committees as in Denmark and Norway. Each department decides for itself which coordinating organs will be established and who will participate. In Finland a large number of consultative EU sections with participation from affected departments and authorities, as well as private interests, have been established and are responsible for coordinating EU-questions. As such, it is only in Denmark that private interests (interest organizations) have attained the right to be represented in formally established decision-making committees.
8. It is naturally not without problems to include independent experts under the category private interests. I do so in this case as the data clearly reveal that the administration is in a situation where a decision must be made whether to include organizations, corporations or independent experts in the management of EU-related matters. The competition becomes apparent in the sense that there are significant differences in the four countries as far as whether organizations and/or corporations and/or experts are involved.
9. Two national Danish surveys asking organizations and private firms to asses their contacts to national administrative agencies and political institutions and to EU organizations affirm these findings (Christiansen and Nørgaard 2003a, pp. 123ff., 2003b, pp. 32ff.). They also point to the fact that the bypass strategy became more important during the 1990s and that especially labour market organizations in 2000 are using the go-through strategy as often as the bypass strategy.
10. While there are not as many groups and committees that have been established to manage EU matters in Denmark, the administrative agencies find that they meet representatives from private interests more often in the existing committees and groups compared to the administration in the other Scandinavian countries.
11. In identifying ideals a number of public primary and secondary sources have been used – laws and other authoritative norms, debates in parliaments, public statements from governments or commissions in parliaments, legal evaluations and decisions by courts and expert commissions (see Højbjerg and Pedersen 2002).

REFERENCES

Almond, Gabriel A. and G. Bingham Powel Jr. (1978), *Comparative Politics: System, Process, and Policy*, 2nd ed., Boston: Little, Brown and Company.

Averyt, William F. (1977), *Agropolitics in the European Community*, London: Praeger.

Christiansen, Peter Munk (1998), 'Interesseorganisationer, centraladministration og udviklingen af nye indflydelsesstrategier', in Karsten Ronit (ed.), *Interesseorganisationer i dansk politik*, Copenhagen: Jurist- og Økonomforbundets Forlag, pp. 119-54.

Christiansen, Peter Munk and Asbjørn Sonne Nørgaard (2003a), *Faste forhold – flygtige forbindelser: Stat og interesseorganisationer i Danmark i det 20. århundrede*, Århus: Aarhus University Press.
Christiansen, Peter Munk and Asbjørn Sonne Nørgaard (2003b), *De som meget har ... Store danske virksomheder som politiske aktører*, Århus: Magtudredningen.
Christiansen, Peter Munk and Niels Chr. Sidenius (2000), 'Interesseorganisationerne', in Tim Knudsen (ed.), *Regering og embedsmænd: Om magt og demokrati i staten*, Århus: Systime, pp. 305-30.
Esmark, Anders (2002), 'Skyggeorganisering i Erhvervsministeriet', in Ove Kaj Pedersen (ed.), *EU i forvaltningen. Broen fra Slotsholmen til Bruxelles*, Copenhagen: Jurist- og Økonomforbundets Forlag, pp. 211-54.
Greenwood, Justin (1997), *Representing Interests in the European Union*, London: Macmillan.
Hansen, Lene and Michael C. Williams (1999), 'The myths of Europe: Legitimacy, community and the "crisis" of Europe', *Journal of Common Market Studies*, **37** (2), 233-49.
Hayes-Renshaw, Fiona and Helen Wallace (1997), *The Council of Ministers*, London: Macmillan.
Hayward, Jack (ed.) (1995), *The Crisis of Representation in Europe*, London: Frank Cass.
Hermansson, Jörgen (1993), *Politik som interessekamp: Parlamentariskt beslutsfattande och organiserade interessen i Sverige*, Stockholm: Norstedts Juridik.
Hermansson, Jörgen et al. (1999), 'Av-korporatisering och lobbyism – konturerna till en ny politsk modell', Stockholm: *SOU 1999:121.*
Hirschman, Albert O. (1970), *Exit, Voice and Loyalty: Responses to Decline in Firms, Organizations and States*, Cambridge: Harvard University Press.
Hirschman, Albert O. (1981), *Essays in Trespassing: Economics to Politics and Beyond*, Cambridge: Harvard University Press.
Højbjerg, Erik (2002), 'Processen om EMAS', in Ove Kaj Pedersen (ed.), *EU i forvaltningen: Broen fra Slotsholmen til Bruxelles*, Copenhagen: Jurist- og Økonomforbundets Forlag, pp. 255-314.
Højbjerg, Erik and Dorthe Pedersen (2002), 'Det danske koordinationssystem', in Ove Kaj Pedersen (ed.), *EU i forvaltningen: Broen fra Slotsholmen til Bruxelles*, Copenhagen: Jurist- og Økonomforbundets Forlag, pp. 63-118.
Jacobsson, Bengt, Per Lægreid and Ove Kaj Pedersen (2001), *Europaveje. EU i de nordiske centralforvaltninger, Nordisk Projekt*, Copenhagen: Jurist- og Økonomforbundets Forlag.
Jacobsson, Bengt, Per Lægreid and Ove Kaj Pedersen (2004), *Europeanization and Transnational States. Comparing Nordic Central Governments*, London: Routledge.
Laffan, Brigid (1996), 'The politics of identity and political order in Europe', *Journal of Common Market Studies*, **34** (1), 81-102.
Lewin, Leif (1992), *Samhället och de organiserade interessena*, Stockholm: Norstedts Juridik.
Lodge, Juliet (1994), 'Transparency and democratic legitimacy', *Journal of Common Market Studies*, **39** (3), 342-68.
Lowi, Theodore J. (1979), *The End of Liberalism: The Second Republic of the United States*, New York: W.W. Norton & Company.
Micheletti, Michelle (1994), *Det civila samhällat och staten: Medborgarsammanslutningarnas roll i svensk politik*, Stockholm: Publica.

Obradovic, Daniela (1996), *National Parliaments and the European Union*, London: Frank Cass.

Pedersen, Ove Kaj (1995), 'Nye demokratiske udfordringer', in P. Lübcke (ed.), *Miljøet, markedet og velfærdsstaten*, Copenhagen: Fremad, pp. 219-37.

Pedersen, Ove Kaj (1998), 'Interesseorganisationer og den parlamentariske styreform', in Karsten Ronit (ed.), *Interesseorganisationer i dansk politik*, Copenhagen: Jurist- og Økonomforbundets Forlag, pp. 197-232.

Pedersen, Ove Kaj (1999), 'Den danske stat og Grundloven', in Henrik Zahle (ed.), *Kommenteret udgave af Grundloven*, Copenhagen: Jurist- og Økonomforbundets Forlag, pp. 22-8.

Pedersen, Ove Kaj (2001), 'Interesseorganisationer og europæisk integration', in B. Jacobsson, Per Lægreid and Ove Kaj Pedersen, *Europaveje. EU i de nordiske centralforvaltninger*, Nordisk Projekt Vol. IV, Copenhagen: Jurist- og Økonomforbundets Forlag, pp. 191-216.

Pedersen, Ove Kaj (ed.) (2002), *EU i forvaltningen. Broen fra Slotsholmen til Bruxelles*, Copenhagen: Jurist- og Økonomforbundets Forlag.

Pedersen, Ove Kaj and Dorthe Pedersen (2001), 'The Europeanization of local interests in Denmark: The strategic choice – to "go-through" vs. to "by-pass" national institutions', in Janerik Gidlund and Magnus Jerneck (eds), *Local and Regional Governance in Europe*, Aldershot: Edward Elgar, pp. 51-75.

Rothstein, Bo (1992), *Den korporativa staten: Interesseorganisationer och statsförvaltning i svensk politik*, Stockholm: Norstedts.

Rothstein, Bo and Jonas Bergstrøm (1999), *Korporatismens fall och den svenska modellens kris*, Stockholm: SNS Förlag.

Scharpf, Fritz W. (1997), *Games Real Actors Play: Actor-Centered Institutionalism in Policy Research*, Boulder: Westview Press.

Sidenius, Niels Chr. (1998), 'Interesseorganisationer og Europa: En status', in Karsten Ronit (ed.), *Interesseorganisationer i dansk politik*, Copenhagen: Jurist- og Økonomforbundets Forlag, pp. 155-96.

Wallace, Helen and William Wallace (eds) (1996), *Policy-Making in the European Union*, Oxford: Oxford University Press.

Weiler, J.H.H. (1996), 'Legitimacy and democracy of union governance: The 1996 intergovernmental agenda and beyond', Oslo: *ARENA Working Paper, no. 22.*

Williamson, Peter J. (1989), *Corporatism in Perspective: An Introductory Guide to Corporatist Theory*, London: Sage Publications.

PART II

Executive Decision-making and National Parliamentary Scrutiny

7. Undermining Democratic Governance in the Member States? The Europeanization of National Decision-making

Tanja A. Börzel and Carina Sprungk

FROM THE EUROPEAN TO THE NATIONAL DEMOCRATIC DEFICIT

The last decade has witnessed a continuous debate over the legitimacy problems of the European Union (EU). Most politicians, students of the European politics and European citizens believe that the EU suffers from a severe democratic deficit. While there is some disagreement on the extent to which the EU lacks democratic legitimacy, the problem is mainly located at the EU level. The EU is criticized for its complex and non-transparent decision-making processes and weak mechanisms of democratic representation, reinforced through the absence of a European public sphere and a collective identity as the *sine qua non* for the formation of a European *demos* (see e.g. Scharpf 1999, Schmitter 2000, Moravcsik 2002).

Some have argued that the EU's democratic deficit is related to a misfit between national conceptions of democratic power and authority on the one hand, and the new institutions and practices of postnational or transnational governance on the other hand (Grande 2000, Schmitter 2000, Zürn 2000, Schmidt 2003). The democratic quality of the EU as a transnational polity should not be judged by the same criteria as the nation states, which form its members.

We argue, by contrast, that neither strengthening democratic representation at the EU level nor adapting national conceptions of democratic governance to the postnational quality of the EU is likely to remedy the democratic deficit. EU governance certainly needs to become more democratic. But the current debate on how to democratize the EU and according to what criteria tends to overlook that EU institutions and processes themselves have a significant impact on democratic governance in the member states. Europeanization[1] can affect both societal and state-centric processes of democratic governance. In our chapter, we focus on the impact of Europeanization on national decision-making procedures and show that it undermines one of the core mechanisms for ensuring the democratic legitimacy of domestic politics: the horizontal and vertical division of power.

On the one hand, Europeanization has affected the *horizontal* division of power in the parliamentary democracies of the member states, where decision-making powers are shared between the different branches of government. The transfer of domestic competencies to the European level strengthens the executive branch of government by resulting in the restriction or even the partial loss of traditional parliamentary functions providing for input legitimacy. What is more, Europeanization reinforces the fusion of legislative and executive powers as it is already implied in parliamentary democracies. Some national parliaments have acquired important *ex ante* scrutiny rights as compensation for the substantial loss of competencies. However, the effective use of these rights depends on an intensive cooperation with the central government as the 'gatekeeper' at the European level, which has to provide the parliament with necessary information about EU policy-making processes.

On the other hand, Europeanization has changed the *vertical* division of power in strongly decentralized member states, where political power is shared and divided between the central state and its subnational authorities, such as regions, Länder, provinces and communities. The transfer of domestic competencies to the European level empowers the central state vis-à-vis the subnational levels of government. Some regions have been able to cut their losses through obtaining co-decision rights in the formulation and representation of the national bargaining position in Brussels. Yet, the resort to cooperative federalism comes at a price, too. It strengthens regional governments vis-à-vis their legislatures thereby reinforcing the disempowerment of parliaments at the national level.

Europeanization undermines a core feature of democratic governance in the member states by challenging the horizontal and vertical balance of powers in favour of the executive. Thus, the EU has infected the member states with a major symptom of its alleged democratic deficit: executive dominance.

In order to state our argument we proceed in three steps. The first part sets out a conceptual framework to analyse the impact of Europeanization on democratic governance in the member states. Drawing on resource-dependence approaches, we maintain that the transfer of policy competencies to the EU has significantly changed the balance of power between the executive and legislature on the one hand, and the central state and the regions on the other.

In the second part, we illustrate our argument using the Federal Republic of Germany as a critical case. Compared to other parliamentary democracies, the German *Bundestag* is a relatively powerful legislature; likewise the German *Länder* belong to the institutionally most entrenched regions in Europe. Therefore, a strengthening of the executive appears less likely than in member states with a less powerful parliament and weak subnational authorities, for example France, Greece or Portugal. Finally, we summarize our findings and discuss their implications for the EU democratic deficit.

EUROPEANIZATION AND THE DIVISION OF POWER IN THE MEMBER STATES

The division of power is a key principle of liberal democracy. It aims at constraining and checking the use of power of the state to avoid usurpation, arbitrary action and undue expansion. The classical liberal understanding of checks and balances is based on the horizontal division of power between the different branches of government (Locke 1690, Montesquieu 1748). The Fathers of the American Constitution, however, developed a system of checks and balances, in which the horizontal division of power between legislature, executive and judiciary is complemented by a vertical division of power between the central government and regional governments (Hamilton et al. 1787). The vertical or federal dimension of the division of power gained prominence in the 20th century to ensure the transition to democracy of authoritarian regimes such as Germany, Austria and Spain. A powerful regional level of government was to prevent the re-emergence of a strong central state.

There is a growing literature analysing the impact of European integration on the member states. Several studies have identified conditions, processes and outcomes of Europeanization pressures on domestic policies, politics and polity, thus covering all dimensions of the domestic political system (Héritier et al. 1996, Héritier 2001, Knill 2001, Cowles et al. 2001, Börzel 2002, Featherstone and Radaelli 2003). Most works on the domestic impact of Europe refer to certain aspects of the domestic polity by focusing on Europe-induced change in specific domestic institutions, both formal and informal (see Börzel and Risse 2003). However, only little attempts have been made so far to analyse how Europeanization has changed the domestic polity *as a whole*, examining changes in the overall 'constellation of institutions, procedures and rules associated with parliamentary democracy in each of the member states' (Anderson 2002, p. 794).

Moreover, the few existing works strongly disagree on the system-wide effects of Europe on the nation state. While proponents of liberal intergovernmentalist approaches have argued that Europeanization has strengthened the central state vis-à-vis other domestic actors, including parliaments and regions (Moravcsik 1994), others have claimed exactly the opposite, namely that the EU tends to reinforce the separation of powers between the three branches of government and has weakened the central state since domestic actors are able to circumvent them in EU decision-making by directly accessing the EU political arena (Marks 1993, Sandholtz 1996, Schmidt 1999, 2003). A third group of scholars expects neither a withering away of the state nor its obstinate resilience but a fundamental transformation of the state in terms of the emergence of a European system of multi-level governance where European, national and subnational actors share rather than compete for political power (Grande 1996, Kohler-Koch 1996, Rhodes 1997).

Finally, while there is still no consensus on whether Europe strengthens, weakens, transforms or does anything at all to the member states (on the latter see Anderson 2002), the normative implications of the domestic impact of Europe have hardly been explored. What does Europe do to democratic governance in its member states?

This chapter takes a broader view on the system-wide changes that the EU induced in the member states by focusing on a key principle of liberal democratic polities: the horizontal and the vertical division of power.

The impact of Europeanization on the division of power in the member states can be conceptualized in terms of a redistribution of resources between the different branches and levels of government (Hix and Goetz 2000, cf. Börzel 2002, pp. 18-26). Europe constitutes a political opportunity structure that provides domestic actors with new constraints and opportunities, providing some with additional resources while depriving others. National parliaments and regions, however, face different constraints and opportunities resulting from Europeanization.

Undermining the Horizontal Division of Power: National Parliamentary Scrutiny and the Challenge of Europeanization

A basic feature of all democratic political systems is the distribution of power on a horizontal level, which aims at dividing sovereignty between the executive, the legislative and the judicial power. The respective decision-making power is based on specific *functions* attributed to each branch of government. By exerting their specific executive, legislative and judicial functions autonomously and independently from each other, the different governmental powers mutually control and might counteract decisions made by the other branches. In the following, we focus on the executive-legislative relationship as a core aspect of democratic governance.

There is an emerging literature on how the domestic legislatures participate in EU decision-making (Norton 1996, Smith 1996, Katz 1999, Maurer and Wessels 2001, Auel and Benz 2005). Moreover, the European Convention has established a special working group on the future role of national parliaments, and the Constitutional Treaty would have provided for new *ex ante* scrutiny mechanisms. Both scholars and political actors perceive that the severe loss of competencies national parliaments faced in the 1990s challenges the legitimacy of European politics. In particular with the ratification of the Maastricht Treaty, several domestic policy areas have been completely or partially transferred to the European level (for details, see Raunio 1999), where members of the national government and European actors are responsible for policy-making.

However, the EU provides national parliaments not only with new constraints, but also with new opportunities. Most domestic legislatures have acquired specific scrutiny rights in EU affairs as a reaction to their disempowerment (Maurer and Wessels 2001). These new powers generally include better access to information about EU legislation processes. Yet, better access to information does not compensate for the loss of substantial influence. Moreover, national parliaments might lack the resources and even the willingness to counteract the central government by using their new rights (Sprungk 2003).

In order to assess the impact of Europeanization on the horizontal division of power between executive and legislative branches of government, we analyse to what extent the new constraints and opportunities affect the autonomous and effective exertion of parliamentary functions.[2]

New constraints: restricting the autonomy of the parliament

Modern parliaments usually exert an elective, a legislative, a control and a communication function. First, parliaments *elect* the government or the head of government. Second, their *legislative function* consists of the right to initiate a bill, to participate in the legislation process and to formally decide on each law. Third, parliaments have to *control* the politics of the government, which requires precise information, the capacity to deal with and to evaluate it and the competence to react on this information by articulation, cooperation or sanction (Schüttemeyer 1978, p. 270). Fourth, parliaments have to guarantee a permanent *communicative* exchange between parliament and citizens as a necessary condition for providing legitimacy to parliamentary activities (Ismayr 2001, p. 41, Patzelt 1995).

Domestic parliaments as national institutions have no formal competencies to exert an elective function for all political actors involved in EU policy-making processes (except the respective national minister). Concerning the legislative function, the transfer of domestic competencies to the

European level affects its exertion in two ways. First, the participation in the EU legislation process is restricted on a legal basis. There is no legally binding provision on the European level providing for an involvement of domestic legislatures at the beginning or during the EU legislation process.[3] Domestic legislatures are formally involved only at the last stage of the European legislation process, in which they are supposed to ratify treaty changes or to implement European law (for details, see Raunio 1999, p. 189). But even these participation rights *ex post* may not be exerted in the traditional sense, since national parliaments do not have the power to either amend an EU legal act (primary law) or to reject it (secondary law). Thus, regarding formal competencies, national parliaments are not able to have an impact on the content of European legislation in the same way as on domestic legal acts.

Second, the exertion of a legislative function in EU politics by national parliaments faces structural restrictions. In contrast to domestic policy processes, European legislation processes include multiple actors on different levels of governance. National parliaments may actively contribute to this process only via one of those actors, namely the relevant minister in the Council. But on the one hand, members of government are not obliged[4] to consider the parliament's position during Council meetings.[5] On the other hand, even if a Council member takes the national parliament's position into account, it might not be considered in the legislation in case of majority voting or 'package dealing'.[6]

There are similar restrictions on the exertion of a *control function*. First of all, it is more difficult for national parliaments to *acquire* information about European issues, since government is favoured in the information process at the expense of the parliament. Moreover, since EU politics often concern several policy sectors (Fuchs 2001), its control requires intensive cooperation and sharing of responsibilities of domestic experts. Second, the *handling* with numerous documents that concern several policy sectors at the same time (Weber-Panariello 1995, p. 267) challenges the institutional organization. In addition, parliamentarians need specific 'European' expertise about structures, procedures, timetables and so on. (Rometsch 1996, p. 78). Furthermore, as EU documents correspond to a different political agenda, the deputies face temporal restrictions for their evaluation. Third, national parliamentarians are also less able to *react* on the information they receive about European issues. In fact, they can neither demand *ex ante* that their position to a legislative document is considered, nor sanction the government *ex post* for not having considered it. In sum, parliaments can only react on European information by articulating their position (Schüttemeyer 1978).

Equally, the exertion of a *communication function* in European issues demands increased efforts of national parliaments. The area of 'European' communication exceeds the traditional domestic policy-specific discourses, since it may also include institutional and integration-specific questions. Moreover, in European affairs, MPs can only articulate citizens' demands, but they cannot guarantee that these demands will have an impact on the legislation process. Consequently, if the characteristics of EU politics do not put restrictions on the simple exertion of the traditional communication function by national parliaments, they might impede its effective use.

In sum, the transfer of competencies to the European level leads to the restriction (control and communication function) or even the partial loss (elective and legislative function) of traditional parliamentary functions providing for input legitimacy. Even for the effective exertion of the remaining functions, increased efforts and additional activities are necessary compared with domestic politics.

Thus, by restricting the autonomy of the parliament and favouring executive dominance, Europeanization undermines one important aspect of the horizontal division of power, namely the equal standing of each branch government in the decision-making process. Moreover, while providing new opportunities to counteract parliamentary disempowerment, Europe affects yet another aspect of the division of power.

New opportunities: towards an ever closer fusion?

As a reaction to the partial loss and substantial restriction of parliamentary functions, several mechanisms of compensation have been introduced in the 1990s. First, regular meetings of COSAC (*Conférence des organes spécialisés dans les affaires communautaires*) have been institutionalized in order to establish mutual contacts between national parliaments and to improve exchange of information. Second, most domestic legislatures have acquired specific rights for information about the EU legislation process by the government and for scrutinizing European politics. Third, all national parliaments have finally created specific European Affairs Committees (EAC)[7] for dealing with documents and other information about the EU legislation processes. In sum, all the mechanisms aim at enabling national parliaments to influence EU legislation *ex ante* via better access to information or improving the capacity to deal with and react on the information. They thus focus on strengthening the parliamentary function of controlling the executive branch of government.[8]

However, the possibility of acquiring information about EU politics through exchange with EU institutions or other national parliaments does not necessarily improve the capacity of parliaments to have an impact on EU politics, since these institutions have no decision-making powers in EU legislation and might thus lack important information. When it comes to having complete, early and precise information necessary for an effective parliamentary control, national parliaments still depend on the transmission by their respective governments as members of the Council. Therefore domestic scrutiny rights generally oblige the government to provide early and precise information about EU legislation and to take the parliament's position into account (Maurer and Wessels 2001). Thus, paradoxically, (re-)enhancing the autonomy of the parliament vis-à-vis the government requires cooperation between the two branches of government.

Moreover, the new opportunities for national parliaments also do not compensate for the substantial loss of competencies, since they do not imply effective sanction mechanisms. The new powers mainly guarantee that parliaments are better informed about EU issues and can articulate their position before a legal act is decided, but represent no effective means to impose the consideration of their position. Again, this results in a stronger cooperation between executive and legislative power. On the one hand, the parliament depends on the government for having a maximal impact of national parliaments on European legislation, which can still only be achieved through the articulation of the parliament's position and its immediate transmission to the respective Council members (Laprat 1995, p. 8, Maurer 2001, p. 20). On the other hand, the government is now actually solicited to transmit information to the parliament and to take its position into account during Council meetings.[9]

Finally, the efforts to counteract the disempowerment of domestic legislatures may intensify the relationship between legislative and executive power in yet another way. All EU member states are parliamentary democracies, which already imply the mutual dependence and strong cooperation between the two powers, that is the government and the parliamentary majority, whereas division of power is usually stricter in presidential systems (see Lijphart 1999). Therefore, parliamentarians belonging to the party in government or to the coalition parties might be less inclined to invoke formal powers vis-à-vis the government, even though they faced a severe loss of competencies. But since the government has the relevant information about decision-making processes, it is likely that the parliamentary majority uses its existing informal contacts in order to have a 'say' in EU policy-making – thereby intensifying the mutual exchange between the two powers.

Moreover, the likelihood that the new opportunities lead to a closer fusion between government and parliament instead of re-enhancing the autonomy of the legislature is not only determined by the willingness, but also by the level of capacity of parliamentarians (Sprungk 2003). Again, if parliaments lack the organizational resources to effectively acquire, deal with and react on information about EU issues, the most effective way to have an impact on EU legislation is to draw on informal contacts with the government.

Thus, instead of rebalancing the division of power by enhancing the autonomy of the parliament vis-à-vis the executive, the effective use of new opportunities tends to favour an 'ever closer fusion' of the two branches of government, thereby undermining yet another core feature of the horizontal division of power – the clear distinction and separation of the different branches of government.

Undermining the Vertical Division of Power: Federalism and the Challenge of Europeanization

Generally, federalism refers to a spatial or territorial division of power between two (or more) levels of government in a given political system. Both levels have to hold some autonomous decision-making powers, which they can exercise independently of each other. Finally, the federal units (regions)[10] are represented in central decision-making processes, usually through the second chamber of the central state legislature. In a nutshell, federalism provides for a 'guaranteed division of power between central and regional governments' (Lijphart 1999, p. 186).

The EU provides the regions with both new constraints and opportunities.[11] On the one hand, Europeanization creates an unequal distribution of 'say' and 'pay' that favours the central state over the regions. On the 'say' side, the regions lose powers when national and regional competencies are transferred to the EU where central state executives and European actors dominate decision-making. On the 'pay' side, the regions are often the main implementers of EU decisions and have to bear the implementation costs (*pay without say*).

On the other hand, European institutions, such as the Commission, the European Parliament and the Committee of the Regions act as additional access points to the policy process which the regions can exploit independently of, and even against the interests of, their central governments. Yet, not all regions have been able to explore these additional opportunities nor does direct access to the EU policy process provide a compensation for regional power losses. As a result, the uneven distribution of say and pay changes the distribution of power in favour of the central state.

New constraints: the uneven distribution of say and pay

Because they enjoy a relatively high degree of legal, administrative, and fiscal autonomy, the German, Austrian, Belgian and Spanish[12] regions have more powers to lose when domestic policy competencies are transferred to the EU than do regional and local authorities with purely administrative functions. At the same time, the institutionally better entrenched regions have the resources to establish and exploit direct relations with European institutions. Subnational authorities in unitary and weakly decentralized states not only often lack the organizational capacity (e.g. manpower, financial means and expertise) to access the European policy-making arena directly, but normally their constitutions do not permit them to conduct external relations, including official relations with European institutions. The regions of the four federal member states have established direct channels of access to the European policy arena. However, (informal) consultations with the Commission and the European Parliament, or with the collective representation in the Committee of the Regions together with 200 other subnational authorities, have hardly compensated for the loss of their formal, domestic decision powers.

The regions have not only lost power in absolute terms; Europeanization has also changed the relative balance of power between them and the central state. Both the central state and the regions lose policy-making power ('say') when their competencies are transferred to the EU. Yet, unlike the central state, whose government is compensated for the loss of its competencies by decision-making powers in the Council of Ministers, the regions have no formal influence on the exercise of their former competencies at the European level. Moreover, by Europeanizing regional competencies, the central state gains access to areas of regional responsibility that were removed from its reach by the national constitution. While the central state may be weakened vis-à-vis the EU, Europeanization strengthens its domestic position vis-à-vis the regions.

At the same time, the regions are the main implementers of EU policies. They often have to bear the lion share of the implementation costs ('pay') of policies in whose decision-making they do formally participate ('pay without say').

At first sight, the uneven distribution of say and pay tends to strengthen the power of the central state even vis-à-vis the powerful regions of federal member states. Yet, at the same time, the central state depends on them for the effective implementation of EU policies. The central governments have only limited means for directly intervening in the way their regions apply and enforce European law. In order to ensure uniform implementation across the country, central governments have, therefore, centralized the transposition of European policies into national law and have prescribed detailed national regulations limiting the regions' discretionary powers in implementation and reinforcing the centralization of their competencies.

The centralization of legal implementation has had little effect, however. Even detailed national legislation has only limited influence on the way the regions implement European policies. As the main implementers, they have to provide, or build up, the administrative infrastructure to apply, monitor and enforce European law. High costs, both material and political (i.e.

opposition by powerful societal interests), are often a major source of implementation problems. Although the central government is liable to the EU for implementation failures, it cannot command the amount of resources (i.e. manpower, expertise, technology and money) the regions dedicate to the implementation of European regulations. In view of rising implementation problems, the central state has been increasingly seeking the cooperation of the regions in the formal and practical implementation of European policies.

New opportunities: compensation through participation

While the central state relies on the regions' resources for effectively implementing EU policies, the regions increasingly realized that they depend on the central state for the effective representation of their interests in EU decision-making. Direct contacts with the Commission and the European Parliament where regions have to compete with hundreds of pressure groups for access have proved ineffective to compensate for the regional losses of power. As a result, the Belgian, German, Austrian and Spanish regions have increasingly sought cooperation with their central governments to inject their interests into the European policy-making process. As members of the national delegation, regional representatives participate in European committees and sometimes (with the exception of Spain) even in the Council of Ministers. Domestically, they cooperate with the central government in formulating the national bargaining position on European issues.

Instead of strengthening one level of government over the other, then, Europeanization increases the mutual dependence of the central state and its regions in the four federal states in European policy-making. In all four federal member states, central state and regions have established institutions to facilitate intergovernmental cooperation in EU policy-making. Even in Spain and Belgium, where the relationship between central state and regions are traditionally ridden by conflict and tension, the Autonomous Communities and the Belgian regions participate in the formulation and implementation of EU policies (Börzel 2000, cf. Börzel 2002).

Regional co-decision rights in formulating and representing the national bargaining position provide an effective compensation of regional losses of competencies caused by Europeanization. The cooperation of the central state and regional governments should also improve effective implementation of European policies. But by providing an institutional solution to one challenge of Europeanization (the uneven distribution of say and pay), compensation through participation appears to reinforce another – executive dominance. The compensatory co-decision powers are exercised by the regional governments, which, at best, inform and consult their parliaments on important European issues. Unlike in domestic policy-making, the regional parliaments have no formal powers in the formulation and decision-making of European policies. The disempowerment of regional parliaments reinforces the general trend of deparliamentarization at the national level discussed in the previous section. In other words, containing the undermining effects of Europeanization on the vertical division of power has substantially reinforced the erosion of the horizontal division of power between executive and legislature.

The next section illustrates our general argument using Germany as a critical case. The empirical study shows that Europeanization has seriously affected the functioning of the democratic polity by strengthening the executive at both the national and the regional level.

UNDERMINING DEMOCRATIC GOVERNANCE IN THE MEMBER STATES? GERMANY AS A CRITICAL CASE

Europeanization and the Horizontal Division of Power: Towards an Ever Closer Fusion

New constraints: restricting the autonomy of the Bundestag

Compared to other European parliaments, the *Bundestag* is a relatively powerful legislature. It is the only directly elected institution at the federal level and has a high level of autonomy vis-à-vis the other branches of government thanks to its important organizational, financial and human resources. Since it is fully involved in all stages of the legislation process and has to decide on each legal act, it is one of the most active legislatures in the world (Pilz and Ortwein 2000). Moreover, members of the *Bundestag* – and especially the parliamentary opposition – dispose of numerous rights for controlling and sanctioning the politics of the government (for details, see Ismayr 2000). Yet, despite its strong position in the institutional structure, the process of Europeanization has significantly weakened the autonomy of the *Bundestag*.

First, the transfer of domestic competencies to the European level deprives the *Bundestag* of its significant impact *ex ante* on the contents of all legal acts which are supposed to be in force at the national level. The high level of autonomy of the *Bundestag* in domestic affairs is characterized by the fact that the federal government depends on the parliament's agreement in the legislation process and thus has to consult it at every stage of the legislation process and justify changes of position. Compared to domestically 'weak' parliaments, which contribute less actively to the legislation process due to the government's frequent regulatory activity, the loss of a formal decision right in formerly domestic policy areas is more important for the powerful *Bundestag*. Europeanization restricts this autonomy by giving more independent decision-making powers to the federal government.

Second, the difficulties in controlling EU policy-making discussed in the previous section are particularly important in the case of the German parliament. In domestic affairs, the parliamentary organization reflects exactly the functional division between ministerial departments of the Federal Government. Each parliamentary committee has its counterpart at the level of the executive and vice versa. Thus, the control of some 750 officially transmitted EU documents per year on average,[13] which concern several policy sectors at the same time, challenges the institutional structure of the *Bundestag*. The multi-sectoral character of European politics requires not only systematic coordination between several parliamentary committees. It also challenges the cooperation between *Bundestag* and the Federal Government, since there is no Federal Ministry with exclusive responsibility for European Affairs. Moreover, the *Bundestag* used to *receive* information about European issues relatively late in the legislation process. The duration for transfer of EU documents could go up to 42 days (Maurer and Wessels 2001, p. 447). Since the introduction of a digital transmission system in the 15th electoral term, however, transmission is far more quickly, with a maximum duration of 14 days.[14] In sum, the analysis shows that even the *Bundestag* as a domestically powerful parliament is restricted in its autonomy as a result of Europeanization.

New opportunities: towards an ever closer fusion between Bundestag and Federal Government

As a result of its loss of competencies, the *Bundestag* has acquired constitutionally guaranteed participatory rights in the context of the ratification of the Maastricht Treaty. The most important legal provision is Article 23 of the Basic Law (GG), which obliges the Federal government to 1) provide 'comprehensive' and 'earliest possible' information about the European legislation process; 2) enable the *Bundestag* to vote on a resolution before a decision is taken in the Council; and 3) take the parliament's position into account. Moreover, Article 45 GG provides the institutionalization of a 'Committee for the Affairs of the European Union' (EAC), which might be authorized to represent the *Bundestag* as a whole in order to react quickly on EU documents. Compared to other European parliaments, the *Bundestag* thus has relatively good opportunities to re-enhance its autonomy vis-à-vis the Federal Government. However, it hardly invokes its new rights (Sprungk 2003).

Concerning the acquirement of information about EU issues, the *Bundestag*, that is the EAC is very active. The EAC frequently holds EU expert hearings, and delegations of the committee travel regularly to EU institutions. In addition, members of the EAC frequently consult the ministers participating in the council meetings. However, they do not necessarily insist on an earlier transmission of relevant EU documents.[15] Moreover, MPs do not frequently use their interpellation rights or initiate public debates about EU issues (Sprungk 2003, Auel and Benz 2005) In general most public debates on EU issues take place after a government's information about European Council meetings. German MPs in the *Bundestag* not only obviously prefer to get European information by questioning experts rather than by putting additional pressure on the government. The rare use of interpellation rights also demonstrates that even the parliamentary opposition does not intensively use its opportunities to counteract the government.

Even at the stage of dealing with EU documents within parliamentary committees, the *Bundestag* tends to rely on its contacts with the Federal Government rather than using its own resources. While the EAC has the best organizational and human resources compared to other parliamentary committees and is the committee with the most frequent meetings in the *Bundestag* (and even in the EU; see Maurer 2001, p. 22), most documents are only taken notice of in committee meetings.[16] The lack of intensive deliberation despite frequent meetings can be explained by the numerous hearings and the regular questioning of government members who participate more often in EAC meetings than in other committee meetings. Indeed, the EAC has never used its right to hold special meetings to deal with EU documents, but only to hear the government on current EU topics (Hölscheidt 2000, p. 19).

Finally, the parliamentary reaction on information about EU issues is also affected by a cooperation of *Bundestag* and Federal Government rather than by confrontation. First, parliamentarians usually inform the government about their position in an *informal* way during plenary or committee meetings (Hölscheidt 2000). But even when a parliamentary resolution is officially declared, it rarely contradicts the position of the Federal Government (Fuchs 2001, Hölscheidt 2000). Second, if it is decided to make a resolution on an EU document the object of a public debate, the debate often includes other, even national, bills (*verbundene Debatte)*, which does not favour the consideration of the parliamentary position on the European level. On the one hand, the position of the *Bundestag* on one specific EU document is difficult to seize for the government. On the other hand, a resolution might not be voted on before a Council's decision because the plenary is waiting for other bills until it holds a public debate (Weber-Panariello 1995, p. 254). Third, the EAC has only rarely made use of its special powers to officially demonstrate the parliament's autonomous activity by voting on a resolution at the place of the plenary. In sum, the *Bundestag* does not explicitly insist on a consideration of its own position by the government. Even in the follow-up of resolutions, the *Bundestag* does not request a regular report by the ministers in times of heavy work loads.

Thus, to have an impact in EU policy-making, the *Bundestag* relies on and intensifies its contacts with the Federal Government instead of actively using its relatively powerful opportunities vis-à-vis the executive branch of government for regaining autonomy.

Europeanization and the Vertical Division of Power: Reinforcing Executive Federalism[17]

New constraints: the uneven distribution of say and pay between federal government and *Länder*

The vertical distribution of power in Germany was most affected by the transfer of regional policy competencies to the European level. This process caused substantial change in the federal balance of power in favour of the central state.

First, when exclusive *Länder* competencies are transferred to the EU, the *Länder* are deprived of any formal influence on the exercise of these competencies at the European level. The central state, on the contrary, whose executive represents Germany in the Council of Ministers, is directly involved in the policy formulation and decision-making. As a result, the central state gains access to regional competencies at the European level, which the German Constitution placed beyond its reach at the domestic level.

Second, when federal or shared competencies are transferred to the European level, the formal input of the *Länder* is reduced from a co-determination right in formulation and decision-making to the participation in the implementation of European policies. The central state, however, which also loses decision-making power, still has a major influence on policy formulation and decision-making in the Council of Ministers.

There is hardly any policy area in which the exclusive or shared competencies of the *Länder* have not been affected by Europeanization. Fifty per cent of all issues dealt with in the *Bundesrat*, the regional chamber of the national parliament, are related to European issues. The shift of competencies is most significant in culture, educational and vocational training, media (exclusive competencies), research and technology, transport, environment, regional and structural policy (shared competencies, cf. Börzel 2005).

But the *Länder* not only lose power on the 'say' side (legislative competencies). As the *Länder* have the responsibility for implementing the vast part of European policies, they have to bear the lion share of implementation costs of European policies without participating in the formulation and decision-making at the European level. Moreover, unlike in domestic policy-making, the *Länder* have little discretion in implementing European policies. Contrary to the principles of German legislation, European Regulations and Directives do not allow the *Länder* to implement legislation as they see fit.

The uneven distribution of 'say and pay' applies in favour of the central state and seriously disturbs the vertical distribution of power between central state and regions. Since European rules and procedures concentrate decision-making powers in the hands of the national governments, the transfer of domestic policy competencies to the EU results in a centralization of regional competencies not only at the European, but also at the central state level.

New opportunities: compensation through participation of the *Länder*

From the very beginning of European integration, the German *Länder* have been aware that Europeanization would cause them significant losses of power. In trying to redress the territorial balance of power, the *Länder* consequently pursued a strategy that aimed at the compensation of their losses of formal decision-making powers through participation in European decision-making mediated through the central state. This 'intrastate' participation of the *Länder* in European decision-making is based on the cooperation of the *Länder* with the central state in the formulation and representation of the German bargaining position at the European level.

The *Länder* started asking for co-determination powers of the *Bundesrat* in European affairs already in 1951. The Federal government discarded these demands as an unconstitutional intervention into its foreign policy prerogative. Yet, the *Länder* were not left completely without influence on European policy-making. In 1957, the Federal Government granted the *Länder* some initial possibilities of participating in European policy-making, which they successfully managed to expand over the following years. These intrastate state channels of access to European institutions were based on:

1. information to the *Bundesrat* of projects, initiatives and proposals of the European Commission;
2. access to informal and formal European documents;
3. the right of the *Bundesrat* to make recommendations the federal government has to give due consideration;
4. participation of the *Länder* Observer and other *Länder* representatives in European decision-making bodies (Council, COREPER, committees) as members of the German delegation;
5. ratification of European Treaty revisions by the *Bundesrat* (veto power).

In a continuous process of multilateral bargaining with the central state, the *Länder* subsequently succeeded in enhancing their intrastate participation European decision-making. But these intrastate channels of influence proved insufficient to compensate the *Länder* for their losses of domestic decision-making powers. Information and consultation in European decision-making is not a substitute for self-determination and co-determination rights in domestic decision-making.

In 1987, however, the *Länder* achieved substantial co-determination powers in European affairs by threatening to veto the ratification of the Single European Act (SEA) in the *Bundesrat*. A new intrastate procedure was introduced by the law ratifying the SEA. The so-called *Bundesratsverfahren* reinforced the obligation of the Federal Government to inform the *Bundesrat* comprehensively and as soon as possible of all European issues of interest for the *Länder*. The *Bundesrat* obtained the possibility of making formal recommendations on EC proposals that affected the exclusive jurisdiction or essential interests of the *Länder*, from which the Federal Government could only depart for due reasons which had to be justified before the *Bundesrat*. Finally, the Federal Government was obliged to call in *Länder* representatives at the negotiation stage when important interests of the *Länder* were involved. These formal co-determination rights in European decision-making provided a first step in effectively compensating the *Länder* for their losses of domestic power.

With the Maastricht Treaty, the *Länder* definitively succeeded in redressing the territorial balance of power between them and the Federal Government in European policy-making. Threatening again to veto ratification, the *Länder* finally got what they had always wanted: comprehensive, legally binding co-determination powers in EU policy-making. For the first time, the transfer of both national and regional competencies to the EU requires the consent of the *Länder* (*Bundesrat*). A two-thirds majority of *Bundestag* and *Bundesrat* has to ratify any changes in the EU Treaty or similar regulations. When *Länder* interests are affected by an EU decision, the Federal Government has to take into account the opinion of the *Bundesrat*, which, however, is not ultimately binding. But when former administrative or legislative *Länder* competencies are involved, the *Bundesrat* has the final decision on the German bargaining position in the Council of Ministers. And whenever exclusive legislative competencies of the *Länder* are concerned, a *Länder* minister represents Germany in the Council negotiations.

The increasing intrastate participation of the *Länder* in European policy-making redressed the vertical balance of power, which had been disturbed by Europeanization causing a double shift of competencies in favour of the central state. On the 'say' side, the *Länder*'s losses of autonomous and shared competencies are compensated by co-determination rights in European policy-making. On the 'pay side', the *Länder* are involved in the formulation and decision-making of essentially every European policy, which they later have to implement.

Compensation through intrastate participation resulted in an externalization of cooperative federalism to European policy-making by which the

German central state has been neither strengthened nor weakened nor transformed. Rather, Europeanization has led to incremental adjustments of the system of interlocking politics, extending it to the European level, which has ultimately reinforced rather than fundamentally changed cooperative federalism.

Externalizing cooperative federalism to EU policy-making may contain the undermining effects of Europeanization on the vertical distribution of power. But it comes with a price attached: executive dominance. The Europeanization of legislative *Länder* competencies, which used to be exercised by the *Länder* parliaments, was compensated by co-decision rights for their executives exercised through the *Bundesrat*. Even compared to the *Bundestag*, the *Landtage* hardly play any role in European policy-making. Besides some general information rights, the *Länder* parliaments are left with an *ex-post* control of the European activities of their governments (Straub and Hrbek 1997).

DEPARLIAMENTARIZATION AS THE PRICE OF PREVENTING CENTRALIZATION?

Our findings confirm that the emergence of supranational governance has altered the systemic functioning of democracy in the member states (Anderson 2002). Europeanization has affected the horizontal division of power in the member states in two ways.

First, as domestic policy areas become increasingly subject to European policy-making, the executive branch of government is strengthened, while national parliaments face a severe loss of competencies. Domestic legislatures not only lose formal participation rights. Even in areas where parliamentary participation is required, the non-transparent character and the specific functioning of EU decision-making procedures (package dealing, QMV) as well as the complex multi-level structure of the EU impede its effective influence. In sum, the transfer of competencies to the European level leads to the restriction or even partial loss of traditional parliamentary functions providing for input legitimacy.

Second, Europeanization reinforces the fusion of legislative and executive powers as it is already implied in parliamentary democracies. Some national parliaments have acquired important *ex ante* scrutiny rights as compensation for the substantial loss of competencies. However, the effective use of these rights depends on an intensive cooperation with the central government as the ‘gatekeeper’ at the European level, which has to provide the parliament with necessary information about EU policy-making processes.

The disempowerment of parliaments at the national level is reinforced through the impact of European integration on the vertical division of power. Like the national legislatures, Europeanization has inflicted significant losses of power on the regional level of government in the member states. Some of the regions have been able to compensate their losses by obtaining co-decision rights in EU policy-making. This compensation through participation implies a shift towards cooperative federalism, in which central state and regional executives closely cooperate in the formulation and representation of the national bargaining position. The regional parliaments remain on the sidelines. The tendencies of executive dominance and fusion are even more pronounced at the regional level.

Our findings seem to contradict some of the Europeanization literature. A recent study claims that core features of the democratic polities of the member states have proved 'quite resilient' (Anderson 2002, p. 795). Employing a comparative framework based on Arend Lijphart's analysis of democratic regimes, Anderson discovers only a modest increase in majoritarian characteristics on the executive-legislature dimension, which would still support an albeit weak strengthening of the executive. These changes are less attributed to Europeanization and more to the decline of ideology (Anderson 2002, p. 816). And the equally modest increase on the federal-unitary dimension points in the opposite direction, namely a strengthening of the regional level of government. The trend is due to decentralization processes found in Belgium, Italy and the UK (Kerremans and Beyers 1997, Keating and Elcock 1998, Desideri and Santantonio 1997). Yet, these processes also have less to do with Europeanization pressures, and appear to be driven by domestic politics (Keating and Elcock 1998); for a contending view see Schmidt 1999). Moreover, even or precisely if Europeanization is a main cause of decentralization, it is the regional executives rather than the parliaments that will be strengthened.

Finally, the undermining effect of Europeanization on democratic governance challenges the general perception in the academic literature and the public alike that Europe has a positive impact on democratization. The EU entails a strong commitment to the preservation of democratic values in Europe, and its collective identity is firmly based on democratic institutions and practices (see preamble to European Treaties, Copenhagen criteria for membership). We do not deny that EU membership has played a supportive role in the transition to democracy in several European countries, including the Federal Republic of Germany, Greece, Spain, Portugal and, more recently, the former communist states in Central and Eastern Europe. But there appears to be a 'dark side' of Europeanization that has not been sufficiently paid attention to.

Moreover, if we look at the European level, one aspect of the perceived 'democratic deficit' of the EU consists of the same lack of division of power. Not only is the fusion of the legislative and the executive branch of government already implied in the Council's activities, but the autonomy of the European Parliament is also rather weak within the institutional structure. However, by introducing aspects of presidential systems in the EU (like the position of the president of the European Council and the Union Minister for Foreign Affairs) the Constitutional Treaty had provided for a clearer distinction between and balance of powers. Thus, further research has to analyse whether changes in the future institutional structure of the EU will have a more positive effect on democratic governance in the member states.

NOTES

1. We define Europeanization as a process by which domestic policy areas are increasingly subjected to European policy-making. On the different definitions of Europeanization see Featherstone (2003) and Olsen (2002).
2. The following is based on Sprungk (2003).
3. Their participation is only mentioned in the 'Protocol on the role of national parliaments in the European Union' attached to the Amsterdam Treaty.
4. Except Denmark, where ministers get legally binding mandates of the European Affairs Committee of the Danish parliament (see e.g. Laursen 2001).
5. However, its point of view might have an impact if ministers argue that they are politically bound by the decision of their parliament (Putnam 1988). But, as 'executives who can tie their hands can just easily untie them' (Phare 1997, p. 147), the parliament's contribution to the European legislation process fully depends on the cooperation of the government.
6. In addition, institutionalist approaches (Sandholtz and Zysman 1989, Pierson 1996) stress that EU policy processes have their own dynamics and can no longer be under the full control of executives.
7. These institutions are not always referred to as 'committees'. We use the term for reasons of simplicity.
8. However, more and better information also improve the parliament's capacity to communicate EU affairs.
9. This refers to all national governments of the EU member states, since it is stated in the 'Protocol on the role of national parliaments in the European Union' attached to the Amsterdam Treaty.
10. In EU member states the (semi-)federal units are called Länder (Austria, Germany), Autonomous Communities (Spain) and regions (Belgium, Italy). For the sake of simplicity, we use the term 'regions'.
11. The following draws on Börzel (2002).
12. Strictly speaking, Spain does not fully qualify as a federal state as Article 2 of the Spanish Constitution declares the sovereignty of the Spanish state indivisible. Yet, as territorial public corporations which have their own legislature, executive and judiciary, the autonomous communities carry state qualities. Moreover, their right of existence is not merely derived from the Spanish Constitution but grounded in the *estatuto de autonomía* of each Autonomous Community, which do not have the status of a constitution but are not mere state laws either.
13. Information obtained by the *Europabüro* on 29 November, 2005; see also http://www.bundestag.de/ausschuesse/archiv15/a20/bilanzen/bilanz_15wp.html (Novem-

ber, 29, 2005). Adding the respective annexes and corrigenda, the *Bundestag* receives about 25 000-30 000 documents annually.
14. Information obtained by the *Europabüro* on 29 November, 2005.
15. Interview with a member of the EAC on 23 May 2002.
16. Only about 5 per cent of the transferred documents enter the stage of deliberation (Hölscheidt 2000, p. 28).
17. On the following see Börzel (1997, 2002).

REFERENCES

Anderson, Jeffrey (2002), 'Europeanization and the transformation of the democratic polity', *Journal of Common Market Studies*, **40** (5), 793-822.

Auel, Katrin and Arthur Benz (2005), 'The politics of adaptation: The Europeanisation of national parliamentary systems', *Journal of Legislative Studies*, **11** (3-4), 372-93.

Börzel, Tanja A. (1997), 'Does European integration really strengthen the state? The case of the Federal Republic of Germany', *Regional and Federal Studies*, **7** (3), 87-113.

Börzel, Tanja A. (2000), 'From competitive regionalism to cooperative federalism: The Europeanization of the Spanish State of the Autonomies', *Publius, the Journal of Federalism*, **30** (2), 17-42.

Börzel, Tanja A. (2002), *States and Regions in the European Union: Institutional Adaptation in Germany and Spain*, Cambridge: Cambridge University Press.

Börzel, Tanja A. (2005), 'Mind the gap: European integration between level and scope', *Journal of European Public Policy*, **12** (2), 1-20.

Börzel, Tanja A. and Thomas Risse. (2003), 'Conceptualising the domestic impact of Europe', in Kevin Featherstone and Claudio Radaelli (eds), *The Politics of Europeanisation*, Oxford: Oxford University Press, pp. 55-78.

Cowles, Maria Green, James A. Caporaso and Thomas Risse (eds) (2001), *Transforming Europe: Europeanization and Domestic Change*, Ithaca, NY: Cornell University Press.

Desideri, Carlo and Vincenzo Santantonio (1997), 'Building a third level in Europe: prospects and difficulties in Italy', in Charlie Jeffery (ed.), *The Regional Dimension of the European Union: Towards a Third Level in Europe?*, London: Frank Cass, pp. 96-116.

Featherstone, Kevin (2003), 'Introduction: In the name of Europe', in Kevin Featherstone and Claudio Radaelli (eds), *The Politics of Europeanization*, Oxford: Oxford University Press, pp. 3-36.

Featherstone, Kevin and Claudio Radaelli (eds) (2003), *The Politics of Europeanisation*, Oxford: Oxford University Press.

Fuchs, Michael (2001), 'Der Ausschuss für die Angelegenheiten der Europäischen Union des Deutschen Bundestags – kein Ausschuss wie jeder andere!' http://www.bundestag.de/parlament/gremien15/a20/oeffentlichkeitsarbeit/pdf_dateien/wie_kein_anderer.pdf.

Grande, Edgar (1996), 'The state and interest groups in a framework of multi-level decision-making: The case of the European Union', *Journal of European Public Policy*, **3** (3), 318-38.

Grande, Edgar (2000), 'Postnational democracy in Europe', in Michael T. Greven and Louis W. Pauly (eds), *Democracy Beyond the State: The European Dilemma and the Emergning Global Order*, Toronto: Lanham, pp. 115-38.

Hamilton, Alexander; John Jay and James Madison (1787), *The Federalist: A Collection of Essays, Written in Favour of the New Constitution, as Agreed Upon by the Federal Convention Sept. 17, 1787*. New York: John &Archibald McLean, no. 41, Hanover-square, 1788, reprinted in Rossiter, Clinton (ed.) (1999) The Federalist Papers, New York: Mentor.

Héritier, Adrienne (2001), 'Differential Europe: National administrative responses to community policy', in Maria Green Cowles, James A. Caporaso and Thomas Risse (eds), *Transforming Europe: Europeanization and Domestic Change*, Ithaca, NY: Cornell University Press, pp. 44-59.

Héritier, Adrienne, Christoph Knill and Susanne Mingers (eds) (1996), *Ringing the Changes in Europe. Regulatory Competition and the Redefinition of the State: Britain, France, Germany*, Berlin and New York: de Gruyter.

Hix, Simon and Klaus H. Goetz (2000), 'Introduction: European integration and national political systems', *West European Politics, Special Issue*, **23** (4), 1-26.

Hölscheidt, Sven (2000), 'Die Behandlung von Europaangelegenheiten im Deutschen Bundestag von 1993 bis 1999', *Infobrief Nr. 51/00 der Wissenschaftlichen Dienste des Deutschen Bundestages.*

Ismayr, Wolfgang (2001), *Der Deutsche Bundestag*, Opladen: Leske und Budrich.

Katz, Richard S. (ed.) (1999), *The European Parliament, the National Parliaments, and European Integration*, Oxford: Oxford University Press.

Keating, Michael and Howard Elcock (1998), 'Devolution and the UK state, regional and federal studies', *Special Issue on the Remaking of the Union. Devolution and British Politics in the 1990s*, **8** (1), 1-9.

Kerremans, Bart and Jan Beyers (1997), 'The Belgian sub-national entities in the European Union: Second or third level players?', in Charlie Jeffery (ed.), *The Regional Dimension of the European Union: Towards a Third Level in Europe?*, London: Frank Cass, pp. 41-55.

Knill, Christoph (2001), *The Transformation of National Administrations in Europe. Patterns of Change and Persistence*, Cambridge: Cambridge University Press.

Kohler-Koch, Beate (1996), 'The strength of weakness: The transformation of governance in the EU', in Sverker Gustavsson and Leif Lewin (eds), *The Future of the Nation State: Essays on Cultural Pluralism and Political Integration*, London: Routledge, pp. 169-210.

Laprat, Gérard (1995), 'Parliamentary scrutiny of Community legislation: An evolving idea', in Finn Laursen and Spyros A. Pappas (eds), *The Changing Role of Parliaments in the European Union*, Maastricht: European Institute of Public Administration, pp. 1-20.

Laursen, Finn (2001), 'The Danish Folketing and its European Affairs Committee: Strong players in the national policy cycle', in Andreas Maurer and Wolfgang Wessels (eds), *National Parliaments on their Ways to Europe: Losers or Latecomers?*, Baden-Baden: Nomos, pp. 99-116.

Lijphart, Arend (1999), *Patterns of Democracy. Government Forms and Performance in Thirty-Six Countries*, New Haven and London: Yale University Press.

Locke, John (1690), *Two Treaties of Government*, reprinted in Peter Laslett (ed.) (1988), *Two Treatises of Government*, Cambridge: Cambridge University Press.

Marks, Gary (1993), 'Structural policy and multilevel governance in the European Community', in Alan W. Cafruny and Glenda G. Rosenthal (eds), *The State of the*

European Community II: Maastricht Debates and Beyond, London: Boulder, pp. 391-410.

Maurer, Andreas (2001), 'National parliaments after Amsterdam: Adaptation, recalibration and Europeanisation by process', paper for Working Group Meeting, XXIVth COSAC, 8-9 April, http://www.cosac.org/en/meetings/previous/24/working_group/mauer/

Maurer, Andreas and Wolfgang Wessels (eds) (2001), *National Parliaments on their Ways to Europe: Losers or Latecomers?*, Baden-Baden: Nomos.

Montesquieu, Charles Louis de (1748), *De l'Esprit des Lois 1748*, reprinted in Jean Ehrard (ed.) (1969), *Les classiques du peuple*, Paris: Éd. Sociales.

Moravcsik, Andrew (1994), 'Why the European Community strengthens the state: Domestic politics and international cooperation', *Working Paper*, *52*, Cambridge, MA: Harvard University.

Moravcsik, Andrew (2002), 'In defence of the "democratic deficit": Reassessing legitimacy in the European Union', *Journal of Common Market Studies*, **40** (4), 603-24.

Norton, Philip (ed.) (1996), *National Parliaments and the European Union*, London: Frank Cass.

Olsen, Johan P. (2002), 'The many faces of Europeanization', *Journal of Common Market Studies*, **40** (5), 921-50.

Patzelt, Werner J. (1995), 'Vergleichende Parlamentarismusforschung als Schlüssel zum Systemvergleich. Vorschläge zu einer Theorie- und Forschungsdebatte', *Zeitschrift für Parlamentsfragen*, Sonderband, **1** (95), 355-85.

Phare, Robert (1997), 'Endogenous domestic institutions in two-level games and parliamentary oversight of the European Union', *Journal of Conflict Resolution*, **41** (1), 147-74.

Pierson, Paul (1996), 'The path to European integration: A historical institutionalist analysis', *Comparative Political Studies*, **29** (2), 123-63.

Pilz, Frank and Heike Ortwein (2000), *Das politische System Deutschlands*, München: Oldenbourg.

Putnam, Robert D. (1988), 'Diplomacy and domestic politics: The logic of two-level games', *International Organization*, **42** (3), 427-60.

Raunio, Tapio (1999), 'Always one step behind? National legislatures and the European Union', *Government and Opposition*, **34** (2), 180-202.

Rhodes, R.A.W. (1997), *Understanding Governance: Policy Networks, Governance, Reflexivity and Accountability*, Buckingham and Philadelphia: Open University Press.

Rometsch, Dietrich (1996), 'The Federal Republic of Germany', in Dietrich Rometsch and Wolfgang Wessels (eds), *The European Union and Member States: Towards Institutional Fusion?*, Manchester and New York: Manchester University Press, pp. 61-104.

Sandholtz, Wayne (1996), 'Membership matters: Limits of the functional approach to European institutions', *Journal of Common Market Studies*, **34** (3), 403-29.

Sandholtz, Wayne and John Zysman (1989), '1992: Recasting the European bargain', *World Politics*, **42**, 95-128.

Scharpf, Fritz W. (1999), *Governing Europe: Effective and Legitimate?*, Oxford: Oxford University Press.

Schmidt, Vivien A. (1999), '"European federalism" and its encroachments on national institutions', *Publius*, **29** (1), 19-44.

Schmidt, Vivien A. (2003), 'The Europeanization of governance in larger European democracies', paper presented at the Biannual Conference of the European Studies Association held in Nashville, Wisconsin, 26-29 March.

Schmitter, Philippe C. (2000), *How to Democratize the European Union... and Why Bother?*, London: Boulder.

Schüttemeyer, Suzanne S. (1978), 'Funktionsverluste des Bundestages durch die europäische Integration?', *Zeitschrift für Parlamentsfragen*, **9** (2), 261-78.

Smith, Eivind (ed.) (1996), *National Parliaments as Cornerstones of European Integration*, London: Kluwer.

Sprungk, Carina (2003), 'National parliamentary scrutiny in the European Union: The German Bundestag and the French Assemblée Nationale – key players or side shows?', paper presented at the 8th European Union Studies Association Biennial Conference, 27-29 March, Nashville Tennessee, http://aei.pitt.edu/archive/00000581/.

Straub, Peter and Rudolf Hrbek (eds) (1997), *Die europapolitische Rolle der Landes- und Regionalparlamente in der EU*, Baden-Baden: Nomos.

Weber-Panariello, Philippe A. (1995), *Nationale Parlamente in der Europäischen Union: Eine rechtsvergleichende Studie zur Beteiligung nationaler Parlamente an der innerstaatlichen Willensbildung in Angelegenheiten der Europäischen Union im Vereinigten Königreich, Frankreich und der Bundesrepublik Deutschland*, Baden-Baden: Nomos.

Zürn, Michael (2000), 'Democratic governance beyond the nation-state', in Michael T. Greven and Louis W. Pauly (eds), *Democracy Beyond the State: The European Dilemma and the Emerging Global Order*, New York and Oxford: Rowman & Littlefield, pp. 91-114.

8. The Europeanization of National Executives: Changing Capacities and Ambivalent Effects on Democracy

Ignacio Molina and César Colino

EUROPEANIZATION, NATIONAL EXECUTIVES' CAPACITY AND DEMOCRACY

Since the early studies on Europeanization, the predominant focus of this fast expanding approach seemed to be the impact that the European Union (EU) had on sectoral policies rather than on nation state polities and domestic politics (see the general discussion on the concept in Anderson 2002, Olsen 2002a or Featherstone and Radaelli 2003). Now it is increasingly recognized that supranational processes also have an effect on the democratic political process where national actors interact around traditional liberal-democratic institutions of government. It is now commonplace, although also contested with regard to its extent and nature, to affirm that European integration has entailed a significant transformation of the internal political systems of the member states.

This chapter examines the extent of the impact EU membership has on central executives of the member states. National executives are among the most significant institutions in the European multi-level system of governance. No other domestic institution or actor comes closer to their enormous constitutional and leadership power regarding both internal and European policy-making and implementation; even the political importance of national parliaments, courts or autonomous agencies actually consist in trying to check and counterbalance the executives rather than in developing a policy-making role on their own. With regard to the position of executives as institutional channels between the domestic and the EU level of policy-making, it is important also to underline their key importance as hubs of national EU coordination at home and in Brussels. They do this through the Council, to which the 25 national executives belong, and through its associated structures of intergovernmental negotiation in committees or working groups (Kassim 2003a, Peters and Wright 2001). Moreover, the EU Council of Ministers and the European Council also have a privileged position in the supranational decision-making process. Their procedures, based on a diplomatic and not very transparent logic, reinforce national executives in them.

The chapter complements the analysis related to the Europeanization of decision-making and its effects on democratic governance initiated in the previous chapter (see Börzel and Sprungk, Chapter 7). It seeks to analyse the Europeanization of national executives in its intra-institutional facet – the reactions and changes taking place within the executives themselves – putting special emphasis on its political and administrative components. They include especially the linkage institutions and agencies in charge of connecting and coordinating the domestic and European stages of the process and the effects of membership in the policy output of national governments.

Conceived as a broad review of the topic, the analysis is illustrated with comparative cross-country evidence that will enable us to establish the extent to which national executives have taken advantage of its privileged position in the EU system. Additionally, conceding that EU-induced deparliamentarization is a prevailing trend in member states, the chapter tentatively engages in the issue of the effects of Europeanization on democratic governance from a slightly different perspective, a more output-oriented conception of democratic legitimation.[1] It thus seeks to qualify and differentiate the hypothesis that EU integration erodes democratic legitimacy by reinforcing executive dominance and encroaching on vertical and horizontal division of powers. This is done along two tracks: first, by including findings about the situation of executives in Central Eastern and Southern European member states and, second, by examining another decisive aspect of democratic governance, majority rule and collective problem-solving capacity.

In this way, the chapter assesses differences among member states and reaches a more ambivalent appraisal of the effects of Europeanization on democratic governance. We argue that European integration not only produces limited structural alterations but also affects the programmatic action of governments at the national level. That means that, according to the different national domestic circumstances, the output-oriented legitimacy within member states may be differently affected, and in some cases in which the overall effect of the integration process is positive and public opinion favours closer union, democratic rule may be enhanced by membership. We refer not only to an indirect role in encouraging and preserving democratic values and practices in new European democracies, but also to a more direct effect. The EU can be said to have provided national governments with compulsory global collective goals, with successful models to emulate, or with important stimuli to launch internal overdue structural reforms avoiding veto points.

Thus, EU membership facilitates national governments to augment their political and policy capacity and, hence, the fulfilment of majoritarian policy choices.

The chapter thus presents the discussion on Europeanization of national executives in terms of governmental capacity – that is to say, whether executives are under better conditions to translate their initial preferences with coherence and effectiveness into policy outputs, even though their scope of actions is now narrower and more complex. Following Painter and Pierre (2005, p. 2) policy capacity may be defined as the 'ability to marshal the necessary resources to make intelligent collective choices about and set strategic directions for the allocation of scarce resources to public ends', and it is closely connected to administrative capacity – the ability to efficiently manage the human and physical resources required for delivering the outputs of government. Moreover, we argue that new variables should be incorporated, such as horizontal learning, blame avoidance and so on that may facilitate reforms, reinforce executive capacity. In some cases of Southern and Central Eastern Europe they imply more than simple modest institutional transformations. That means that the consequences of Europeanization may not be as inertial or weak as asserted in the literature, which is usually based on the situation in northern or western member states.

Since the mid-1990s different studies have debated whether national executives have been reinforced because of EU membership. Some assert that they have been empowered vis-à-vis other national actors (Moravcsik 1994) or that Europeanization has meant more national government rather than less (Metcalfe 1994), while others contradict that conclusion (Schmidt 1996, Kurzer 1997). On the one hand, the ill-defined term Europeanization can refer to the top-down impact of EU institutions and policies on national governments and designate the domestic arrangements that reshape the political position of national governments – accommodation and adaptation. On the other hand, it also refers to the bottom-up process through which member states' governments 'hit Brussels' uploading or projecting their preferences to the EU level (Beyers and Trondal 2003, van Keulen 2003). It is therefore an interactive process in which both senses should be taken into consideration (Börzel 2003, Dyson and Goetz 2003, Colino and Molina 2005).

Recent research is dominated by the view that Europeanization does not amount to a significant alteration of the structure or the operation of the national executives in Western and Central Eastern Europe. Indeed, most empirical studies of national decision-making processes rather lend greater support to the hypothesis of persistent divergence both at the internal level of the executives and in the systemic relationships between them and the rest of the domestic actors than to the idea of convergence around a common European model.[2] Corroborating the main assumptions of historical institutionalist thought, the impact of Brussels is normally found to be path-dependent, reinforcing previous national divergences. Although a general reinforcement of the executive may be detected, it may indeed have very different implications for institutional processes and outcomes when occurring in majoritarian or in consociational systems, in corporatist or statist countries, depending on the strength of parliamentary institutions, or depending on the type and degree of decentralization within which subnational bodies operate (be it symmetrical federal systems, heterogeneous federalisms, systems in transformation from unitarism or hardly deconcentrated administrative systems).

The policy capacity approach has analytic advantages compared with discussions that usually characterize theories of the European integration and Europeanization (Knill 2005). Debating whether the EU reinforces or weakens the power of states and their governments may make an interesting argument but remains practically unresolvable. This may explain the endless dispute between intergovernmentalists and neofunctionalists on the issue of whether the EU rescues or empties the nation state. If the question is, on the contrary, centred on the capacity, the issue is no longer stated as a zero sum question, and if capacity is correctly measured, it allows for a better empirical accumulation of case studies that will be able to refute and generate hypotheses on EU impact. In sum, the Europeanization of executives presents us with a much more suggestive intellectual problematique and empirical puzzle than it seems at first sight.

We proceed, in the next section, to describe the specific linkage processes and structures between the national and supranational governmental tiers. In particular, we look at the domestic structures of interministerial coordination and permanent representations in Brussels. The third section examines the general transformations that EU membership produces on national executives, distinguishing on the one hand between the effects on several sectors of public activity and governmental agencies, where the dominant trend is towards departmentalization and therefore sectoral fragmentation of executives and, on the other, the effects on high politics and more politicized issues as a result of Europeanization, where there is clearly an increase in the political power of core executive actors such as first ministers or finance ministers. Finally, before presenting some conclusions to assess the effects of these transformations on democratic governance, a fourth section outlines the need to go beyond the transformations in structures and policy-making and examining governmental action, as well as actors, ideas and discourses on the integration process.

ATTEMPTS TO COORDINATE THE COMPLEXITY AT HOME AND IN BRUSSELS

EU membership demands internal mechanisms to organize the national involvement in the European policy-making process. First, keep in mind that the EU does not possess its own implementing administrative organizations, and therefore it does not directly implement its policies even in its domain of exclusive competencies (Kassim 2003b). The European institutions' role consists mainly in regulating and only in some cases in monitoring and inspecting, while the administrative apparatuses of the member states assume the functions to execute European law and policies. As we know, this arrangement, which is analogous to that of some cooperative federations, clearly shapes the relationships between the EU and the member states. This section, however, will revolve around the upward dimension of the interaction, which is more politically relevant. That is to say, how the different member states participate in European decision-making through their national executives that have to define and coordinate the internal decision-making processes and have to make their presence felt in Brussels.

Wallace (1973) was probably the first author to defend a domestic perspective to explain the nature of the European organization and to stress that integration followed the logic of domestic processes rather than the other way around. Besides that, it was from the start obvious that in the domestic stage of European decision-making it was the central executives – both derived from the domestic coordination arrangements and from their control of the permanent representations in Brussels – who channelled the political communication between the EU and the member states. Intervention by national parliaments in EU policy-making is very constrained, not only by national structures and rules, but also by national party strategy and interactions (Wessels and Rometsch 1996), and only the most vital issues or those that become politicized reach the public debate. That is the reason domestic formulation of European policies is confined to the executive and administration of the 25 member states.

In fact, all the states have organized a coordination structure that attempts to guarantee both interministerial coherence and aggregation of different views at the domestic level and the subsequent defence of national interests in the many negotiation forums at the supranational level. The member states diverge in terms of which ministries a designated to coordinate the domestic stages of the process (Kassim et al. 2000, Wright and Hayward 2000). Some countries tend to assign the general conduction of EU policy to the ministry of foreign affairs (e.g. Portugal, Denmark, Spain, Ireland or Hungary). In other cases current general management of EU affairs is entrusted to the prime minister's office (the European Secretariat in the United Kingdom, the

SGCI in France, the Office of European Integration in Estonia)[3] or the Ministry of Economy and Finance (Germany and Greece, although sharing powers with the foreign ministry and the prime minister).

Besides these specific departments for the conduction of EU policy, which are sometimes equivalent in rank to a junior ministry, parallel interministerial committees are also common in the national capitals (and standing committees to coordinate positions with the subnational authorities in decentralized systems without federal second chambers to handle this task). Both horizontal departments and arenas, normally staffed by a reduced and qualified team of officials from different ministries, often have more coordination ambitions than real capabilities to achieve them. The explanation of this weakness is twofold: (i) internal fragmentation and jealous defence of jurisdictions and negotiation strategies among line ministries and (ii) the decisional features of the EU. With the functional specialization that is implicit to the enormous range of European policy action assumed and developed by each ministerial department, they may follow their own criteria, thus occasionally jeopardizing the coherence of the national position in the policy process. The task of coordination may then be hampered, but informal mechanisms of coordination (basically, the networks of personal contacts of the small team of officials in positions involving the EU policy-making) help to maintain the effectiveness in arbitration.

In addition, and regarding responsibility for the pursuit of both sectoral and institutional policy-making in Brussels, all EU countries have ambassadorial teams with explicit responsibility for coordinating the national negotiators' actions in the different branches and spheres of the Union (see Kassim et al. 2001). These Permanent Representations follow the intergovernmental negotiations that take place in the Council meetings, their preparatory Committee of Permanent Representatives – commonly known by its French acronym COREPER – as well as in the myriad of working groups and committees attached to the Council and the European Commission. Since final decisions are made in Brussels, it is not only vital that the overall national interest be identified internally, but that it be reflected – in theory, faithfully –in the position defended at the European level.

Member states' representations in Brussels, normally staffed by between 50 and 100 elite officials, attempt to ensure unity of action, functional hierarchy and coordination with the rest of the executive and, in order to fulfil this task, they enjoy a theoretical exclusive right to establish and channel all contacts with EU institutions. However, they have in fact faced many difficulties in their attempt to maintain a monopoly, not only due to other national actors (such as regions or private groups, which are also present in Brussels), but to the authority retained by all the line ministries that, at least during the initial phase of EU decision-making, often directly carry out negotiations in the working groups in Brussels. In any event, the problems derived from departmentalization are particularly acute with respect to politically less significant issues, as well as during the initial stages of the process – that is before the COREPER intervenes. In addition to the gatekeeper role played by the ambassador and his deputy during the most important phase of EU decision-making, hierarchy and exchange of information are also enforced through sectoral coordinators and constant meetings within all the various sectoral units into which the Representation is divided.

These two bodies of member states' EU coordination – one in the national capital and the other in Brussels as Permanent Representation – operate in, and are influenced by, a dual context, in that they form part of both European and domestic polities. On the one hand, as cogs in the EU machinery, these offices – specially the mission in Brussels – represent the member states' interests and inform the domestic arena about developments in the European institutions. On the other, they form part of national executives and therefore retain many of the features derived from the domestic political and administrative systems. Thus, they vary among the member states in size, composition, ministerial location and centralizing capacity. A fundamental distinction can be drawn between states where departmentalization reduces interministerial coordination organs to mere arenas, and other states with a clear coordinating function that allows authentic corporate and hierarchical national EU policy-making.

However, given the enormous complexities of the multifaceted European integration, they will never be able to assure complete governmental coherence. In addition, national variations in coordination approach will also depend on the varying salience of EU issues in domestic politics and on the diverse national administrative styles of coordination. Even coordination imperatives vary as well: member states that favour integration are less keen on speaking with one voice than Euro-sceptic member states; those with a clear output preference – for example maximizing EU funds – will rather focus on policy coherence to avoid a segmentation that, on the contrary, may be functional to states with comprehensive interests in the process (Kassim 2003a).

Furthermore, it should not be forgotten that the procesual context in which these structures work is extremely problematic (Kassim 2003b, Peters and Wright 2001) given the high and unclear institutional density of the EU, which is reflected in the complexity of procedures and voting rules in the EU Council. Since there are no real European political parties or other channels of stable coordination, member states depend on bargaining and coalition building with other states in the Council or individually (Beyers and Dierickx 1998). In those negotiations, the lines of conflict may follow different cleavages such as cohesion versus contributors, North versus South, large versus small, Europeanists vs. those who to prefer an intergovernmental model or statists vs. free marketers and so on. The Representation, however, far from restricting its contacts with the Council and its counterparts, develops constant relations with other actors that also participate during the process: first of all, with the European Commission, which shapes EU policy-making as much as the Council, and, to a lesser extent, with the European Parliament and other actors who are present in Brussels. It should be taken into account that the EU agenda is evolving and the initiative is no longer controlled by the national governments in the EU Council of Ministers, which now have to act in a reactive fashion, as the unanimity rule is, at least legally although not in practice, applied less and less. From the point a proposal is launched by the Commission until it is finally approved in the Council, it has to go through the amendments of the European Parliament and a whole array of committees with diverging status, permanence and membership around the European Commission or the working groups in the EU Council.

In addition, clear differences can be found among different sectors of public activity depending on the type of issue: institutional, distributive, regulative, redistributive, high politics (e.g. IGCs, EMU, competition, agriculture, foreign policy) and so on so that the capacity of the states to give coherence to its positions, for example in the COREPER, is constrained. Even the Council itself, to a certain extent, cannot be said to enhance coordination. This is due, in the first place, to its dynamics of sectoral operation, in which line ministries have the final word in the decision-making process. Second, there exists a certain administrative incongruence between the composition of sectoral EU Councils and the departmental division in national cabinets; and third, in some cases competencies are shared with subnational authorities. Finally, and from a bureaucratic point of view, the effective operation depends heavily on negotiators with linguistic proficiency, technical information and legal skills (see Colino and Molina, 2005).

EUROPEANIZATION OF EXECUTIVES: POLITICAL AND BUREAUCRATIC LEVELS

After an analysis of the specific linkage mechanisms through which the executives try to coordinate national action in EU matters at home and connect with Brussels, this section attempts a more comprehensive assessment of the Europeanization of executives. Beyond the specific arrangements for managing EU matters and the existence of top bureaucrats specialized in dealing with supranational issues, European membership also acts as a general external adaptive pressure affecting and transforming the national executive in its broadest sense. These reactions and changes are either required by the supranational organization or respond to the adjustment willingness to anticipate or to grasp the opportunities and face the challenges of the new situation.

As mentioned in the previous chapter, Europeanization has systemic implications for the institutional balance of powers, which seem to reinforce the general position of the national executives vis-à-vis parliaments or regions, and it has internal implications for the executive itself both at the political and administrative levels. Europeanization brings about an important set of transformations, although with variation across the EU members depending on distinctive domestic traits (see Wessels et al. 2003). Europeanization has produced important effects on executives, but it has not diluted their characteristic features. Many authors even argue that Europeanization in most cases reinforces the original characteristics of the national government. However, it can be argued that the strengthening of the most important core executive actors (prime minister and, to a lesser extent, finance and foreign minister) stands out as a common finding in all the member states. This trend towards centralization of power around main coordinators can be explained, apart from the general reinforcement of leadership and administrative capacity of these actors in national executives, by specific EU reasons such as the growing importance of the European Council and ECOFIN Council (while General Affairs Council is losing some importance) or the fact, already outlined, that national coordinating mechanisms for EU affairs are under their control in all members.

However, centralization does not preclude that most sectoral ministries are also increasingly involved in EU matters since fragmentation is inherent to the complex European policy-making process. This is the consequence of the sectoralized functioning of the Council – the final decision on the national position is adopted by the minister with functional competence on the matter – and the practice of direct linkage between line ministries and the EU arena. Progressively, the different ministries feel more mature and self-confident to act by themselves without the necessity of external orientation or coordination. The direct and non-mediated presence of ministerial negotiators from the early stages of policy elaboration by the Commission stimulates vertical multi-level policy networks rather than horizontal policy coordination. This leads to frequent clashes between sectoral departments and overall national preferences normally supported by the coordinators.

But changes in the national executives, apart from the creation of organisms in charge of the general conduction of EU policy or this contradictory pattern of high political coordination with growing fragmentation, also imply the progressive involvement of almost all ministries in European affairs and their internal adaptation to EU policies and processes. Effects concentrate mainly in the design of certain organizational features, although it should not be forgotten that supranational influence concurs with modernization, privatization, new public management or general ideological factors to shape governmental changes in similar directions.

Firstly, the EU has stimulated the creation and design of government portfolios in a form more consistent with supranational policies. This influence is felt directly in the creation of new ministries or their redesign, particularly in countries suffering a greater misfit with EU policies in areas like the environment or competition. The second (and most evident) type of effect is the internal reorganization of departments. The *leit motif* is almost generally a better adaptation of functional units to specific EU policies including the creation of special ministerial units to coordinate European business. Finally, a third clear effect is the progressive autonomization of certain organs that traditionally belonged to the domain of the ministry of economics. This is the case, obviously, of central banks as a consequence of Economic and Monetary Union (EMU), but also of deregulation of monopolies and privatization of public firms. It is also important to note that the level of Europeanization may vary significantly from sector to sector. While the independence of the central bank is a direct result of the demands of European monetary policy, other policy sectors and their governmental organizations may be less influenced by the European context.

Finally, if we consider the general administrative transformation in, for example, style of decision, or bureaucratic culture and so on, no great organizational changes, formal or informal, have occurred (Page 2003). EU working procedures and policy processes have not stimulated substantial reform of bureaucracies, and low specialization on EU affairs is still considered a general characteristic of all member states. Moreover, recruitment and training of officials has not incorporated tests of extensive knowledge of EU affairs or skilful command of European languages. Training in negotiation techniques, experience with network organizations and even willingness to leave home are rarely considered in civil servants' career. So far, there is no formal European Administrative Space (Olsen 2002b), although there is some progress in what we may call the informal administrative Europeanization as an indirect consequence of integration and the result of constant contact and interaction between the European Commission and different national administrations (Burnham and Maor 1995).

BEYOND STRUCTURAL CHANGES: EU MEMBERSHIP AND EXECUTIVE CAPACITY

Although the original assumption during the 1990s was that national executives of member states had been profoundly Europeanized, the most widely held and authoritative conclusion in the recent institutional literature is quite different. According to several authors (Goetz 2000, Kassim 2003a, Page 2003), the relevance of the impact and adaptation to EU integration on national executives outlined in the previous sections – the coordination mechanisms that coexist and attempt to compensate the ever more fragmented and complex European policy-making or the transformation in the national administrative style and apparatus of the member states – might have been exaggerated. Without denying the existence of organizational consequences, recent research underlines that changes in governmental structures and procedures are quite limited in nature and extent to the specific management of the membership obligations or the need of practical involvement and linkage between the internal and supranational levels of decision-making.

Thus, although the main coordinating actors in the core executive have certainly been empowered to deal with horizontal issues and despite the countervailing pattern of sectoral fragmentation in low politics and sectoral issues, the political position of the executive in the more general domestic opportunity structure has hardly altered. Rather, high political coordination, strong sectorization, internal bureaucratic adjustment or even deparliamentarization as a consequence of Europeanization should be considered modest phenomena[4] and, furthermore, these impacts are decisively shaped by the structural path dependencies of national polities. Certainly, there is very little evidence of convergence among the member states around a common model of government, which has not emerged either. On the contrary, it is more correct to speak about 'domestication' of European executive decision-making than Europeanization of the domestic executive organizations (Kassim 2003b, Olsen 1997). National governments are not growing more and more alike or coming closer to a sort of common EU model; rather they retain their distinctive structures and operating procedures (Harmsen 1999).

This said, and precisely because of the contingent effects produced by Europeanization, the transformation of the executive is much more far-reaching in some cases, that is the peripheral and backward member states, than in the North Western countries, which are usually the main object of this literature. For instance, Central Eastern and Southern executives have been much more intensively transformed and their capacity enhanced as a result of European integration. It is indeed true that from a mere structural perspective, looking only at the institutional arrangements that they have set up explicitly to meet the demands of EU membership, their Europeanization can be considered weak as well. There are, however, at least two additional elements already theorized in much of the Europeanization literature that largely reinforce the importance of EU membership as a fundamental variable that changes, and usually enhances, the national executives in those countries: institutional misfit and strategic behaviour of political actors.

The first, as mentioned in the previous section, is the larger institutional misfit that exists between these executives and EU law and policies in comparison with the founders and northern states, which regardless of their participation in European integration already benefited from qualified bureaucracies and executives' action in areas such as the environment or consumer protection and the promotion of competition policy. That is to say, many adaptations are required where the mismatch is significant and, therefore, changes in the national executive should be much more expected there than in countries with insignificant divergence between domestic arrangements and EU requirements.

The second element, and perhaps the most fundamental, has to do with a dimension that goes beyond the attention to the specific development of effective coordination structures to represent national interests in Brussels or to the limited institutional compliance with EU prescriptions in policies of positive integration: the strategic use of EU membership. This factor helps to alter more decisively the position of national executives in their domestic opportunity structure. As Knill (2001, p. 215-27) points out, the institution-based perspective needs to be supplemented by an agency-based approach with primary focus on the preferences, beliefs and strategic interaction of domestic actors (see also Börzel and Risse 2003). When this second point of view is also considered in the analysis, the weight of the European factor to explain to what extent the political position of executives is changing grows considerably – in particular, in member states where the combination of the ideological pro-Europeanism and the perception of the material benefits extracted from membership is especially favourable, e.g. Spain and, to a lesser extent, other Southern and Central Eastern countries.

Executives in these countries are usually not well equipped to face the perspective of launching structural reforms that may imply confrontation with important sectoral groups or that require coordination of their strongly departmentalized administrative apparatus. Inertia and veto points are difficult to overcome, but this state of affairs may be altered due to special impacts – for example, the remarkable substantive EU goals such as the 1992 Single Market Project, the EMU process or the accession itself that can be considered as *critical junctures* redefining the institutional position of and within the national executives (Laffan 2003) – or due to the accumulation of several factors. Among them, the appearance of new economic ideas supported by an epistemic community, the unavoidable need to carry out reforms to compete in more interdependent markets, the possibility to receive external structural funds, the exclusion of certain traditional options that may be discarded from the range of national policy choices because of the free-market stance of the European process of negative integration, or the advantage of diverting the responsibility for unpopular measures towards non-elected supranational authorities can be mentioned. For example, and regarding liberalization, it is probable that without the help of EU law and policies, which provided explicit calendars of deregulation, *blame avoidance* and structural funds, the sectoral interests of strong policy communities opposed to deregulation or privatization would have defeated any strategy designed by the core executive in those countries.[5]

Europeanization implies – or, rather, may imply – the provision of strategic resources that reinforce the executive capacity and, therefore, the possibilities for setting and maintaining priorities – policy innovation – for ensuring effective coordination on conflicting objectives, for representing diffuse and unorganized interests or for imposing losses to entrenched interest groups (Weaver and Rockman 1993). Surely, when the executive acts as a promoter of political changes and as a policy entrepreneur the implications for democratic legitimacy are ambivalent. The pattern of executive dominance facilitated by Europeanization may erode the role of institutional checks and balances, but in some countries it may also reinforce, or simply permit, the achievement of policy choices firmly supported by or beneficial to a large majority of citizens, thereby promoting democracy in output and executive capacity. For instance, tangible benefits in the relatively poorest member states – modernization as a consequence of EU liberalization and budgetary allocations – have helped to build a consistent social consensus about the convenience of being part of Europe. Executives may take advantage of it to avoid clientelistic, short-term or sectoral preferences of some groups, parties, regions and bureaucratic agencies.

Therefore, although the European impact on the executive political power seems limited at first sight, its measurement should rather be made considering agent-based and endogenous elements. As already pointed out, a balanced conclusion on the real effect of Europeanization should differentiate factors explaining governmental change and avoid attributing to the EU what is actually caused by other general trends and global forces (Goetz 2000). However, it is also necessary to go beyond the formal appearance of the structures and consider the most dynamic effects that supranational integration is promoting in some cases. Thanks to Europe, the institutional opportunities of policy departure may be strengthened, for example the supposed vigour of the executives often found in the constitutions of Southern and Central Eastern European states can be activated in practice, and the political restrictions – weak and fragmented bureaucracies, sectoral policy networks or other veto players – may weaken.

Thanks to these critical transformations, or rather as a process of maturation and policy learning, the executives reinforce their capacity, in particular when their priorities coincide with those backed by the European institutions. It is not easy, and probably not useful either, to determine which factor is more important – the national governments as policy shapers or as policy takers (Börzel 2003) – or which one is previous to the other (Moravcsik 1994). However, it is indeed undeniable that EU membership has facilitated some fundamental changes in the operation of the executives in some countries. Accession implies anchoring the state to a programme of structural reforms facilitated by the supremacy of EU law, the unavoidable need to compete in wider markets, or the framing of domestic beliefs and expectations that compel modification of traditional and protectionist policy choices. Europeanization also favours the effectiveness of hierarchical coordination in the core executive for horizontal and high political matters or the appearance of bureaucratic islands of excellence in the mediocre panorama of the low capacity general state administration (Goetz 2001). Nevertheless, it is likely that a persistent, when not growing, fragmentation in routinized issues and complex policy networks will prevail over the central coordinators as a natural consequence of the sectoral and fluid nature of the EU policy-making.

This segmentation between politicized issues – intergovernmental conferences to reform treaties, enlargement or negotiations of financial perspectives – and routine policy issues may encourage central core executive actors to politicize sectors previously managed by a routine logic. A clear political will, combined with the structural and strategic elements provided by Europeanization, leads to a reinforced political capacity for the governments. For example, in Spain, the growing politicization of the need to curb public expenditure (reducing state aids and privatizing public firms) and the convenience to concentrate on other spending (physical and human capital) was progressively linked to the objective of improving competitiveness, achieving macroeconomic convergence or receiving structural funds (Molina 2004). Very difficult objectives in an ordinary domestic context – tough fiscal austerity and coordination of ministries in reducing subsidies and in optimizing the budgetary revenues from the EU – were gradually achieved in what can be considered a good example of reinforced capacity in a Europeanized executive.

CONCLUSIONS

The issue of democracy and the problems of democratic legitimacy have usually been associated with discussions of supranational decision-making. To date, however, the issue of how membership in the EU affects the operation of democracy within national polities, in other words, the question of Europeanization of democratic governance at the national level was largely neglected. We have argued that there is evidence that the impact of EU membership on national democracy has so far been neither outstanding nor univocal, nor has necessarily led to convergence among the 25 member states. In the first place, it is not outstanding because, among the different national actors and within their institutions, few existing traditions have undergone radical reorientation. Nowhere have cultural changes in approaches and democratic working practices taken place. Arguably, a far-reaching Europeanization of domestic organizations may only be discerned among actors operating in sectors particularly affected by European integration (e.g. central banks as a consequence of the EMU, agrarian organizations due to the full *communitarization* of agricultural policies, ministerial departments in charge of infrastructures or the environment, in the recipient states or regions of structural funds in countries that had to decentralize to administer regional policies). The remaining traditional domestic institutions and actors (parties, unions, employer associations or the media, as well as most government agencies, bureaucracies, parliaments, subnational authorities and all judicial powers of member states) seem to have loosely adapted their organization and internal operation to respond to a somewhat changed context, without basically altering neither their structures nor their national cultural patterns.

It is not a univocal impact either, since depending on the member state in question, the operation of democracy displays different models and traditions. It would thus be misleading to compare the recent Europeanization of a democracy like the British or the Scandinavian, where the supranational element is superimposed to a pre-existing and very consolidated complex of social and institutional factors, with the steady and persistent Europeanization taking place in the six founding member states from the start, or finally, with the rapid Europeanization of national systems of the Mediterranean countries, occurring practically simultaneously with democratization in the 1980s, or to Central Eastern Europe countries, which have just been incorporated in the EU (Anderson 2002).

This said, although Europeanization of national democracies has not significantly altered domestic actors individually, for many it has indeed implied noticeable adjustment in the balance of the system, in the relationships and existing balances between some specific actors and institutions, leading, for example, to increasing influence for some EU-oriented actors, which have gained influence at the expense of democratically elected institutions. It is true, however, that at least three common patterns are in most member states: (i) deparliamentarization, (ii) increased fragmentation in everyday issues due to sectoral operation and the multi-level logics of European policy-making, and (iii) enhanced coordination in high politics and more politicized issues; manifested in growing implication of first ministers or finance ministers. However, it can be argued that these three trends are brought about by other structural factors alongside the supranational factor that are likely to be more consequential than membership, such as globalization, territorial devolution, the articulation of new citizens' demands on the public sector, the shift from hierarchical government to *governance*, a more and more leadership-oriented high politics, privatization and the reshaping of state-market relationships in general, agencification, new public management, and so on (Colino and Molina, 2005).[6]

This analysis looks at the internal adaptation of the central executives to Europe. The heightened sectoralization of the EU has apparently made national coordination more difficult, and this has affected the political and institutional capacities of central executives to effectively negotiate in Brussels and to translate policy ambitions into coherent programmes (Peters and Wright 2001). This constitutes an opportunity to assess which domestic groups are emerging as winners and losers from EU integration; and, furthermore, to gauge whether the central government as a unitary actor is getting weaker or stronger, more autonomous or more dependent vis-à-vis these other actors (e.g. certain firms, unions, regions, parties or sectoral administrative departments, which now interact in particular policy areas through transnational and multi-level networks). Depending on whether we look at the political or bureaucratic level, Europeanization produces centralized coordination of the countervailing trend towards sectoral fragmentation.

Similarly differentiated or ambivalent is the effect of integration on democratic governance. It is true that Europeanization may entail loss of parliamentary accountability or control, less transparent decision-making through package deals and the creation of closed policy networks in some sectors. EU membership may, on the other hand, facilitate national executives to augment their political capacity, in terms of their increasing possibility of effectively implementing majoritarian policy choices. The increase of capacity detected in the executives in some countries – since coordination tends to impose itself against departmentalization in the most important issues – vis-à-vis subnational units or parliaments – by successfully seeking to monopolize the government's representation of the member state in the Council of the EU – and vis-à-vis private interest groups or political parties – through the production of a legitimizing discourse that presents governmental actions as irreversible, thus avoiding domestic vetoes by shifting the blame for the costs of unpopular policies towards Brussels.

Logically, and in accordance with the aforementioned thesis of persistent divergence across countries, the conclusion that the EU can positively affect the capacities of national executives must be qualified by stressing that the extent of this effect will vary depending on national variables such as the level of ideological pro-Europeanism, the perception of the material benefits extracted from membership or, again, on the institutional framework in question. Whilst the combination is particularly favourable in some member states like Spain, where a certain permissive pro-European consensus has existed, some palpable returns through the European funds, a parallel growth of income and welfare policies, or an institutional structure that favours the concentration of power in the central executive vis-à-vis parliament, political parties or civil society, it is less propitious in the UK or especially the Scandinavian countries, just for the opposite reasons. Between the two, other member states represent a wide range of logically possible intermediate cases. In addition, other factors push the picture away from increasing capacity, since the growing delegation of sectoral competencies to Brussels, the reaction of the parliaments and above all of regions, creates multi-level policy networks that are more and more difficult to coordinate and hardly more hierarchical or central government directed.

NOTES

1. For the distinction between input- and output-oriented conceptions of democracy see Scharpf (1999, 2003).
2. The possible convergence was suggested by Wessels and Rometsch considering that all EU member states were undertaking 'similar innovations and adaptations which lead towards one common model and, as a result, to the disappearance of pre-existing differences among member states' (1996, p. 328). Olsen confronts that *isomorphy hypothesis* with the autonomy hypothesis since 'all institutions develop robustness towards changes in their functional and normative environments, as well as towards reform attempts' (1997, p. 161).
3. The fact that the interministerial coordination department for EU affairs may be located in the prime minister's or the cabinet office allows a more horizontal view and sometimes a hierarchical logic of coordination, but it does not imply the direct intervention of the prime minister and his/her closest aides, who restrict their EU activity to lead those policies and issues with high political salience (e.g. CFSP, European Council or the semesters of EU presidency). Moreover, in some examples that prefer 'prime ministerial' coordination, the foreign ministry (e.g. in Italy or the UK) or a specific European ministry (France) also intervenes in national EU policy-making while, on the contrary, active involvement by the premier can be frequent in countries in which he/she has no formal role in EU matters, but exerts constant indirect supervision and arbitration (e.g. Spain, due to the quasi-presidential nature of the system).
4. Moreover, other factors besides EU membership are likely to be more consequential in explaining the structural changes of national executives. The interpretations that contest the importance of the European explanation as a factor behind governmental transformation highlight the impact of private sector models (new public management, agencification, privatization, and the reshape of state-market relationships in general) or mention other main political trends such as globalization, territorial devolution, the articulation of new citizens' demands on the public sector, the shift from hierarchical government to *governance*, a more and more leadership-oriented high politics etc. 'European-level changes are just one among several drivers of domestic change' (Olsen 2002a, p. 937).
5. The concept of blame avoidance refers to the mechanism used by the national governments as a means of legitimizing and securing agreement at home on controversial decisions. By *blaming* Brussels, given the compulsory nature of EU legislation and the popular consensus on the benefits of membership of the organization, central policy makers *avoid* pressures of sectoral networks that not only include private groups that benefit from protection (some firms or unions), but also certain public actors (some bureaucrats, some regional authorities or sectoral departments such as industry). For example, as accession to the third phase of EMU was conditioned by the fulfilment of the Maastricht criteria, these central

actors (prime ministers or economy and finance ministers) could use this *external discipline* to achieve previously unseen levels of budgetary rectitude and control of spending departments (Kassim et al. 2000).

6. Conversely, it is interesting to note that executives of non-member states can also become Europeanized, not only for foreseeable accession (Goetz 2001), but for an impact based on the European Economic Area agreement (Lægreid et al. 2004).

REFERENCES

Anderson, Jeffrey. J. (2002), 'Europeanization and the transformation of the democratic polity, 1945-2000', *Journal of Common Market Studies*, **40**, 793-822.

Beyers, Jan and Guido Dierickx (1998), 'The working groups of the Council of the European Union: Supranational or intergovernmental negotiations?', *Journal of Common Market Studies*, **36**, 289-317.

Beyers, Jan and Jarle Trondal (2003), 'How nation states hit Europe – Ambiguity and representation in the EU', *European Integration Online Papers*, **7** (5), full text.

Börzel, Tanja A. (2003), 'Shaping and taking EU policies: Member state's responses to Europeanisation', *Queen's Papers on Europeanisation, no 2.*

Börzel, Tanja A. and Thomas Risse (2003), 'Conceptualizing the domestic impact of Europe', in Kevin Featherstone and Claudio M. Radaelli (eds), *The Politics of Europeanization*, Oxford: Oxford University Press, pp. 57-80.

Burnham, June and Moshe Maor (1995), 'Converging administrative systems: Recruitment and training in EU member states', *Journal of European Public Policy*, **2**, 185-204.

Colino, César and Ignacio Molina (2005), 'National governments and the EU', in Peter van der Hoek (ed.), *Handbook of Public Administration and Policy in the European Union*, New York: Dekker, pp. 341-54.

Dyson, Kenneth and Klaus H. Goetz (2003), 'Living with Europe: Power, constraint and contestation', in Kenneth Dyson and Klaus H. Goetz (eds), *Germany, Europe and the Politics of Constraint*, Oxford: Oxford University Press, pp. 3-35.

Featherstone, Kevin and Claudio M. Radaelli (eds) (2003), *The Politics of Europeanization*, Oxford: Oxford University Press.

Goetz, Klaus H. (2000), 'European integration and national executives: A cause in search of an effect?', *West European Politics*, **23** (4), 211-31.

Goetz, Klaus H. (2001), 'Making sense of post-communist central administration: Modernization, Europeanization or Latinization?', *Journal of European Public Policy*, **8**, 1032-51.

Goetz, Klaus, H. (2003), 'The federal executive: Bureaucratic fusion versus governmental bifurcation', in Kenneth Dyson and Klaus H. Goetz (eds), *Germany, Europe and the Politics of Constraint*, Oxford: Oxford University Press, pp. 55-72.

Harmsen, Robert (1999), 'The Europeanization of national administrations: A comparative study of France and the Netherlands', *Governance*, **12**, 81-113.

Kassim, Hussein (2003a), 'Meeting the demands of EU membership: The Europeanization of national administrative systems', in Kevin Featherstone and Claudio M. Radaelli (eds), *The Politics of Europeanization*, Oxford: Oxford University Press, pp. 83-111.

Kassim, Hussein (2003b), 'The European administration: Between Europeanization and domestication', in Jack Hayward and Anand Menon (eds), *Governing Europe*, Oxford: Oxford University Press, pp. 139-61.

Kassim, Hussein, Anand Menon, B. Guy Peters and Vincent Wright (eds) (2001), *The National Co-ordination of EU Policy: The European Level*, Oxford: Oxford University Press.

Kassim, Hussein, B. Guy Peters and Vincent Wright (eds) (2000), *The National Co-ordination of EU Policy: The Domestic Level*, Oxford: Oxford University Press.

Knill, Christoph (2001), *The Europeanisation of National Administrations; Patterns of Institutional Change and Persistence*, Cambridge: Cambridge University Press.

Knill, Christoph (2005), 'The Europeanization of national policy capacities', in Martin Painter and Jon Pierre (eds), *Challenges to State Policy Capacity: Global Trends and Comparative perspectives*, London: Palgrave, pp. 52-71.

Kurzer, Paulette (1997), 'Decline or preservation of executive capacity? Political and economic integration revisited', *Journal of Common Market Studies*, **35**, 31-56.

Lægreid, Per, Runolfur S. Steinthorsson and Baldur Thorhallsson (2004), 'Europeanization of Central Government Administration in the Nordic States', *Journal of Common Market Studies*, **42**, 347-69.

Laffan, Brigid (2003), 'Managing Europe from home: Impact of the EU on executive government: A comparative analysis', paper prepared for the ECPR General Conference, Marburg.

Metcalfe, Lawrence (1994), 'International policy co-ordination and public management reform', *International Review of Administrative Sciences*, **60**, 271-90.

Molina, Ignacio (2004), *Capacidad gubernamental y pertenencia a la UE: Un análisis de la adopción de decisiones económicas europeizadas en España* (Executive Capacity and EU Membership: An Analysis of Spanish Decision-making on Europeanised Economic Issues), Ph.D. Thesis, Madrid: Autonomous University of Madrid.

Moravcsik, Andrew (1994), 'Why the European Community strengthens the state: Domestic politics and international cooperation', *Working Paper 52*, Center for European Studies, Harvard University, Cambridge, MA.

Olsen, Johan P. (1997), 'European challenges to the nation state', in Bernard Steunenberg and Frans van Vught (eds), *Political Institutions and Public Policy*, Dordrecht: Kluwer.

Olsen, Johan P. (2002a), 'The many faces of Europeanization', *Journal of Common Market Studies*, **40**, 921-52.

Olsen, Johan P. (2002b), 'Towards a European administrative space?', *Working Paper 02/26*, Oslo: ARENA, University of Oslo.

Page, Ed (2003), 'Europeanization and the persistence of administrative Systems', in Jack Hayward and Anand Menon (eds), *Governing Europe*, Oxford: Oxford University Press.

Painter, Martin and Jon Pierre (2005), 'Unpacking policy capacity: Issues and themes', in Martin Painter and Jon Pierre (eds), *Challenges to State Policy Capacity: Global Trends and Comparative Perspectives*, London: Palgrave, pp. 1-18.

Peters, B. Guy and Vincent Wright (2001), 'The national co-ordination of European policy-making: Negotiating the quagmire', in Jeremy Richardson (ed.), *European Union: Power and Policy-Making*, London and New York: Routledge, pp. 155-78.

Scharpf, Fritz W. (1999), *Governing in Europe: Effective and Democratic?* Oxford: Oxford University Press.

Scharpf, Fritz W. (2003), 'Problem-solving effectiveness and democratic accountability in the EU', *MPIfG Working Paper, 03/1*.

Schmidt, Vivien A. (1996), 'Loosening the ties that bind: The impact of European integration on French government and its relationship to business', *Journal of Common Market Studies*, **34**, 223-54.

Van Keulen, Mendeltje (2003), 'How "home" hits Brussels: Exploring an "input"-oriented Europeanisation research agenda', paper presented at the ECPR General Conference, Marburg, 18-21 September.

Wallace, Hellen (1973), *National Governments and the European Communities*, London: Chatham House.

Weaver, R. Kent and Bert A. Rockman (eds) (1993), *Do Institutions Matter? Government Capabilities in the United States and Abroad*, Washington, DC: Brookings Institution.

Wessels, Wolfgang and Dietrich Rometsch (1996), 'Conclusion: European Union and national institutions', in Dietrich Rometsch and Wolfgang Wessels (eds), *The European Union and Member States: Towards Institutional Fusion*, Manchester: Manchester University Press, pp. 328-65.

Wessels, Wolfgang, Andreas Maurer and Jürgen Mittag (eds) (2003), *Fifteen into One? The European Union and its Member States*, Manchester: Manchester University Press.

Wright, Vincent and Jack Hayward (2000), 'Governing from the centre: Policy coordination in six European core executives', in R. A. W. Rhodes (ed.), *Transforming British Government*, Vol. II, London: Palgrave Macmillan, pp. 27-46.

9. Adapting to Europe: Strategic Europeanization of National Parliaments[1]

Katrin Auel

INTRODUCTION

Considering the literature on the role of national parliaments in the European Union (EU), most scholars would probably reply to a hypothetical Eurobarometer question that European integration was rather 'a bad thing' for national parliaments. The process of European integration, it is generally argued, has led to a transfer of legislative power not only from the national to the European level, but, even more importantly, also from parliaments to the executive (Moravcsik 1994). From this point of view, the Europeanization of national parliaments seems to mean only one thing: they find themselves on the losing end of the integration process.

Yet, national parliaments have realized their decline, and 'backbenchers have learnt to fight back' (Raunio and Hix 2000) by adapting to the challenges of European integration. As a first reaction, national parliaments reformed their institutional structures to create the means and instruments for parliamentary scrutiny of EU affairs. It will be argued, however, that this institutional Europeanization has been only partly effective in restoring parliamentary power vis-à-vis their governments. In some parliaments, the institutional reforms provide parliamentarians with scrutiny rights that are too weak to effectively influence the executive. But even for stronger and more influential parliaments the reforms might prove dysfunctional as they may confront MPs with a structural dilemma: The more effectively they influence and scrutinize their government, the more they bind their representatives negotiating at the European level to specific interests. Parliaments strictly supervising their governments and thus tying their hands in multi-level negotiations must face the possibility that outcomes of negotiations are inferior to compromises that might have been obtained if the government had enough room for manoeuvre. It will be shown, however, that national parliamentarians are quite aware of the disadvantages and dysfunctional effects of the institutional reforms and therefore develop strategies to cope with them. Thus, with regard to the Europeanization of parliamentary democracy, we need to distinguish between (a) the institutional reforms aimed at parliamentary scrutiny of European affairs as institutional Europeanization and (b) the adaptation strategies as a strategic form of Europeanization.

The chapter is divided in three parts: After a short presentation of the institutional context as well as the institutional Europeanization of four parliamentary systems, I discuss the ambivalent consequences of these institutional reforms from a theoretical point of view, and provide first evidence on the 'strategic Europeanization' of members of parliaments. Taking the example of four member states that represent different and specific types of parliamentary systems, the UK, France, Germany and Denmark, it is argued that both the institutional reforms and, consequently, the strategies parliamentary actors develop to cope with coordination problems resulting from the multi-level structure are influenced by the overall institutional context of the respective parliamentary system.

INSTITUTIONAL EUROPEANIZATION OF NATIONAL PARLIAMENTARY SYSTEMS

The term 'Europeanization' is mainly[2] used to characterize processes of 'domestic adaptation to pressures emanating directly or indirectly from EU membership' (Featherstone 2003, p. 7). This definition includes both, the impact the European integration process has upon the role and position of national parliaments (*passive Europeanization*) and the reaction of national parliaments to these changes in the form of institutional or strategic adaptation (*active Europeanization*).

As regards the passive Europeanization of national parliaments, there seems to be at least one consensus, namely that it has severely weakened national legislatures and redistributed political power from the legislatures to the national executives. In the process of European integration, policy-making competencies were transferred from the national to the European level. National parliaments still control important steps of the integration process through the ratification of Treaty agreements (as far as Treaty changes are not subject to referenda), but they are not directly involved in European policy-making. They hold discretionary power with regard to the transposition of European legislation into national law, but can only indirectly influence European decisions. As a consequence, national parliaments were and still are losing a growing part of their sovereignty as legislatures while national executives are strengthened due to their direct involvement in European policy-making. National parliaments, either 'losers or latecomers' (Maurer and Wessels 2001), have been 'left behind in the rush' (Norton 1996a, p. 192).

This, however, is only one side of the process of Europeanization of parliamentary democracy. Over the centuries, parliaments have proved to be highly adaptive institutions that can cope quite well with changes in their environment. And indeed, we can observe continuous processes of adaptation of national parliaments to the challenges of European integration. First and foremost, the debate about the democratic deficit of the EU, and above all their interest to maintain their power has motivated national parliaments to adapt to the changing environment through institutional reforms of their infrastructure (Laursen and Pappas 1995, Maurer and Wessels 2001, Norton 1996b, Smith 1996). This *institutional Europeanization* had three basic objectives (Auel and Benz 2004):

- It was meant to entitle national parliaments to obtain comprehensive information on European issues by their government. While this right at first applied mainly to the 'first pillar' of the EU, it was later expanded to the 'second' and 'third pillar' in most national parliaments.
- It aimed at enhancing parliamentary capacities to handle and process this information. All national parliaments have reformed their infrastructure by setting up one or more special European Affairs Committees and by implementing a scrutiny procedure for European documents and decisions.
- It intended to establish participation rights that parliaments hold vis-à-vis the government within the national arena for European affairs as well. This includes the right to draft resolutions on European issues before a final agreement is reached ('scrutiny reserve').

Although the reforms were all meant to achieve these basic objectives, the institutional provisions implemented in the different national parliaments vary considerably. This variation reveals a path-dependent development, which reflects the institutional context of different parliamentary systems (Dimitrakopoulos 2001). Using the example of four national parliaments, which represent distinctive types of parliamentary systems, the British House of Commons, the German Bundestag and the French Assemblée Nationale,[3] it will be shown that parliaments have chosen procedures based on existing institutional repertoires.

United Kingdom: Institutional Reforms in the House of Commons

The British House of Commons[4] stands for the classic Westminster model of democracy characterized by a clear parliamentary majority as well as an almost complete symbiosis of government and its parliamentary majority. The immense power originating from the traditional principle of absolute parliamentary sovereignty[5] is transferred to the executive via a disciplined party system. As a result, the House of Commons is regarded as a relatively weak 'policy influencer' (Norton 1994, see also Mény and Knapp 1998, p. 181, Helms 2002). Characterized as an 'arena legislature' (Polsby 1975), the House of Commons has mostly communicative functions, while the committee work plays only a minor role (Sturm 2003). Standing committees are set up, contrary to what their name suggests, only for the debate of a bill and dissolved once the legislative process is finished. The permanent Departmental Select Committees, on the other hand, are not involved in the legislative process. Their task is the critical scrutiny of governmental action, that is of the implementation of policies (Rush 2000), which is underlined by the fact that the Committees normally sit in public.

The scrutiny procedure for European affairs closely mirrors these institutional arrangements. European documents are first transferred to the *European Scrutiny Committee* (ESC) whose task is to examine the documents, to report its opinion on their legal and political importance and to consider any issue arising in the documents or related matters (Standing Order 143). For this task, the Committee not only obtains information in form of *Explanatory Memoranda* from the responsible department, but also has the right to ask for further information and to question the responsible minister. Once the ESC has determined the political and/or legal importance of a document, it can be deferred for debate to one of the three European Standing Committees or – by a motion put down by the government – to the Committee of the Whole House. According to Standing Order 119, the com-mittees, which generally sit in public, then have the possibility to debate the document and the respective governmental motion, on which they can move amendments. However, for the amendments to become effective the Committees have to rely on the government, as it is the government that formulates and puts down the final motion on the Floor of the House (House of Commons 2002), where it is normally voted on without further debate. To ensure that parliament has the opportunity to deal with European matters before they are agreed upon at the European level, the House of Commons adopted a resolution on a scrutiny reserve stating that no minister should give agreement to any proposal for European Community legislation that is still subject to scrutiny or is awaiting consideration by the House.[6]

France: Institutional Reforms in the Assemblée Nationale

Like the House of Commons, the French Assemblée Nationale is generally considered a rather weak parliament. This is due to the Constitution of the V. Republic of 1958 which rigorously pursued the aim to replace the instable and inefficient parliamentary system of the III. and IV. Republic by governmental stability and efficiency. Although the Assemblée Nationale has a more sophisticated standing committee structure, its influence on governmental policy-making is severely restricted as the government controls the parliamentary agenda as well as the legislative process. At the same time, the Constitution severely limits parliamentary control over governmental policy-making. It 'restricts and gags parliament, in fact preventing it from exercising its powers of control' (Cot 1980, p. 11). The effects of the new constitutional and procedural constraints were summed up by Frears as follows: '. . . complete executive supremacy in the legislative process, severely limited opportunities for general debates criticizing government, virtually no opportunities for scrutinizing executive acts and making the executive give an account of them [...] executive power is a little too immune from proper scrutiny' (1990, p. 33).

During the first decades, the Assemblée Nationale (as well as the Sénat) paid only little attention to the process of European integration (Nuttens and Sicard 2000, p. 61, Szukala and Rozenberg 2001, p. 229). The first direct elections to the European Parliament, however, and especially the debate on the Single Market Programme, raised parliamentarians' awareness and fears of losing their prerogatives. In 1979, after a serious conflict over the transposition of a European directive,[7] both Houses set up a *Délégation pour les affaires européennes*, albeit with powers limited to monitoring European legislation and keeping parliament informed.

During the course of the ratification of the Maastricht Treaty, which necessitated a constitutional reform, the new Article 88-4 was inserted into the French Constitution. It obliged the government to 'lay before the National Assembly and the Senate any proposals for Community instruments which contain provisions which are matters for statute as soon as they have been transmitted to the Council of the Communities'. The article also included a right to table explicitly non-binding[8] resolutions, which was limited, however, to drafts for legislative community acts that fell within the limited sphere of parliamentary responsibility according to Article 34.[9] This restriction[10] was at least partly abolished with the amendment of Article 88-4 in January 1999 (Hourquebie 1999, p. 78). Now Article 88-4 *obliges* the government to submit all European drafts of legislative nature of all 'three pillars' of the EU, but also *enables* the government to submit all other EU documents, thus giving parliament the opportunity to vote a resolution on the latter as well. In addition, a parliamentary scrutiny reserve was established in 1994. To be able to deal with European documents effectively and to analyse them in detail, the Delegation can designate one or more *rapporteurs* to draw up a detailed report (*rapport*). The outcome may be the tabling of a resolution, but the report may also remain informative in character (*rapport d'information*).

Germany: Institutional Reforms in the Bundestag

The German parliamentary system resembles the Westminster model insofar as the government and its supporting parliamentary majority form a functional unit vis-à-vis the opposition (Döring 1994, Schütt-Wetschky 2000). At the same time, however, the *Bundestag* is characterized as more of a 'transformative legislature' (Polsby 1975) and a solid policy influencer, which finds its expression in the independent agenda power of the parliament, the extensive control rights of the opposition as well as in the transfer of parliamentary policy-making to numerous committees and subcommittees. These working structures are also mirrored at the parliamentary party group level through corresponding working groups (Ismayr 2001). In addition, the German electoral system, a combination of majority and proportional representation, favours the development of a multi-party system where (at least at the national level) government is regularly formed by coalitions. In contrast to the Westminster model, executive dominance is therefore clearly more restricted.[11]

The participation rights of the German Bundestag were tied down in the German Basic Law (Grundgesetz, GG) in the course of the ratification of the Maastricht Treaty.[12] According to Article 23 GG the Bundestag cooperates with the government in affairs of the EU. The Bundestag has the right to receive all relevant information on European matters as well as a right to draft a resolution on European draft proposals before the government agrees to a European decision. It clearly states that the 'federal Government takes account of the Bundestag's resolution in the negotiations' (Article 23 para. 3 clause 2 GG).

As provided for in Article 45 GG, the European Affairs Committee was set up in December of 1994 (and thus rather late[13]). Just like the Foreign Affairs Committee, the Defence Committee and the Petitions Committee, the establishment of the European Affairs Committee is constitutionally demanded and thus not subject to the Bundestag's Parliamentary Standing Orders. It is the central arena for the Bundestag's dealings with European affairs. As a classic 'cross-section committee' it deals with all important integration decisions, while all specific policy decisions are, as in domestic policies, dealt with in the sectoral standing committees. As a rule, all committees hold closed sessions, but may by decision admit the public.

Denmark: Institutional Reforms in the Folketing

The *Folketing* in Denmark stands for a parliament in a consensus democracy (Lijphart 1999, Nannestad 2003, p. 55). In contrast to the other three countries, Denmark has a highly fragmented multi-party system (Nannestad 2003, p. 81). Parliament's power vis-à-vis the government is relatively strong, because Danish governments are generally formed by minority coalitions unable to act without a supporting majority (Laursen 1995). According to Article 15 of the Danish constitution, a government may remain in office as long as it does not have a majority in parliament *against* it (*'negative parliamentarism'*, Laursen 2001, p. 99). Against minority governments, the opposition is in a rather powerful position. It is not only able to change or even obstruct governmental policy-making, but can also – at least in theory – push its own agenda (Damgaard 1997, p. 80). This opposition power is partly balanced by the government's right to dissolve parliament at almost any time and call for new elections.[14]

As a result, the *Folketing* is regarded as a highly 'transformative' and 'policy-making' parliament, where committees and commissions play a major role in legislation (Nannestad 2003, p. 60). It is therefore not surprising that 'EU affairs are serious business in the domestic politics of Denmark, and the Parliament has tried from the very beginning of Denmark's EC membership to control the Government rather tightly' (Laursen 2001, p. 99). With Denmark's accession to the European Community (EC) in 1972, a Market Relations Committee (*markedsudvalg*)[15] was established as a permanent committee to implement the Accession Act and to scrutinize the government's European policies. Since early 1973, the Committee has had the power to mandate the government's negotiation position in European Affairs.[16] According to the logic of 'negative parliamentarism', the aim of this provision was to prevent the government from agreeing to a European decision that might not be supported by a majority in the Folketing (Damgaard and Nørgaard 2000, p. 42). In practice, the procedure entitles the Committee to formal veto rights vis-à-vis the government in European policy-making, and 'a government wanting to survive politically knows it will have to listen to the Committee' (Laursen 2001, p. 105). The Committee is further strengthened by the fact that its members are often experienced MPs and even former ministers who have served on the Committee for a long time and have acquired considerable expertise in European affairs (Dosenrode 1998, p. 60).

THE DILEMMA OF PARLIAMENTARY CONTROL IN MULTI-LEVEL GOVERNANCE

The institutional Europeanization described above was meant to counterbalance the redistribution of political resources between the executive and the legislature caused by the process of European integration: The aim was to obtain the same information as the government and to be able to influence European decision-making before the stage of formal ratification or implementation. Yet, this institutional Europeanization did not completely make up for the structural disadvantages. Parliaments still depend on their government as the main information source, they are still not directly involved in European policy-making and – as a consequence – have neither complete control over the agenda setting at the European level, nor can they directly influence European decisions.

Nevertheless, the institutional reforms have enabled national parliaments to have more control over European policy-making by opening up the possibility to influence and control the negotiation position of their national government. In this respect, however, the institutional reforms vary considerably. The European Affairs Committee of the Danish Folketing undoubtedly has the most extensive powers due to its right to mandate the government's negotiation position, but the constitutional obligation of the German government to take parliamentary resolutions into account puts the Bundestag in a quite powerful position as well. On the other hand, neither the French Assemblée Nationale nor the British House of Commons can exert great influence on their government's European policy-making. In France, the Conseil Constitutionnel explicitly ruled out any binding effect of parliamentary resolutions, and in the UK, the parliamentary rules allow the government to completely ignore motions voted for in the European Standing Committees: 'if the motion is amended and the Government dislikes the amended motion it can move a different motion in the House. It casts doubt on the value of serving in European Standing Committees if their decisions can simply be ignored' (HC 152-xxx, para. 70).

A simple formula to overcome the weakness of these parliaments would be to strengthen their institutional rights to influence their governments' negotiation position, for example by institutionalizing a mandating procedure. This, however, is hardly an option. Not only would the governments in both countries reject such a limitation of their power, but parliamentary mandates would also entail a structural disruption, as the legislatures would acquire rights in European policies, which they lack in domestic politics. However, a second reason seems to be even more important. As has been discussed extensively elsewhere (Benz 2001, 2003, Auel and Benz 2004, 2005), stronger participation rights of national parliaments do not inevitably contribute to advancing parliamentary control and democratic accountability of national governments, but may lead to the manifestation of a structural dilemma: A binding mandate may hamper European decision-making by restricting the necessary scope of action of the negotiating governments. Governments bound to a clear-cut negotiation mandate lack the necessary flexibility to search for the best realization of national interests that can be achieved in cooperation with other governments (Benz 2001, Czada 1997).

This is even true in cases where national parliaments have no formal veto right, but the right to draft only non-binding resolutions on European issues. According to the basic norm of parliamentary systems the government is ultimately bound to the will of the parliamentary majority. Governmental action in a parliamentary system is only legitimate if subject to parliamentary control and open for parliamentary veto, because only then can it be guaranteed that the will of the electorate is actually transformed into policy-making. Therefore, if a parliament raises its voice publicly on a European issue through a clear-cut parliamentary resolution, it can hardly be ignored by the government and can have the effect of politically binding the government.

What then are the consequences of the institutional Europeanization of national parliaments? At first sight, the institutional reforms seem to have dysfunctional effects in all national parliaments. Either the parliamentary powers of influence and control remain too weak to be more than a symbolic measure to disguise the actual loss of parliamentary power, or parliamentary scrutiny and control are effective, but may have the unwanted effect of diminishing the effectiveness of the government's European negotiations and policy-making.

In the following, it will be argued that in reality neither is the case. The decisive point is that parliamentary actors themselves are indeed well aware of the limitations and disadvantages connected with their institutional reforms. Therefore, they develop strategies to cope with the disadvantages resulting from the institutional Europeanization and, at the same time, to avoid getting caught in the dilemma described above. In the literature on multi-level governance in federal systems and in the EU, there is ample evidence of the ability of actors to develop strategies to circumvent dilemma situations (e.g. Benz 2003, Héritier 1999, Scharpf et al. 1976). While these studies mainly focus on executives, the development of strategies by members of parliament can be observed as well.

From a theoretical point of view, several potential strategies of national parliaments can be identified (Auel and Rittberger 2006):

- First, they can focus on holding the government publicly accountable. Thus, instead of trying to influence the government's negotiation position, they subject it to public scrutiny. In this case, the parties supporting the government leave the responsible minister sufficient room for manoeuvre in European negotiations but induce him to act as a representative of the electorate and give him no opportunity to shift the blame or disguise his responsibility. Such a strategy can be used ex ante as well as ex post by publicly scrutinizing the government's negotiation position as well as the results obtained by the government in the European negotiations.

- Second, they can turn into forums of public deliberation. In this case, they do try to influence the government's European policy, but not through institutionalized participation rights, which might establish veto positions and provoke mutual blockades. Public deliberation of European matters rather aims at changing decision premises or contexts through information, ideas and arguments.
- Third, MPs can cooperate informally with the responsible minister before and during the process of European negotiations. This enables them to influence the government's European policy without binding the government to a specific mandate. At the same time, they can adjust the parliamentary position to the opportunities or constraints arising during the negotiation process.
- Finally, MPs may try to completely bypass the government. By establishing direct contacts to actors at the European level or in other member states they can try to open up their own independent channels of influence in EU policy-making.

Although more comparative research is needed, it can be shown that the strategies, which MPs in the four parliaments develop to cope with their disadvantages in European multi-level governance and the inadequacies of their institutional reforms, are influenced by the overall institutional context of the respective parliamentary system and therefore quite different: 'After all, the institutions provide venues for the interactions between MPs and ministers, rules for behaviour of participants and above all, role models for the "inmates" of the parliamentary/governmental complex' (Andeweg and Nijzink 1995, p. 157). Above all, the strategies reflect both the type of executive – legislative relations and the dominant parliamentary function. The greater the independence of the executive and the less significant the 'transformative' or 'policy-influencing' power of the legislature, the more parliamentarians seem to adopt a more public strategy to strengthen their position.

MANAGING THE DISADVANTAGES: STRATEGIC EUROPEANIZATION[17]

The House of Commons: Public Control

In the classic Westminster model of parliamentary democracy, characterized by a single party majority as well as an almost complete fusion of government and its parliamentary majority, parliament traditionally acts as an institution controlling the government. Corresponding to this type of government regime, the strategies that parliamentarians develop are aimed less at influencing the negotiation process or at circumventing the government's position in multi-level governance than at holding the government accountable. MPs in the House of Commons abstain from challenging the central position of the executive in European policy-making, but aim at preventing the government from exploiting its power position and at making the use of this position more transparent to parliament and the electorate. Consequently, parliament develops strategies aimed at publicity, it forces the government to respect parliamentary rules, to fully expose, explain and defend its negotiation position as well as the respective decisions achieved in the European negotiations.

According to the MPs themselves, the main aim of the whole scrutiny process is not 'to tell the government what to do, but to see that the government explains what it is doing and follows the rules properly' (personal interview majority MP). The Committees' aim to hold the government publicly accountable is achieved by a strategy of continuous and vociferous demand for information, by constantly 'breathing down the governments' necks' (Carter 2001, p. 412). Both the European Scrutiny Committee and the European Standing Committees make frequent use of asking the Government for additional information and of 'inviting' ministers to public sessions to question them on European matters and the government's stance on them.

In addition, MPs do not shy away from publicly embarrassing the government if it has failed to adhere to parliamentary information rights or parliamentary rules, such as the scrutiny reserve. For example, from 1994 to 1998 the ESC kept a 'Black Book' where the government's failures to provide the European Scrutiny Committee with information on time were meticulously listed by name and later published (HC 791/98, Annex G). Since the beginning of 2000 the departments are obliged to issue a monthly declaration on information not made available to the Committee (HC-152-xxx/02, para. 47). The most effective strategy, however, is to regularly cite ministers before the Committee to question them on certain issues or to hold them accountable for incomplete information or breaches of the scrutiny reserve. 'Our job is to hunt them' (personal interview majority MP). These public '*evidence sessions*' can be quite uncomfortable for the ministers, as they generally have to face the Committee alone, that is without a large staff, to answer to questions not known beforehand. In the interviews with members of the ESC it was often pointed out that ministers who make a bad impression in these evidence sessions because they are unable to defend the government's position properly, may even damage their standing in the cabinet. Nevertheless, even their own party members often attack ministers quite fiercely, causing the opposition to admit that the Labour members in the Committee 'act as a group of parliamentarians, not as party members' (personal interview opposition MP).

Strategies aimed at improving direct parliamentary influence, on the other hand, are hardly developed in the House of Commons. In the parliamentary party groups,[18] for example, which generally provide arenas of coordination between the majority and government, European issues are only rarely flagged up by MPs. Similar observations apply to other strategies of informal influence available to MPs such as contacting the relevant minister. Almost all MPs declared that they practically never used these strategies in connection with European issues or questions. As the transfer of information in European Affairs is regarded as the vital element of the government's formal accountability, and requests for better or more information and questioning of ministers are an essential part of the scrutiny process, MPs hardly ever try to open up alternative information sources. Most of the members of the Com-mittee declared to have practically no contacts to European institutions and only few to members of other national parliaments.

The French Assemblée Nationale: Public Deliberation

In the 'rationalized' French parliament the rigid framework of the constitution strictly limits the influence on and the scrutiny of governmental policy-making both in domestic and European affairs. While the Standing Committee System allows for the development of parliamentary expertise and more legislative influence than the British ad hoc committees, the Assemblée Nationale is in a much weaker position than the German Bundestag or, in particular, the Danish Folketing with regard to the legislative process. At the same time, the parliamentary control function is not as pronounced as in the House of Commons. Thus, the main parliamentary function seems to lie in acting as '*instrument de vigilance*' and in providing an arena of public deliberation of government policy. 'L'information et la diffusion sont à la racine du pouvoir' (Kessler 1999, p. 243).

Accordingly, the French parliament has resorted to the strategy of influence through information and public deliberation using the formal instrument of the parliamentary *rapports*. Although information reports are a common feature of the French legislative system, the Delegation of the Assemblée Nationale has made special use of them, not only in number but also in content.[19] Contrary to the reports elaborated by other European Affairs Committees, these reports frequently have paperback dimensions and are often profound studies on a specific European issue. As interviews in the different ministries revealed, the government now regards these reports as important sources of information and as finely tuned seismographs of parliamentary opinion. By drafting these extensive and detailed reports on important European issues the French parliament not only provides information on European affairs for the general public, it is also able to argue for parliamentary views and standpoints and to formulate indirect demands without directly determining or criticizing the government's negotiation position.

In addition, both Delegations have begun to improve their relationships with representatives of European institutions and other national parliaments to be more independent of the government as the main information source in European matters. In 1999 the French Senate was among the first national parliaments to set up a representation (*antenne administrative permanente*) in Brussels. In recent years the French parliament has also become more active in building up interparliamentary relationships. Especially the bilateral cooperation between the Assemblée Nationale and the Bundestag has been intensified, and the Delegation regularly holds sessions with German European Affairs Committee.[20] Similar developments can also be observed at the party level where, for example, the conservative UMP and the German conservative CDU/CSU decided to convene regularly to discuss common positions on European issues and to give the Franco-German relationship a new impetus.

The German Bundestag: Informal Cooperation and Bypassing

The German Bundestag with its sophisticated standing committee structure is regarded as a more powerful policy influencer than the British and the French parliaments. The fact that legislative function and the involvement in governmental policy-making clearly dominate is also reflected in the parliamentary participation procedure in European affairs (Judge 1995, p. 82). Accordingly, article 23 of the German Basic Law speaks of 'collaboration' (*Mitwirkung*), the respective accompanying law of 'cooperation' (*Zusammenarbeit*) of the Bundestag with the German government in European affairs.

It is therefore not surprising that in the European policy process, parliamentarians have the objective to be involved in policy-making, too. However, as parliamentarians are aware of the dilemma connected to parliamentary participation in multi-level structures, they use their formal rights quite strategically. Generally, the government's request for a broad scope of action in the European negotiations is respected. Thus, the majority either completely abstains from drafting a parliamentary resolution or drafts it in close cooperation with the government in order to strengthen the latter's negotiation position in Brussels. Only in exceptional situations does the Bundestag use its powers to force the government to adopt the parliamentary position. Instead, majority MPs have taken recourse to strategies aimed at influencing European policies without tying the government's hands in the European negotiation process, partly by informal cooperation with and partly by bypassing the government.

Internal coordination in the majority parties offers ample opportunities to influence the government beyond the drafting of formal resolutions. The most important coordination bodies in the Bundestag are the sectoral working groups of the parliamentary parties consisting of the party members that sit in the respective standing committees. The main purpose of these meetings is the preparation of the upcoming Committee meeting and the coordination of the party line to be represented there. 'Generally, we get prepared for the standing committee meetings in form of a parliamentary party meeting, a working group meeting, [...] where we really fight for positions. Here, the government will most likely be willing to make concessions' (personal interview majority MP, translation K.A.).

The most important precondition for effectively influencing the government, however, is independent access to information. Only then does parliament have a chance to question the agenda and the normative justifications set by the government. Therefore, several MPs build up interparliamentary networks as well as contacts to European institutions. 'In terms of transparency, much is still to be desired, so you have to get active as an MP to get the information, either through the government or through other sources' (personal interview majority MP). Especially MEPs, but also European Commission officials increasingly serve as a kind of 'burglar alarm' to some German MPs by informing them on important Commission initiatives as early as possible. Building up interparliamentary networks with other national parliamentarians, too, primarily serves to access information, especially on the negotiation positions of other member states, to enable MPs to evaluate the negotiation situation in the run-up to the Council meetings.

However, contacts to the European level not only serve as information sources. A small but growing number of parliamentary 'euro wizards' also try to bypass the government by influencing European policies directly through contacts at the European level. 'One example is, of course, the development of EU directives. There you have the possibility to influence this process by informally contacting Commissioners or Commission officials that share our views. This has worked astonishingly well' (personal interview majority MP).

The Danish Folketing: Cooperation in the Shadow of a Formal Mandate

While the institutional reforms generally turned parliaments into 'external veto players' (Benz 2003) in European governance, who may obstruct decisions made by other institutions but are not themselves involved in the decision-making and can therefore only *react* to processes and their outcome (Benz 2003, pp. 231-2), the situation in Denmark is rather special. Due to the formation of minority governments and the particular rights of the Committee for European Affairs, Danish MPs can exert much more immediate influence on the European decision-making process.

As a result, the government and the European Affairs Committee cooperate very closely. For the government, fully explaining negotiation situations at the European level and its strategic options in these negotiations is an advantage, because the European Affairs Committee may refuse a mandate as long as it is not satisfied with the information and explanations by the government. In addition, the Committee has the possibility of controlling ex post whether the government has stayed within the confines of the parliamentary mandate. 'It is a security for the minister to seek the mandate in the parliament before he goes to Brussels, because otherwise he risks his life when he comes back' (personal interview opposition MP). In return, members of the European Affairs Committee mainly focus its deliberations on the strategic questions of what would be in Denmark's best interest and, even more importantly, on what is achievable with what kind of coalition in the Council. Party politics, on the other hand, play only a minor role in the European Affairs Committee, which ensures a more informal and consensual style of debate (Nannestad 2003, p. 63).[21]

The fact that the Folketing is well informed on European issues and is able to negotiate and control the Danish negotiation position generally makes it unnecessary for the Committee to bind the government to very narrow mandates as the members are aware of the negotiation situation and the government's options and objectives. 'If there is a good minister, he or she can say: Please give me a mandate where I can negotiate! And if we have confidence in that minister he'll get it' (personal interview opposition MP). As a result, mandates approved by the European Affairs Committee generally do not define a fixed position the government has to represent in the Council. Instead, they outline the broad strategy the government wants to pursue in the Council negotiations and provide rather flexible guidelines.

Given their powerful position, members of the Danish European Affairs Committee feel no need to develop strategies of bypassing the government by opening up independent information sources or channels of influence at the European level. On the other hand, the issues and mandates debated in the Committee are highly confidential, which rules out the development of strategies of holding the government publicly accountable. Thus, the only strategy observed in the Danish European Affairs Committee so far is to selectively veto the government's mandate, that is to refuse to give a minister any kind of mandate when it feels that it has not been properly informed or involved.[22] This ensures the Committee's influence on European policy-making and guarantees that the government respects parliamentary participation rights.

CONCLUSION

'Europeanization' is not something national parliaments simply endure passively. Undeniably, the process of European integration has weakened national parliaments. They have not only lost substantial areas of legislation to the European level, they are also weakened by the executives' gatekeeper position between the national and the European arena. However, parliamentarians have not simply accepted their decline, but try to actively counterbalance this shift in power and search for ways to manage the challenges of multi-level policy-making.

In a first step, national parliaments implemented institutional reforms aimed at recovering the rights they hold in domestic politics. But this institutional Europeanization has its flaws. In France and the UK, for example, the institutional reforms could not counterbalance the dominance of the executive in European decision-making. The legislatures' right to draft resolutions on European issues seems to be little more than symbolic politics to disguise the actual loss of parliamentary power. The German Bundestag and, in particular, the Danish Folketing, on the other hand, are much more powerful vis-à-vis their governments in European politics. However, given the problematic consequences of external interventions in the multi-level process, even these strong parliaments may be restricted in the use of their institutional rights.

The comparative study has shown that MPs are quite aware of their disadvantages in the European multi-level system. In a second step they have therefore tried to develop adequate strategies to exploit the opportunities provided by the institutional reforms. In contrast to the wide variety of strategies executive actors can utilize in two-level games (Putnam 1988, Evans et al. 1993), the strategic options of parliaments, which are not directly involved in European policy-making, are much more limited, but they exist. Which strategies parliaments develop seems to depend on the particular parliamentary-executive relations in the respective parliamentary system. Rather than challenging these traditional relations, MPs focus their efforts on strengthening their capacity to fulfil the parliamentary function that dominates in domestic politics as well. Legislatures with less influence on governmental policy-making appear to take recourse to strategies with a more public impact to enhance their power. Allegedly weak parliaments thus gain their relative strength by acting as an intermediary public arena between Europe and the citizens. Strategies of bypassing the government in order to gain access to independent information or to influence policy-making directly at the European level, on the other hand, are rarely developed. More 'transformative' legislatures, in contrast, cooperate more closely with their respective government, either formally or informally. Thus, they develop strategies that enhance their influencing capacities, either by bypassing the government or through the use of selective vetoes to remind the government of their power.

More research is needed before the actual effectiveness of these strategies can be evaluated. This is especially true with regard to strategies aiming at influence either through public deliberation, informal cooperation with the government or through direct channels of influence at the European level. The different strategies can, however, be evaluated from a democratic theory point of view. Parliamentary legitimacy cannot only be achieved through parliamentary influence on the government's policy-making, but also requires public parliamentary deliberation and scrutiny of governmental action. Only then can parliaments truly serve as an intermediary arena between the government and the citizen. From this point of view, the strategic European-ization of national parliaments can have its flaws as well. In particular in the Danish, but also in the German case, cooperation with the government seems to ensure parliamentary influence on governmental policy-making. However, this cooperation takes place behind closed doors. In Denmark, the mandating procedure even requires confidentiality among the partners including the opposition, which rules out effective public scrutiny of governmental policy-making. In Germany, cooperation takes place informally within the majority parties, and the direct but informal influence exerted by German MPs at the European level is likewise neither transparent nor subject to public scrutiny. In both parliaments, this opaqueness of the parliamentary process is not sufficiently counterbalanced by parliamentary debates in the plenary. Both parliaments therefore cannot adequately fulfil their functions of *public* control and deliberation.

In France, on the contrary, the Assemblée Nationale provides extensive information on important European issues. As such, it fulfils the parliamentary function of keeping the general public informed about European issues and the parliament's view on them. At the same time, however, public parliamentary involvement in France is focused on the communication of *parliamentary* arguments and less on parliamentary control of *governmental* policy-making. The British House of Commons, despite its weak institutional position, seems to fulfil this parliamentary control function best, because it concentrates on forcing the government to explain and defend its negotiation position publicly. However, as both parliaments mainly depend on their government as the key source of information, they cannot adequately prevent their government from exploiting their gatekeeper position through a strategic transfer of information (Schelling 1960). This asymmetry can only be overcome if parliaments have access to independent information about future and current developments at the European level, the negotiation position of other governments as well as the negotiation behaviour of their own government.

To sum up, if we want to study the active Europeanization of national parliaments in reaction to the challenges of European integration we have to look beyond the formal institutions and take the strategic adaptation of national parliaments into account. At the same time, it has been shown that this strategic Europeanization does not always enhance the democratic quality of European politics. Cooperation behind closed doors does provide for more effective parliamentary influence, but it also reduces the democratic quality of European policies in general. Strategies that aim at public deliberation and scrutiny, on the other hand, contribute to the transparency of policy-making processes and enhance public control. They remain insufficient, however, as long as parliaments rely only on their governments to provide information on European issues. Thus, in order to guarantee democratic legitimacy in European policy-making, national parliaments may have to re-evaluate their roles and search for a combination of different strategies.

NOTES

1. This article is an extended version of my contribution to Auel and Rittberger 2006.
2. This is certainly not the only way that the term 'Europeanization' is used. For a review of different definitions offered in the literature see Featherstone 2003 and Olsen 2002.
3. The article focuses mainly on the Assemblée Nationale but also provides some information on the second chamber of the French Parliament, the Sénat.
4. Due to the relative insignificance of the House of Lords the UK is regarded as an almost-one-chamber-system (Mény and Knapp 1998, p. 185). Still, especially the Lord's Committee on European Legislation has earned high merits with regard to the scrutiny of European matters (Sturm 2003).
5. The competencies of the Parliament may not be limited, not even by Parliament itself. Parliamentary legislation takes absolute priority and hence cannot be revoked by British courts.
6. The first resolution on the scrutiny reserve had been adopted as early as 1980. The current scrutiny reserve is based on the resolution of 18 November 1998; see ESC 2001: Appendix

III, online: http://www.parliament.uk/documents/upload/ESC%20GreenGuide.pdf.

7. In 1978 the Assemblée Nationale rejected a 'projet de loi' (bill) introduced by the government for the transposition of the 6th TVA directive (Nuttens and Sicard 2000, p. 62). Although the government made sure to adopt the bill in another form some days later, the Assemblée was successful 'de porter un coup d'arrêt à la conception peu démocratique que le gouvernement français a de l'Europe' (Laurent Fabius, cf. Nuttens and Sicard 2000, p. 63).
8. Decision DC 92-314 of the Conseil Constitutionnel, 17 December 1992.
9. Certain matters concerning the constitutional order must be regulated by law (a complete list is found in Article 34 of the French Constitution). All other matters fall within the realm of directives according to Article 37.
10. All other European documents (including, for example, the 'Agenda 2000' documents) were transferred as information (*communication*) only, thus preventing parliament from tabling a resolution on them (Assemblée Nationale 1998). Between 1993 and 1998, for example, only 43.7 per cent of the 'First Pillar' documents were formally submitted to Parliament (Sauron 1999, p. 179).
11. In addition, the decision-making process is strongly determined by the federal structure, the specific role of the Bundesrat and its involvement in the legislative process.
12. Until the Maastricht Treaty, the ratification law on the Treaties of Rome (of July 1957 in BGBl. II, p. 753) had been the legal basis for the Bundestag's involvement in European legislation. The government was obliged to 'keep the Bundestag and the Bundesrat informed on developments in the Council of the European Economic Community and the Council of the European Atomic Community', with the information to be given before a decision in the Council in those cases where 'a decision has to be transposed into German law or is directly applicable in Germany'.
13. Several earlier attempts to set up an effective European Affairs Committee failed due to the rivalry with the established standing committees. For details see Bila et al. (1998).
14. The threat to call for early elections can be effective, since elections might lead to the loss of a parliamentary seat for some members, but not necessarily to the formation of an alternative government (Eysell 1996, p. 387ff.) And indeed, elections ahead of schedule are quite frequent (Jesse 1994, p. 185).
15. In 1994, after the Maastricht Treaty took effect, the name was changed to European Affairs Committee (*Europaudvalget*).
16. The decisive provision, which lays down the competence of the Committee, is found in he first *Report* of the Market Relations Committee of 29 March 1973:

    > The Government shall consult the Market Relations Committee of the Folketing in questions relating to EC policy of a major importance so that the regard for the influence of the Folketing as well as the freedom to negotiate are respected. Prior to negotiations in the EC Council of Ministers on decisions of a wider scope, the Government submits an oral mandate for negotiation to the Market Relations Committee. If there is no majority against the mandate, the Government negotiates on this basis (quoted from Folketinget 2002, p. 2).

    The distinction between questions of 'major importance', about which the Government shall inform the Committee, and decisions of 'a wider scope', to which the mandating procedure applies, has become more blurred over time. Today, the Government submits negotiation mandates for practically every European legal document.
17. The following is based on the empirical evidence derived from 68 interviews conducted with Members of the House of Commons, the Assemblée Nationale, the Bundestag and the Folketing.
18. The 16 Departmental Committees of the Parliamentary Labour Party (PLP) cover specific policy fields. While the Committees are not all similarly active, most of them convene about once a month to discuss topical issues. Attendance of the MPs varies with some meetings being attended by just a handful and others by more than a hundred MPs. Although the influence of these Committees on governmental decision-making is disputed,

at least they signal the general parliamentary opinion to the government 'because the MPs who are interested enough in a subject to attend the relevant backbench grouping are also the ones who could cause trouble in more public arenas' (Cowley 2000, p. 16).

19. In the 11th election period, for example, the Delegation produced 101 *rapports d'information*. A complete list of the *rapports d'information* of the Delegation is available at http://www.assemblee-nationale.fr/europe/index-rapinfo-11leg.asp.
20. On 24 September 2003, for example, both committees met in Paris to discuss issues such as the European Constitution and the upcoming Intergovernmental Conference, developments of the CFSP and the new European security strategy as well as aspects of the cohesion policy with regard to EU enlargement.
21. Foreign and European policy-making in Denmark is traditionally based on a broad coalition between the four 'old' parties: The Conservatives (Konservativt Folkeparti), the Liberals (Venstre), the Social Liberal Party (Det Radikale Venstre) and the Social Democrats (Socialdemokratiet). This is also true for the current Folketing, where the liberal-conservative minority government of Prime Minister Anders Fogh Rasmussen is, for the first time, generally supported by the Danish People's Party (DPP) in domestic politics. In European affairs, however, this 'governing coalition' changes. As the nationalistic DPP is violently anti-European, the government cannot and will not rely on its support in the European Affairs Committee but rather forms the traditional 'grand coalition' with the Social Democrats and the Social Liberal Party, currently the main opposition parties.
22. As interviews revealed, this was the main reason in several of the cases in which the Committee completely refused to provide a minister with any mandate.

REFERENCES

Andeweg, Rudy B. and Lia Nijzink (1995), 'Beyond the two-body-image: Relations between ministers and MPs', in Herbert Döring (ed.), *Parliaments and Majority Rule in Western Europe*, Frankfurt a.M. and New York: Campus, pp. 152-78.

Assemblée Nationale (1998), La mise en œuvre de l'article 88-4 de la Constitution et les modifications susceptibles de lui être apportées, rapport d'information n° 1189, présenté par Henri Nallet.

Auel, Katrin and Arthur Benz (2004), 'National parliaments in EU multi-level governance: Dilemmas and strategies of adaptation', *polis-Arbeitspapiere No. 59*, Hagen: FernUniversität, Institute for Political Science, http://www.fernuni-hagen.de/POLALLG/index.htm.

Auel, Katrin and Arthur Benz (2005), 'The politics of adaptation: Europeanisation of national parliamentary systems, *Journal of Legislative Studies*, **11** (3-4), 372-93.

Auel, Katrin and Berthold Rittberger (2006), 'Fluctuant nec merguntur: The European Parliament, national parliaments, and European integration', in Jeremy Richardson (ed.), *European Union: Power and Policy-Making* (3rd ed.), London: Routledge, pp. 121-45.

Benz, Arthur (2001), 'Postparlamentarische Demokratie und kooperativer Staat', in Claus Leggewie and Richard Münch (eds), *Politik im 21. Jahrhundert*, Frankfurt a.M.: Edition Suhrkamp, pp. 263-80.

Benz, Arthur (2003), 'Konstruktive Vetospieler in Mehrebenensystemen', in Renate Mayntz and Wolfgang Streeck (eds), *Die Reformierbarkeit der Demokratie: Innovationen und Blockaden*, Frankfurt and New York: Campus, pp. 205-36.

Bila, Jacqueline, Uwe Gehlen, Hartmut Groos and Beate Hasenjäger (1998), *Der Ausschuss für die Angelegenheiten der Europäischen Union des Deutschen Bundestages*, Bonn: 'Sekretariat des Ausschusses für die Angelegenheiten der Europäischen Union' (2nd ed.).

Carter, Catríona (2001), 'The parliament of the United Kingdom: From supportive scrutiny to unleashed control?', in Andreas Maurer and Wolfgang Wessels (eds), *National Parliaments on their Ways to Europe: Losers or Latecomers?*, Baden-Baden: Nomos, pp. 395-423.

Cot, Jean-Paul (1980), 'Parliament and foreign policy in France', in Antonio Cassese (ed.), *Parliamentary Control over Foreign Policy*, Aalpen an der Rijn: Sijthoff and Noordhoff, pp. 11-24.

Cowley, Philip (2000), 'Can sheep bark? British Labour MPs and the modification of government policy', paper presented at the ECPR Workshop on Parliamentary Control of the Executive, Copenhagen, 14-19 April.

Czada, Roland (1997), 'Vertretung und Verhandlung: Aspekte politischer Konfliktregelung in Mehrebenensystemen', in Arthur Benz and Wolfgang Seibel (eds), *Theorieentwicklung in der Politikwissenschaft – eine Zwischenbilanz*, Baden-Baden: Nomos, pp. 237-60.

Damgaard, Erik (1997), 'The political roles of Danish MPs', *Journal of Legislative Studies*, **3** (1), 79-90.

Damgaard, Erik and Asbjørn Sonne Nørgaard (2000), 'The European Union and Danish parliamentary democracy', *Journal of Legislative Studies*, **6** (1), 33-58.

Dimitrakopoulos, Dionyssis G. (2001), 'Incrementalism and path dependence: European integration and institutional change in national parliaments', *Journal of Common Market Studies*, **39** (3), 405-22.

Döring, Herbert (1994), 'Parlament und Regierung', in Oskar W. Gabriel and Frank Brettschneider (eds), Die *EG-Staaten im Vergleich. Strukturen, Prozesse, Politikinhalte* (2nd ed.), Opladen: Westdeutscher Verlag, pp. 336-58.

Dosenrode, Søren Z. von (1998), 'Denmark: The testing of a hesitant membership', in Kenneth Hanf and Ben Soetendorp (eds), *Adapting to European Integration: Small States and the European Union*, London and New York: Longman, pp. 52-68.

Evans, Peter B., Harold K. Jacobson and Robert D. Putnam (eds) (1993), *Double-Edged Diplomacy: International Bargaining and Domestic Politics*, Berkeley: University of California Press.

Eysell, Maria (1996), 'Der dänische Minderheitsparlamentarismus der achtziger Jahre', *Zeitschrift für Politikwissenschaft*, **6** (2), 375-407.

Featherstone, Kevin (2003), 'Introduction: In the name of "Europe"?', in Kevin Featherstone and Claudio M. Radaelli (eds), *The Politics of Europeanization*, Oxford: Oxford University Press, pp. 3-26.

Folketinget (2002), *The European Affairs Committee of the Folketing: Parliamentary Control of Government Policy in the EU*, Copenhagen: EU Information Centre of the Folketing.

Frears, John (1990), 'The French parliament: Loyal workhorse, poor watchdog', *West European Politics*, **13** (3), 32-51 (special issue on: Parliaments in Western Europe, ed. by Philip Norton).

HC 791/98: Select Committee on the Modernisation of the House of Commons Seventh Report on 'The Scrutiny of European Business', 17.06.1998.

HC 152-xxx/02: European Scrutiny Committee Thirtieth Report on 'European Scrutiny in the House of Commons', 22.05.2002.

Helms, Ludger (2002), *Politische Opposition: Theorie und Praxis in westlichen Regierungssystemen*, Opladen: Leske und Budrich.

Héritier, Adrienne (1999), *Policy-Making and Diversity in Europe: Escaping Deadlock*, Cambridge: Cambridge University Press.

Hourquebie, Francis (1999), *Organes spécialisés dans les affaires communautaires des parlements nationaux: Le cas français et allemande*, Paris: ed. l'Harmattan.

House of Commons (2002), *Standing Orders of the House of Commons*, Public Business, London.

Ismayr, Wolfgang (2001), *Der Deutsche Bundestag im politischen System der Bundesrepublik Deutschland*, Opladen: Leske und Budrich.

Jesse, Eckhard (1994), 'Wahlsysteme und Wahlrecht', in Oskar W. Gabriel and Frank Brettschnei-der (eds), *Die EG-Staaten im Vergleich: Strukturen, Prozesse, Politikinhalte*, 2nd revised and extended ed., Opladen: Westdeutscher Verlag, pp. 174-93.

Judge, David (1995), 'The failure of national parliaments?', *West European Politics*, **18** (3), 79-100.

Kessler, Marie-Christine (1999), La *politique étrangère de la France : Acteurs et processus*, Paris: Presses de Sciences Po.

Laursen, Finn (1995), 'Parliamentary bodies specializing in European Union affairs: Denmark and the European Committee of the Folketing', in Finn Laursen and Spyros A. Pappas (eds), *The Changing Role of Parliaments in the European Union*, Maastricht: European Institute of Public Administration, pp. 43-60.

Laursen, Finn (2001), 'The Danish Folketing and its European Affairs Committee: Strong players in the national policy cycle', in Andreas Maurer and Wolfgang Wessels (eds), *National Parliaments on their Ways to Europe: Losers or Latecomers?*, Baden-Baden: Nomos, pp. 99-115.

Laursen, Finn and Spyros A. Pappas (1995) (eds), *The Changing Role of Parliaments in the European Union*, Maastricht: European Institute of Public Administration

Lijphart, Arend (1999), *Patterns of Democracy: Government Forms and Performance in Thirty-six Countries*, New Haven: Yale University Press.

Maurer, Andreas and Wolfgang Wessels (eds) (2001), *National Parliaments on their Ways to Europe: Losers or Latecomers?*, Baden-Baden: Nomos.

Mény, Yves and Andrew Knapp (1998), *Government and Politics in Western Europe: Britain, France, Italy, Germany*, Oxford: Oxford University Press.

Moravcsik, Andrew (1994), 'Why the European Community strengthens the state: Domestic politics and international cooperation', *Working Paper Series No. 52*, Cambridge, MA: Center for European Studies, Harvard University.

Nannestad, Peter (2003), 'Das politische System Dänemarks', in Wolfgang Ismayr (ed.), *Die politischen Systeme Westeuropas*, Opladen: Leske und Budrich, pp. 55-92.

Norton, Philip (1994), 'The legislative powers of parliament', in Cees Flintermann (ed.), *The Evolving Role of Parliaments in Europe*, Antwerpen: Maklu, pp. 15-32.

Norton, Philip (1996a), 'Conclusion: Addressing the democratic deficit', in Philip Norton (ed.), *National Parliaments and the European Union*, London: Frank Cass, pp. 177-93.

Norton, Philip (ed.) (1996b), *National Parliaments and the European Union*, London: Frank Cass.

Nuttens, Jean-Dominique and François Sicard (2000), *Assemblées parlementaires et organisations européennes*, Paris: La documentation Française.

Olsen, Johan (2002), 'The many faces of Europeanization', *Journal of Common Market Studies*, **40** (5), 921-52.

Polsby, Nelson W. (1975), 'Legislatures', in Fred I. Greenstein and Nelson W. Polsby (eds), *Governmental Institutions and Processes* (*Handbook of Political Science*, vol. 5), Reading, MA: Addison-Wesley, pp. 257-319.

Putnam, Robert (1988), 'Diplomacy and domestic politics: The logic of two-level games', *International Organization*, **42** (3), 427-60.

Raunio, Tapio and Simon Hix (2000), 'Backbenchers learn to fight back: European integration and parliamentary government', *West European Politics*, **23** (4), 142-68.

Rush, Michael (2000), 'Parliamentary Scrutiny', in Robert Pyper and Lynton Robins (eds), *United Kingdom Governance*, Houndsmill, Basingstoke and London: Macmillan, pp. 107-37.

Sauron, Jean-Luc (1999), 'Le contrôle parlementaire de l'activité gouvernementale en matière communautaire en France', *Revue trimestrielle de droit européen*, **35**, 171-91.

Scharpf, Fritz W., Bernd Reissert and Fritz Schnabel (1976), *Politikverflechtung: Theorie und Empirie des kooperativen Föderalismus in der Bundesrepublik Deutschland*, Kronberg: Scriptor.

Schelling, Thomas (1960), *The Strategy of Conflict*, Cambridge: Harvard University Press.

Schütt-Wetschky, Eberhard (2000), 'Gewaltenteilung zwischen Legislative und Exekutive?', *Aus Politik und Zeitgeschichte*, B-**28**, 5-12.

Smith, Eivind (ed.) (1996), *National Parliaments as Cornerstones of European Integration*, London: Kluwer Law.

Sturm, Roland (2003), 'Das politische System Großbritanniens', in Wolfgang Ismayr (ed.), *Die politischen Systeme Westeuropas* (3rd ed.), Opladen: Leske und Budrich, pp. 225-62.

Szukala, Andrea and Olivier Rozenberg (2001), 'The French parliament and the EU: Progressive assertion and strategic investment', in Andreas Maurer and Wolfgang Wessels (eds), *National Parliaments on their Ways to Europe: Losers or Latecomers?*, Baden-Baden: Nomos, pp. 223-50.

10. National Parliamentary Scrutiny: Comparing Rules, Institutions and Behaviour

Ronald Holzhacker

The national parliaments of the member states of the European Union (EU) have been losing power. Decisions that parliaments traditionally had the right and power to decide are increasingly being made either within the institutions of the EU or by the national executives of the member states. The law making powers of national parliaments in important areas of policy are being tightly circumscribed by the EU. This is the case not only for agricultural policy, trade policy, competition policy, indeed in many aspects of economic policy, but also for areas reserved until recently for national decision-making, such as justice and home affairs. But as the EU has been extended to include more and more policy areas, national parliaments and parliamentary party groups acting therein began to realize the loss and adapted their institutional structures to claw back some lost power. This process intensified after treaty revisions in the late 1980s and early 1990s further deepened European cooperation. Today, all national parliaments in the member states have established some kind of European affairs committee (EAC) within their parliament to improve parliamentary scrutiny over the decision-making of their own government concerning EU matters. These committees typically focus on the negotiating position taken by their government in Council of Minister meetings.

National parliamentary scrutiny over EU matters must be seen within the perspective of the overall relationship – legal, institutional and behavioural – which exists between any parliament and its government. Nevertheless, the power to scrutinize the national government varies from the traditional law-making powers of parliament, and in many cases emerges from specific legal rules, institutional structures, and party behaviours unique to this type of parliamentary activity. The purpose of this chapter is to construct a model for comparatively assessing national parliamentary power over EU decision-making in the member states. This essay proposes a set of eight criteria for assessing this power. It then uses this model to assess the power of the national parliament to scrutinize their government's EU decision-making in four member states: the UK, Netherlands, Germany and Denmark.

METHODOLOGY

To understand an institution and analyse its relation to other institutions in a system of government, we must understand the formal rules which give it delineated powers, the institutional structure developed to exercise these powers, and gain an understanding of how strategic actors use these rules and institutions to achieve their objectives.

These three levels of analysis require different methodological approaches. The study of formal rules governing relations between actors, including constitutional provisions, statutory law and rules of procedure is traditionally the work of legal scholars. Here the analysis proceeds in the first instance from the rules themselves – the language and construction of the law. The analysis may continue by looking at supporting documents *preceding* the rules' creation, such as reports and debates, in an attempt to understand the intent of the parties. The analysis may continue through an analysis of events *antecedent* to the rules, to see how the rules have been interpreted and used by the parties themselves. In this case that would mean not only how parliament and the government have interpreted a certain legal rule governing their relationship, but also how competent judicial authorities have interpreted the rule. Moving to the next level of analysis, research into institutional structures is a traditional focus of political science. Here, an analysis of the institutional structures created by parliament for scrutinizing the government is necessary. Finally, the analysis of how actors use these institutions, an important scholarly focus since the behavioural revolution in political science, is done here through intensive interviewing in order to understand the actions and motivations of the actors.

The chapter first presents the set of criteria for evaluating parliamentary power to scrutinize EU decision-making by national governments and then analyses four parliaments using these criteria. Because the power of scrutiny over EU matters must be seen in the context of the overall relationship of executive-legislative relations in a country, the four countries have been chosen to represent a country with a majority government, two coalition governments (that differ in their typical coalition characteristics) and a minority government. Traditionally the type of government formed in a country has a great deal of influence on its executive-legislative relations, and the four countries were thus selected based on the expectation that important differences will also emerge in the analysis of national parliamentary scrutiny over EU decision-making.

REPRESENTATION AND LEGITIMACY AND THE POWER TO SCRUTINIZE

Representation and legitimacy of government decision-making emerges in the first instance from parliament – the body directly elected by the people in periodic, competitive elections. It is not sufficient that a parliament installs a government at the beginning of the term or holds the ultimate power to dissolve government. Representation and legitimacy demands an ongoing, continual role for parliament. Networks of interest groups, either within nation states or across borders, and forms of participatory democracy like referendums, initiatives and consensus-building consultations do not replace the central role of parliament in a democratic system.

Traditional concepts of executive-legislative relations emphasize two formal powers of parliament: (1) installing a government and powers of dissolution, and (2) law-making powers.

But parliamentary oversight and scrutiny over government decision-making is becoming an increasingly important power of parliaments. One of course needs to understand the formal constitutional powers and laws that give parliaments powers to conduct scrutiny over the government – but these are just the starting point, the rules of the game, in which a very important strategic game is played. The players are the governing and opposition parties in parliament. This game works quite differently in systems with a one-party majority government, those with a coalition government or systems with a minority government.

One of the reasons that national parliamentary scrutiny is so important for increasing the legitimacy and participation in the process of European decision-making is that it is the primary institutional source for receiving input from opposition parties. In the Council of Ministers, only governments – elected from governing parties – are represented and participate in setting European policy. Yet traditional democratic structures normally allow some opportunity for opposition parties to discuss and debate laws and policies set by the government. They are normally given power to pose written and oral questions, to raise matters in committee, and to place matters on the agenda for general debate. It is important that the voice of opposition parties is heard at the national level, because the voice of opposition parties is non-existent or weak within the EU institutions themselves.

The voice of these non-governing parties is not heard in the Council, or the Commission, and only rather weakly in the European Parliament (EP).

Because the EP does not formally vote a government into office in the way a national parliament does, it lacks the traditional division of parliament into governing and opposition party roles. To understand how national parliamentary scrutiny over EU matters functions in the member states, we must analyse the interaction between governing parties and opposition parties in the process of scrutinizing their national executive.

Parliamentary scrutiny is the exercise of power by the legislative branch to control, influence or monitor government decision-making. These three terms refer to various degrees of influence that parliament may have on the government. Dahl defines the term 'influence' as 'a relation among actors such that the wants, desires, preferences or intentions of one or more actors affect the actions, or predisposition to act, of one or more other actors' (Dahl 1989).[1] Dahl furthermore states that this influence may either be 'manifest', in which parliament explicitly acts to achieve a given outcome, or 'implicit', in which parliament is successful in achieving a given outcome without taking any overt actions because a government may act in anticipation of reactions from parliament.

Parliamentary scrutiny may occur publicly in the formal institutions of parliament, such as committees, public hearings, the submission of written or oral questions and plenum debate. These activities may also occur privately within the various institutions of parliamentary groups, such as parliamentary party group meetings, committees or working groups of the party groups, and informal consultations between specialists in the party group and government ministers.

CHAINS OF REPRESENTATION IN THE EU AND THE MEMBER STATES

Modern representative democracy is based on an institutional structure in which parliaments elected by the people enact laws and hold executives responsible for government decision-making and the policy outputs of the political system. It is believed that representation and democratic legitimacy emerge from the process of political parties competing for the people's vote, forming a government from this parliament thereafter and then ensuring that both governing and opposition parties may play an active and ongoing role in passing laws and scrutinizing government decision-making and policy outputs. Traditionally these policy outputs are national laws and policies (and treaties with foreign countries), but now must include the government's position taken within the EU, principally actions and votes taken in the Council of Ministers.

Figure 1.1 in the introduction to this book illustrates an abstracted and simplified view of the two chains of representation within the formal institutional system of democracy in the EU and the member states. A chain of representation should link voter preferences through a series of deliberative (parliamentary) and decision-making (government) institutions to the policy outputs of the system to assure democratic representation and legitimacy.

If we first follow the path of representation through the EU institutions, we see the input of the views and preferences of the citizens (at least those who chose to vote in the elections) of the EU being expressed during the elections for the EP. Then, to the extent that the EP has various rights and powers, from consultation to co-decision within the institutional structure of the EU, the voice of the citizens are heard through the individual members of the EP and the party family groups which they form. However, because the EP does not directly decide and elect a European government like a national parliament does, but instead is given only limited rights and powers vis-à-vis the European Commission, the chain of representation is incomplete (or indeed, broken). This means that the chain of representation through the EU institutions, linking voter preferences and choice expressed during elections to decision-making and policy outputs, is incomplete because of the limited powers of the EP over the two executive institutions of the EU, the European Commission and the Council of Ministers. This institutional structure is a primary cause of the 'democratic deficit' in the EU.

But there is another chain of representation that could potentially link the Council of Ministers into a democratic chain of representation. If we now follow the left-hand side of Figure 1.1, a chain of representation which exists in each of the member states is illustrated. Here the citizens' preferences are expressed in national elections, in which candidates, or more typically polit-ical parties, are competing for the national parliament. This national parliament then elects a national government, a Prime Minister and a cabinet, which is responsible for both national policy-making and casting a vote in the Council of Minister meetings of the EU. These national parliaments not only directly elect a government at the beginning of the term and have lawmaking powers, but also have the power to scrutinize the government's positions taken in the Council of Ministers.

Of course, some matters are decided exclusively within the EU institutions themselves, principally the European Commission, and do not appear on the agenda of the Council of Ministers. Democratic representation through the national parliaments does not occur for these matters.

THE COMPARATIVE ASSESSMENT OF PARLIAMENTARY POWER TO SCRUTINIZE

Formal Rules

The first base of parliamentary rights of scrutiny to be discussed is the formal rules. These rules – including constitutional provisions, statutory law and procedural rules – give parliament formal powers, and may be cited by parliament in their dealings with the government. These rules normally are given the utmost respect by government, and are sometimes enforceable by involving other constitutional bodies, such as the highest court of the land, in any disputes over their application. Legal rules are especially important and valuable for opposition parties, for they provide rights to the parliament which are not easily waived by the governing parties through pressure by the government.

Constitutional provisions
The highest of these legal rules, and the first criteria for assessing parliamentary powers of scrutiny, are constitutional provisions or decisions from the highest court in the land concerning parliamentary rights of scrutiny over EU decision-making in the country. These provisions and decisions could provide parliament with important rights of timely information, consultation, and decision-making powers over the government when acting at the EU level. These give certain powers to parliament which it may claim vis-à-vis the government and which would be difficult for the government to violate.

Constitutional structure: existence of second chamber with competency
The second criteria for assessing parliamentary powers of scrutiny has to do with the constitutional structure of the state. In countries with a strong second chamber which possesses some competency to scrutinize the government and must pass laws related to EU directives, the powers of the first chamber are strengthened. This may occur because of different strengths of the parliamentary party groups in the two chambers. For example, whereas members of one party may be in opposition in the lower chamber, if their party is part of the majority coalition in the upper chamber, it can be expected that the lower chamber has more power to scrutinize the government because the position of the opposition parties are increased.

Laws and procedural rules of parliament
The third criteria are laws and rules, which although below the level of constitutional provisions, have either been agreed to by government and passed into law by parliament or are procedural rules decided by the parliament to

structure its relationship with government and acquiesced to by successive governments. These laws and rules provide formal rules to proscribe the relationship between parliament and government in the conduct of scrutiny over EU decision-making. Like constitutional provisions, these laws and rules are especially important to opposition parties, because their rights of scrutiny cannot be waived by the governing parties upon government pressure. Because of the alternation of power between governing and opposition parties over successive elections, parties see the advantage that these laws and procedural rules have for preserving the powers of parliament and the interest of the various political parties represented therein, whether at the moment in government or in opposition.

Institutions

Establishing specialized institutional bodies within parliament, like the EACs (with various names, but similar functions) which all the parliaments of the member states have now created, is a way to focus the power of parliament to scrutinize the decision-making process of the government on EU matters. These particular committees play an especially important role in fulfilling this function of parliament because the parliament as a whole rarely gets the chance to consider these matters, unlike the situation when parliament is acting within its law-making powers. Before their universal creation, having such a specialized committee or not, would have been an important criteria for evaluating the power of parliament vis-à-vis its government when scrutinizing on EU matters. Now that all parliaments have established such a committee, the two criteria presented focus on how the membership of this committee is selected and the extent to which other committees in parliament also play a role in this scrutinizing function beyond the EAC.

Overlapping membership

The fourth criterion for evaluating the power of a parliament to scrutinize is the extent that membership on the EAC overlaps with the membership of other important committees in parliament. This is a way of bringing diverse expertise to the committee, which broadens and strengthens its knowledge and allows the committee to understand the implications of policy in one area and prepared by one ministry, with other policy areas. Overlapping membership also allows knowledge learned about the EU and its operation from service on the EAC to be used when the member of parliament is acting on another committee. A system of overlapping membership both focuses a diverse expertise on the committee, and it distributes expertise on the EU to the other committees of parliament, thus involving larger parts of the parliament in the process of scrutiny when necessary. This institutional feature clearly strengthens the power of parliament vis-à-vis the government.

Involvement of other committees

The extent that other committees in parliament also discuss EU matters and upcoming business on the Council of Ministers agenda is another indicator of parliamentary power. It allows a specialized committee to consider matters arising for the government at the EU level, in terms of the committee's own institutional expertise of the policy area. Thus, the involvement of other committees proceeds even further than a system of overlapping membership, but allows the full institutional competency of the specialized committee to analyse EU matters, increasing parliamentary power as a result.

Party Behaviour

The final base of parliamentary power emerges from the actions of the most important collective actors in parliament, the political parties. The power of parties emerges not only from the collective ability of like-minded MPs to stand together and from institutional rules and procedures to conduct scrutiny. The power emerges from their democratic legitimacy, as the object of vote choice from the electorate, and their role in electing the government or standing as the loyal opposition. The power of parliament vis-à-vis their government to scrutinize emanates from three organizational relationships: the one between governing parties and their government, between governing and opposition parties, and between members of parliament within each parliamentary party group.

Power of governing parties for agenda-setting

The relationship between the governing parties and government is the sixth indicator of parliamentary power. Here the question is, how much power do the governing parties have to set the agenda in parliament, and how much power does the government have? Here we see a progression from governing parties where the power of the parliamentary power group is fused with government power, giving governing parties great power to set the parliamentary power because their power is fused with that of the power of the government, to systems with a separation of powers and thus a competition to set the agenda, to systems where the agenda is clearly set by the government and enforced through a whip system in parliament.

Power of opposition parties

The role of opposition parties in a parliamentary system is very important in holding the government accountable and challenging the government with policy alternatives, in ways the governing parties may be unable or unwilling to accept. As such, opposition parties play an essential role in a democratic system, and ensure that alternative views in society are heard during government decision-making. Although differences in the formal rights of op-position parties are apparent between various parliaments, for example how much time they are given to determine the agenda in the plenum or their ability to place oral or written questions to challenge the government, their greatest power emerges when the governing parties need the support of opposition parties in support of their own aims. For example, opposition parties in countries with a minority government have a great deal of power because the governing parties need their support to pass legislation or to effectively scrutinize the government and give government a mandate to negotiate. In countries with coalition governments, occasionally a governing party will temporarily side with an opposition party to bring government policy closer to its own preferences, thus giving opposition parties power in the system. The power of opposition parties is most limited in countries with a majority government; here the opposition may rely only on its formal powers of op-position contained in the rules and traditions of the parliament.

A final source of power for opposition parties in the lower chamber emerges if the party has real power in the second chamber. In such cases, an opposition party may argue that the governing parties should discuss and compromise matters in the lower chamber, because otherwise the party will use its strength in the upper chamber to block or modify the government's proposal. Thus, the type of government formed out of a parliament (whether majority, coalition or minority) and the formal powers and the distribution of party strength in the upper chamber, has a great deal of impact on the power of opposition parties to set the agenda and thus on the overall power of parliament.

Distribution of power within the parliamentary parties

The final criteria for judging parliamentary power to scrutinize the government is the distribution of power within the parliamentary party groups in the parliament. A system that both organizes the parliamentary party members to discuss and act collectively in their committee work, and when necessary to share information and build consensus in meetings of the entire parliamentary party group, combines the advantages of specialization and expertise with the power of the entire party. This system increases the power of parliament vis-à-vis the government by allowing members of parliament to approach or surpass (by having knowledge of activities across different policy areas by different ministries) the expertise of the ministries, and then rallying the rest of the parliamentary party group around this position to add the power of numbers.

THE EMPIRICAL ASSESSMENT OF POWER IN FOUR COUNTRIES

We are now ready to evaluate the power of four parliaments when scrutinizing their government's decision-making on EU matters in terms of their formal rules, institutions and party behaviour. The information in this section was gathered by an analysis of materials produced by the EACs in the four countries and interviews conducted by the author with the leading member of parliament from most of the parties serving on their parliament's EAC.[2]

Formal Rules

Constitutional provisions

Germany's Basic Law, which serves as its constitution, contains specific provisions that structure the relationship between parliament and government for purposes of conducting scrutiny over EU matters. The German method of structuring such scrutiny with constitutional provisions, statutory law and procedural rules of parliament is consistent with their tradition of clearly delineating powers in a *Rechtstaat*.

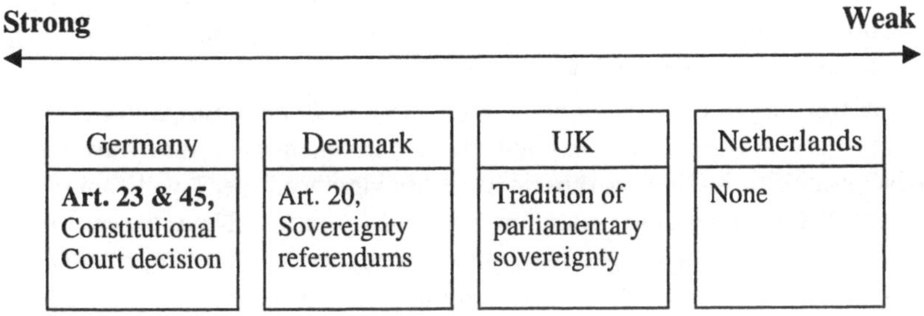

Figure 10.1 Constitutional provisions

Two articles were added to the Basic Law during the ratification process of the Maastricht Treaty, a time that corresponded with a general rethinking and reappraisal of the constitutional organization of German democracy following reunification. Article 23 of the Basic Law has specific provisions that give the Bundestag powers of information and the power of *Mitwirkungsrechte*. This concept lies somewhere between the ideas of consultation and codecision between parliament and government, the true nature of which will only be determined over time by the behaviour and practices of government and parliament. That is, either through the development of tradition or through appeal and interpretation by the other constitutional body involved, the *Bundesverfassungsgericht* (Constitutional Court). Article 23 also gives the Bundesrat special powers to approve EU measures in fields where the Länder have competency.

Article 45 of the Basic Law establishes the European Affairs Committee (*Der Ausschuss für die Angelegenheiten der Europaeischen Union des Deutschen Bundestages*) and allows it to act decisively and authoritatively when the parliament is in recess or unavailable to consider pressing matters.

Articles 23 and 45 were given additional weight and importance because the *Bundesverfassungsgericht* issued an unusually strong decision that indicated that increased rights of oversight by the parliament over the government's EU decision-making was necessary to protect the Basic Law's enshrinement of democratic principles of representative government. In its Maastricht Decision (issued 12 October 1992) the court warned that principles embodied in the Basic Law mean that transfers of German sovereignty to the EU depend on the appropriate development of democratic institutions and procedures (*demokratischen Grundlagen*) over time (*schritthaltend*) at the EU level, but that nevertheless the Bundestag must continue to play a substantial role in democratic legitimation. The decision of the court puts the other constitutional bodies, the Bundestag and Bundesrat, as well as the government on notice that it stands behind and will enforce if necessary the constitutional provisions enshrined in the two articles, as well as the general principles of democratic representation, legitimacy and the protection of individual rights found in the Basic Law.

The wording of the constitutions of the three other countries under consideration here are much less explicit about parliamentary scrutiny over EU decision-making by their governments, not having been specifically amended to take the contemporary situation into consideration. Nevertheless, next in order of parliamentary power provided by constitutional principle is Denmark, where Article 20 of the constitution states that there should be no transfer of Danish sovereignty unless a referendum is held. This provision has given the Danish parliament and government constitutional arguments for consulting with the people before agreeing to new EU treaties among the member states.

But the provision may also be seen as insinuating a general constitutional preference for parliamentary scrutiny over important EU matters when reached by the government, even when today these decisions are accomplished by routine decision-making by the EU and the member states, instead of being party of a treaty between sovereign states, as envisioned when this provision of the Danish constitution was written. Thus national parliamentary scrutiny over government decision-making in EU matters can be interpreted as emanating from a constitutional principle (or preference) which holds that measures that give up Danish sovereignty be carefully reviewed and approved by the parliament or the people. Some scholars will certainly argue that this argument goes too far as a matter of law, but certainly it could be argued that strong parliamentary scrutiny over EU matters is part of the spirit of the Danish constitution and the rights of the people enshrined therein.

Next in line in terms of constitutions giving power to parliament is the UK. While the UK has no written constitution, it has a strong tradition of parliamentary sovereignty, which is considered a fundamental tenet of the unwritten constitution. This gives parliament and the people a strong argument for the power to scrutinize government decision-making related to the EU. The political and societal arguments about British sovereignty certainly emerge in part from this fundamental tenet of the constitution.

The Dutch constitution is the weakest of the four countries in terms of specific constitutional provisions that could provide the parliament with arguments for strong parliamentary control over EU decision-making. Instead the general ideas of parliamentary democracy and government accountability, and traditions of government consultation and consensus decision-making, must be cited as the constitutional frame for parliamentary scrutiny over EU decision-making by the government.

Constitutional structures – second chamber

The powers of an upper chamber in a parliament to conduct parliamentary scrutiny over EU decision-making may influence the power which the lower democratically elected chamber has through the political interactions between the two chambers.

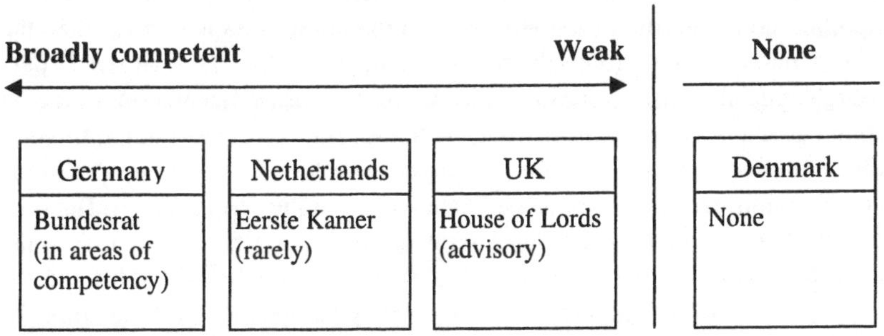

Figure 10.2 Constitutional structures – second chamber

The existence of a strong second parliamentary chamber with specific powers exists in Germany because of the federal nature of the state. In terms of its role in EU decision-making, Article 23 gives the Bundesrat the right to be provided with information concerning EU proposals and government decision-making towards EU matters, and even to take the place of the government in EU institutions for issues that under the constitution the Länder are given exclusive competency.

The number of votes each Land is given in the Bundesrat is determined by agreement and is roughly dependent on the population of each Land. How these votes will be cast as a block is decided by each Land government, which is elected from their Land parliament. Thus, because of the different polities in the Länder and different election periods, there are often different political majorities in the Bundestag and Bundesrat. The effect of this institutional arrangement is to strengthen the role of opposition parties in the Bundestag itself and give them enhanced power to scrutinize the government. The governing parties in the Bundestag and the government have an incentive to consult and make compromises with opposition parties in the Bundes-tag if they know that their political brethren in the upper chamber could block or amend the government proposal.

The Netherlands is a distant second in the measurement of power which an upper chamber may provide to a lower chamber. The Dutch Eerste Kamer, consisting of representatives from the provinces, only occasionally discusses EU matters.

The British House of Lords, despite reforms diminishing the power of hereditary life peers and providing for government appointment of some of the Lords, the body remains unelected and non-democratic. In terms of parliamentary scrutiny over EU matters, the body may be able to influence the views of political parties or the public. It may also play a role in the interpretation of law when sitting as the highest court in the land. The most important concrete role of the House of Lords in this area is to scrutinize the EU's general policy proposals contained in the White and Green Papers through special hearings organized by its committees. The subcommittee on foreign policy headed by Sir William Wallace, also a professor at the London School of Economics, has been especially notable. The periodic committee and subcommittee reports on broad areas of EU policy have been influential with the EAC (called the Select Committee on European Legislation) in the House of Commons and more broadly within British political circles and the public. This work of the House of Lords may be seen as strengthening the tradition of national parliamentary scrutiny over both the EU and national government decision-making towards the EU, and thus indirectly strengthening the power of the House to scrutinize.

Denmark does not have a second chamber, so there are no interaction effects between two parliamentary bodies to discuss.

Formal institutional laws and rules of parliament

At the time of accession to the EU, Denmark passed a specific law signed by the government. It governs the interaction between parliament and the government and gives the parliament powers to scrutinize the government in its EU decision-making. The Accession Act of 1972 reads in part: 'The Government informs a committee set up by the Folketing about proposals for Council decisions which become directly applicable in Denmark, or the fulfilling of which requires the approval of the Folketing' (Section 6, subsection 2).

Strong ←——————————————————→ **Weak**

Mandate Required	To be Consulted and to Guide	To be Informed and Time for Debate	To be Informed and Time for Debate
Denmark Netherlands (3rd pillar) 'Mandate'	Germany *'Mitwirkungs-rechte'* *'Begleiten'*	UK 'Scrutiny Reserve' (1st pillar)	Netherlands (1st and 2nd pillars)

Figure 10.3 Formal institutional laws and rules of parliament

However, the decisive provision which establishes the unique form of national parliamentary scrutiny which the Folketing possesses, requiring the government to receive a mandate for the government negotiating position before a Council of Minister meeting, is found in an agreement reached between the parliament and government and announced in the first Report of the EEC Committee (forerunner to the present committee) on 29 March 1973: The Government shall consult with the EEC Committee of the Folketing in questions relating to EC policy of a major importance so that the regard for the influence of the Folketing as well as the freedom to negotiate are respected.

Prior to negotiations in the EC Council of Ministers on decisions of a wider scope, the government submits an oral mandate for negotiation to the EEC Committee. If there is no majority against the mandate, the government negotiates on this basis'.

The EAC (called *Europaudvalget*) in a report issued October 1996 notes that the interpretation of the expressions 'major importance' (requiring the government to inform the committee) and 'decisions of a wider scope' (requiring the government to submit an oral mandate for negotiation) have undergone development over time.[3] Thus, Danish governments in practice now submit all questions of 'major importance' to the committee. In fact, the committee argues: 'The provision which says that the EAC takes a stand on the mandate for negotiation of the Government prior to the meetings in the Council of Ministers in the EU has been observed indisputably by all Governments since 1973. Thus the provision has become part of the existing *constitutional law of Denmark*' (p. 3, italics in the original).

Next in line in terms of laws and parliamentary regulations that give parliament power to scrutinize their government's decision-making in EU matters is Germany. The German parliament passed a law entitled the *Zusammenarbeitsgesetz Bundesregierung – Deutcher Bundestag* (EUZBBG) (Cooperation Law Federal Government – German Bundestag), which adds details to the general framework agreed to in Article 23 and makes the rights of parliament more concrete and enforceable. It requires the government to provide the Bundestag not only with documentation from the EU from the very earliest stages of proposals, but also to inform the parliament of the government's own position in these negotiations, as well as those of the EP, the European Commission and the other national parliaments. This information greatly strengthens the possibility of effective national parliamentary control because it allows the parliament to see 'political' arguments on various sides of a proposal, instead of merely the EU proposal. Additionally, by hearing about the prospective points of view of other national governments, members of the European affairs committee (normally referred to as the *EU-Ausschuss*) can better judge on which issues their scrutiny may most effectively affect the final outcome of the EU decision-making process.

In addition to the constitutional articles and laws, there are formal parliamentary procedures of the German parliament (Sections 93 and 93a *Geschaeftsordnung des Deutschen Bundestages*, 15 December 1994 edition) and of the EAC (*Verfahrensgrundsaetze*, 25 October 1995), which delineate in ever greater detail how the German Bundestag will exercise its powers of parliamentary scrutiny.

Whereas Denmark's Folketing has the right to control the government's positions taken in Council of Minister meetings by requiring the government to seek a mandate in the EAC, and the German Bundestag has the right to be consulted and to guide the government, the British House of Commons claims only a 'Scrutiny Reserve'. This applies only to first pillar decision-making (the original European Community, with the creation of a Single Market as principal goal). The claim of a right to this scrutiny reserve has generally, but not without occasional lapses, been respected and adhered to by the government. This power, originally resting on the undertakings of successive governments, was formalized by Resolution of the House on 30 October 1980 and then broadened and strengthened in a new Resolution on

24 October 1990.[4] The scrutiny reserve requires that a minister of the government normally may not give agreement in the Council of Ministers to any proposal for EC legislation which is still being examined by the Select Committee on European Legislation or has been sent to one of the two European Standing Committees or to the whole House for further debate. Thus the Scrutiny Reserve requirement gives the parliament the right to demand that the government grants it time to consider matters and debate them before the government may vote in the Council of Ministers. After the House has been given the time, the government is entitled to vote as it wishes in the Council of Ministers. Any further control the parliament may exercise substantively over the issue may happen only through political means by criticizing the position taken in the Council of Minister meeting by the government, either in one of the House committees, the floor of the House or in the media. Of course, the parliamentary majority also has the ultimate power to express its displeasure with a government decision through a vote of non-confidence and the dissolution of Parliament.

Additional parliamentary procedures, found in Standing Order 127, call on the government to deposit certain documents related to the first pillar of the EU and to attach an 'Explanatory Memorandum'. These are prepared by the government department responsible for the subject and signed by the responsible minister and summarizes: the subject matter of the document, the legal basis for EU decision-making in the area and procedural issues for how the document will be considered, an assessment of the document in terms of the principle of subsidiarity, the government's policy towards the proposal, including any criticism, financial implications for Britain (including in some cases, a detailed Compliance Cost Assessment, showing the impact of the proposal on business or a cost–benefit analysis), the timetable of the decision-making process in the EU institutions and indications of previous considerations by Parliament.

The Standing Order also requires the government to transmit certain documents related to the two intergovernmental decision-making pillars under the Treaty on European Union (TEU), the second pillar (Common Foreign and Security Policy) and third pillar (Justice and Home Affairs).

Both Houses of Parliament have special powers that control the UK's possible entry into the third stage of the European Monetary Union (EMU) and the adoption of the Euro as the national currency. According to the European Communities (Amendment) Act of 1993, which incorporated the Treaty on European Union into British law, an Act of Parliament must be passed to enter the third stage of EMU and adopt the Euro.

The Netherlands has the thinnest statutory basis to guide its conduct of scrutiny, with the notable exception of decision-making under the third pillar, among the four countries under consideration here. Instead parliamentary procedures guide how the government shall consult with parliament, requiring documents from the EU and a short form called 'fiches', which briefly describes the proposal, indicates the possible consequences for national law and lists the ministry that has been given primary responsibility for conducting the negotiations on behalf of the Netherlands.

There is a statutory basis for the power of the Tweede Kamer to scrutinize the government's position taking on issues in the third pillar (Justice and Home affairs). An amendment to the bill approving the TEU adopted in November 1992 declares that the government is obliged to make public and provide to the States-General with draft proposals and to obtain the consent of (or be given tacit consent if no action is taken within 15 days of the draft being submitted) the States-General (Tweede Kamer and Eerste Kamer) before the Council of Ministers makes any decisions under Title VI of the TEU.

Parliamentary Institutions

The second set of criteria in the model establishing criteria to assess parliamentary powers vis-à-vis the government concerns the specific institutional arrangements made in the parliament to scrutinize the government's EU decision-making. The two criteria concern; first, concentrating expertise from throughout the parliament onto the EAC so that a single committee has a broad degree of knowledge of the EU across many important policy areas, and second, distributing consideration across the specialist policy committees (i.e. justice and home affairs, environment or transportation committee) to involve their in-depth knowledge of the policy area. This process of concentrating and distributing power need not be contradictory, because consideration by different committees may be consecutive or simultaneous.

Overlapping membership

Overlapping membership with the specialized committees gives the EAC overall knowledge of and expertise in EU institutions and procedures, and the government's cross-ministerial decision-making, giving it the power to understand the connections and developments at the EU and national government levels across different policy areas. This knowledge and experience of the specialized institutions, procedures and latest developments, which cross policy fields, give a committee knowledge to construct persuasive arguments necessary after breaking through the government's superior ability to have a broader overview of developments at the EU level. In reality, at times the EAC because of the longer tenure of some of its members and the broad discussions the committee has with different ministers, the committee may be more aware of the connections between issues than a particular ministry or minister. Ministries are hierarchical organizations with specialized competencies, and interministerial rivalries exist in developing and managing specific policy areas, resulting in situations where the committee may see connections that the government has not thought through. Overlapping membership also aids the dissemination of both information and political arguments between the EAC and the policy committees, and vice versa.

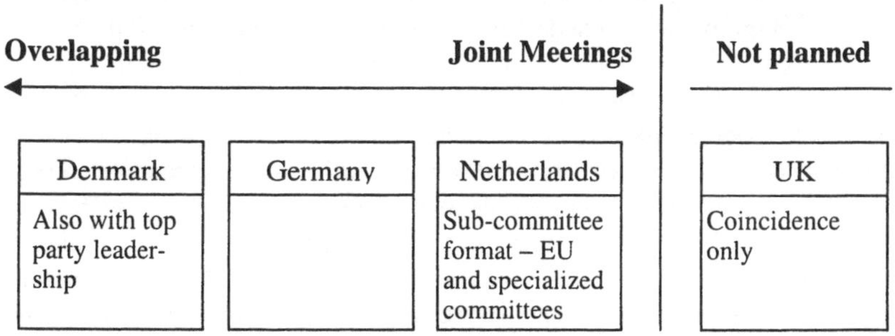

Figure 10.4 Overlapping membership

The Danish EAC consciously attempts to bring MPs from various committees into the Committee, concentrating its policy expertise. Furthermore, the Committee attracts MPs from the top leadership in the various parties, thus concentrating political authority in the Committee and giving it a strong mandate to act in many cases on behalf of the whole parliament, thus further strengthening its authority.

In Germany, the EAC also attempts to assure overlapping membership from the important policy committees. However, it does not necessarily attract the very highest political leaders.

The EAC in the Netherlands (called *the Algemene Commissie voor EU-Zaken*) at first glance appears to have overlapping membership, but the advantages of structuring the institution in this way are eviscerated by normally meeting to perform scrutiny in what is technically a joint meeting of the EAC and a specialized policy committee. In reality, however, only one person appears from each party who serves on the committee and the specific policy committee which routinely oversees a particular ministry. The whole committee normally only meets to scrutinize the foreign minister, finance minister and the prime minister. This is an example that once again shows the importance of a careful analysis of the actual practice of institutions, instead of merely looking at the formal institutional structure.

The British House of Commons has not institutionalized a system of overlapping membership between the EAC and the specialized policy committees; this only occurs haphazardly and by coincidence. However, the political parties themselves attempt to find MPs to serve on a committee with various sectoral interests, such as agriculture or business.

Involvement of other committees

In terms of the fifth criteria, the involvement of other committees in EU affairs, none of the four parliaments can be ranked very high on this measure of parliamentary powers of scrutiny. None has systematically institutionalized a system of review encompassing both the EAC and any applicable specialized committees. Nonetheless, the specialized committees in Denmark, the Netherlands and Germany will pick up issues that become particularly salient to a committee or a political party by interest group activity or through media attention. This is most apparent in the environmental committees, but also increasingly in justice and home affairs committees because of the increasing saliency of decision-making in this area. Furthermore, the commerce committee of these parliaments will address EU issues at times, although the great bulk of the measures to create the Single Market have now been completed. Finally, there are times when the foreign relations committees of the three countries assert themselves, refusing to allow the EAC to complete domination to scrutinize decision-making in EU matters. These committees especially discuss development in the second pillar (Common Foreign and Security Policy) and also during periods when treaty changes for the EU are being actively discussed.

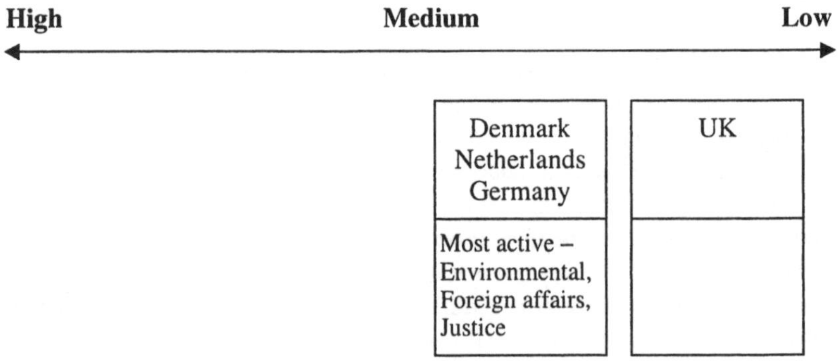

Figure 10.5 Involvement of other committees

The committees in the British parliament outside of the EAC generally stay away from addressing EU issues in any systematic way. European issues can be quite sensitive for both the Labour and the Conservative Parties, so avoiding the discussions even within one's own parliamentary party group is desired. Many in parliament seem to be pleased that EU subjects scheduled for general debate are normally now sent to one of the two specialized Standing Committees on Europe, instead of the normal committee system or the floor of the House.

PARTY BEHAVIOUR

Agenda-setting Power of Governing Parties

The almost daily necessity of the minority governments in Denmark to obtain support from both governing and opposition parties to obtain a mandate for Council of Minister negotiations and to pass legislation, gives the governing parties in parliament a great deal of influence over the setting of the agenda. The success of the government depends on the ability of the governing parties in parliament to discuss and persuade and compromise with op-position parties to obtain a working majority on a given issue. In Denmark, the power of the governing parties is thus to a great extent fused with the government, because it is necessary for government success to continuously negotiate with other parties in parliament.

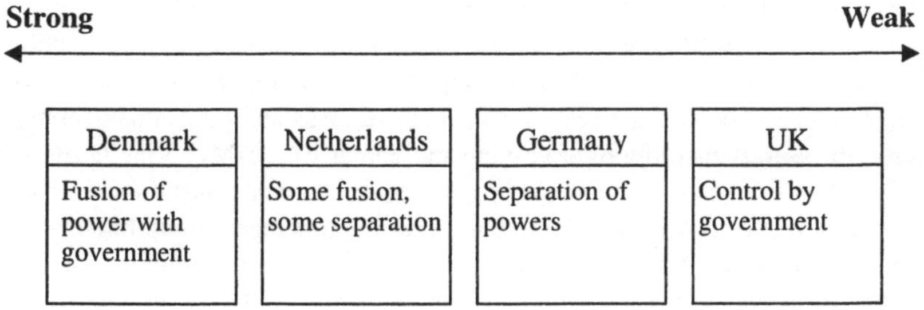

Figure 10.6 Power of governing parties for agenda-setting

In the Netherlands, with a coalition government consisting of two relatively equal parties and one smaller one, the government also needs to consult frequently with parliament to make sure that it maintains these broad coalitions. There have been times when portions of the parties within the governing coalition will threaten to temporarily defect and side with an opposition party to bring a policy proposal closer to their own party's view and away from the politically mixed bag coalition (at the time of this research, prior to the recent elections) combining labour (PvdA) and conservative liberal (VVD) parties with a smaller social liberal party (D66). This need, and the traditions of consensus decision-making in Dutch political culture, results in a fusion of power with the government to set the agenda in parliament. This does not reach the level seen in Denmark, with the situation of a minority government requiring continuous bargaining between the parties in parliament, but nonetheless the need to keep the broad, politically mixed coalition together and avoid temporary defections gives the governing parties a measure of agenda-setting power in parliament.

In Germany, with the coalition government (SPD and Greens, 1998-2005) under study here, consisting of the typical constellation of a larger, more dominant party and a smaller coalition partner, the government itself has more agenda-setting power in parliament. The government can be fairly confident in support from the governing parties in parliament, especially the larger party with the prime minister from its ranks, but also its smaller coalition partner, which has few alternatives if it desires to remain a governing party. There is more of a division between the governing party in parliament and the government ministers, more of a separation of powers than in Denmark or even the Netherlands. Put simply, the government in Germany has less need to cede agenda-setting power in parliament to the governing parties themselves. Occasional disputes break out between the SPD and the Greens over EU policy, and the SPD-dominated government must temporarily cede power to the parliamentary party to hammer out a compromise with the coalition party in parliament and soothe ruffled Green feathers.

The agenda-setting power of the British government in parliament is legendary, and a whole institutional apparatus involving whips with a heavy bag of carrots and sticks has evolved. These rewards and punishments extend through various institutions involving the career of the MP – including the MP's standing in parliament, the party and his or her constituency. These devices are normally quite effective in keeping most members in line most of the time. In these situations of majority government, the government to a great extent controls parliament and sets the agenda. Of course, when a real revolt among members of the governing party emerges, as it did a number of times during the rule of Prime Minister Margaret Thatcher with a deeply divided Conservative Party on European issues, the debate is bitter and the very leadership of the prime minister over the party is questioned. The only protection that an individual member of parliament has in such situations is to be part of a strong minority faction within the governing party, which makes it difficult for the government to use its normal whip enforcement mechanisms against them as individuals. They must also hope that they have a chance to win, to topple the current party leadership and elect a new prime minister.

The Danish opposition parties have the highest level of power to influence the parliament's agenda in scrutinizing the government's decision-making on

EU matters because the government needs their support to receive a mandate to negotiate in the Council of Ministers.

Next in line is Germany, where the power of opposition parties emanates from the party's strength in the upper chamber, the Bundesrat. If the government knows that a particular measure must also be approved by the Bundesrat, or that other issues which the Bundesrat has the power to decide may be influenced by the government's position on another issue, parties which determine outcomes in the Bundesrat also have increased agenda-setting powers in the Bundestag. Thus in the government under study here, although the SPD and Greens had a majority in the Bundestag, the Bundesrat had a different constellation of power with many Länder governed by (or in coalition with) the CDU or the FDP. This gives these parties additional powers they can also exercise in the Bundestag. This strengthens the position of opposition parties in the parliament.

The power of the Dutch opposition parties to set the agenda emerges not only from formal rights of the opposition parties which all these parliaments enshrine in their procedural rules, but also from their occasional ability to persuade one of the governing parties to temporarily defect and amend the government proposal closer to their own preferences. A governing party will not do this if the coalition agreement between the parties has spoken on this matter, but many EU issues are not envisioned at the start of a government's term and are thus not part of the written coalition agreement. Thus, at times a proposal of the current government, which has emerged from a compromise from this politically mixed bag coalition, will be modified by either the Green-Left Alliance opposition party encouraging the governing PvdA Party to temporarily defect from the coalition, and steer policy more to the left. Similarly, at times the Christian Democratic Party (CDA) has persuaded the VVD to defect on issues and steer policy more to the right. This happened a number of times during the current government, with the Green-Left Alliance party bringing environmental policy closer to its preferences, and the CDA bringing agricultural policy closer to its preferences. Normally, the temporarily defecting governing parties try to accomplish this without voting against a formal proposal of the government, so these actions are discussed during preliminary discussions between government and parliament or perhaps in a resolution on an issue to the government, which is less binding than passing a law.

The power of the British opposition parties to set the agenda in parliament is limited. They of course have procedural rights to question the prime minister and ministers during Question Time or may use their scheduled opposition debate time to raise European issues. Additionally, the British opposition parties are especially good at raising European issues for public discussion, which the British press is more than willing to carry to the public, with many Eurosceptics among them.

Power of opposition parties to influence agenda

Denmark and Germany have highly efficient parliamentary party structures to focus expertise in working groups and to disseminate this knowledge and position taking to the members of the parliamentary party. In both Denmark and Germany, a working group consisting of the MPs from each party in the EAC meets before the committee meeting to hammer out the parties' position in private. Often a minister who is scheduled to appear at the subsequent committee meeting will first appear at this working group meeting. This is a very effective way of increasing the power of parliament to scrutinize the government's decision-making power in EU matters. The members of the working group from each party can normally take a position on behalf of the whole party, but will raise the issue in the general weekly meetings of the parliamentary party group if he or she needs to consult others before a common party position can be taken, or to build support with the party for a position he or she expects to be controversial.

Strong ←→ **Weak**

Denmark	Germany	Netherlands	UK
Minority government needs opposition support	Power emanates from opposition party strength in Bundesrat	Power to persuade governing parties to temporarily defect and amend government proposal	Limited to questioning government during Question Time or using opposition debate time

Figure 10.7 Power of opposition parties to influence agenda

In the Netherlands, this formal system of concentrating control and oversight, and then channelling and dissemination through the parliamentary party is less developed. Normally the party spokesperson on a given issue area is given authority to decide on the party's position on a given EU matter. Thus a single person may often decide, instead of a special working group of the parliamentary party of those serving on the EAC.

The distribution of power in the House of Commons is quite different. One has a strong whip system controlling the power of the parliament, and relatively atomized members of parliament serving on the EAC with no institutional vehicle for forging their own common position towards EU matters independent of the government and the whips. There are groups of MPs, including cross-party groups, that can forge positions and apply pressures to the government over EU decision-making.

CONCLUSION

National parliaments and the strategic actors in the parliaments, the political parties, have had to react to the advent of multi-level government in the EU. Decision-making power of the most democratic branch of government has been lost to the EU institutions and national executives.

A qualitative, fundamental change in the relations between parliament and government has occurred in the member states of the EU. The initial gradual erosion of parliamentary power as more and more decision-making sovereignty was transferred to the EU level was followed by a clawing back of power by the strategic actors in the system. Political parties acted in their parliaments to create new institutional mechanisms designed not to pass laws, but to scrutinize their governments' negotiating positions in Council of Minister meetings.

Parties had an incentive to do this because scrutinizing the government is an increasingly important activity a party can offer voters as the multi-level government of the EU and the member states continues to expand into new policy areas. The Europeanization of domestic systems of representation, led by political parties competing for electoral support in national polities, have created new rules, institutions and party behaviours to attempt to regain lost power. This strategic action by political parties to adapt their parliamentary institutions was necessary because of institutional development from above at the EU level and electoral pressure from below.

This chapter proposes a model with a set of eight criteria for comparatively assessing the power of parliaments to scrutinize their government's decision-making in EU matters. The criteria are organized into three categories: formal rules, institutions and party behaviour. It then empirically analyses parliamentary scrutiny in four member states, selected based on type of government formation – minority, coalition or majority.

We have seen from this analysis that parliaments with minority governments have the greatest power to scrutinize their government, followed by parliaments with coalition governments. Parliaments with majority governments have the least power. In parliaments with coalition government, those with broad and diverse coalitions that must rely on the parliament to continually discuss and negotiate, have more power and thus edge a bit toward the power enjoyed by parliaments with a minority governments. Coalitions with a dominant party and a junior partner may be expected to rely less on discussions and negotiations in parliament to keep the coalition together, and thus edge a bit towards the power parliaments have with a majority government. Nonetheless, the power these parliaments have vis-à-vis their governments is more similar to other parliaments with coalition governments than it is to either of the two more extreme cases.

In the four countries examined here, the Danish parliament clearly has the most power to scrutinize government decision-making on the EU. Although it does not have great powers enshrined in the constitution, it has a strong statutory framework giving it the right to give or refuse a mandate to negotiate in the Council of Ministers. It has a system of overlapping membership between the EAC and the specialized policy committees, thus concentrating expertise on the scrutiny committee. Additionally, from a party behaviour perspective, the agenda-setting power of the governing parties is very high because it is fused with the government, there is a heightened power of opposition parties to also set the agenda, and there is an effective distribution of power in each parliamentary party. The Danish parliamentary parties are uniquely well organized to scrutinize the government.

Next in line are the two countries with coalition governments, with the German parliament having greater power than the Dutch parliament. The German parliament has a strong constitutional and statutory base for its powers, with another constitutional body – the *Bundesverfassunggericht* – having signalled its great desire to back the power of parliament. Additionally, the existence of the Bundesrat strengthens the power of opposition parties in the Bundestag. Although the German parliament and its EAC do not have the right to give or refuse a mandate, they do have the right to be consulted and to guide EU policy (*Mitwirkungsrechte*). The system of overlapping membership with the EAC strengthens oversight. The organization of the parliamentary parties themselves, with working group meetings of each party serving on the EAC and periodic discussions in the whole party, are very effective in asserting the power of parliament vis-à-vis the government.

The Dutch parliament has considerably less power than the German Bundestag. The Netherlands has less of a constitutional and statutory framework specifically designed to give parliament power to scrutinize the government's decision-making in EU issues. A notable and very important exception to this is in the area of the third pillar, where the Dutch parliament's right to give or withhold a mandate over justice and home affairs issues is found in the statute approving the TEU. In terms of the way the parliamentary institutions are organized, although the Dutch formally have an overlapping membership between their EAC and their specialized committees, in reality only one member from each party normally appears at the joint committee meetings, thus obliterating most of the advantages gained from overlapping membership. There is some fusion with the government of the power to set the parliamentary agenda, which strengthens parliamentary power. Finally, there are times when opposition parties are able to assert themselves and attract the support of one of the governing parties to influence the government, increasing parliamentary power.

The power of the British House of Commons to scrutinize their government's decision-making over EU matters is normally quite low. Certainly the parliamentary institutions as well as the political party institutions are designed to control dissent and not give parliament much power to scrutinize the government in any real, meaningful way, beyond the exchange of words. The constitutional and statutory basis for scrutiny is weak. And instead of institutional structures designed for effective scrutiny, there are institutional structures designed to bury debate and keep it off the floor of the House; and party structures designed to control and stifle debate, not encourage scrutiny.

However, meaningful, powerful scrutiny does sometimes occur in the House of Commons. It breaks out of the institutional attempts at constraining it when groups of MPs head right for the jugular, right for the Prime Minister's ability to continue to lead his or her party and parliament. This is an *extraordinary* power, which the British parliament is able to muster occasionally to great effect in a quite Eurosceptic country. However, these extraordinary episodes are not part of the *ordinary* powers one sees when examining the rules, institutions and the organization of party behaviour for conducting scrutiny.

Finally, returning to the issue of the democratic deficit raised in the opening of this chapter. The diminished powers of national parliaments to make law has only been somewhat replaced by increasing powers to scrutinize national government inputs into the making of EU directives. Because each national parliament is only one of fifteen, and a national government may be outvoted when majority voting procedures are used in the Council of Ministers, there remains a net loss of national parliamentary control over laws implemented in a given country. This loss of national democratic control, which is *necessary* to create a new multi-level system of government, must be compensated for by European-wide forms of democratic representation to represent the emerging *Demos* of European people.

It must be said that there is more scrutiny occurring in the national parliaments of the member states that many commentators and the public are aware of. This is a function of the fact that much of the routine scrutiny occurs out of the public's earshot within the governing parties themselves. And there are institutional limits on the power of opposition parties to scrutinize the government. This activity by the national parliaments, regaining some of their powers, which then must be exercised quite differently than their former law-making powers, are beginning to reduce the 'double democratic deficit'. However, it only reduces one side of the democratic deficit, the side conferring democratic representation and legitimacy on the decision-making of national governments and their position taking in the Council of Ministers.

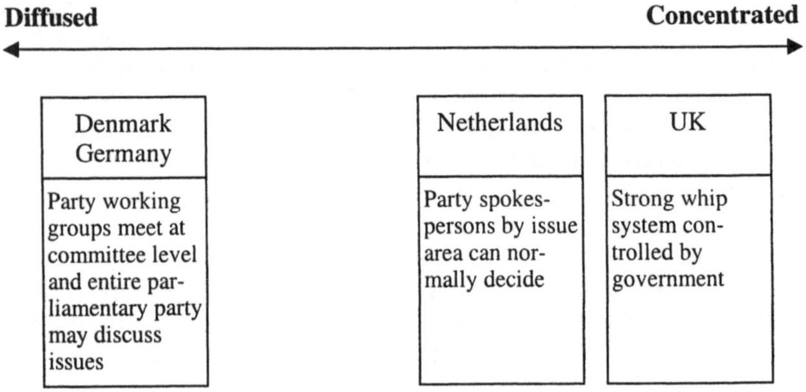

Figure 10.8 Distribution of power within the parliamentary power group

No amount of national parliamentary scrutiny over national government decision-making in the Council of Ministers will replace the necessity of democratic legitimacy at the EU level of government. The current institutional structure between the Council, Commission and the EP clearly does not fulfill the requirements. While increased national parliamentary scrutiny over council decisions can reduce one side of the 'double democratic deficit' in the EU, it does not solve the fundamental institutional democratic deficit in the EU itself.

NOTES

1. Dahl, Robert A (1989), *Democracy and its Critics,* New Haven: Yale University Press, p. 32.
2. Interviews with members of parliament serving on their parliament's European Affairs Committee were conducted in Germany in the period from November 1999 to January 2000, in the Netherlands in February 2000, in the UK June 2000 and in Denmark from September to October 2000.
3. The Danish report is entitled *The European Affairs Committee* and was signed by the Head of the Secretariat of the Committee, Bjorn Einersen, October 1996.
4. See Information Sheet No. 56, The House of Commons and European Communities Legislation, revised April 1999, House of Commons Information Office.

11. A Model for the Strictest Scrutiny? The Danish European Affairs Committee in a Party Group Perspective

Henrik Jensen

When it comes to parliamentary control with the executive, the European Affairs Committee of the Danish Parliament – the *Folketing* – is often considered among the most powerful European Affairs Committees of the member states in the European Union (EU) (Arter 1995, p. 121, Laursen 1995, p. 43, Fitzmaurice 1996, p. 95, Hegeland and Mattson 1996, p. 198, Jensen 1996, p. 43, Mouritzen 1997, p. 86, Dosenrode 1998, pp. 60-61, Raunio and Hix 2000, pp. 156-7, Raunio and Wiberg 2000, pp. 345-6, Jensen 2001, p. 135, Holzhacker 2002, p. 105). 'The Danish model' has served as a role model in the sense that parliaments from some of the countries entering the EU after Danish entrance in 1973 have looked towards Denmark. An obvious reason for the high esteem of the Danish European Affairs Committee with regard to parliamentary control is that the Danish government, that is the ministers, are obliged to show up in the committee and orally present a negotiation proposal, and thus secure the support of the European Affairs Committee before they go to Council Meetings, whenever matters of a wider scope are to be discussed or adopted.[1] Accordingly, the committee can block a minister's stance on a particular issue in the EU if a majority of the committee members, representing half or more of the seats in the Folketing, refuses to accept the mandate submitted by the minister.

Bearing this picture of the influence of the European Affairs Committee in mind and remembering that Danish governments usually are minority governments, it would be a great temptation to treat the committee as an actor vis-à-vis the ministers, when analysing the scrutiny activities of the European Affairs Committee as part of the multi-level governance processes in the EU and its member states. Notwithstanding the fact that the European Affairs Committee can be analysed as an actor, this chapter follows another methodological approach. I attempt to show that the European Affairs Committee is characterized by lines of demarcation that are running – not outside, between the committee and the ministers, but – *inside* the committee. The purpose of this chapter is to analyse, that is to describe and explain, the two most important decisional activities in the committee: policy decisions and institutional decisions, in a party group perspective. I do this by analysing the European Affairs Committee as an institution, in which the party groups – and not the committee – are the real actors, while the committee members as well as the ministers are considered representatives of party groups.

I start in the first section with a few methodological remarks mainly by discussing the meaning of 'analysing the European Affairs Committee in a party group perspective'. The second section gives a brief close-up of the European Affairs Committee by contrasting it to the other standing committees of the Folketing. This section shows that the European Affairs Committee, as a committee in the Folketing, is 'something special'. In the third section, I turn to institutional matters, namely the process of building institutional instruments for parliamentary control of the government and its EU policy. I do this by looking at an important series of reports submitted by the European Affairs Committee over the years, dating back to the Danish entrance into the EU in 1973. The reports – regarded by the committee as 'the procedural reports' – have been the primary source for regulating the pro-cedures and competence of the European Affairs Committee, as well as its general relations to the government and to other committees. It will be clear that the party group dimension should not be ignored if one wants to understand the behaviour of committee members in institutional matters. The fourth section turns to matters of policy and analyses the European Affairs Committee's practice of parliamentary scrutiny, mainly by mapping out 'who is in practice doing the scrutiny of the ministers' and which party groups do not support the policy of the government by refusing to accept the ministers' negotiation proposals. Here, it will also be clear that the party group dimension is crucial. The fifth section compares the two patterns of committee behaviour found in sections three and four and tries to explain the patterns of behaviour by relating them to the party group level. Finally, I close with a few substantial comments on the relevance of the party group perspective in multi-level analyses on parliamentary processes related to Europeanization. But first, what does it mean to analyse the Folketing's European Affairs Committee in a party group perspective?

METHODOLOGY

First, we have to ask how the European Affairs Committee can be analyzed as a parliamentary institution, if the party groups and their members in the committee are the actors? One very simple way of doing this is to look at the European Affairs Committee as well as the other committees of the Folketing as if they were arenas for the actors. The arena concept is a metaphor as the committees are not arenas per se, and the concept therefore needs to be clarified. Two different meanings will be put into the arena concept. The committee can be seen as an institutional instrument for the actors that enables them to do things that they would not otherwise be able to do, and the committee can be seen as a structure that affects the actors.

For instance, a member of the committee can use the committee as an instrument by denying a minister the support of his or her party group in relation to the minister's proposal for negotiation in the hope of influencing the government's policy position. The same committee member could also try to reach exactly the same goal by putting critical questions to the minister to show the minister as well as the other members in the committee that the government's position is not tenable. Such behaviour hits one classical meaning of parliamentary control, that is, to influence the government. Committee members may also pose questions outside the committee meetings on matters within a minister's jurisdiction. For instance, a member might be interested in gathering information on how the government has formerly responded to an initiative from the Commission, and can do this by posing written questions to the minister through the committee. Such behaviour hints at another classical meaning of parliamentary control, that is, to gather information on the government's behaviour. These examples all illustrate how the committee can be seen as an institutional instrument for the members as actors.

At the same time the committee can, however, also be seen as a structure that in a soft sense, that is in a non-causal way, affects the actors. For instance the committee coordinates the individual behaviour of committee members as well the ministers and their civil servants in time and space. It does so by requiring them to concentrate and work in the committee with the same EU items on the agenda of the Council – before the meetings take place. In addition, this is accomplished by urging them to show up at the same time in the same room – usually a Friday at 10 or 11 a.m. But the committee does not only affect the actors' behaviour at the individual level, it also affects them at the party group level per se and does so in a less visible manner. Together with the other permanent committees of the Folketing the European Affairs Committee lays down a division of labour within each party group. In every party group the members and the leadership will decide who will join which committee. A party group can change its composition of representatives in the committee from day to day if it wants to, but usually the party group will have one spokesperson as a more or less permanent member in the committee. As the division of labour within a party group not only determines who is doing what, but also determines who receives information and makes de-cisions in what policy areas, the European Affairs Committee and the other permanent committees affect the distribution of power and expertise among the members of a party group. To sum up, analysing the European Affairs Committee in a party group perspective means treating the committee as if it were an arena that can be seen both as a means and a structure for the party groups and their members in the committee.

Second, as the European Affairs Committee makes decisions in different types of matters it is necessary to be explicit about which types of decisional activities are being analyzed. Two different types of decisions will be taken up. The first is decisions on institutional matters, that is matters that concern the committee as an institution in terms of its competence, procedures, working routines and its general relations to other actors and institutions. These include for instance the European Parliament, the Commission, EU affairs committees in other countries, the government, the Danish Ministry of Foreign Affairs or other ministries, the party groups in parliament, the other permanent committees and so on. The second type of decisions regards matters of policy related to the EU, for instance whether Turkey should be a member of the EU; should tobacco advertisements be prohibited; should the use of single-hulled tank vessels be restricted? The hard core of the European Affairs Committee's decisional activities is to mandate Danish ministers prior to negotiations in the Council and these decisions are usually of the second type, that is policy decisions.

In the following sections I attempt to show how the European Affairs Committee makes decisions in these two types of matters and how important the party group dimension is in order to understand the decisional activities. However, to give an idea of what the European Affairs Committee is like in a Danish context, I just give a brief introduction to the European Affairs Committee by comparing it to the typical resort committee of the Folketing, before I begin the analysis.

THE EUROPEAN AFFAIRS COMMITTEE – A SPECIAL COMMITTEE

Tables 11.1 and 11.2 respectively show the composition of the European Affairs Committee before and after the latest election in November 2001. The election resulted in a change from a government of the Social Democrats and the Social Liberals to a government of the Liberal Party and the Conservative

Party. The tables show that both coalition governments constituted a minority in the committee. The Social Democrat/Social Liberal government had 6 out of 17 members of the committee, and the Liberal/Conservative government held 7 out of 17 seats after the election. Government party groups constituting a minority in the committee as well as in the Folketing are a typical trait

Table 11.1 Composition of the European Affairs Committee according to size of party group (number of seats in the Folketing, including North Atlantic mandates), October 2000

	Members	Substitutes	Seats
Soc. Dem.*	5	2	64
Lib. Par.	4	2	43
Cons. Par.	3	2	16
Soc. Peo.	1	1	13
Dan. Peo.	1	1	10
CD	1	0	8
Soc. Lib.*	1	1	7
Red-Gr.	1	1	5
Chr. Dem.	0	1	4
Total	17	11	170

Note: * Government party.

Table 11.2 Composition of the European Affairs Committee according to size of party group (number of seats in the Folketing including North Atlantic mandates), December 2001

	Members	Substitutes	Seats
Lib. Par.*	5	2	55
Soc. Dem.	5	2	52
Dan. Peo.	2	2	22
Con. Par.*	2	1	16
Soc. Peo.	1	1	12
Soc. Lib.	1	1	9
Chr. Dem.	0	1	4
Red-Gr.	1	1	4
Total	17	11	174

Note: * Government party.

of the Danish parliamentary system. The tables also show another trait, which is very typical not only of the European Affairs Committee, but of all the other standing committees of the Folketing: All members and all substitutes in the committees are representatives of party groups.

The composition of the committee is just one of many ways of picturing the European Affairs Committee as an institution. Table 11.3 gives a very rough impression of what the European Affairs Committee is like in a Danish parliamentary context. The table shows along four basic dimensions and in an oversimplified way some important similarities and differences between the European Affairs Committee and the 'typical' specialized committee. The Folketing has 25 permanent committees. Nineteen of the twenty-five committees would count as specialized standing committees. They are typically dealing with one policy area such as defence, labour market, housing, transport, health care and so on. The first dimension in Table 11.3 is the composition of the committee, and the three others dimensions are committee meetings, competence/decisional procedures and policy area.

The distribution of member seats in a committee is more or less dependent on the size of the party groups in the parliament as a whole (see Tables 11.1 and 11.2), whereas a party group normally has one or two substitutes in a committee. The formal difference between committee members and substitutes is that only members are allowed to make decisions in a committee, though in practice this difference is usually not important. If a party group has more than one person in a committee it can benefit from a division of labour among the group members in the committee, though one person, the spokesperson, will normally be responsible to his or her party group for coordinating the group's activity in the committee.

In the European Affairs Committee this group of persons, the EU spokesmen for all the party groups, together with the chairman of the committee, are the most stable part of the committee and constitute the subcommittee of the European Affairs Committee. Contrary to the typical specialized committee, the European Affairs Committee has for years had a tradition of having a subcommittee that deals with institutional matters, for instance drafts to procedural committee reports.

The party groups' work with the EU policy can differ and is influenced by the size of the party group, its (lack of) relations to the government and the party group's internal traditions. On a day-to-day basis however, all party groups have the possibility of replacing a member or substitute on a committee. Even though the specialized committees have been far more involved in EU matters by the European Affairs Committee in recent years, figures indicate that some party groups, in particular the Socialist People's Party, have also used the possibility of bringing in 'experts' on an ad hoc basis; party group representatives from a specialized committee represent the party

Table 11.3 Comparison between the European Affairs Committee and the 'typical' specialized committee

	European Affairs Committee	Specialized Committee
Composition:		
Members/substitutes	17/10-11	17/10-11
Members and substitutes are party group representatives	Yes	Yes
One of the members is normally spokesperson for his/her party group	Yes	Yes
Division of labour among a PG's members and substitutes	Yes	Yes
Number of replacements	High	Low
Subcommittee	Yes	No
Status of the committee among members	Higher	Lower
Proportion of front-benchers	Higher	Lower
Committee meetings:		
Meeting activity	Higher	Lower
Length of meeting	Longer	Shorter
Rhythm of meeting follows	The EU	The Folketing
Work load	Bigger	Smaller
Competencies:		
Competency in practice on behalf of the Folketing	Yes	No
A committee member can count for the party's seats in the Folketing	Yes	No
A party group's absence can count in favour of the minister	Yes	No
Degree of institutional autonomy	Higher	Lower
Degree of 'institutional patriotism'	Higher	Lower
Policy aspects:		
Policy area	Transversal	Sectoral
Elements of foreign policy	Higher	Lower
Amount of committee documents	Higher	Lower
Reading of bills	No	Yes

group at the meetings in the European Affairs Committee when matters related to the specialized committee in question have been dealt with. Accordingly the result is a far higher number of replacements in the European Affairs Committee than in the typical specialized committee. In the parliamentary year 1998-99 the number of replacements, that is changes in the composition of the committee, was more than three times higher in the European Affairs Committee than in the typical specialized committee (Jensen 2003, p. 124).

Two final traits relating to the composition of the European Affairs Committee are worth mentioning. The European Affairs Committee is more or less a high status committee. Hence, research results from the 1990s indicate that the committee was considered the most attractive by the MPs (Jensen 1995, p. 61). The European Affairs Committee also attracts more frontbenchers than the typical specialized committee. In the parliamentary year 1998-99 the proportion of leading figures from the party groups was twice as high as the average of the typical specialized committee, and a similar pattern has been observed earlier (Damgaard 1977, p. 155, Arter 1995, p. 115, Jensen 2002, p. 76). As a consequence the authority of the committee's decisions is typically higher.

Regarding the committee meetings, which are the second main dimension of Table 11.3, the number of meetings, the length of the meetings, the usual meeting day as well as meeting period of the year for the European Affairs Committee are heavily influenced by the rhythm of the EU. The numbers of meetings of the European Affairs Committee are normally among the highest if not the highest of the permanent committees. The parliamentary year 2000-01, in which the European Affairs Committee held 44 meetings, was no exception (*Folketingstidende, Årbog & Registre* 2000-01, p. 25). But members of the European Affairs Committee not only have to go to more meetings and in that sense work more than their party group members, they have to do it in a different rhythm. The European Affairs Committee meetings usually take place on Friday, that is before the Council meeting of the following week, but Friday is generally not a meeting day in other committees. The length of the meetings is different, too, as most meetings of the typical specialized committee are far shorter. At the beginning of the 1990s, 4 per cent of the meetings of the typical specialized committee lasted more than two hours. The corresponding figure for the European Affairs Committee was 44 per cent (Jensen 1995, p.109)! Considering the growing activity of the EU, the meetings have probably grown longer since then.

The way the meetings of the European Affairs Committee take place is also different. In general meetings in the committees of the Folketing are highly standardized, but this is even more the case with the European Affairs Committee. Experienced ministers as well as experienced members of the

European Affairs Committee are familiar with the decisional procedures of the committee, which confirms that: 'If a committee is to make hundreds of decisions it will have to standardize its tasks' (Fenno 1973, p. 47). The meetings usually take place behind closed doors, and most of the time is spent on consultations with ministers who prior to meetings in the Council need to brief the committee and/or submit a mandate. In the latter case the attention of the members will usually be higher, and they will be better prepared for the oral consultation with the minister.

The minister will describe the negotiation situation and the Danish position including the negotiation proposal, the chairperson will 'open' for questions and the members in the committee, mainly the spokespeople from the opposition party groups, will pose more or less critical questions to the minister. The minister will answer and members might pose additional questions. In the meantime a civil servant who keeps the records of the committee will produce a stenographic record of the meeting. As ministers can be held responsible for the information given to the European Affairs Committee, they are usually careful and are well aware that members from the opposition might later in the process confront them with the oral information that appears in the committee's confidential minutes. When there are no more questions to the minister, the chairperson ends the consultation by asking who in the committee opposes the negotiation proposal. If party group representatives from party groups constituting a majority in the Folketing do not oppose the minister's negotiation proposal, the minister receives a mandate when the chairman states that 'there is no majority against the negotiation proposal', and the other members remain silent and thereby tacitly agree with the chairperson. If the minister does not go beyond the mandate during the negotiations in the EU he or she should *ceteris paribus* not expect political trouble such as public critique in Parliament from the majority constituted by party groups supporting the minister's mandate. This highly standardized way of making decisions on behalf of the Folketing is not found in any of the specialized committees. The specialized committees do have consultations with the minister in question before the minister shows up in the European Affairs Committee, but the European Affairs Committee is the only committee capable of turning the ministers' negotiation proposals into mandates.

The decisional activity of accepting or denying a minister's negotiation proposal reflects the competency of the European Affairs Committee, and hence regards the third dimension of Table 11.3. In practice this competency enables the committee to make decisions on behalf of the Folketing. Disregarding the Finance Committee, the competency of the European Affairs Committee is unique. First, the members of the typical specialized committee are only able – typically in committee reports – to produce recommendations to the Folketing, for instance on the fate of a bill. So the final decision of the

Folketing on a bill is taken when the MPs vote, not when the committee submits a report on the bill. Second, when a committee makes a decision whether to submit a report, a committee member counts for the party group's number of members in the committee and not in plenum. The unique competence of the European Affairs Committee and the related decision-making principle implying that a member in the committee counts in the party group's number of seats in the Folketing is a smooth way of making decisions. It prevents that a proposal from a minister who has formerly received a mandate from the European Affairs Committee will see a majority in the Folketing block the directive if this has to be implemented through a bill. It should, however, also be clear that the principle implies that members on the European Affairs Committee are legitimate representatives of their party groups. This means that the principle is based on the precondition that party groups, through their representatives on the European Affairs Committee, act as unitary actors, which they usually do – they do not split the party group's votes. Third, still another remarkable decisional principle of the European Affairs Committee should be noted. If a party group is not represented at a meeting when a minister is to put forward a negotiation proposal, the party group is counted in favour of the minister's negotiation proposal, unless another agreement is made with the chairperson of the committee. This principle protects minority governments in the sense that it prevents a situation where minister gets no mandate at all due to a lack of quorum in the committee. In the typical specialized committee a member's absence does not 'automatically' count in favour of the government. Finally, if one combines the higher degree of competency of the committee with the fact that more front-benchers are found on the European Affairs Committee, it is no surprise that the European Affairs Committee's degree of decisional autonomy is higher than that of the typical specialized committee. The decisional autonomy is normally also defended by the members of the committee in spite of all partisanship. For instance, ministers should not play tricks on the committee but are supposed to show the committee respect. This phenomenon, which is not easy to prove, can also be characterized as a higher degree of so-called 'institutional patriotism' (Matthews 1980, pp. 101-2). In the eyes of a recently appointed minister it probably makes the European Affairs Committee look more 'scary' than the average specialized committee dealing with the same policy area as the one for which the minister is responsible.

The question of which ministers show up in the committee is to a wide extent related to the character of the policy area, which is the fourth and final dimension of Table 11.3. The normal pattern of interaction between the specialized committees and the ministries is one of 'sectoral' interaction in the sense that the typical specialized committee interacts with one or sometimes two ministries covering the same policy area as the committee in question.

As a result a specialized committee will more or less have consultations with the same one or two minister(s). This is not the case with the European Affairs Committee, as the policy area of the European Affairs Committee is far more transverse in character. The difference is reflected in the fact that members of the European Affairs Committee will have consultations before the Council meetings with maybe more than half of the government's ministers – including the prime minister and, of course, the minister for foreign affairs.

Despite the fact that EU policy increasingly influences 'domestic politics', elements of foreign policy are still present. The Danish Ministry of Foreign Affairs, though under pressure for decentralization, is still the main coordinator on the government's side of the street of the Danish EU policy. Coordinating efforts are continuously made in order to make sure that Denmark speaks with one tongue in the EU (Mouritzen 2003, p. 244). An argument for closed doors at the meetings of the European Affairs Committee is that Danish ministers and Danish national interests benefit from keeping the Danish bargaining position secret. This is also reflected in the fact that negotiation proposals are worded orally by the minister at the meetings and are in principle not known to the committee members beforehand; in practice representatives from the party groups in government are better informed.

Finally, a final difference between the European Affairs Committee and the typical specialized committee deserves mentioning as it is related to aspects of the policy area. Though the fate of a negotiation proposal is decided upon at the meetings, the members in the committee are heavily burdened with paper, mostly notes from the ministries that are sent out before the meetings. The European Affairs Committee is usually among the top three when it comes to the annual amount of documents, even though it does not – contrary to the typical specialized committee – read bills, which is usually a paper-consuming activity. In the parliamentary year 2000-01 the European Affairs Committee received the highest amount of documents (*Folketingstidende, Årbog & Registre* 2000-01, p. 25), which suggests that its members have a greater workload than members of the typical specialized committee.

To sum up, the brief illustration of the European Affairs Committee captured in Table 11.3 shows first and foremost that the European Affairs Com-mittee is not only a standing committee in the Folketing – it is also an outstanding committee. The differences at the institutional level between the European Affairs Committee and the typical specialized committee are far more conspicuous than the similarities. The European Affairs Committee is beyond doubt a special committee. However, we cannot ignore the party group dimension: The European Affairs Committee is, like all the other committees, composed of party group representatives; the subcommittee mainly consists of one representative, the EU spokesperson, from each party group; the composition of and changes in the committee are solely a result of decisions in the party groups; majority decisions on ministers' negotiation proposals are weighted according to the size of the party groups; committee members are legitimate representatives of their party groups and so on. So it is not a surprise if the committee's institutional decisions to some extent mirror the partisan dimension.

INSTITUTIONAL DECISIONS – BUILDING INSTRUMENTS FOR PARLIAMENTARY CONTROL

When the European Affairs Committee was founded in 1972 as one of 22 permanent committees, the Accession Act stated that: 'The government has a duty to inform a standing committee of the Folketing concerning proposals for Council decisions that will be directly applicable in Denmark or for whose fulfilment the assistance of the Folketing is required'. A political crisis occurred shortly after the Danish entrance into the EU when the Social Democratic minister of agriculture was criticized by the opposition parties for not having informed the Folketing about a negotiation result that was reportedly detrimental to Danish agricultural interests. The crisis resulted in the first report from the European Affairs Committee containing the crucial statement that: 'Prior to negotiations in the EC Council of Ministers on decisions of a wider scope, the government submits an oral mandate for negotiation to the Market Committee [the European Affairs Committee, HJ]. If there is no majority against the mandate, the government negotiates on this basis' (European Affairs Committee 2002, p. 2). Now, this is the basic element of the Danish 'mandating model', a 30-year-old instrument for parliamentary control still being used and *ceteris paribus* still preventing ministers of a minority government who once received a mandate at the meeting with the European Affairs Committee from afterwards being opposed by a majority.

However, the report from the European Affairs Committee was not only important because it laid down the core of the competency of the committee, that is to deny a minister a mandate. In several ways the report was also typical for the reports to come: The draft was hammered out in a subcommittee composed of the chairman and one representative from each party group; the report was worked out in close contact with representatives of the government, and the content was the result of an agreement between the government and the committee; and the report dealt with institutional matters.

Including the first report from 1973, the European Affairs Committee has submitted 32 reports. Twenty-three are procedural reports that reflect decisions in institutional matters, that is regulate the competency, procedures and working routines of the European Affairs Committee and its general relations to other actors and institutions, especially the government. The procedural reports can be seen as parts of, and reactions to, the Europeanization process. I shall focus on some aspects of the procedural reports that put the party group dimension of the reports up front, and refrain from an in-depth analysis of the contents of the procedural reports.[2] Suffice it here to note that the procedural reports among other things have expanded the competency of the committee; following the development of the EU and the corresponding spread of EU involvement in more policy areas, the competency of the committee has primarily been expanded by a spread of the use of the mandating model, that is more areas in which Danish ministers are obliged to present an oral negotiation proposal in the committee. They have involved other external actors than the government, for instance the specialized committees, but the focus of the reports is the general relationship between the committee and the government in EU matters.

Now, turning to the party group aspects of the procedural reports one might, first, ask how procedural committee reports – which are neither formally binding in the same way as for instance a law, nor submitted by parliament as such – can regulate not only the internal procedures of the committee, but also its general relations and interactions with surrounding actors and institutions alike. From where does the political authority of the reports stem, so that the reports affect the behaviour of members of the committee as well as ministers and civil servants? The authority of the reports does not stem from the fact that the committee members are committee members per se. Rather, it stems from the fact that the committee members are party group representatives, and are regarded as legitimate representatives of a majority of the Folketing; besides, as the focus of the reports is the relationship between the committee and the government, the involvement and acceptance by the government of changes in 'the rules of the game' is important because it increases the likelihood that ministers and their civil servants will keep in line with the reports.

Second, it should be noted that at least 16 of the 23 procedural reports were prepared by a subcommittee. As the subcommittee usually consists of one person, the EU spokespeople, from each party group the subcommittee becomes a centre for consensus building and coordination among the party groups when drafts of procedural reports and corresponding changes in the way the committee works are to be discussed. The previously mentioned involvement of the government in the drafting of the reports, typically via the minister for foreign affairs or a leading civil servant from the Ministry of Foreign Affairs, ensures that institutional changes are not forced upon the government. In connection with institutional changes there is typically high pressure in the subcommittee to reach a unanimous agreement not only with the government, but also among the party groups in the committee.

Third, in spite of the pressure for consensus in institutional decisions, nine of the twenty-three procedural reports contain minority statements that usually express more or less critical views on the majority's positions promoted in the reports. Table 11.4 gives an overview of the pattern of the minority statements. In the table the party groups are divided into four different 'super groups': left-wing party groups, right-wing party groups, actual government party groups and former government party groups.

Table 11.4 Minority statements in the European Affairs Committee's procedural according to the position of the party group, 1973-2001[a]

Opposition	Left wing	13
	Potential government	4
	Right wing	16
Government		1

Notes:
[a] Left wing: The Unity List – the Red-Green Alliance, the Socialist People's Party, the Danish Communist Party. Right wing: the Danish People's Party, the Progress Party, the Danish Single Tax Party (Retsforbundet). the Liberal Party, the Social Democrats, the Conservative Party, the Social Liberals, the Christian Democrats and the Centre Democrats are classified as either (actual) government or potential (former) government depending on their position as government party group respectively party in opposition at the time of the release of the report in question.

First, Table 11.4 shows that only once has a government party group come up with a minority statement. Remembering that minority (coalition) governments are the most frequent type of government in Denmark, this means that party groups in government stick together, whereas critical views stem from party groups in opposition. Second, potential (former) government party groups, however, have produced only a modest amount of minority statements. So far we have a picture of changes in the European Affairs Committee's procedures and relations to the government that are primarily supported by the party groups who already are in government or expect to be in government in the future. As these party groups – mainly consisting of the Social Democrats, the Liberal Party, the Conservative Party and the Social Liberals – form a vast potential majority, the effect hereof is *ceteris paribus* a higher degree of actor support to 'the rules of the game'. Finally Table 11.4 shows that the lion's share of minority statements have been put forward by the party groups on the wings, indicating that these party groups are most critical of the way the committee works.

If we then take a quick look at the content of the minority statements from the party groups on the wings there is a rather high degree of overlapping wishes as well as critique and dissatisfaction with the committee's working conditions. Over the years, the party groups on the wings have most often – and most critically – pointed to the need for classical instruments of parliamentary control like open meetings, written mandates, meticulous minutes of the consultations and so on. A couple of times party groups on the left wing and the right wing have even joined forces and put forward common and critical minority statements on the committee's competence and way of working. So, all together we see a decisional pattern in institutional matters where the demarcation lines are running between the government party groups and the party groups in opposition as well as between the actual and potential government party groups on one side and the party groups on the wings pushing for more and stronger instruments of parliamentary control on the other side. The next section describes who in practice uses the instruments of parliamentary scrutiny that the committee places at the members' disposal when the committee is to decide on a minister's negotiation proposal, that is to make policy decisions.

USING THE INSTRUMENTS – THE PRACTICE OF PARLIAMENTARY SCRUTINY IN POLICY MATTERS

The highly standardized procedure that ministers and committee members follow when a minister presents a negotiation proposal and answers questions from the committee members implies that the ministers will do most of the talking at the meetings. But how do the committee members in practice perform scrutiny vis-à-vis the government? The politically most important instruments of scrutiny at the committee members' disposal are the possibilities of questioning a minister on his/her negotiation proposal and, of course, of accepting or rejecting the proposal on behalf of one's party group. Who, then, uses these two instruments? Tables 11.5 and 11.6 give a partial answer.

Table 11.5 Proportion of questions, comments and so on from representatives on the European Affairs Committee according to the position of the party group, 1991-92 (minority government of the Conservative Party and the Liberal Party; N = 619 = 100.0 %). Proportion of seats on the committee in brackets (N = 100 % = 28 = 17 members + 11 substitutes)

Opposition	Left wing	15.7	(7)
	Potential government	52.3	(50)
	Right wing	24.7	(7)
Government		7.3	(36)

Table 11.6 Proportion of questions, comments and so on from representatives on the European Affairs Committee according to the position of the party group, 1998-99 (minority government of the Social Democrats and the Liberals; N = 647 = 99.9 %). Proportion of seats on the committee in brackets (N = 100 % = 28 = 17 members + 11 substitutes)

Opposition	Left wing	38.9 (18)
	Potential government	33.5 (39)
	Right wing	24.1 (11)
Government		3.4 (32)

Tables 11.5 and 11.6 show for two parliamentary years with two different minority coalition governments how the speech acts of questioning and commenting on ministers' negotiation proposals were distributed – once again divided into left-wing party groups, potential government party groups, right-wing party groups and government party groups (cf. Table 11.4). The behavioural patterns are not completely identical in the two tables, but it appears, first, that the representatives from the government parties, although they have about one-third of the seats, pose far less than one-tenth of the questions. They are to a great extent silent. Second, the balance is better when it comes to the potential government. Holding 50 per cent of the seats in 1991-92 and 40 per cent in 1998-99 their representatives on the committee pose respectively half and one-third of the questions. Third, the party groups on the wings are responsible for a disproportionately high share of the activity. Holding 14 per cent of the seats in 1991-92 and 29 per cent of the seats in 1998-99 their share of the questioning activity is no less than 41 and 63 per cent respectively. In other words the committee members from the government's party groups are obviously not the ones performing scrutiny in the committee. The parliamentary scrutiny is carried out by the representatives from the party groups in opposition and especially from the party groups on the wings.

Now, turning to the second institutional instrument, that of not accepting a negotiation proposal, Tables 11.7 and 11.8 show who most frequently opposed a minister's policy stance. It should be noted that the two tables, out of necessity, cover recent and rather short periods. They do, however, concern two different minority coalition governments, a Social Democrat/Social Liberal government before the November 2001 election and a Liberal/Conser-vative government after the November 2001 election.

Table 11.7 Party group rejections of ministers' negotiation proposals according to the position of the party group, 1 January-20 November 2001 (minority government of the Social Democrats and the Liberals)

Opposition	Left wing	64
	Potential government	6
	Right wing	22
Government		0

Table 11.8 Party group rejections of ministers' negotiation proposals according to the position of the party group, 21 November – 26 June 2002 (minority government of the Liberal Party and the Conservative Party)

Opposition	Left wing	40
	Potential government	3
	Right wing	13
Government		0

In short the decisional patterns of Tables 11.7 and 11.8 show that the committee members from the government party groups never opposed a ministers' policy stance no matter which party groups were in government. The former government party group did, but only to a very limited extent. The opposition to the government's EU policy is first and foremost found in the party groups on the wings. The figures are in harmony with the fact that Danish governments find their way, that is avoid a majority against a negotiation proposal, in 'the middle of the road'. And as matter of fact it happens seldom that a majority in the committee turns down a minister's negotiation proposal (Jensen 2003, p. 156, Nedergaard 2000, p. 335).

Though we should be careful because the data stems from different periods, Tables 11.5 through 11.8 show that the practice of parliamentary scrutiny in the Danish European Affairs Committee is not a story of 'the European Affairs Committee against the ministers'. The tables show that in practice the opposition party groups in general and the party groups on the wings in particular carry out the scrutiny in the committee. As the party group representatives from the government party groups remain more or less silent and support the government's negotiation proposals the tables also indicate that the government party groups and the ministers act as one unitary actor in the committee.

INSTITUTIONS – AND POLICY – MATTER

Now if we combine the behavioural patterns in policy matters (Tables 11.5-11.8) and institutional matters (Table 11.4), well aware that the tables cover different periods, we by and large see that government party groups wholeheartedly support their ministers' negotiation proposals and tend not to pose critical questions; in addition they tend not to put forward critical minority statements in the procedural committee reports. Among the opposition parties the potential government party groups are least inclined to reject ministers' negotiation proposals; they take an active part in the questioning activity and put forward only a small number of minority statements. The party groups on the wings most often refuse to accept the ministers' negotiation proposals, are very active in the questioning activity and tend to put forward most of and the most critical minority statements in the reports. How are we to understand these patterns?

Recalling that in Denmark the EU-sceptical opinions in parliament are found on the wings, the behavioural patterns in institutional matters and policy matters might not be particularly surprising. It is only to be expected that party groups that most frequently oppose the government and the rest of the majority at the policy level would be critical of the procedures that in the end rest with the same majority. Recalling, too, that the party groups on both wings have no government experience and, so far, have had no expectations of becoming part of the government, the committee members' behaviour can also be seen in a slightly different way, that is explained in terms of both policy and institutions. The arguments rest partly on counterfactual thinking.

Imagine that EU policy/politics had a left-right dimension going from a leftist 'let's get out of the EU – a shield for multi-national companies – as quickly as possible' to a rightist 'we want faster, deeper and more integration into the EU – the only democratic shield against another war in the heart of Europe'; imagine, too, that all party groups were neighboured along this dimension and with the minority government party group(s) somewhere in between. Then a minority government would have to either go left or right in parliament in order not to have a majority against its EU policy. If it goes right it will be met by critical voices from the left and vice versa. Juxtaposing attitudes and interests, left- and right-wing party groups would simply have non-symmetric interests in policy matters. In institutional matters, however, the picture would be different. The party groups on the left would want a strong parliament as an institutional instrument for pulling the government out of the EU and, accordingly, the right-wing party groups would want a strong parliament to push the government into the EU. In other words their interests will be symmetrical in institutional matters.

Now, turning to the Danish party groups the rather high degree of EU scepticism in both the left and right wing parties is in harmony with the fact that they have put forward partly similar and critical point of views on the European Affairs Committee's way of working. A couple of times they have even joined forces in institutional matters in order to have a stronger committee and more efficient instruments for parliamentary control with the government. In addition, this is in harmony with the fact that they are highly depen-dent on the committee as an instrument for influencing the government's EU policy, as they have neither access to nor expectations of gaining access to the ministries.

Regarding the actual government party groups they are more or less in the opposite situation. They are hardly dependent on the committee as an instrument for policy shaping. In this respect they are way ahead of the opposition parties because they have – via the ministers – direct access to ministries and the EU and do not need the committee as an institutional instrument for influencing the EU policy or collecting information in EU affairs. Due to the fact that representatives from the government party groups, in particular the EU spokespeople, are usually in close contact with the ministers and their civil servants before the committee meets, the government party groups normally are united behind the minister when he or she shows up in the committee. The EU spokespeople from the government party groups will know and have accepted the negotiation proposals and normally do not have to intervene in the committee's dialogue with the ministers.

Finally, the potential government party groups are somewhere in between. They are generally closer to the government's line of policy and closer to the possibility of becoming government party groups themselves, but are usually not directly involved in the formulation of the negotiation proposal. Hence they have to scrutinize the minister's proposal and arguments at the committee meetings. Accordingly, the representatives from the party groups in opposition and especially from the party groups on the wings have the motive to carry out scrutiny at the committee meetings.

CONCLUDING REMARKS

I set out to analyse the Danish European Affairs Committee's decisional activities in institutional matters and policy matters in a party group perspective. This perspective meant looking at the committee, not as an actor, but as an arena, that is as an institution that analytically could be seen as a structure and an instrument for party groups and their representatives on the committee.

In both institutional matters and policy matters we see decisional patterns that indicate that the lines of demarcation are running inside the committee, between party groups, and not between the committee as such and the ministers. These decisional patterns can, among other things, be explained as a combination of the party groups' different attitudes towards the EU and their different degree of dependence on the European Affairs Committee as an institutional instrument for influencing the government's EU policy.

Though other permanent committees of the Folketing to an increasing extent have been involved in the mandating process, the European Affairs Committee still pulls the trigger when it comes to accepting the government's negotiation proposal before negotiations in the EU. In this, and several other respects, the European Affairs Committee is a special committee with a unique competence compared to the other committees of the Folketing. In comparison to most of the other European Affairs Committees it is also considered a strong committee.

Keep in mind, however, that the institutional strength of the committee is dependent on the party groups and their relations to the government. Danish governments are typically minority governments. If a stable majority government came into power, the government would still be obliged to submit an oral mandate for negotiation to the committee. And the party groups in government would continuously have the possibility and, most likely, the need to act as a unitary actor, hence forming a majority behind the minister before the meetings in the committee. This would diminish the strength of the committee as an instrument in the hands of the party groups in opposition. Representatives from the opposition would still have the possibility of posing critical questions and point out weak spots in the government policy, but would not be able to block the minister.

So, the different political value of the European Affairs Committee as a political instrument to the opposition party groups under a minority government and under a majority government should be kept in mind if 'the Danish model' should be considered the strictest possible scrutiny. In general, the picture painted here of the European Affairs Committee gives partisanship a prominent role and tones down the European Affairs Committee's role as an actor in Danish EU policy. Studying processes of Europeanization in a multilevel perspective the Danish experience shows that the role of parties and party groups should not be ignored.

NOTES

1. The model has been in place almost since Denmark's entrance into the EU (EEC) in 1973. Hence, the following is stated in the first report from the European Affairs Committee, which in 1973 laid down the substance of the committee's competency: 'Prior to negotia-

tions in the EC Council of Ministers on decisions of a wider scope, the Government submits an oral mandate for negotiation to the Market Committee [the European Affairs Committee, HJ]. If there is no majority against the mandate, the government negotiates on this basis' (the European Affairs Committee 2002, p. 2).

2. The analysis of the institutional decisions in this section is mainly based on the public data from 'the procedural reports' submitted by the European Affairs Committee, though part of the analysis is also based on confidential material. The analysis of policy decisions in the next section draws mostly on the minutes from the committee and to some degree on participant observation from a dozen or more committee meetings. Access to the minutes as well as to the meetings was granted due to my former employment as a committee secretary in the Folketing and to a research project on the European Affairs Committee. The results from the project are published in Jensen (2003), on which this chapter draws.

REFERENCES

Arter, David (1995), 'The Folketing and Denmark's "european policy": the case of an "authorising assembly"?', *The Journal of Legislative Studies*, **1** (3), pp. 110-23.

Damgaard, Erik (1977), *Folketinget under forandring: Aspekter af Folketingets udvikling, virkemåde og stilling i det politiske system*, Copenhagen: Samfundsvidenskabeligt Forlag.

Dosenrode, Søren von (1998), 'Denmark: the testing of a hesitant membership', in Kenneth Hanf and Ben Soetendorp (eds), *Adapting to European Integration*, London and New York: Longman, pp. 52-68.

European Affairs Committee of the Folketing (2002), *Parliamentary Control of Government Policy in the EU, 2002*, Copenhagen: EU Information Centre of the Folketing.

Fenno, Richard F. (1973), *Congressmen in Committees*, Berkeley: Institute of Governmental Studies Press.

Fitzmaurice, John (1996), 'National parliamentary control of EU policy in the three new member states', *West European Politics*, **19** (1), 88-96.

Folketingstidende, Årbog & Registre, 2000-01, Copenhagen: The Folketing.

Hegeland, Hans and Ingvar Mattson (1996), 'To have a voice in the matter: a comparative study of the Swedish and Danish European committees', *The Journal of Legislative Studies*, **2** (3), 198-215.

Holzhacker, Ronald (2002), 'Nationale parlamenter i Den Europæiske Union: En model til komparativ vurdering af demokratiske kontrolbeføjelser', in Thomas Pedersen (ed.), *Europa for folket? EU og det danske demokrati*, Aarhus: Aarhus University Press, pp. 83-107.

Jensen, Henrik (1995), *Arenaer eller aktører? En analyse af Folketingets stående udvalg*, Copenhagen: Samfundslitteratur.

Jensen, Henrik (2002), *Partigrupperne i Folketinget*, Copenhagen: Jurist- og Økonomforbundets Forlag.

Jensen, Henrik (2003), *Europaudvalget – et udvalg i Folketinget*, Aarhus: Aarhus University Press.

Jensen, Jørgen Albæk (1996), 'Prior parliamentary consent to Danish EU policies', in Eivind Smith (ed.), *National Parliaments as Cornerstones of European Integration*, London, The Hague and Boston: Kluwer Law International, pp. 39-48.

Jensen, Jørgen Albæk (2001), 'Folketinget og udenrigspolitikken', in Gorm Toftegaard Nielsen (ed.), *Parlamentarismen – hvem tog magten?*, Copenhagen: Jurist- og Økonomforbundets Forlag, pp. 117-46.

Laursen, Finn (1995), 'Parliamentary bodies specializing in European Union affairs: Denmark and the Europe Committee of the Folketing', in Finn Laursen and Spyros A. Pappas (eds), *The Changing Role of Parliaments in the European Union*, Maastricht: European Institute of Public Administration/Institut européen d'administration publique, pp. 43-60.

Matthews, Donald R. (1980), *U.S. Senators And Their World* , Westport, Connecticut: Greeenwood Press.

Mouritzen, Hans (1997), *External Danger and Democracy: Old Nordic Lessons and New European Challenges*, Aldershot: Dartmouth Publishing Company.

Mouritzen, Hans (2003), 'Sammenfatning, perspektiver og reform', in Hans Mouritzen (ed.), *Er vi så forbeholdne? Danmark over for globaliseringen, EU og det nære*, Aarhus: Aarhus University Press, pp. 242-74.

Nedergaard, Peter (2000), *Organiseringen af Den Europæiske Union*, Copenhagen: Handelshøjskolens Forlag.

Raunio, Tapio and Simon Hix (2000), 'Backbenchers learn to fight back: European integration and parliamentary government', *West European Politics*, **23** (4), 142-68.

Raunio, Tapio and Matti Wiberg (2000), 'Parliaments adaptation to the European Union', in Peter Esaiasson and Knut Heidar (eds), *Beyond Westminster and Congress: The Nordic Experience*, Columbus: Ohio State University, pp. 344-64.

12. The Southern European Pattern of Parliamentary Scrutiny of EU Legislation: Emulating the French Model

José M. Magone

THE THEORETICAL CONTEXT

One of the aspects that make the study of top-down 'Europeanization' so interesting is that each political system adjusts differently institutionally and strategically to the pressures put on them. Indeed, as Katrin Auel makes clear in Chapter 9, it is important to compare different countries, so that one can learn how institutions, in this case parliaments, adjust to the growing pressures from the supranational level. Quite important is the fact that the historical and institutional context of each country is different, leading in some way to path-dependent responses to this new phenomenon (Dimitrakopoulos 2001).

The approach in this chapter is inspired by Auel's chapter, but with very important qualifications. First, we are analysing the impact of Europeanization on the southern European parliaments, which can be grouped as among the weakest of the European Union (EU) due to their late emergence in the case of Portugal, Spain and Greece, or due to manipulation and corruption in the pre-1992 'First' Republic in Italy. Second, the mismatched interaction among the institutions clearly prevented the development of a parliament that prides itself on controlling the executive. On the contrary, the executive is more or less unrestricted, protected in general by strong majorities in the corresponding parliaments. Third, the southern European political elites are not challenged by Eurosceptic populations. Southern European populations are in fact among the most pro-Europeanist in the EU (Magone 2002). Nevertheless, this support has to be qualified by the fact that southern European populations, particularly the Spanish and Portuguese, are among the least knowledgeable about the institutions and policies of the EU (Magone 2003, pp. 236-7).

Fourth, the southern European legislatures were not proactive in developing mechanisms of at least post-facto EU legislation parliamentary scrutiny. In comparison to the cases presented by Auel, southern European parliaments were reactive to the developments after protocol 13 in the Treaty of Maastricht and the Treaty of Amsterdam was ratified respectively in 1993 and 1999.

All four southern European parliaments tried to emulate other parliaments, following mainly the French pattern, but still characterized by lack of resources, dependent on high-quality individuals and quite discontinuous in their engagement. Indeed, it never reached the levels of institutionalized and professionalized work as can be found in the British, German and French cases. This is related to the overall culture of parliamentarianism in these countries. Despite these similarities, note that Italy, in spite of the collapse of the previous political class in 1992, is making large efforts to move towards a more pro-active pattern, but it is too early to say if the new political class of this new 'Second Republic' will be able to achieve this.

After this theoretical contextualization, the following sections deepen the insight by contextualizing the role of parliament in the political system, particularly in relation to the executive and, last but not least, the way parliament adjusted institutionally and strategically to the pressures of Europeanization.

THE PLACE OF PARLIAMENT IN THE SOUTHERN EUROPEAN POLITICAL SYSTEMS: THE DOMINANCE OF THE EXECUTIVE

Apart from the historical legacy of weak discontinuous parliamentarianism and the strong pro-European integration attitudes of the population, two further factors may explain the low profile of southern European parliaments: the attitude of political parties towards European integration and the pattern of executive-legislative relations.

Parties and Party System

In comparison to the Nordic countries, southern European party systems are not characterized by cleavages related to the European integration process as all main parties are more or less pro-European. Moreover, all four party systems are characterized by a polarization of two main parties or coalition of parties. The European integration process is not a factor of polarization for any of them. In Portugal, there are two large parties, the Socialists (*Partido Socialista-PS*) and the liberal Social Democrats (*Partido Socialdemocrata-PSD*), and two small parties, the People's Party (*Partido Popular-PP*) and the Communists (*Partido Comunista Portugues-PCP*). While the larger parties are uncritically committed to the European integration process, the smaller parties tend to present moderate Euro-sceptic positions. The PP under the leadership of Manuel Monteiro and then Paulo Portas resisted the Treaty of the EU and subsequent developments. Nevertheless, in the elections in 2002 the PP had no difficulties forming a coalition with senior partner, the PSD although parts of the party continued to be Eurosceptic. The Communists were for a long time opposed to European integration, but after accession they became positive, emphasizing the 'social Europe' aspect in the European project.

Table 12.1 Results of legislative elections in southern Europe (lower house)

	Parties/coalitions	Share of votes	Seats
Portugal (2005)	PS	46.4	121
	PSD	29.6	75
	PCP-PEV	7.7	14
	PP	7.5	12
	BE	6.5	8
Spain (2004)	PSOE	43.3	164
	PP	37.8	146
	CiU(incl. ICV-EUIA)	3.3	10
	IU	4.1	4
	ERC	2.6	8
	PNV	1.7	7
	Other	3.7	11
Italy (2006)	Union	49.8	341
	House of Freedoms	49.7	277
	Other		1
Greece (2004)	ND	45.5	165
	PASOK	40.5	117
	KKE	5.9	12
	Synaspismos	3.3	6

In Spain, the three national parties are pro-European. There are two large parties, the Christian Democratic People's Party (*Partido Popular-PP*) and the Social Democratic Socialists (*Partido Socialista Obrero Español-PSOE*), which are uncritical about the European integration process. While the PP tends to moderately emphasize the national interest, the PSOE sticks to a more integrationist pro-European line similar to other socialist parties in Europe. The third party, the small communist-led coalition United Left (*Izquierda Unida-IU*) is pro-European, but tends to be more critical than the two main parties. Apart from these three main national parties, there are over ten tiny regionalist parties represented in the Cortes and in the respective regional parliaments. By far the most important ones are the Catalan Convergence and Union (*Convergencia i Unió-CiU*) and the Basque Nationalist Party (*Partido Nacionalista Vasco-PNV*). They can become pivotal parties if any of the two main parties are unable to achieve a working majority. Most regionalist parties are very pro-European, with the exception of the Nationalist Galician Block (*Bloque Nacionalista Galego-BNG*), which has always presented a Eurosceptic left wing anti-capitalist position against the EU.

In Greece, there are two large parties, the Socialists (*Panneliniko Sosialistiko Kinima-PASOK*) and New Democracy (*Nea Dimokratia-ND*), which uncritically support European integration, and two small communist parties; one orthodox (*Kommounistikó Kómma Elládas-KKE*), which is quite anti-European integration, and another reformist, which candidates under a more loose umbrella organization, which is called Greek Left (*Kommunistikó Kómma Elládas-esouterikou-KKE-es/Synaspismos*) and is more pro-European.

After the *tangentopoli* affair of 1992, a new party system emerged in Italy. In spite of a mushrooming of political parties, due to a new mixed electoral system, which is predominantly majoritarian (75 per cent of seats) and only partly proportional (25 per cent seats), they had to group themselves around the two main pre-electoral coalitions on the left or right. Despite this overhaul of the Italian party system, the electoral coalition and the parties in it, with some discontinuity, are pro-integrationist. In December 2005, a further reform of the electoral system returned to a proportional representation system with blocked lists.

While the left-centre coalition Olive Tree/Democratic Party (*Ulivo/Unione*) under the leadership of Romano Prodi, comprising Social Democrats (*Democratici di sinistra-DS*), the Christian Democrats/Liberals (*Margherita*) and the Greens (*Girasole*) are very pro-European, the right–centre coalition House of Freedoms (*Casa delle Libertá*) under leader Silvio Berlusconi comprising his Christian Democratic catch-all party *Forza Italia*, the Northern League (*Lega Nord-LN*), the post-fascist National Alliance (*Alleanza Nazionale-AN*) and a small group of Christian democrats (*Biancafiore*), may express attitudes of national interest or even Euro-scepticism. This is normally associated with the leader of the Northern League, Umberto Bossi, whose spontaneous declarations have sometimes caused conflicts with parliament, the president or even within the coalition government. Nevertheless, these individual expressions of national interest or Euro-scepticism have never acquired a consistent strategy. On the contrary, they remained isolated in the mainstream discourse of the Italian political class (Di Virgilio 2002, p. 85).

Parliament in the Political System

Although all four parliaments may be considered weak in terms of controlling and shaping the work of the government, it is important to distinguish between the four countries. First, Portugal, Spain and Greece can be grouped into a category of parliaments that had to undertake a process of transition, consolidation, institutionalization and professionalization. Such processes cannot be accomplished over a short period; on the contrary there is still a low level of professionalization if we look at the high levels of rotation from legislature to legislature. Moreover, lack of human and material resources play a role in undermining any challenge to the government of the day. In Spain, MPs are asking for a research support office to scrutinize properly the budget presented by the government. Moreover, they are still waiting for a proper reform of the Senate, the Upper House of the Spanish Cortes. Prime Minister José Luis Zapatero is engaged in introducing these reforms in Spain. Indeed, he has been negotiating with all parliamentary parties for a substantial revision of the constitution towards a genuine federal structure. The Federal Republic of Germany has been presented as a possible model (*El Pais*, 16 May 2004, p. 16, 19 September 2004, p. 18). In Greece and Portugal insufficient human resources allocated to the committees allow only a very superficial control of the policies of the executive.

Table 12.2 The parliaments of southern Europe

	Portugal	Spain	Italy	Greece
Structure	Unicameral Assembleia da Republica(230)	Asymmetrical Bicameral Cortes Senate(258) Congress of Deputies(350)	Symmetrical Bicameral Parliament Senate (315) Chamber of Deputies (630)	Unicameral Vouli(300)

Since 1992 the Italian parliament has been better prepared to move towards an institutionalized, professionalized pattern than the other three legislatures. Although the rotation of MPs was very high in the 12th legislature (1994-96) reaching 77 per cent evenly distributed among all parties (Verzichelli 1996, pp. 116, 122), subsequently the bicameral parliament has been able to draw on the experience of pre-1992 parliamentarianism. Reform so far has been piecemeal, but most recently there has been a will to reform the Senate in the direction of the German Bundesrat, transform it into a genuine territorial chamber and move the political system towards a genuine federal system (*La Repubblica*, 9 October 2003, p. 7).

Executive–Legislative Relations

Between 1987 and 1995, Portugal was governed by absolute majority governments, which helped institutionalize and routinize the interaction between the institutions, but at the same it strengthened the executive in relation to parliament (Bandeira 2004). During the socialist governments under Prime Minister Antonio Guterres between 1995 and 2002, parliament was able to gain in more profile, but remained far from being a hard-working parliament. This pattern did not alter considerably under the coalition government of prime ministers Manuel Durão Barroso and Pedro Santana Lopes since the legislative elections of 17 March 2002 and the present Socialist government elected after the legislative elections of 18 February 2005.

A similar verdict can be made about the Spanish parliament. The absolute majorities of the socialist government between 1982 and 1993 fostered cooperation between the parties in terms of amendments to government legislation, but also helped to strengthen the executive (Capo Giol 1994). Between 1993 and 2000, both main parties were dependent on the support of the regionalist parties allowing for a stronger role for parliament, but after the absolute majority of the PP in the March 2000 elections, the dominance of the executive prevented a stronger engagement of parliament in the overall system.

In Greece, the Papandreou governments in the 1980s and 1990s weakened parliament considerably. Ninety-eight per cent of all legislation was pushed through by the government without proper consultation of the legislative. There was a brief revival of parliament in 1989-90, during which no party was able to achieve absolute majority and enquiry committees were set up to investigate the corruption scandals of the socialist governments, but the activism was abruptly stopped soon afterwards. In 2001, a constitutional revision slightly improved the position of parliament in the political system, but it is too early to say if this will affect the weak culture of parliamentarianism (Zervakis 1999, p. 651).

In the 13th legislature (1996-2001) of the new Italian 'Second' Republic, parliament was quite active in pushing forward necessary reforms of the constitution and it remained active throughout the legislature. The unstable Olive Tree coalition government allowed for a stronger prominence of parliament. Since 2001 the activism has become more rationalized in the 14th legislature. One reason is the strong cohesive majority of the House of Freedoms coalition government under Silvio Berlusconi. There were also cases of abuse of parliamentarianism from which Prime Minister Berlusconi gained personally, such as granting immunity for the top positions of the state and the regulation of private interests while serving in public office (Fabbrini 1998, 1999, Cotta and Verzichelli 2003, pp. 66-9).

In sum, southern European parliamentarianism can in many ways be grouped within a pattern of weak legislatures dominated by very pro-integrationist political parties. Compared to their counterparts in the Nordic countries and western Europe, they are characterized by a lower level of professionalization and routinization and are embedded in a very pro-European public opinion environment.

INSTITUTIONAL AND STRATEGIC EUROPEANIZATION: A SOUTHERN EUROPEAN PATTERN OF PARLIAMENTARY SCRUTINY OF EU LEGISLATION

During the Delors Commission, southern European political systems in general and parliaments in particular were under pressure to adjust to the new challenges from the implementation of the Single European Market (SEM) and Economic and Monetary Union (EMU). A crucial turning point was the adoption and ratification of the Treaty of the European Union (TEU) in 1992 and 1993, which led to an upgrading of the scrutiny structures in each parliament. The inclusion in the TEU of protocol 13 on the role of national parliaments in the European integration process led to a reactive upgrading. The ratification of the Treaty of Amsterdam in 1999 can be regarded as a further turning point for the strengthening of the scrutinizing role of parliaments in southern Europe. The final draft of the Constitutional Treaty envisages a stronger role for the national parliaments.

This process was more or less reinforced by the continuing informal debates at the Conference of European Affairs Committees (CEAC), which have been taking place twice a year since 1989.

Institutional Europeanization: An Evolutionary Reactive Pattern

Before 1985, the Italian parliament did not deal with EC issues, because it was seen as foreign policy and thus exclusively in the realm of the government. The SEM Programme put the Italian parliament under pressure to play its part in the transposition of EC legislation into national law. Italy has had committees dealing with EU affairs since the 1960s, emulating the example of the German Bundesrat, which created a committee in 1957. The Italian committee was established in July 1968. The so-called Consultative Committee for EC Affairs (*Giunta consultativa per gli Affari delle Comunità Europee*) only had consultative powers and played only a minor role in the process of EU scrutiny. It was able to offer advice on draft laws and prepare its own reports on European Community issues, and it worked closely with the Committee of External Affairs of the Senate. The counterpart in the Chamber of Deputies, the so-called Standing Committee for Community Affairs (*Comitato Permanente per gli affari communitari*), was created in February 1973 as a subcommittee of the powerful External Affairs Committee. It prepared reports on different issues related to the European Community (Millar 1979, pp. 191-2). The irrelevance of the two committees is due to the slow pace of the European integration process. It was Jacques Delors, the president of the European Commission, who changed the pace and nature of the EC considerably. Between 1987 and 1992 Italy had to catch up with the transposition of the directives related to the SEM. The constant pressure from the European Commission and the Constitutional Court led to changes in the previously unorganized approach of parliament in relation to EU affairs. Quite crucial was the adoption of the Fabbri Law (Law n°183 of 1987), which was designed for a fast transposition of directives into national law. It also allowed for a stronger involvement of the regions in the process of European integration through the newly created Council of State-Regions designed to facilitate the exchange of information. This was then further rationalized by the La Pergola Law (Law n°86 of 9 March 1989) and other laws accompanying this aspect. The La Pergola Law is still today the main legal framework for EU scrutiny. It clearly gives a more organized integrative framework to the process of EU legislation transposition.

As a consequence, institutional changes were introduced in the Italian parliament. The *Giunta* was able to more or less preserve its format, but in the Chamber of Deputies the subcommittee was upgraded, and Community matters became part of the strong External and Community Affairs Committee (*Commissione Affari Esteri e Communitari*) in July 1987. By 1990 it had been granted even more autonomy from the field of external relations, and it became the Special Committee for EC Policies (*Commissione speciale per le politiche communitari*). The final autonomy and upgrading of Community matters in the Chamber of Deputies took place in August 1996, when the committee finally became a standing committee. In some sense, adjustment to the European integration process started before the Protocol on National Parliaments enshrined in the Maastricht Treaty of 1993. The Italian parliament was able to steadily improve its position in the political system in terms of scrutiny of EU legislation. Indeed, in August 1996 and July 1999, respectively, the relevant Committee for EU Policies was upgraded to a standing committee with full law-making powers (Chamber of Deputies 2000). The whole process of post facto scrutiny is enshrined in Articles 126 and 127 of the parliamentary standing order of the Congress of Deputies (Camera dei Deputati 2001, pp. 174-9) and in Articles 142 and 143 of the parliamentary standing order of the Senate (Senato 2003, pp. 231-9), but there is no mention in the constitution.

In Spain, a Joint Committee for EC Affairs (*Comisión Mixta del Congreso y del Senado para las Comunidades Europeas*) was established in 1985 as a joint committee of Senate and Congress. After Maastricht its role was reinforced, and it became known as the *Comisión Mixta para la Unión Europea* (Joint Committee for EU Affairs). In spite of this upgrade, the dominance of the executive clearly prevented a strong role for the *Comisión*. Moreover it is defined as a non-legislative committee, which is highly dependent on other committees to act in a legislative manner, particularly the external affairs committee. Its main role is control. The whole process of transposition of directives is monopolized by the government, although the *Comisión* may be able to express opinions related to the transposed legislation. The main work of the *Comisión* has been concentrated on oral questions to the government or requests for debates on specific EU legislation (Cienfuegos Mateo 1995, pp. 78-91, 2001, pp. 203-5). This naturally shows that European legislation is firmly under government control, and that parliamentary scrutiny of EU affairs is not regarded as important in the Spanish Cortes. The *Comisión* has a low status in both houses of parliament (Closa 1996, pp. 147-8).

In Portugal, a Committee for Community Affairs (*Comissão de Assuntos Comunitários*) was established in 1985, shortly before Portugal joined the EC. Some control of EU legislation was established in 1987 (Law 29, 29 June 1987) and revised in 1988 (Law 111, 15 December 1988), but parliament was not able to play a major role in the period between accession and the adoption of the Maastricht Treaty. The introduction of Law 20 of 15 June 1994 clearly strengthened the oversight role of the Portuguese parliament. The Committee of European Affairs (*Comissão de Assuntos Europeus*) became more active under the leadership of Jorge Braga de Macedo. In contrast to Spain and Italy, the competence to scrutinize EU legislation has been enshrined in the Portuguese constitution since its third revision of 1992 under Articles 166 and 167. It was changed in the fourth revision of the constitution in 1997 to Article 161n in a direct response to the Treaty of Maastricht. This led to a considerable improvement of executive-legislative relations in EU matters (Assembleia da República 2000, Braga de Macedo 1995). Since the last legislative elections of 17 March 2002, the Committee of European Affairs has merged with the Committee of External Affairs (*Comissão de Assuntos Exteriores e Europeus*) due to the difficult budgetary situation in Portugal (Interview with Ana Fraga, 13 July 2002).

Although Greece joined the EC/EU in 1981, it was not until 1990 that the Greek parliament established a Committee of European Affairs (*Epitropi Evropaikón Ypothésseon*), which was enshrined in the rules of procedure under article 32a in 1993. It was updated in the revision of the rules of procedure of the chamber in 1997. Since then the government has been obliged to report all EU proposals to all permanent committees of parliament through its president (Zervakis and Yannis 2001, p. 159). In spite of this formal institutional upgrading of the Greek Committee of European Affairs, its work has been characterized by discontinuity. Between 1990 and 1996 it was completely inactive, but since 1996 a procedure has been in place in which the committee just submits reports to parliament and government (Zervakis and Yannis 2001, p. 160, Dimitrakopoulos 2001). The recent constitutional revision of 2001 enhanced the role of parliament in EU affairs, but it seems that the behavioural pattern has not changed very much.

The number of people sitting in the different committees varies from country to country. In Italy, the *Commissione* has 48 members, while the *Giunta* has about 25 members. The Spanish *Comisión* has about 36 members; the Portuguese *Comissão* has 25 to 30. The Greek *Vouli* consists of 31 members, 16 of which are MPs and 15 are MEPs. The committee is chaired by an ex officio non-elected member of parliament. In all parliaments, proportional representation of all relevant political groups is used to select the members.

According to Ana Fraga, the Portuguese *Comissão* in 1999 had a support staff of three persons, two of whom were specialized in EU affairs and one who was an administrator. In spite of a merger between the committee of external and European affairs after the legislative elections of 2002, the staff did not increase. This naturally put a huge workload on the few staff members, who were really committed to what was happening in the EU (interview with Ana Fraga, 13 July 2002).

According to the final report of the 6th legislature (1996-2000) Spain had two to four legal assistants (*letrados*) working for the *Comisión* and additional secretarial staff comprising four secretaries. They all came from a pool of staff allocated to the committee directorate comprising 22 legal assistants, 13 technical staff and 19 secretarial staff (Congreso de los Diputados 2001, pp. 1162-4)

In Italy, the Chamber of Deputies has 20 staff members attached to the *Commissione*. According to Federiga Bindi and Stefano Grassi there is a Service for Community and International Affairs inside the Research Unit, which monitors institutional and legislative processes, drafts legal opinions and background documentation. The service has three higher civil servants, six assistants and three secretaries, and additional staff, one administrator and six assistants are allocated to the *Commissione*. The *Giunta* has only five staff members: two technical and three administrative staff (Bindi-Calussi and Grassi 2001, pp. 277-8).

There are no exact data on the Greek parliament, but the low level of meetings and activity suggest a weak allocation of human and material resources to the committee of European affairs.

Strategic Europeanization: Towards a Discontinuous, Reactive 'French' Pattern

According to Auel in Chapter 9, the French parliament focuses its work on preparing excellent documentation on aspects of European legislation in order to make the process of European integration more transparent to French civil society. The French parliament is less interested in bypassing or rivalling the government at the supranational level, but provides French society with an alternative source of information. Discontinuous reactive elements of this French pattern can be found in all four southern European countries. Nevertheless, we can differentiate between the Italian and Portuguese parliaments, which have shown signs of ambition and improvement in the second half of the 1990s, and the more reactive and modest performance of Spanish and Greek parliaments.

The Italian *Commissione* is now in theory better equipped to deal with EU legislation both in the so-called ex ante decision making process (*fase ascendente*) as well as the post facto implementation process (*fase descendente*). There was some ambition in the 13th legislature to play a stronger role in the scrutiny of EU policies, but dependence on the cooperation of the government makes it difficult to play a systematic long-term role. The *Commissione* has now become central to the whole process of EU scrutiny. Quite central to this process is the so-called Community Law (*Legge Communitaria*) enshrined in the La Pergola Law. The Community Law is a systematic balance of all the legislation which was transposed until July of the previous year. This is submitted by the government to the Italian parliament for scrutiny. The Community Law was devised to overcome the backlog of directives, which were not transposed into national law in the early 1980s. It is a very flexible instrument including all forms of legislative acts for more complicated directives and administrative acts for less relevant technical issues coming from Community legislation. In some sense, the La Pergola Law has been considered a success, because it decreased the backlog of directives. Moreover, parallel to that, Law 400/1988 also changed the Presidency Office of the Council of Ministers by adding a so-called general directorate for European Integration (*Dipartimento per il Coordinamento delle Politiche europee*) to better coordinate the process of legislation transposition. The whole confusion about Italian EU policy coordination starts with confusion as to which ministry is responsible for internal coordination work and which ministry is responsible for external coordination work. According to David Hine, a shift of power from the Ministry of Foreign Affairs to the Prime Minister's Office took place during the 1980s and 1990s. Today the DPCE is in a certain sense the coordinating institution in the preparation of the *legge communitaria*, although it is not always clear if it has the position of a quasi ministry (Berlusconi I, D'Alema I and II) or an under-secretariat (Prodi) (Hine 2001, pp. 31-41, Bindi-Calussi 1999, pp. 208-13). In the Italian parliament the *Giunta* and *Commissione* play a more active role. Their main task is to scrutinize legislation within a time frame of 30 days. In reality it lasts much longer, because the *Giunta* and *Commissione* send it to different committees according to issues to evaluate the right transposition into national law. This naturally does not tell us a lot about the quality of legislation. Indeed, Alessia Donà and Sergio Fabbrini found in a study that the MPs' lack of expertise in terms of the technical nature of the directives leads to very superficial work in the committee system. More or less, there is a tendency to accept the community law as it was originally presented by the executive. Apart from the fact that MPs' lack experience in scrutinizing directives, there is also a lack of resources in the house to undertake it. In some sense, there is an asymmetrical relationship in terms of information gathering between the executive and parliament (Fabbrini and Donà 2002, Guizzi 2000, pp. 559-69). According to Bindi and Grassi, some efforts were made to improve the situation in terms of this asymmetrical information. The Italian parliament now has an office attached to the European Parliament and in the 13th legislature government was more forthcoming in transferring EU documentation to the Secretariat. One major problem, however, is the lack of technical comments attached to the respective EU documents. This is related to the fact that the Italian government is still not up to speed in dealing with the growing number of documentation produced by the European institutions (Bindi-Calussi and Grassi 2001, pp. 287-9).

Between 1991 and 1999, seven annual community laws were adopted allowing for an improvement of the transposition of EU directives into national law. According to the statistical data attached to the Annual Community Law 2000, the transposition rate had improved from 76.5 per cent of total at the end of 1991 to 96.8 per cent on 24 November 2000.

In spite of this improvement Italy was not able to overcome the backlog in transposing EU legislation (Giuliani 2001). In fact, Italy along with Greece and France are the laggards of transposition of EU legislation (Börzel 2001, p. 819). Reforms are under way to speed up not only transposing, but also compliance with EU legislation by decentralizing the political system further and increasing the competencies of the regions in this respect.

The Italian parliament's ambitions to achieve some kind of parliamentary reserve in the ex ante phase of crucial EU legislation proposals led to increased cooperation between the government and parliament in the late 1990s. The Annual Community Law of 2000 further strengthened the position of parliament in relation to the government. Documentation was transferred to the *Comissione*, which allowed for some very restricted influence in the whole process. Article 6 of Annual Community Law 422 of 29 December 2000 allows for a flexible ex ante scrutiny of EU proposals, in which parliament can present its amendments before the bill is tabled at EU level. If there is no reaction by that date, the government is free to adopt its own position. Most of this was undertaken by hearings of EU proposals and less so by a more sophisticated actual scrutiny of EU legislation. In the 13th legislature there were 32 meetings with different ministers. Eleven EU proposals were scrutinized by the standing committees, ten of them by the *Comissione* in the Chamber of Deputies. Many EU proposals are reviewed by the other standing committees according to the different issues. In the same period 33 resolutions were adopted on EU issues by standing committees and 35 by the plenary (Bindi-Calussi and Grassi 2001, pp. 290-2).

The ambition of the Italian parliament to regain some importance in the overall decision-making process was more or less frustrated by Silvio Berlusconi's government, which intended to strengthen the role of the executive in the overall Italian political system. In the 14th legislature, the Italian parliament was marginalized by the majority obtained by Berlusconi in the elections on 13 May 2001.

Similarly, the Portuguese Committee of European Affairs never achieved a major role in the process of EU legislation. The whole process of scrutiny is ex post, meaning that at the beginning of each year the Committee of European Affairs receives an annual report of the transposition of legislation made by government in the previous year. This is forwarded to the relevant committees. After a period of one month the committee just collects the opinions of the individual committees and writes a report, which is presented and approved in a plenary session. A representative of government, normally the State Secretary for European Affairs, or even the Foreign Minister, is normally present to respond to any questions or criticisms in the report of the *Comissão*. Between 1994 and 2001, seven reports were presented to the plenary session. There is a general feeling that the governmental reports are mere compilations of data from the main institutions without any real institutional input from the Directorate General for European Affairs in the Ministry of Foreign Affairs. Parliamentary reports have several times criticized the lack of quality of the government reports. Parliament was not able to play a genuine proactive role in creating a research culture of European integration studies, which would counterbalance the poor quality of the reports by the Ministry of Foreign Affairs.

The Portuguese parliament has a more realistic assessment of its role in scrutinizing legislative proposals. The lack of practice and need for training in EU legislation scrutiny are quite evident. Although executive-legislative relations in terms of transfer of information have improved, it is still unsystematic and selective. It leaves parliament highly dependent on internet sources (Assembleia da República 2000, p. 1).

In the legislative session of 1999-2000 the Committee monitored the Portuguese presidency of the Council of the EU and the Intergovernmental Conference, which would lead to the Treaty of Nice, prepared by the COSAC, it monitored the Convention on drafting a Charter of Fundamental Rights and it scrutinized both the budget and the legislative programme of the European Commission. During this period of the presidency, it had 15 meetings with members of the government, particularly with the Secretary of State for European Affairs, Francisco Seixas da Costa (DAR 2.7.2001, n°32, 128).

During the past few years, the *Comissão* has improved its internet site, so that it may reach a larger public. Public hearings and debates have been going on since 1994 in relation to the Treaty of Maastricht (Assembleia da Republica 1995), the consequences of Economic Monetary Union (Assembleia da Republica 1998), the Treaty of Amsterdam (Assembleia da Republica 1995) and the future of the EU. The Committee for External and European Affairs (*Comissão de Assuntos Exteriores e Europeus*) monitored the European Convention and the role for national parliaments in it. In spite of the lack of resources and insufficient training of MPs, the Committee of European Affairs of the 8th legislature (1999-2002) worked quite hard to monitor the work of the government. This became quite evident in the process towards the Treaty of Nice. Rapporteurs were nominated to monitor the work of the government in the Intergovernmental Conference. The outcome was an excellent and detailed report which was made available to the wider public on the website of the Committee of European Affairs (Moura and Pereira 2001).

The Spanish *Comisión Mixta* has a similar task of informing the public about the developments in the EU. Similar to the Portuguese and Italian cases, the *Comisión* is not able to play a major role in the decision-making process. Indeed, Amsterdam did not lead to major changes of the role of the

Comisión within the overall decision-making process (Parlément Espagnol 2000). Most of the activities of the *Comisión Mixta* are related to preparing questions to the government on aspects of European integration which may affect Spain. According to the data provided by the Cortes, in the 6th legislature (2000-2004) 55 such questions were addressed to the government between June 2000 and June 2002. They deal with various subjects, but predominantly structural funds, internal market regulation and the external economic relations of the EU as part of pillar I.

The *Comision Mixta* also made 118 requests for hearings of members of government. The minister of foreign affairs appeared in the *Comisión Mixta* once to explain the position of the government before the final negotiation of the Nice Treaty. In 2001, the Secretary of State for European Affairs appeared three times in the *Comisión Mixta*. In April 2002, it also had hearings with Spanish representatives at the European Convention. Furthermore, hearings with EU officials and the ambassadors of the candidate countries were part of the programme. In this period, the *Comisión Mixta* presented 16 so-called resolutions (*proposiciones no de ley*), which is something between a bill and a control instrument, in order to influence the government in particular policies, e.g. the role of the regions in the decision-making process, the status of community law in the ultra-peripheral regions, enlargement and the presidency in the first half of 2002.

In sum, the influence possibilities of the Spanish Cortes are quite limited. According to the former Speaker of the Congress of Deputies, Luisa Fernanda Rudi Ubeda, there is a need to improve the relationship between parliaments and governments in the process of transmission of legislative proposals by the Commission. In her contribution to the COSAC in Madrid, she clearly wanted the procedure of transmission towards the parliaments to be better defined, instead of developing new institutions such as a proposed second chamber of national parliaments at EU level. It clearly makes the point that the main institution for national parliaments is not the European Parliament, but the Council. In spite of that, the procedures among parliaments are still too divergent. She pleads for minimum rules so that a level playing field can be created (Rudi Ubeda 2002).

Although the role of the *Comisión Mixta* was upgraded after 1994, it is in reality marginalized from the overall decision-making process. In comparative terms, one would estimate that the Spanish possibility of influence and level of activity is lower than in the Italian and Portuguese cases.

The Greek parliament has an even lower profile than the other three parliaments. The Committee of European Affairs scrutinizes EU legislative proposals, which have to be submitted by the government according to the rules of procedure. It may decide not to act and just allow the government to act without any parliamentary input. If it decides to act, it may submit a report to the plenary after consulting the government. This is discussed in the plenary, but not voted on and it is not binding for the foreign ministry. The government may voluntarily report back to parliament. One of the main problems with the process is that the government may delay submission of EU legislative proposals, so that parliamentary scrutiny remains at an absolute minimum. In spite of reforms, the Greek parliament remains marginalized from the whole EU legislative decision-making process at national level (Zervakis and Yannis 2001, p. 162).

A way of measuring the importance of committee work among the southern European parliaments is the number of sessions dedicated to EU matters. Here again there is a major distinction between the Italian and Portuguese parliaments on the one side and the Spanish and Greek parliaments on the other.

More concretely the *Comisión* had 34 sessions (comprising 105 hours) in the 3rd legislature (1986-89), 29 sessions (comprising 82 hours and 48 minutes) in the 4th legislature (1989-93), 35 sessions (comprising 82 hours and 12 minutes) in the 5th legislature (1993-96) and 38 sessions (comprising 99 hours and 23 minutes) in the 6th legislature (1996-2000) (Basabe Lloréns and González Escudero 2001, p. 208, Congreso de los Diputados 1991, p. 100, 1995, p. 110, 1997, p. 107, 2001, p. 165).

The Portuguese Committee of European Affairs met around 40-50 times per legislative period between 1995 and 2002, which led to 150-200 meetings per legislature, if we compare the data with the Spanish case. Exact data on the activities of the committee exists only since the 2nd legislative session of the 7th legislature (1995-99). According to the figures, the committee met 43 times in the legislative session of 1996-97, 48 in 1997-98, and 54 times in 1998-99. In the first legislative session (1999-2000) of the 8th legislature, which includes the period of the Portuguese presidency of the EU, the Committee met 47 times (DAR, 7.8.1998, n°38, p. 253, 5.7.1999, n°29, p. 175, 11.11.2000, n°7, p. 15, 2.7.2001, n°32, p. 328).

Quite amazing is the workload of the Italian *Commissione*, which reached three days a week after 1998. According to Andreas Maurer, the Italian *Commissione* may work up to 160 days a year. If we extrapolate his figures, the *Commissione* would have about 200-300 meetings per legislative session. In contrast, the *Giunta* has less than two meetings per month. Nevertheless, according to the response of the Italian parliament to the questionnaire to the XXIIIrd COSAC in Paris in the 13th legislature (1996-2001), meetings of the Committees increased by 700 per cent, and the number of propositions and law projects to be examined in relation to their compatibility with the community law increased more than 200 per cent. Moreover, the number of legislative proposals forwarded for scrutiny by the relevant committees increased by 1000 per cent (Sénat Italien 2000, p. 1). In the 13th legislature the *Commissione* met 618 times (comprising 337.15 hours) until July 2000 (Bindi-Calussi and Grassi 2001, p. 287). In comparison to previous legislatures this is a considerable increase. According to the statistical data of the Chamber of Deputies, the *Commissione* met 54 times (comprising a period of 56.5 hours) during the 12th legislature (1994-96), 76 times (comprising a period of 78.1 hours) during the 11th legislature (1992-1994) and 112 times during the 10th legislature (1987-1992) (Camera dei Deputati, no year, pp. 84-5, 94-5, 104-5).

The Greek Committee of European Affairs meets infrequently, only eight times per legislative period. Compared to the other parliaments, its parliament works the least.

In sum, southern European parliaments increased their scrutiny work in the 1990s compared with the previous decade, but their performance is discontinuous, irregular and above all more reactive than proactive.

CONCLUSIONS: THE SOUTHERN EUROPEAN PATTERN OF PARLIAMENTARY SCRUTINY OF EU LEGISLATION

Despite the differences between the southern European parliaments, they have the same approach to scrutiny of EU legislation. To a certain extent all four parliaments attempt to emulate the French pattern of EU legislation scrutiny, that is they want to be an important forum for the respective civil societies to discuss the latest developments in the European integration process. None of the four southern European parliaments is able to achieve the level of sophistication and continuity achieved by the French parliament. On the contrary, they struggle to keep pace with European developments. There is some mismatching in the information flows between government and parliament. Most of the work has been quite reactive and emulating patterns of behaviour presented by more professionalized legislatures in the semestral meetings of the CEAC. In spite of this lower level of quality of the southern European parliaments, one has to acknowledge that some parliaments work harder and are more ambitious than others. While the Spanish and Greek scrutiny committees are quite weak and members make only modest efforts to change the situation, the Italians and Portuguese committees work very hard. The Italian *Commissione* conducts ex ante hearings, which allows for some influence on the Italian position in relation to legislative acts, while Portuguese MPs focus predominantly on interacting with civil society to make the whole process more transparent.

REFERENCES

Assembleia da República (1995), *Acompanhamento Parlamentar da Revisão do Tratado da União Europeia na Conferencia Intergovernmental de 1996*, 2 vols., Lisboa: Comissão de Assuntos Europeus.

Assembleia da República (1998), *Opções Europeias de Portugal: União Económica e Monetária*, Lisboa: Comissão de Assuntos Europeus.

Assembleia da República (2000), *Scrutiny of European Policy by Member States National Parliaments: Answers to the Questionnaire for XXIIIrd COSAC*, Versailles, 16-17 October, http://www.cosac.org.

Bandeira, Cristina Leston (2004), *From Legislation to Legitimation.: The Role of the Portuguese Parliament*, London: Routledge.

Basabe Llorens, Felipe and Maria Teresa González Escudero (2001), 'The parliament of Spain: Slowly moving onto the European direction?', in Andreas Maurer and Wolfgang Wessels (eds), *National Parliaments on their Ways to Europe: Losers or Latecomers?*, Baden-Baden: Nomos, pp. 199-221.

Bindi-Calussi, Federiga (1999), 'L'influenza italiana nei processi decisionali europei', *Europa, Europe*, **8** (3), 207-25.

Bindi-Calussi, Federiga and Stefano B. Grassi (2001), 'The parliament of Italy: From benevolent observer to active player', in Andreas Maurer and Wolfgang Wessels (eds), *National Parliaments on their Ways to Europe: Losers or Latecomers?*, Baden-Baden: Nomos, pp. 269-99.

Börzel, Tanja (2001), 'Non-compliance in the European Union: Pathology or statistical artefact?', *Journal of European Public Policy*, **8** (5), 803-24.

Braga de Macedo, Jorge (1995), 'Acompanhamento e Apreciação Parlamento dos Assuntos Europeus', *legislação*, **13/14**, 157-77.

Camera dei Deputati (2001), *Constituzione della Repubblica: Regolamento della Camera*, Roma: Camera dei Deputati.

Camera dei Deputati (no date), *Notiziario della Camera die Deputati: Attività legislativa, di indirizzo, controllo e informazione dati statistici e quantitativi. Compendio statistico dalla I alla XII Legislatura*, Roma: Camera dei Deputati.

Capo Giol, Jordi (1994), 'Oposición y Minorias en las Legislaturas Socialistas', *Revista Española de Investigaciones Sociologicas*, **66**, 91-113.

Chamber of Deputies (2000), *Scrutiny of European Policy by National Parliaments of Member States*, XXIIIrd COSAC, Versailles, 16-17 October 2000, Response to questionnaire, p. 1.

Cienfuegos Mateo, Manuel (1995), 'O controlo parlamentar sobre o governo nos assuntos relativos às Comunidades Europeias em Espanha', *legislação*, **13/14**, 65-105.

Cienfuegos Mateo, Manuel (2001), 'Las Cortes Españolas ante la integración Europea', in Carlos Closa (ed.), *La europeización del sistema politico español*, Madrid: Istmo, pp. 197-221.

Closa, Carlos (1996), 'Spain: The Cortes and the EU – a growing together', in Philip Norton (ed.), *National Parliaments and the European Union*, London: Frank Cass, pp. 136-50.

Congreso de los Diputados (1991-2001), *Memórias de las Legislaturas*, Madrid: Congreso de los Diputados.

Cotta, Maurizio and Luca Verzichelli (2003), 'Il governo Berlusconi II alla prova: un anno di complicazioni' in Jean Blondel and Paolo Segati (eds), *Politica in Italia: I Fatti dell'Anno e le Interpretazioni. Edizione 2003*, Bologna: il Mulino, pp. 49-71.

Di Virgilio, Aldo (2002), 'L'Offerta Elettorale: La Politica delle Alleanza si institutionaliza', in Roberto D'Alimonte and Stefano Bartolini (eds), *Maggioritario finalmente? La transizione elettorale 1994-2001*, Bologna: il Mulino, pp. 79-129.

Diário da Assembleia da República (DAR) II-Série C (various years).

Dimitrakopoulos, Dionyssis (2001), 'Incrementalism and path dependence: European integration and institutional change in national parliaments', *Journal of Common Market Studies*, **30** (3), 405-22.

Fabbrini, Sergio (1998), *Chi Guida L'Esecutivo? Presidenza della Repubblica e Governo in Italia (1996-1998)*, Siena: Centro Interdipartimentale di Ricerca sul Cambiamento Politico. Occasional Papers, no. 3.

Fabbrini, Sergio (1999), 'Dal Governo Prodi al Governo D'Alema: continuità o discontinuità?', in David Hine and Salvatore Vassallo (eds), *Politica in ltalia: I Fatti dell'Anno e le Interpretazioni. Edizione 99*, Bologna: il Mulino, pp. 139-59.

Fabbrini, Sergio and Alessia Donà (2002), 'Europeanization of the governmental system as strengthening of domestic executive power: The Italian experience and the case of the "Legge Comunitaria"', paper presented at the ECPR Joint Sessions workshop on 'Europeanization and Political Institutions', University of Turin, 22-27 March.

Giuliani, Marco (2001), 'Europeanization and Italy: A bottom-up process?', in Kevin Featherstone and George Kazamias (eds), *Europeanization and the Southern Periphery*, London: Frank Cass, pp. 47-72.

Guizzi, Vincenzo (2000), *Manuale di Diritto e Politica della Unione Europea*, Roma: Editoriale Scientifica.

Hine, David (2001), 'European policy-making and the machinery of Italian government', in Kevin Featherstone and George Kazamias (eds), *Europeanization and the Southern Periphery*, London: Frank Cass, pp. 25-46.

Magone, José M. (2002), 'The attitudes of southern European citizens before and after accession(1974-1999)', in Antonio Costa Pinto and Nuno Severiano Teixeira (eds), *Southern Europe and the Making of the European Union*, New York: Columbia University Press, pp. 209-36.

Magone, José M. (2003), *The Politics of Southern Europe: Integration into the European Union*, Westport, CT: Praeger.

Millar, David (1979), 'Treatment of European Community matters by committees of the national parliaments', in Valentine Herman and Rinus van Schendelen (eds), *The European Parliament and National Parliaments*, Westmead: Saxon House, pp. 189-200.

Moura, José Barros and António Nazaré Pereira (2001), *Relatório sobre a proposta de resoluçã o n°59/VIII que aprova para ratificação, o Tratado de Nice que altera o Tratado da União Europeia, os Tratados que instituem as Comunidades Europeias e alguns actos relativos a esses tratados assinado em Nice, em 26 de Fevereiro de 2001*, Lisboa: Comissão de Assuntos Europeus, 24 Outubro.

Parlément Espagnol (2000), *Réponse du Parlément espagnol au questionnaire du Parlément francais pour la XXIIIéme COSAC*, Versailles, 16-17 octobre.

Rudi Ubeda, Luisa Fernanda (2002), *El Papel de los Parlamentos Nacionales en la Unión Europea.Ponencia Para La Conferencia de Presidentes de la Union Europea*, Madrid, 8-9 June.

Sénat Italien (2000), *Réponses du Comité pour les affaires européennes du Sénat italien*, XXIIIeme, COSAC, Versailles, 16-17 October www.cosac org.

Senato (2003), *Regolamento del Senato*, Roma: Senato.

Verzichelli, Luca (1996), 'The new members of parliament', in Richard S. Katz and Piero Ignazi (eds), *Italian Politics: The Year of the Tycoon. A Review Vol. 10*, Boulder, CO: Westview Press, pp. 115-33.

Zervakis, Peter A. (1999), 'Das politische System Griechenlands', in Wolfgang Ismayr (ed.), *Die politischen Systemen Westeuropas*, Opladen: Leske & Budrich, pp. 637-72.

Zervakis, Peter A. and Nikos Yannis (2001), 'The parliament of Greece: Slow but constant moves towards European integration?', in Andreas Maurer and Wolfgang Wessels (eds), *National Parliaments on their Ways to Europe: Losers or Latecomers?*, Baden-Baden: Nomos, pp.147-71.

13. The Role of ECE Parliaments in EU Integration

Attila Ágh

INTRODUCTION

This chapter deals with the parallel process of the Europeanization of East Central European (ECE) parliaments and the parliamentarization of Europeanization.[1] ECE parliaments have had to undergo profound changes in the EU accession and post-accession periods, and at the same time they have played a very active role in making their countries more adapted to the EU. This dual process has produced some negative features from the very beginning such as the cultural shock of arriving in Europe, the lack of information and low interest in the EU institutions, the language barrier of MPs, and a general 'EU-phoria' which has substituted for more practical approaches. Among the positive features are the strong parliamentary traditions in the ECE and the very active public opinion focusing on the EU. At present new negative and positive factors are emerging as party over-competition has distorting effects on all EU issues, many well-informed organized interest groups discuss the issue of EU transfers, and there is an intensified public discourse on EU matters in general. Actually in the ECE these two different party blocs have an increasingly diverging view on Europeanization: a pro-EU left and a Eurosceptic right seem to emerge as the ECE left has focused on the EU-type modernization and the ECE right on the 'Europe of nations'.[2]

The parliamentarization of the EU in recent years has basically changed the tasks of parliaments in the new ECE member states as they have to get used to the new situation with the increased competencies of the European Parliament (EP). Reinforcing this external challenge, there are three internal factors pushing the ECE parliaments to change. First, although the basic legislation on democratization and marketization as the legal systemic change is more or less over, the ECE parliaments are still faced with the huge legislative task of the detailed legal and political harmonization bills or 'Euro-legislation'. This legislative task is much bigger now than it was for the latest entrants (Austria, Finland and Sweden). Second, ECE parliaments have a decisive role in formulating national interests in the post-accession period by aggregating the interests of social groups. This task has also turned out to be more difficult than before because ECE governments have almost completely monopolized the representation of national interests, although its aggregation by the parliaments has to resolve the problems of increasing conflicts among social groups due to the emerging considerable mass of people hurt by of EU integration. Third, the parliaments have to communicate the results of the accession negotiations and the new tasks assuring an effective membership to the population at large. ECE parliaments are in a unique position to perform this communicative function because of their high visibility as political forums; at the same time their public trust is low because of their poor performance.

Political-legal analyses of the ECE accession capacity typically focus on the performance of governments and state administration, but this is an elitist approach or vision of EU integration. For a non-elitist approach the major political problems in the ECE are associated with 'the integration of people in the process of European integration' as indicated above: (1) communication with the population, (2) national interest aggregation and (3) Euro-legislation. The case of the most recent entrants proves that the only way to solve these problems is the parliamentarization of EU accession. In this regard the paper analyzes three issues: (1) external or communication capacity – how parliaments can mobilize the population to support Europeanization; (2) aggregation or social capacity – how parliaments create a national interest from the conflicting interests concerning EU accession; (3) internal or organizational capacity – how the ECE parliaments manage EU affairs. Accordingly, the role of ECE parliamentarization in Europeanization has appeared in (1) its communicative function, since these parliaments are the populations' windows to the EU in an accession process guided by elites; (2) the aggregation function of national interests, to involve social and territorial actors, since these parliaments historically have a well-developed committee system; (3) the legislative and the scrutiny function has only been partially effective since EU issues constitute an overload and MPs are relatively unfamiliar with EU policy. Policy transfer and policy learning have accelerated the learning process because despite low rates of MP re-election, there is a very high continuity of experience in the standing committees. These functions fit well into the structure of this book as described in the Introduction, since it deals with opinion formation, interest intermediation, national decision making and parliamentary scrutiny. This chapter is also structured in that order.

First, however, a brief analysis of the external challenge of Europeanization and the role of ECE parliaments in general, which has been a dual task of coping with globalization and accession (Tang 2000, p. 3). Parliamentarization has been a central element of Europeanization in the ECE in both the anticipatory and adaptive periods, since it has performed a coordination function among various aspects of European integration and has played a vital role in political harmonization (Ágh 2003). Political harmonization in and by ECE parliaments cannot be limited to the establishment, 'domestication' and 'copying' of Western constitutional models and major institutions, including those of the EU. Beyond this, in early consolidation as a second phase after democratic transition, political harmonization increasingly requires both political and administrative modernization to raise the 'poli-technical' capacity of the ECE political systems to cope with EU issues effectively and efficiently, and to implement them with high efficacy as a real 'working' democracy. The low EU capacity in ECE polities has been caused by the state or government overload in general, and in the management of EU affairs in particular. It has therefore not only been politically counter-productive by creating a democratic deficit by alienating the population, but also functionally inefficient and, finally, ineffective as well by not producing the desirable results. As to the constitutional structures of democratic institutions, above all parliaments, ECE polities are already more or less structurally homogeneous with the EU and its member states. But ECE countries still have to enhance their political capacity to domesticate and apply EU decisions and basic policies efficiently. Therefore they have to break from the narrow horizon of a government's activities and broaden it to a multi-actor approach, with these actors represented and mediated mostly by ECE national parliaments.

The same goes for the main political and social actors, parties and organized interests, which are closely involved in parliamentary activities. Again, paradoxically, the serious treatment of EU issues in ECE parliaments was hindered in the 1990s not so much by the anti-European parties but by an overly vague commitment of the parliamentary parties to Europeanization, since they had no definitely outlined Europeanization policies, programmes or profiles of their own in concrete terms of the EU policy universe. Just a few marginal parties produced anti-European ideas and sentiments, and even some markedly populist parties in ECE parliaments usually avoided direct confrontation with Europeanization. These small, extreme right-wing populist parties found various indirect forms and ways to communicate their resistance against European integration, in most cases by reinterpreting 'Europe' according to their own tastes. Otherwise, there was a vague and nebulous consent about Europeanization that did not allow, directly and publicly, for articulation of anti-European ideas and interests, although the situation changed during the accession negotiations and in the course of preparation for the referendums about accession, since anti-European voices might have been heard more loudly. Even the more consolidated conservative parties have made a populist turn or presented some Eurosceptic ideas:

> By the late 1990s, however, the lack of real debate, and the perception that these countries were kowtowing to an exploitative EU, began to create the opportunities for more populist leaders to arise and succeed, even where populism had earlier been discredited. Thus, in its rightward shift, Viktor Orban's Fidesz in Hungary exploited popular discontent and blamed the EU. Similarly, former Czech prime minister Vaclav Klaus, once ousted from power, turned to Euro-skepticism as a way to regain popularity, speaking out the EU's 'creeping silent unification of the continent'. In Poland, finally, a fourth of the seats in the fall 2001 elections have been claimed by anti-Union parties (Grzymala-Busse and Innes 2003, p. 69).

The vague and fragile ideological and political consent seems to have faded away in the early 2000s. At the same time, more careful and professional treatment of the European policy universe had now begun, with more detailed policy scrutiny. In the spirit of a rather painful integration and under pressure from the ongoing partial integration process, the domestic actors have simply been forced to deal with EU issues more attentively and professionally, which has dissipated the former naïve ideology of 'Return to Europe'. The contours of pro and con arguments have become much clearer, conflicting interests have come more to the fore in public debates and different approaches are more directly supported by the conflicting parties. By the time of the signing of the Accession Treaties, Europeanization 'arrived' in party politics and in the public debates of organized interests. Europeanization did not become a serious political and policy issue for ECE countries until an influential and legitimate policy opposition emerged, enabling the articulation of views and interests for and against Europeanization in concrete matters. This public debate already increasingly reflects a real conflict of interests, and it could create and institutionalize an articulate and structured social support for Europeanization. We are now at this turning point, but the creation of widespread and articulated public support for Europeanization, as a final result of parliamentarization at this stage, may be more difficult in some ECE countries in the near future than the establishment of a system of basic democratic institutions in the former stage of democratic transition.

Since the late 1990s, political modernization and Europeanization have been vital issues in the ECE countries' parliaments. Democratic transition began in the ECE with the institutionalization of parliament and its major actors, the parliamentary parties; therefore, the parliaments and parties have also been consolidated first in the early consolidation period. This consolidation has mostly manifested itself in the emergence of a quasi two-party system, sometimes with large centre-left and centre-right parties, sometimes with two large party blocs. The quasi two-party system has changed the political horizons of MPs as well. In the early 1990s many MPs argued that the left–right division had lost its validity and these terms were empty. Nowadays, most MPs have returned to these terms and they use the left-right division for their own political orientation. This reorientation is part of the parliamentary learning process, the subjective side of parliamentarization. Thus, parliamentarization has been a very complex process during which the political system as a whole has been democratized in its contacts with, or under the influence of, ECE parliaments. Moreover, parliamentarization includes its own institution-building process as part of a gradual overcoming of its own institutional and cultural deficits. The parliamentarization of parties (and their MPs) may be essential in this general process with the creation of party cohesion and discipline.

Altogether one can suggest an evolutive model of ECE parliaments in their Europeanization with the following stages: (1) the 'sleeping' parliament in the early 1990s. The ratification of the Association Treaty did not raise too much interest among MPs and their political parties, and they only acted as 'rubber stamps'; (2) the lenient parliament afterwards, which was still not well informed and rather indifferent towards legislation on EU policy issues until the start of the accession negotiations; (3) the weak parliament, which became more active since the start of negotiations in April 1998, but still very much government dominated. The weak parliament is similar to the South European parliaments described by José Magone in Chapter 12, and it is not yet ready and able to use those new means and measures to balance the government dominance described by Katrin Auel in Chapter 9 on West European parliaments. In general, there are two approaches in the current literature on national parliaments' adaptation to the EU. The first approach argues that the reactions of national parliaments 'display an incremental logic marked by slow, small and marginal changes based on existing institutional repertoires' (Dimitrakopoulos 2001, p. 405). The second approach observes a rather rapid accommodation process in the national parliaments and sees the main trend of turning the 'slow adapters' into 'national players' (Maurer and Dietz 2004, p. 3).[3]

Accordingly, following the second approach, my hypothesis is that ECE parliaments have entered a fourth stage, mainly around the elections to the EP in June 2004. Their legislation passed on the government–parliament relationship on EU issues in the spring 2004 session suggests that the position of ECE parliaments will be stronger than that of the South European parliaments, given the very strong parliamentary tradition in the ECE and the intensive contacts of ECE parliaments with the strong parliaments of the West European member states. It is true that the Joint Parliamentary Committees or the EU Affairs Committees were not very significant political actors in the 1990s because the EP had no interest in the Eastern enlargement until its 1999-2004 cycle. When the EP has developed an interest, the contact has been intensified mainly not through the Committees, but with ECE parliaments as a whole. Nevertheless, the contact with the EP has strengthened the role of ECE parliaments in general and more of the same can be expected in the near future. The new tendency is most pronounced in the Polish Parliament (Sejm and Senate), since an Act was passed on 11 March 2004 on parliamentary scrutiny of the government's activity in EU affairs. The Act stipulates that the Polish government must inform the parliament at least twice a year about the general outlines of the Polish activity in the EU and inform the parliamentary institutions (Speaker, House Committee and the relevant standing committees) about selected matters regularly. The Polish Act indicates the major trends in ECE parliaments, since similar acts have also been passed elsewhere.[4]

COMMUNICATING EU INTEGRATION AS OPINION FORMATION IN A NATIONAL FRAMEWORK

In the case of ECE countries, the basic democratization process has by and large come to an end, and democratic order as a precondition of full membership is taken for granted. Meanwhile more and more problems have surfaced concerning the 'workings' of the political system or the criteria for 'effective' democracy. Therefore, the EU capacity or EU conformity of ECE polities has been increasingly questioned from this angle in terms of institutional deficit, weak administrative capacity or lack of absorption capacity of EU transfers. The new democratic structures, the newly (re)organized or established institutions, so far have only a rather low capacity to transfer and apply (implement) EU policies. In general terms, the actual political performance of new democratic institutions is insufficient, that is, their effectiveness, efficiency and efficacy do not yet meet the requirements of the EU. Thus, the special roles of ECE parliaments and their institutional weaknesses in the current stage of Europeanization need a profound analysis. One has to discuss first of all the role of ECE parliaments in the opinion formation on the EU and for the EU as their communicative and mobilizing function.

The role of parliament in opinion formation is crucial, first of all concerning post-accession issues. Discussing the problems of the losers in systemic change, who are also the virtual losers of EU accession, Polish authors emphasize the importance of opinion formation and communicative function:

> A particularly interesting subject for further studies would be a comparative analysis of communication channels between the state authorities and the society with regard to integration issues. Given a dissonance being a loser in absolute and relative terms and the phenomenon of 'blame transfer' – that is blaming the integra-

> tion process for any misfortunes, which is popular among politicians – the news media and NGOs realized a need for adequate information and educational policies. The number of such organizations is still growing in Poland, and they seem to be the best proponents of integration, thanks to their nature (direct contacts with people) (Karasinska-Fendler et al. 2000, p. 186).

Obviously, EU accession has always been a very complex issue for the public at large, and in addition the authorities have overburdened it with the above-mentioned blame transfer. Thus, ECE parliaments should have had a special role in the opinion formation before the referendums about EU membership correcting the mistakes of the official or state communication, but they could not fulfil this communicative function adequately. Due to the lack of proper communication and mobilization, participation was relatively low and support was rather modest. The President of Poland, Aleksander Kwasniewski, has underlined with justification that not only political and economic transformations were necessary for the accession, but also that a 'mentality change' among citizens was necessary. Thus, he asserts that 'public support for EU membership is also a crucial component of a candidate country's "integration potential"' (Slomczynski and Shabad 2003, pp. 504, 527).[5]

Thus, the representation function of parliament, including interest representation and aggregation, as a whole has to be conceived in a communicative model. The ensuing communication function between the legislators and the population at large as well as among elite groups is central to modern parliaments. It creates a common language for political discourse by explaining the legal applications to a larger public (Hausner and Marody 2000, p. 71). At the same time, 'communicative autonomy' solves the problems of the 'cultural lag' between the governing and the governed. The communicative model ushers in a new period in the understanding of the parliaments in general and in 'political marketing' of EU accession in particular. However, as we know, there is a paradox between the high visibility of and the low trust in ECE parliaments. High visibility is not only a burden that exposes all the vices and contradictions of the new democratic systems through their parliaments. It may also become a great potential for further parliamentarization, that is, it makes possible the elaboration of a communicative model in the case of EU accession. High visibility is very helpful in the creation of a common language for public discourse about the current stage of Europeanization. Parliaments are in a better position than governments as far as political marketing of EU integration as a preparation for effective membership is concerned. Parliamentary work begins in a pre-parliamentary stage of everyday discussions among citizens. Responsiveness to social demands may be one of the most important criteria for the evaluation of parliaments, since it is the major criterion on which the public judges its parliament. Public support is very important for a good performance that has usually been discussed under the heading of political participation and efficacy.[6]

Despite the efforts of ECE parliaments, confidence in public institutions has declined significantly since the early 1990s in all ECE countries, perhaps most dramatically in Poland, and this decline concerns first of all the parliaments:

> . . . public confidence in the Parliament (Sejm) decreased from circa 44 per cent in 1998 to 20 per cent in June 2002 . . . The confidence in the political class is also decreasing. . . . As many as 89 per cent of respondents think that the political class in the parliament represent their own interests or those of the parliamentary clubs . . . In Poland, there is usually low participation in the parliamentary and self-government elections (circa 35 to 50 per cent) (Kolarska-Bobinska 2003, p. 93).

All these data suggest that parliaments have not been able to properly use their huge visibility potential in communicating reforms and accession with the population. However, it would be interesting to investigate the EU's role in this communication failure, since the prolongation and asymmetrical character of the accession negotiations and the 'cheap enlargement' have also contributed to the 'considerable frustration' and 'generate a conviction that Poland, and the farmers in particular, will be treated as second-rate citizens' (Kolarska-Bobinska 2003, p. 97).

From discussing the communication function one can conclude that the ECE countries so far have had an elitist approach to EU integration that has emphasized the economic versus the socio-political side of integration, and they have regarded the government as the dominant partner in contacts with EU institutions. This elitist approach has been one of the major reasons that the EU-phoria turned into EU-fatigue in the ECE, although it is interesting to note that this varies from country to country. According to the 'Eurobarometer Flash' conducted in late June 2003, the Hungarians are among the EU-enthusiasts and the Poles are among the Eurosceptics in the EU25, since more than 80 per cent of Hungarians and less than 40 per cent of Poles are in favour of a truly European Constitution. Similarly, more than 70 per cent of Hungarians and less than 30 per cent of Poles are in favour of an elected president of the European Council. These variations of ECE public opinion might have originated from the different party systems and their differing public discourses, including the debates in ECE parliaments.[7]

The crucial issue in this performance legitimacy is that the public has to have ways and means to exert pressure on parliaments, and the media has to act as a vehicle. The crux of the matter is that so far the new democratic parliaments have exhibited slow or missing responsiveness to popular demands in dealing with issues of popular interest in the EU integration process. Governments have been even slower to respond to popular demands, if at all. As an infantile disease, these macro-institutions have to a large extent become 'ivory towers.' In the new democracies, politics has turned out to be a remote world hovering above the general population. Thus, the reform of parliaments in new democracies has to start and end up with the reform of responsiveness by making parliaments more sensitive to public demands as a precondition for the parliamentarization of EU integration.

AGGREGATING NATIONAL INTERESTS: THE RELATIONSHIP BETWEEN PARLIAMENT AND SOCIETY

The Europeanization of ECE parliaments developing a capacity to aggregate national interests is still high on the agenda for the next decade. The complex representation function of ECE parliaments seems to be the most complicated and the most difficult to achieve. This challenge is now more than ever on the agenda of the new member states in the process of structural accommodation to the EU. This urgent demand has raised the task of aggregating and mediating interests, and providing the concertation of various policy fields in the accession process for ECE parliaments more than ever. Altogether, this problem setting outlines some lessons and solutions for ECE parliaments. First, they still have a limited understanding of representation, and they are stuck between corporative-consensual arrangements and majoritarian-governmental decision making. By broadening the meaning of representation to its full complexity and by completing the corporative-consensual arrangements, ECE parliaments can partly assume the job of EU coordination in the EU post-accession process from governments. Second, parliamentary committees can act as honest brokers between parliaments as representatives of long-term national interests and the organized interests with particular groups of populations behind them.[8]

Civil society is an elusive concept in many analyses, but it has to be made concrete for an operative theory of consolidation in the ECE. In early consolidation, however, there is an asymmetrical development in civil society, since above all the winners of systemic change, the new middle classes, are active in forming civil society associations and top organizations as very efficient pressure groups. The losers are still usually politically 'silent' and organizationally disadvantaged and usually have only an 'exit' option. Thus, most of the non-governmental organizations (NGOs) represent the interests of the new middle classes in a social space left empty by the state, such as organizing functions for themselves in education and health care, and so on. While the disadvantaged social classes are still unable to organize, their interests appear only in NGOs supported by enthusiastic activists in social policy and much less in high politics, including parliaments. Obviously, to improve this situation drastically, the state has to return to these 'abandoned' policies as well. This reinterpretation of the 'absentee' state has been going on in both scholarship and politics, and it has a special relevance for the consolidation of ECE countries. Basically, however, mature consolidation will usher in a period of more balanced civil society associations and NGOs. That is, more enhanced political participation will be accompanied by more intensive social participation also on the part of relative losers. ECE parliaments have to take the lead in including the losers in the political process and policy making, otherwise the lofty goals of effective membership have to be given up.

The analysis of the relationship between parliament and society in aggregating national interests leads to the conclusion that first, democratic transition began with the parliamentarization of the polity. Democratic consolidation has to start with parliamentarization, too, but in a new framework of the parliament–society relationship. This will accomplish the parliamentarization of both politics and policy making. Second, in the ECE, unlike in the Balkan or East European regions, the first tasks of parliamentarization were accomplished in the period of democratic transition with relative ease because of ECE democratic traditions, 'social capacity' and less acute economic crisis. ECE parliaments have performed rather well in constitutionalization and legal harmonization (effectiveness), but have had relatively low efficiency in legislation and efficacy in implementation. Third, the new tasks of parliamentarization in the ECE are nowadays, and will be in the next decade, much more difficult in the post-accession period. In the Europeanization of ECE parliaments it will be so in both ways: in their relationship to the European Parliament externally on one side, and in the parliamentarization of the socio-political life domestically on the other.

LEGISLATING THE EU 'POLICY UNIVERSE': A NEW BEGINNING

ECE national parliaments are only in the initial phase of meeting the challenges presented by the European integration process or legislating about the European policy universe. ECE parliaments must, of course, also 'Europeanize' themselves. They are classical cases of 'institutional' Europeanization on the one hand, and the 'functional' lack of Euro-capacity on the other. However, ECE parliaments have also been overburdened with legislative tasks (hence, I have described them as legislative factories), and they have also failed to perform well in their other functions, primarily in their control or oversight functions over the executive power. It is relatively easy to point out the major features of the 'diseconomies' in ECE parliaments, for example the gap between the legislative agenda and actual legislation, or the very high percentage of poorly prepared acts still passed by these parliaments that have had to be amended afterwards, and so on. I deliberately mention these deficiencies here in order to conclude that the tasks of Europeanization will overburden ECE parliaments in the post-accession period even more.[9]

This overload has appeared so far both in their general handling of EU issues and in the workings of the EU committees. In discussing, processing and implementing EU issues as a complex policy universe, these parliaments have tried to overcome the institutional deficit by creating proper organs, above all the EU Affairs Committees (EACs). However, the activities of these committees have proved that it has been much more difficult to overcome cultural than institutional deficits, that is the lack of professionalism and expertise in the European policy universe. Thus, the contrast between their formal-legal and actual-political powers is significant. In the 1990s, the EACs were usually unable to use their institutional potential, including their control capacity over the negotiations of the national executives with the EU authorities. The EACs lagged behind their full potential, and all the functional weaknesses of the early democratic parliaments in the ECE were concentrated in their EACs in some ways. The basic paradox of Europeanization is that at the moment when parliaments are to assume a more prominent role in the European integration process, they are not only weak in their performance in general, but especially weak concerning the handling of the European policy universe. However, with the start of accession negotiations in 1998 their role increased to some extent (see Győri 2001, Pechacek 2001), and after signing the Accession Treaty in April 2003 they have become important 'work horses' but still not politically relevant bodies (Saad 2003). They show a shocking contrast to the strong 'Grand Committees' of the latest entrants. It is true, however, that ECE parliaments have developed their own staff as an expert community that also represented continuity versus a relatively low incumbency retention rate of MPs, moving from 5-10 per cent to 40-50 per cent in the 1990s and above 50 per cent in the early 2000s.[10]

Nowadays, the ECE parliaments are still not fully able to meet the challenges of Europeanization, but the challenge would provide institutional pressure for them to perform their own internal Europeanization and political modernization. The 'legislative weaknesses' of ECE parliaments have appeared, first, in the EU type of legislation, clearly illustrating that 'legal matters are introduced in a haphazard and chaotic way because the legislators lack a comprehensive vision of a legal order of the state'. Second, it results 'in the propensity to pass "laws amending laws"' (Hausner and Marody 2000, p. 65). Finally, ECE parliaments have only been 'policy-influencing' institutions, since no competing centres have emerged in this respect, although the governments have, in fact, monopolized the major policy decisions. ECE parliaments have been also forced by Europeanization – legal and political harmonization – to play a larger role in the policy-making process than the typical West European parliament. The turn from 'extensive' to 'intensive' legislation may be a general trend in ECE parliaments. In order to accomplish this turn, instead of the narrow political perspective, ECE parliaments have to employ a wider and deeper policy perspective, as some kind of 'policy revolution' to be able to legislate on EU policy universe.

During the democratic transition ECE parliaments moved from the establishment of the constitutional state to the task of EU legal harmonization. In early consolidation a new challenge and a new beginning came about when the accession negotiations began. By the early 2000s they had become more and more important vehicles of political harmonization with the EU; at the same time their main partner, the EP, had also become an important power centre inside the EU. This had led to the 'parliamentarization' of European integration to some extent, including the enlargement issue, although parliaments remain minor players. Whereas the EP had not been active in the enlargement issue in the early 1990s, it became much more involved in the enlargement discussions in its 1994-99 legislative period and turned into a powerful actor between 1999 and 2004. Keith Dowding has argued more recently that 'Academics are increasingly turning to the EP as it takes on a more important policy-making role and the EP is beginning to behave more like a parliament with a party system' (Dowding 2000, p. 133). This greater involvement is partly due to the new competencies and the increasing accountability resulting from the Amsterdam Treaty and partly due to a 'participatory revolution' in the member countries mobilizing citizens and organized interests. It has also intensified the pressure on both the EP and the national parliaments to increase their responsivenes and to exchange more information. With the increasing significance of the EP as a power centre, the contacts with the national parliaments of ECE countries will become more intensive and more important for the post-accession process.[11]

The increasing competence of the EP has made communication with the national parliaments of the ECE new member states more intensive. First, the EP took part very actively in determining the date of entry for the new members by insisting upon the date before the elections for the EP in June 2004, so the date was fixed for 1 May 2004. Second, the EP was very active after the Copenhagen Summit in December 2002 in promoting and voting for accession. Third, it assessed the EU capacity of the new members in detail and with much more empathy than the usual EU documents. Fourth, the EP has passed a series of resolutions – as co-decisions with the Council – on issues directly related to enlargement as the reregulation of the NUTS system (26 May 2003) or on the implementation of commitments of ECE countries on regional policy (16 July 2003). There have been two major events within ECE parliaments. First, the constitution amendment process, which started before the Copenhagen Summit on the transfer of sovereignty (see e.g. Kysela 2001, p. 39) and continues with further constitutional matters arranging the government-parliament relationship while already in the EU. Second, the issue of the enhanced role of national parliaments suggested by the Convention, delivering deeper information and leaving considerable time for discussion, which to a large extent, has facilitated the popular acceptance of the accession process for ECE parliaments.[12]

However, ECE parliaments are much less able to perform their current role in external political harmonization than they were in their previous role in promoting internal democratization. The association with, and accession to, the EU has been considered in this work as two subsequent periods of general and particular Europeanization. That is, in the association period there was a challenge of democratization in general; in the accession period copying and domesticating the concrete rules of the EU polity, and the treaties as its constitutions in particular, have become the major tasks. This shift from the general to the particular Europeanization or Westernization has caused serious problems for ECE parliaments, and so far they have not been able to cope fully with the difficulties of the new situation. The issue of the institutional and cultural deficit has re-emerged in this new context of the Europeanization of ECE parliaments. I have discussed the tasks of overcoming the institutional deficit as the need for establishing (1) a powerful Grand Committee for the management of accession; (2) EU subcommittees in parliamentary committees to provide adequate policy-making expertise; (3) a broad expert base or 'epistemic community' to include professionals in the process; and finally (4) strengthening the present EACs in their coordinating functions inside parliaments as well as its relationship with COSAC and the EP. These institutions have become even more important in the post-accession period with the day-to-day increasing workload of ECE national parliaments.

The inclusion of professionals and the extension of their own independent expert base for ECE parliaments already indicate the main direction for overcoming the cultural deficit. It is certainly more difficult than overcoming that one on the institutional side. The 'opportunity-capacity' paradox appears here as a contradiction between the 'EU-mindedness' and 'EU capacity' of MPs. The EU-mindedness of most MPs has already been formed but the emergence of their EU capacity, their understanding and managing of EU affairs, has lagged behind. The first limitation, namely the language barrier, is rather obvious, followed by the lack of proper knowledge about the workings of EU institutions. There is a big contrast between the Euro-mindedness of MPs and their knowledge of EU affairs, so initially the MPs have to be 'integrated' in EU integration to enable them to integrate the people in EU integration.

The experience of Austria, Finland and Sweden showed that the accession process had three, largely overlapping stages. These stages could not be followed in the case of Eastern enlargement exactly, but their process still helps understanding the inner logic of the accession process. In the first stage governments propose EU membership; they begin to negotiate and prepare the preconditions for structural adjustment to the EU. Even in the first stage public awareness grows to some extent and parliament starts the preparation process in various ways. But the national parliaments become important actors only in the second stage because they are vital during the negotiations for full membership and later on in the ratification process. In the third stage, however, just before the negotiations end, the role of the public turns out to be crucial. They enter the scene as articulated societies with organized interests and civil society associations, and their role culminates in the referendum. These three stages may, of course, be fully separated only analytically, not historically, since they overlap. Certainly, at the beginning of the process the role of the executive is the most important, and at the end both parliament and the public play more decisive roles. The national parliaments are the key actors in the final decision-making process as well as chief intermediaries between the government and the public while discussing and managing the integration process.

CONCLUSION: PARLIAMENTARIZATION AND EFFECTIVE MEMBERSHIP

In the post-accession period the problems of ECE parliaments have been rather similar to those of the existing member states. According to Rizzutto, 'European integration is as much an opportunity as a threat to national parliaments', since they have also played the legitimizing role for the EU and have been shaken by the 'distance issue' and 'the executive dominance issue' (2004, pp. 87, 97). Earlier in the accession period the integration process proceeded in the ECE countries under the guidance of governments with the exclusion of social and territorial actors, which resulted in an 'accession democratic deficit'. The parliamentarization of Europeanization has recently begun and transition from the governmental to the parliamentary stage is more important than in the former enlargements, since ECE governments have much less legitimacy on their own than the EU15 national governments. The parliamentary stage was delayed until the end of negotiations for a number of reasons. First, due to the troubled conditions even in early consolidation, ECE governments attempted to concentrate all actual power in their hands, therefore a recentralization effort can be noticed (Hausner and Marody 2000, p. 102). Second, the EU authorities negotiated exclusively with governments, since social and territorial actors were not invited to the official delegations. The competencies of the EP were very limited at the early stage of the accession negotiations, and its communication with national parliaments was therefore also less instrumental than those of the executives on both sides. Third, national parliaments were relatively weak and their popularity was rather low, and their influence in national decision making highly inadequate. Their 'EU capacity' was also limited since most of the EU experts worked for the governments and not for the parliaments, and the MPs themselves were not yet really prepared to handle complicated EU-issues meaningfully and in detail. ECE administrations have had a series of 'political purges' at the time of a change in government, which have radically reduced the number of experts beyond the small circle of the central government, so even the good EU experts have moved to the private sector (Hausner and Marody 2000, p. 126).

The national public administrations, the parliamentary parties and, even more, the interest organizations were also rather weak in EU policy-making. They did not yet, or only to a very limited extent, have their own EU policies, expert staff and mobilization capacity on EU issues. Thus, ECE governments still tried to control the entire Europeanization process, and they were not ready to assign a greater role to parliaments. Parliaments, in turn, were neither prepared for, nor willing to undertake, the role of managing Europeanization. All in all, there has been an urgent need for the parliamentarization of EU integration and for the Europeanization of ECE parliaments but this challenge has not yet been completely met. At the same time as the transnational parties have played a larger and more conflictual role in the EP (see Hix et al. 2003) and ECE parties are getting more and more integrated; the 'party systems in the region will tend to become more similar to what will come to be considered a 'European standard' (Kostelecky 2002, p. 177). This will transform the workings of ECE parliaments where member parties of EP transnational parties will discuss the EU agenda regularly. The first steps have already been shown by the EP elections and subsequent activity of ECE MEPs in the EP.

The new situation after the accession is at the same time easier and more difficult. It is easier, since the ECE countries receive increased EU assistance in the post-accession process. This can accelerate their socio-economic development, which in some years may lead to the next take-off period. It is more difficult, since the further political harmonization presupposes a deeper penetration of EU politics and policy into ECE polities and it demands a more radical and more detailed transformation of the legal and political systems than before. Thus, it is no longer enough to change the rules 'on paper', but the full implementation of rules and the creation of an effective state have become the requirements of the EU. The new ECE member states have to learn first of all how to properly represent their own national interests in order to become effective members. Substantial capacity of state and societal power is needed for small states as new members to survive in the Brussels jungle. Instead of the consensus of the early 1990s concerning constitution-making, a new consensus is needed in the early 2000s. For an effective membership in the EU, the national interest has to be defined by all important political and social actors in a parliamentary framework as a consensual aggregation process.

NOTES

1. The ECE as a region consists of six states – Poland, the Czech Republic, Slovakia, Hungary, Slovenia and Croatia; in a broader sense the three Baltic states may also be considered part of this region. Many papers and books have been written on the activities of ECE parliaments in general, including the extensive research by the Hungarian Centre for Democracy Studies on ECE and Hungarian parliaments. Our team has analysed the First and Second Hungarian Parliaments in great detail in two volumes (Ágh and Kurtán 1995, 2001) and ECE parliaments in general (Ágh 1994, Ágh and Ilonszki 1996) with an international team. See also e.g. the ECE country chapters and Olson's summary in Kurian (1998), Longley and Ágh (1997), Longley et al. (2000) and finally Kraatz and Steinsdorff (2002). In this chapter I focus on the role of ECE parliaments in the Europeanization process, since this topic is under-researched. I describe the ECE parliaments based mostly on the Polish, Czech and Hungarian cases. I have published a book on the Europeanization in the ECE, including a chapter on parliaments (Ágh 2003) and have edited a book with a lengthy chapter on the role of ECE parliaments in the post-accession period (Ágh 2004).
2. The forms of anti-EU tendencies vary from country to country in the ECE, but the situation has been most complicated in Poland with an increasingly tough EU-scepticism and populist danger. See the Polish parties' relationships to the EU membership in Slomczynski and Shabad (2003, pp. 509-10).
3. There have been two major international projects in the field of national parliaments' accommodation to the recent changes in the EU. The first is summarized in Benz (2004), the second in Maurer and Wessels (2001), and the most recent lengthy summary is found in Maurer and Dietz (2004). I do not discuss these projects in detail, since the relevant chapters of this book deal substantially with the West European developments.
4. In the spring 2004 session, ECE parliaments mostly focused on legislation concerning the EP elections in June 2004 and also concluded the discussion on the general regulation of the parliament–government relationship in EU matters (in Poland on 11 March, in Hungary on 17 May and in Slovakia on 23 June 2004). With regard to the Hungarian debates on the role of the parliament see Győri (2004).
5. In the Czech Republic the participation in the EU referendum was 55.21 per cent with 77.33 per cent yes votes; in Hungary 45.60 and 83.76; in Poland 58.85 and 77.45; in Slovakia 52.15 and 92.46 per cent. It means that in the Czech Republic 42.69 per cent of the electorate voted yes; in Hungary 38.19; in Poland 45.57; and in Slovakia 48.21 per cent. Governments were panicking before the referendums and were relieved by the results, which were formally successful, but it created some disappointment in the West and in EU circles. No doubt the overwhelming majority of these ECE countries supported EU membership, but more than half of the electorate were not ready to get mobilized for a positive vote. It is interesting to compare it with the referendums in the entrants from 1994 where

the mobilization was much higher: 81.3 and 66.4 per cent in Austria; 74.2 and 56.9 per cent in Finland; and 83.3 and 52.3 in Sweden (participation and yes votes respectively).

6. With regard to the low trust in institutions and in parliaments in particular, and/or the significance of social capital for democratization, see the relevant chapters in Pridham and Ágh (2001).
7. See europa.eu.int.comm/public_opinion/index.htm; see also the summary in Commission press release on 25 July 2003.
8. In Hungary, the meso-political or social actors have organized their Euro-contacts, both the trade union confederations and the top employer organizations (Confederation of Hungarian Employers' Organizations for International Co-operation, CEHIC) as memberships in ETUC and UNICE. The Hungarian government also established a European Integration Council in June 1999 as a consultative body for the social partners. The CEHIC was invited to participate in the meetings of the official expert committees as well. However, the social partners only played a very limited consultative role during the Orbán government (1998-2002), and their views were heard neither by the Hungarian government nor by the Hungarian parliament in an official framework. Although they expressed their wish to participate in the accession negotiations several times, the government was not ready to involve them. Consequently, the government maintained its quasi-monopoly of aggregating and representing national interests, which proved to be a bottleneck in both negotiations with the EU and in the mobilization of the Hungarian population for the referendum. The situation was more or less the same in the other new member states.
9. Jan Kysela notes that, 'It is probably infeasible to rank the Parliament of the Czech Republic at the top of the "Europeanised" parliaments. However, the national as well as the European aspects must form important elements in the considerations as to how its future activities will appear' (2001, p. 39). It is more or less valid for all ECE parliaments.
10. The president of the Hungarian Socialist Party, then the largest opposition party, demanded in 1999 that the Hungarian parliament had to control and coordinate the accession process through an all-party Grand Committee, but the Orbán government did not even answer this challenge. The Medgyessy government has returned to this issue and has established the Grand Committee following the Finnish and Austrian models. I have contributed to the institutional design of the Grand Committee by 'domesticating' the Finnish and Austrian models.
11. In the second half of the 1990s the European Parliament (EP) began to cooperate with ECE national parliaments and organized two meetings about the role of parliaments in European integration and the enlargement process (Vienna in March 1996 and Paris in June 1998). In addition, the International Institute for Democracy (Strasbourg) also organized, in cooperation with the German Bundestag, a similar conference in the framework of the East–West Parliamentary Practice Project (Berlin in May 1997). These and other events were supported by several ECE initiatives; two conferences about the same topic in the Hungarian and the Czech parliaments (Budapest in April 1997 and Prague in September 1997). Despite these activities, and the importance of the Joint Parliamentary Committees (JPCs) with their regular biannual meetings, it is clear that this was only the introductory phase in the relationship between the EP and the parliaments of the ECE candidate countries. In the 1990s the EU organized many programmes also for the staff and the members of the Central and East European parliaments.
12. The European Parliament (EP) supported the accession of the new member states on 9 April 2003 with a large majority between 489/39/37 for the Czech Republic and 522/23/23 for Hungary (yes/no/abstention votes). In comparison the same data were on 4 May 1994 374/24/61 for Austria, 377/21/21 for Finland and 380/21/60 for Sweden. This support was relatively worse than in the Eastern enlargement. On 11 March 2003 the European Parliament issued a Draft Recommendation for each of the ten countries separately, analysing its progress (PR/471788EN.doc) and on 16 July 2003 there was a Communication of Commission to the EP and Council on regionalization in the ECE (COM(2003) 433 final). On the EP, see the special issue of *Journal of Common Market Studies* (2003).

REFERENCES

Ágh, Attila (ed.) (1994), *The Emergence of the East Central European Parliaments*, Budapest: The Hungarian Centre for Democracy Studies.

Ágh, Attila (2003), *Anticipative and Adaptive Europeanization in Hungary*, Budapest: Hungarian Centre for Democracy Studies.

Ágh, Attila (ed.) (2004), *Post-Accession in East Central Europe: The Emergence of EU25*, Budapest: The Hungarian Centre for Democracy Studies.

Ágh, Attila and Gabriella Ilonszki (eds) (1996), *Parliaments and Organized Interests: The Second Steps*, Budapest: The Hungarian Centre for Democracy Studies.

Ágh, Attila and Sándor Kurtán (eds) (1995), *Democratization and Europeanization in Hungary: The First Parliament (1990-1994)*, Budapest: The Hungarian Centre for Democracy Studies.

Ágh, Attila and Sándor Kurtán (eds) (2001), *Democratization and Europeanization in Hungary: The Second Parliament (1994-1998)*, Budapest: The Hungarian Centre for Democracy Studies.

Benz, Arthur (2004), 'National parliaments in the European Union – West European experiences and lessons for the new member states', in Attila Ágh (ed.), *Post-Accession in East Central Europe: The Emergence of EU25*, Budapest: The Hungarian Centre for Democracy Studies, pp. 57-68.

Dimitrakopoulos, Dionyssis (2001), 'Incrementalism and path dependence: European integration and institutional change in national parliaments', *Journal of Common Market Studies*, **39** (3), 405-22.

Dowding, Keith (2000), 'Institutional research on the European Union', *European Union Politics*, **1** (1) 125-44.

Grzymala-Busse, Anna and Abby Innes (2003), 'Great expectations: The EU and domestic political competition in East Central Europe', *East European Politics and Societies*, **17** (1) 64-73.

Győri, Enikő (2001), 'The Hungarian parliament and the issue of European integration', in Attila Ágh and Sándor Kurtán (eds), *Democratization and Europeanization in Hungary: The Second Parliament (1994-1998)*, Budapest: The Hungarian Centre for Democracy Studies.

Győri, Enikő (2004), 'How can the Hungarian national assembly preserve its sovereignty after accession to the EU', in Attila Ágh (ed.), *Post-Accession in East Central Europe: The Emergence of EU25*, Budapest: The Hungarian Centre for Democracy Studies, pp. 95-128.

Hausner, Jerzy and Miroslawa Marody (eds) (2000), *The Quality of Governance: Poland Closer to the European Union?*, Cracow: Cracow University of Economics.

Hix, Simon, Amie Kreppel and Abdul Noury (2003), 'The party system in the European Parliament: Collusive or competitive?', *Journal of Common Market Studies*, **41** (2) 309-31.

Journal of Common Market Studies (2003), Special Issue: The European Parliament at Fifty, **41** (2), pp. 373.

Karasinska-Fendler, Maria et al. (2000), 'Poland', in Helena Tang (ed.), *Winners and Losers of EU Integration*, Washington, DC: The World Bank, pp. 162-188.

Kolarska-Bobinska, Lena (2003), 'The EU accession and strengthening of institutions in East Central Europe: The case of Poland', *East European Politics and Societies*, **17** (1) 91-8.

Kostelecky, Tomas (2002), *Political Parties after Communism: Developments in East-Central Europe*, Baltimore and London: The Johns Hopkins University Press.

Kraatz, Susanne and Silvia von Steinsdorff (eds) (2002), *Parlamente und Systemtransformation im postsozialistischen Europa*, Opladen: Leske & Budrich.

Kurian, George Thomas (ed.) (1998), *World Encyclopedia of Parliaments and Legislatures*, Washington, DC: Congressional Quarterly.

Kysela, Jan (2001), 'Deputies and senators after accession into the EU', in Lubomir Brokl (ed.), *Deputies, Senators and Integration of the Czech Republic into the European Union*, Prague: Institute of Sociology, pp. 37-43.

Longley, Lawrence and Attila Ágh (eds) (1997), 'The changing roles of parliamentary committees', *Working Papers on Comparative Legislative Studies II*, Research Committee of Legislative Specialists, IPSA, Lawrence University, Appleton, WI.

Longley, Lawrence, Attila Ágh and Drago Zajc (eds) (2000), 'Parliamentary members and leaders: The delicate balance', *Working Papers on Comparative Legislative Studies IV*, Research Committee of Legislative Specialists, IPSA, Lawrence University, Appleton, WI.

Maurer, Andreas and Daniela Dietz (2004), 'EU Parliaments post-2004: Elements for comparative analysis of national parliamentary participation in EU affairs', paper prepared for the Conference 'National Parliaments in the European Union – Lessons for the Accession Countries', Andrássy University, Budapest, 4 March.

Maurer, Andreas and Wolfgang Wessels (eds) (2001), *National Parliaments on their Ways to Europe: Losers or Latecomers?*, Baden-Baden: Nomos Verlag.

Olson, David (1998), 'The parliaments of new democracies: The experience of Central Europe', in George Thomas Kurian (ed.), *World Encyclopedia of Parliaments and Legislatures*, Washington, DC: Congressional Quarterly, pp. 838-853.

Pechacek, Stepan (2001), 'Committees for European integration of the Chamber of Deputies and the Senate of the parliament of the Czech Republic', in Lubomir Brokl (ed.), *Deputies, Senators and Integration of the Czech Republic into the European Union*, Prague: Institute of Sociology, pp. 29-36.

Pridham, Geoffrey and Attila Ágh (eds) (2001), *Prospects for Democratic Consolidation in East-Central Europe*, Manchester: Manchester University Press.

Rizzuto, Franceso (2004), 'National parliaments and the European Union: Part of the problem or part of the solution to the democratic deficit in the European constitutional settlement?', *The Journal of Legislative Studies*, **9** (3) 87-109.

Saad, Judit (2003), 'EU-integráció a magyar parlamentarizmus tükrében' [EU integration in the mirror of the Hungarian Parliamentarism], *Európai Tükör*, **8** (4-5), 144-157.

Slomczynski, Kazimierz and Goldie Shabad (2003), 'Dynamics of support for European integration in post-communist Poland', *European Journal of Political Research*, **42** (4) 503-39.

Tang, Helena (ed.) (2000), *Winners and Losers of EU Integration*, Washington, DC: The World Bank.

Index

accession stages to EU 262
accountability 20, 55, 56
  of government, UK 167
action plans 53
adaptation, ideal of, Nordic countries 101
administration agencies 19
administrative autonomy 121
administrative capacity 139
administrative systems 90
age, analysis by 33, 36
agencies and private interest organization 94, 95, 97
agenda setting 30, 187, 188
  power of governing parties 199
aggregation of interests 106
agricultural policy 180
agricultural sciences 46
agricultural subsidies of EU 61
Amsterdam School of Communications Research 38
Amsterdam summit 31
anti-party sentiment 72
Assemblée Nationale, France 161–2, 168
  influence 164
asylum 61
audience research 33
Austrian regions 121–3
Austrian No-Citizens Initiative 74
authorities and organizations, contact 92
authorization of political leadership 55
autonomy of parliament, restriction of 117–18

balance of power 16, 145

Basic Law, Germany 189, 190
Belgian regions 121–3
benchmarking 53
British Labour Party 78
British Referendum Party 74
Bundesrat Germany 191, 201
Bundestag, Germany 115, 162–3, 191
  autonomy of 124–5
bureaucratization 102
bypassing governments 173

campaign communication 57
captivity, Nordic countries 104
cartel party thesis 72, 75
centralization of power 145
central state, weakening of 116
Christian Democratic Appeal (CDA), Netherlands 78
Christian Democrats (CDA), Netherlands 59
Christian Democrats (CDU/CSU), Germany 63
citizens 3
  demands and legislation process 119
  of EU 25
  information 54
  and parliament, exchange 117
  and political parties, link 71
  political preferences 54, 70
  voice 18
civil society 9, 257
class as social cleavage 71
  party choice and 72
coalition governments 14, 20, 73, 77–8
  Denmark 220
  Germany 162

co-determination powers, *Länder* 129
collective identity 113
Commitment to European integration 78
Committee for Affairs of EU (EAC) 125–6
committees
  involvement in EU affairs 198
  specialized 196, 212
Common Foreign and Security Policy,

UK 195
communication 48, 118
communication function in European issues 118
communism, fall of, in East Central Europe 6
Community Law 239
compensation mechanisms 119
through intrastate participation 129
competencies, loss of 130
competition policy 180
Compliance Cost Assessment UK 195
Conference of European Affairs Committees (CEACs) 235
constitutional amendment 261
constitutional provisions 185, 189–91
Constitution of V. Republic, France 161
consumer groups' opinions 98
convergence amongst member states 147
convictions, generalized 54
Cooperation Law Federal Government – German *Bundestag* 194
cooperation of member states 53
coordination 141, 142
with EU organizations 93
corporatism 89
arrangements 90
coordination 90–99
decision-making 88
COSAC (*Conférence des organes spécialisés dans les affaires communautaires*) 119
cost-benefit analysis, UK 195
Council of Ministers 4, 5, 53
right to vote 195
Council of Regions 4
cultural deficits 259
culture, policy area 127
Czech Republic 14, 264
newspaper coverage of EU 65, 66
Election 2002 64–6

Danish European Affairs Committee 207–27
Danish *Folketing*, cooperation and formal mandate 171–2
decision-making 2, 11
democratic 55
powers lost to EU 203
decisions 3, 10
ignored 164
institutional matters 210
policy matters in EU 210
obstructing 171
defence, committees for 212
Delors, Jacques, president of European Commission 236
democracy 5
in European politics 174
national policy and 90
Westminster model 160
democratic deficit in EU 10, 57, 113–33, 205, 206
democratic governance 7–8, 30, 114
challenge to 103
in member states 113–33
democratic ideals 102
democratic institutions 53
represent the emerging *demos* of European people 205
democratization of East Central Europe (ECE) countries 254
Denmark 14, 18, 163, 189
agenda-setting power of governing parties 204
constitutional law 193, 194
decision making on the EU 204
European Affairs Committee and specialized committees 210–18
influence in EU matters 171
institutional matters 225, 226
mandates 106, 199
mass media 12, 18, 30, 44–52, 48, 51
party group 207–10
right to refuse a mandate 204
specialized committees 213–17
system of overlapping membership 204
Departmental Select Committees, UK 160
dependence of parties on the state 72
digitalization 48
direct democracy 62
disagreement, degree of 98
division of power 13
horizontal 114, 115–24
vertical 114, 115–24
'domestication' of European decision-making 147
domestic issues 54

domestic legislatures 118
  disempowerment 120
domestic party competition 70
domestic policy areas 130
domestic political continuity 57
domestic situation, Europe-induced change 115, 116
Dutch election campaign 2003 54, 59–63
Dutch media, more reporting on EU 63, 67
Dutch political parties, differences on Europe 62

East Central Europe (ECE) 6
  parliaments 20, 268
Economic and Monetary Union (EMU) 146, 235
economic crises in Germany 63
economic development in Europe 71
economic networks 47
economic policy 180
educational training, policy area 127
education level 33, 36
election campaign
  democracy and 57
  European issues 54, 55
  national 15, 53–67
  political parties, analysis 66
  television news 28
elections 8, 18, 26
  Czech Republic 65
  national 184
  Poland 65
electoral volatility 71, 72
electoral support 26
emotional reactions 54
engineering sciences 45
enlargement of EU 35, 61
  reactions to 35
environmental isues 37, 71, 73, 127
Estonia, Office of European Integration 142
European Union
  affiliation 90
  constitutional transformation 6
  directives 170–71
  enlargement, negative views 37
  foreign policy in NRC 61
  issues in national election campaigns 15, 54, 57, 79, 80
  law, supremancy of 150
  legal act, amendment 118
  legislation, scrutiny, southern Europe 229–45, 249, 250
  membership, strategic use of 148
  news in Dutch newspapers 60, 61, 62
  politics, bureaucratization and poor image 31, 105
  strategies 90
euro
  issue 31
  referendum, news coverage 30
Eurocritical position in UK 80
European Administrative Space 146
European Affairs Committees (EACs) 119, 158, 180, 259
  Bundestag 162
  Folketing 104, 164, 171, 172, 211
  special committee 210–18
'European audiovisal space' 48
European Commission, leader 62
European Community legislation, scrutiny of 160
European Council 30
European Court of Justice 4
European decision-making, influencing 164
'European information area' 48
European integration 7, 17, 100, 258
  destabilizing for national parties 70
  impact 73
  media 25–40
  news reporting and 32
  Nordic countries 88–107
  role of national parliaments and 158
  threat to national parliaments 262
European issues
  in British Parliament 168
  campaigning for 54
  national election campaigns and 53–67
Europeanization 3, 7, 15, 16, 114
  accession period 261
  autonomy of *Bundestag* and 124
  democratic governance and 131
  of East Central European (ECE) parliaments 249–65
  of experts 47–50
  of national decision making 13, 113–33

of national executives 137–53
power division and 116
transformations and 145
European languages, skilful command 146
European level contacts, influencing 170
European media 48
European Monetary Union (EMU) (UK) 195
European Parliament
elections 27
financial benefits for parties 76
voters 53
European party systems, shaping of 71
European policy-making 58, 130, 158
European political affairs 26
European question, divisive 70
European regulation 71
European Scrutiny Committee (ESC) UK 160, 167
European Secretariat, UK 141
European Standing Committee, UK 164, 167
European Union member states 180
Europe, Southern 229–45
Euroscepticism 224, 225, 229, 252
in East Central Europe (ECE) 256
in electorate 14
member states 143
parties 77
Denmark 75, 76
executive 115, 116
legislature and 114
executive dominance 14, 114, 123, 130
in southern Europe 230–35
executive-legislative relations 116, 117
southern Europe 234–5
executives, Europeanization of 144–6
experts 46, 196
independent 93
opinions 47
references in the media 44–52
surveys on EU 70
'Explanatory Memorandum' UK 195
external relations 122
'external veto players' 171

Fabbri Law, Italy 236
Federal Government and *Bundestag* cooperation 126
federalism
balance of power 127
Europeanization and 62, 121
executive 127
Finland 18
corporate coordination 96, 97
informal contacts 106
national interest 98
Finnish Alliance for a Free Finland 74
fire fighting 44
fiscal autonomy 121
flight safety 44
Folketing 104, 163, 193
(European Affairs Committee of the Danish Parliament) 207–8
party group dimension 207
right of mandate
foreign experts 48
foreign policy, Germany 63
foreign social scientists 50
formal rules 181, 203
fragmentation in everyday issues 151
France 75–6, 161–2
department for EU policy 142
documentation on European Legislation 239
Germany, links with 169
Freedom Party, Austria 77
free market 58
French model 229–45
French parliament and EU scrutiny 245
French Senate representation in Brussels 169
Front National party, France 76

Gaullists, France 76
Gazeta Wyborcza (Polish newspaper) 65
gender 33, 36
German Federal Republic 115
Germany
agenda-setting powers 200, 201
Basic Law (*Grundgesetz*, GG) 162
Bundesrat strengthens power of opposition parties 204
Bundestag 169–71
coalition government 200
committee involvement 198
democratic governance and 124–30
departments for EU policy 142
Election 2002 54, 59, 63–6

institutional reforms in the *Bundestag* 162–3
Länder 115
no right to give or refuse mandates 204
opposition parties, power of 201
overlapping membership with EAC 197, 204
parliamentary party structures 202
sovereignty transfer to EU 190
Giddens, Anthony *The Consequences of Modernity* 46, 47
globalization
of experts 47–50
political 44
global regulation 71
government 147
coherence 143
control 103
of parliament, France 161
of parliament, UK 200
instalment and dissolution 182
government party groups Denmark 223
government policy 56
government portfolios, design of 146
government standpoint, Nordic countries 97
government status of green parties 73
government whips in UK 200
Greece 14, 229
and EU legislation 243, 244, 245
Committees of European Affairs (CEA) 238
department for EU policy 142
government 20
political parties 231–5
green ideology and Europeanization 73, 78
green papers, UK parliament 192
Green Party, Germany 6

health care, committees 212
health sciences 45, 46, 50
hierarchy 142, 143
government to governance 152
home affairs 180
horizontal level of power division 116
House of Commons, UK
influence 164
committees of sectoral interests 198
'Scrutiny Reserve' 194
House of Lords, UK 191, 192
housing, committees for 212
humanities 46
human rights issues 71
Hungary 14, 264
attitude to EU 256

ideology
aspects of political parties 58
convergence 72–3
deeper political integration 70
impact on EU politics 119
implementation 122, 164
independent experts, Nordic countries 88–107
influence through public deliberation 173
informal contacts 102, 171
information 46
deficits 54
on European issues 158
France 173
parliamentary reaction 126
European politics 54
independent access to 170
parliamentary control 119–20
public deliberation and, France 168
sources 30
transfer of, UK 174
institutional analysis 12
institutional deficits 259
institutional matters 163, 224
institutions 186, 203
policy and 224–5
integration
democratic governance and 152
disruptive impact 78–9
policies 80
interest groups 9, 18
Nordic countries 88–107
representation 16
interests
opposing 89
private and public 104
intergovernmentalism 4, 6, 36, 53
internal coordination in majority party 170
international bargaining 16
interparliamentary relationships 169

interstate relations 47
Iraq war
controversy on EU policy 66
German parties opinion on 63, 64
Islamic radicalism 44
issues important to voter 56
Italy 14, 20, 76, 229
committees for European affairs 236–9
EU legislation and 239–45
parliament 240
political parties 231–5

judiciary 115, 116
June Movement, Denmark 75
justice 180
Justice and Home Affairs (UK) 195

knowledge 46
Kosovo conflict, role of EU 27

labour
worldwide division of 47
labour market, committees for 212
land development issues 37
Länder (German) 192
loss of influence at European level 127
loss of power by Europeanization 128
language barrier of MPs 249
La Pergola Law, Italy 236, 239, 240
law-making powers 182
laws and rules 185–6
left-right dimension 80–81
legal acts and *Bundestag* 124
legal autonomy 121
legal harmonization 260
legislation 102, 103
and legislative agenda 259

legislative power transfer 157
legislative process, France 168
legislature 115, 116
legitimacy 30, 53, 58
democratic governance and 26
in EU 53, 57
of government decision-making 182
in multi-level governance 66
Liberals (FDP), Germany 64
Liberals (VVD), Netherlands 59
Lidové (Czech newspaper) 65
List Pim Fortuyn Party (LPF), Netherlands 59, 77

Maastricht Treaty, ratification 125, 189
France 161
Länder and 129
majority government 14, 20, 203
in UK 200
mandates 193, 194
from EAC , Denmark 215–17
mandating of Danish ministers prior to negotiations in Council 210
'mandating model' Denmark 164, 173, 218
market competition 150
mass communication 56
mass media 48
mechanisms to scrutinize governments in Council of Minister meetings 203
media 3
coverage of EU issues in German newspapers 64
European integration and 25–40
as key intermediary 36
media coverage
of European elections 54
of German elections 64
media exposure 12
media markets 38
media visibility 30
media, policy area 127
membership
of committees 186–7
overlapping 196–8
middle classes, new, East Central Europe 20
Middle East politics 44
military alliances 47
minority governments 14, 20
in Denmark 226
greatest power to scrutinize 203
minority statements in the EAC's procedural reports, Denmark 220
Mlada Fronta Dnes (Czech newspaper) 65
modernity 47
Members of Parliament
direct channel to EU 166
'evidence sessions' 168

multi-level governance 2, 3, 15, 20, 38, 88
multi-level system, European 172
multi-party system, Denmark 163

National Alliance, Italy 77
national administration 100
nation states 3
representation 57
national contexts and the media 48
national coordination 93–5
Denmark 99
national democratic deficit 113–33
national divergences 140
national election campaigns 5, 18, 57
and EU issues 67
executives 137
power of 139
national governments 6, 120, 147, 180
outvoting of 205
national interest 20, 89, 90, 97–9
in ECE countries 257–8
in EU matters 91, 97–8
Nordic countries 97
representation of 264
national legislatures weakened 158
national news media coverage 26
national parliaments
contacts between 119
disempowerment of 130, 131
EU legislative function and 118
scrutiny 116–17, 180–206
strategic Europeanization 157–74
systems, Europeanization 158–63
voters and 53
weakening of 172
national parties
and European integration 70, 81
national standpoint, Nordic countries 97
national television news 30
national unity 80
natural sciences 45, 46, 50
'negative parliamentarism' Denmark 163
negative sentiments 32
negotiation proposal, non-acceptance 222, 223
negotiation processes 166
Netherlands 14, 189, 196
agenda-setting powers 199, 201
committee involvement 198
Eerste Kamer 192
Green-Left Alliance 201
national election campaigns 54
opposition parties power of 201
overlapping membership 197
Netherlands Christian Democratic Party (CDA) 201
less power than Germany Bundestag 204
Netherlands political party, PvdA, CDA 62
Netherlands (TEU) overlapping membership 202–5
New Europe, expansion of 53
new parties, formation of 75
news coverage, strategic 12, 25, 32, 36
non-governmental organizations (NGOs) 257, 258
Nordic countries 13, 88–107
private interests of 19
Northern League, Italy 77
Norway 18
formal contacts 106
national interest and 98
Norwegian Parliament (*Storting*) 104
NRC Handelsblad (Dutch newspaper) 59, 60, 61

officials, recruitment and training 146
open administration 103, 104
opinion
consensual elite 29
formation 8, 9, 17
polarized 29
opposition parties 182
power of 187–8
power to influence agenda 202
parliament
government and 167, 182
opinion formation and 254
society and 257–8
in southern European political system 230–35
parliamentarization 262–4
parliamentary control
democracy, Europeanization of 158
mandate Denmark 218
in multi-level governance 164–7
parliamentary functions, restriction 119
parliamentary government 100

parliamentary institutions 196
parliamentary majority 160
parliamentary mandates, Denmark 171, 172
parliamentary party groups 188
parliamentary practice 11
  in Europe 11
parliamentary scrutiny 3, 8, 9, 11–14, 180–85
  in Denmark 190, 221–3
  of EU affairs 157
  of EU legislation 239–45
    Southern Europe 235–45
  four member states 203
  France 162
parliamentary sovereignty
  absolute 160
  in UK 191
parliaments in Europe 16
participation 101
participation rights
  German *Bundestag* 162
  of national parliaments 164–5
parties against the EU 74
parties and citizens, losing link 69
parties with coalition governments next 203
parties, small, successful 76
parties, transformed role 69
parties' stance in EU issues 59
partisan dealignment 73
party behaviour 203
  at European level 70
party competition 75
  and campaigns 57–61
party democracy 69
'Party Election Programme', Dutch parties 61
party groups 225, 226
  Denmark 219, 220–24
party identification 71
party interaction 58
party loyalties, weaker 71
party membership, decline of 71
party model, responsible 56–7
party politics, Denmark 171
party system 160
  Europeanization of 57–61
  fragmentation 73
  southern Europe 230–33
patronage 72
People's Movement, Denmark 75
People's Party (ÖVP), Austria 77
People's Party for Freedom and Democracy (VVD) 78
Permanent Representatives (COREPER) 142, 143, 144
Poland 14, 264
  attitudes to EU 256
  public loss of confidence in parliament 256
policy
  capacity 139
  consistency 80
  decisions 210
  implementation 160
  influences, *Bundestag* 160, 162
  innovation 149
  shapers, national governments as 150
  support 32, 36–8
policy-making 122, 169–70
Polish Election 2003 64–6
Polish newspaper coverage of EU 65
political assassination of Pim Fortuyn 59
political communication 31
political cynicism 18, 31, 32, 34–5, 37
political efficacy 31, 32, 34, 35
political harmonization 251, 260
political institutions 19
  and private interests 88–9
political knowledge 32, 34, 35, 36
political parties 9, 18, 187
  new 73
political representation questions 57
political systems, internal 137
politicians and EU-related policies 105
politicization 103
Portugal 14, 229
  committees of European Affairs 237–8
  EU legislation and 241, 242
  government 20
  political parties 231, 232, 233, 234
post-European electorate 4
post-industrial economies 71
power balance 114
power
  distribution 188
  division of 114–24
  efforts to get back 203

of German Bundestag 169
of governing parties 187
horizontal and vertical division of 124, 127
loss of national parliaments 16, 180
power relations 47
press coverage of EU 25
priming effects 31
private corporations, Nordic countries 88–107
private interests 13, 19, 98, 100
European organizations and 93, 97, 104
in Nordic countries 90–96
political institutions and 88–9
problem solving 46
procedural rules 185
public accountability 8
public and private interests 99
public authorities 100
public committees for EU-related matters 92
public debate 26, 166
public expenditure in Spain 150
public funding for party income 72
public opinion formation 25, 26
EU politics 31
news media and 37
public scrutiny 165

questioning ministers, Denmark 221, 222

rapports (reports), France 168–9
ratification, formal 164
referendum 26, 37, 262
in Denmark 190
on European convention 62
internal dissent and 79
participation in ECE countries 264
right of 63
reflexivity, increased, in modern societies 51, 56, 57
regional and structural policy 127
regional co-decision rights 123
regional governments 115
regional level 47
regionalist parties 76
regions of federal member states 122, 123
religion 71
representation 9, 54–8, 182, 184
in multi-level governance 66
representation, chains of 10, 11, 57, 184
representative democracy 62
research and technology, policy area 127
researchers 46, 48, 51
research institutions, independent 45
resolutions on European issues 159
right of consultation, Bundestag 194
rights for information 119
rights of parliament, Bundestag 194
rights over domestic policies 172
rules of procedure 181
Rzeczpospolita (Polish newspaper) 65

sanction mechanisms, effective 8, 120
science, hard 51
scientific researchers 45
scrutiny
of EU legislation, southern Europe 229–45
of EU policies 163
majority voting procedures used in Council of Ministers 205
in policy matters, Denmark, 221–3
procedure for documents 158
reserve requirement 195
structures 235
second chamber 191
Select Committee on European Legislation (UK) 192
separation of powers in Germany 200
single economic market 6
Single European Act (SEA) 6
and *Länder* 129
Single European Market (SEM) 235
Single Market Programme 161
Single Market Project 148
Slovakia 264
Slovenia 264
social cleavage 71
Social Democrats (SPD), Germany 63
Social Democrats, Sweden, minority government 78
social interests 71
social participation 20
social science research 45–51
societal-centred democratic processes 9, 16

society, reflexive 46
southern Europe, pro-European 229, 230
sovereignty 100
loss of, by national parliaments 158
Spain 14, 121–229
and EU legislation 242, 243
government 20
Joint committees for EC Affairs 237, 238
political parties 231, 232, 233, 234
special interests, opinions of 99
specialist policy committees 196
Sputnik, Soviet Union 49
single party majority 167
Standing Committee System, France 168
state administration 13
state-centric approach 6, 9
statutory law 181
steel construction 44
Storting (Norwegian Parliament) 104
strategic adaption of national parliaments 174
strategic behaviour of politicians 147, 148
strategic Europeanization of national parliaments 157–74
strategies for managing interests 89
structural reforms 150
supranational institutions 25, 29
of the EU 53
supranationalism 4
Sweden 18
informal contacts 106
total involvement through contact 92

tax policies, Germany 63
technical-natural sciences 50
technical sciences 45, 46
television news 12, 25–30, 33, 37, 71
as source of political information 33
terrorist attack on US, September 11 44
Thatcher, Margaret, Eurosceptic views 82
trade policy 180
traditional choices, modification 150
tradition in earlier societies 46
transnational state 2
transparency 101
transport
committees for 212
policy area 127
treaty
changes 118
negotiations 18
Treaty of the European Union (TEU) 195, 235
truth serum 49

United Kingdom 14, 18
avoidance of European issues 198
burying debate 205
EAC members of Parliament serving on it 202, 203
Eurosceptic country 202, 205
House of Commons 160–62
distribution of power 202
low power to scrutinize 20
Whip system 202
power of Opposition parties for agenda-setting 200–02
power of parliament controlled 202
scrutiny discouraged 205
Standing Committee on Europe 199
voting behaviour 80
uncertainty about issues 54
unemployment in Germany 63
unity of action 142

vertical division of power 19, 121
vested interests 70
Vlaams Blok party, Belgium 76
vocational training, policy area 127
Volkskrant (Dutch newspaper) 59
voters
media and 59
policy preferences and 56, 72, 184
pro-Europeanism and 79
turnout, decline in 71
voting behaviour 70
voting, direct, for leader of EU 62

welfare state 71
Westminster model, German parliament 162
White papers, UK parliament 192
women in German elections 63
world security situation 53